REAL FARMING, REAL FOOD

P9-CLI-853

The Four
Season Farm
Gardener's
Cookbook

The Four Season Farm

Gardener's Cookbook

From the Garden to the Table in 120 Recipes

Barbara Damrosch & Eliot Coleman

WORKMAN PUBLISHING • NEW YORK

Library of Congress Cataloging-in-Publication Data
is available.

ISBN 978-0-7611-5669-7

Cover and book design by Lisa Hollander
Illustration by Lorna Brown
For photography credits, see page 486.

Workman books are available at special discounts
when purchased in bulk for premiums and sales
promotions as well as for fund-raising or educational
use. Special editions or book excerpts can also be
created to specification. For details, contact the
Special Sales Director at the address below or send
an email to specialmarkets@workman.com.

WORKMAN PUBLISHING COMPANY, INC.
225 Varick Street
New York, NY 10014-4381

workman.com

Workman is a registered trademark of Workman
Publishing Co., Inc.

Printed in the U.S.A.
First printing February 2013

acknowledgments

WE WOULD LIKE to thank the many people who lent their talents and good counsel to this project. We have been grateful to the staff of Workman Publishing for their professionalism, wit, and insane work ethic, as they turned this farm-raised product into a book. In particular: Peter Workman, who invited us to write it; our editor Suzanne Rafer, who shepherded it with her usual skill and dedication; Mary Wilkinson for her kindness, wisdom, and tireless dedication to the manuscript. The book's designer Lisa Hollander was wonderful to work with, and we thank her and Anne Kerman for their expert handling of the photography—and the photographers. Anne, along with food stylist Carrie Ann Purcell and prop stylist Sara Abalan, made Food-Shoot Week more fun than work. Selina Meere and Anwesha Basu, in publicity, have been helpful and understanding of our various quirks. Appreciation also to Cathy Dorsey, our index whiz; Kathie Ness, whose careful eye oversaw the recipes; Barbara Peragine, who set the manuscript, and Carol White, who saw the book through production, along with her proofreading team, Barb Stussy, Susan Hom, Marta Jaremko, and Jayne Lathrop.

Jessica MacMurray Blaine's testing of the recipes, along with her many helpful suggestions, made a huge contribution to the book. During its writing, several dozen crew members at Four Season Farm formed an auxiliary testing panel for the recipes. Matthew Robertson and Chad Conley, in particular, offered sound culinary advice. Robert Johnston Jr. gave important feedback with regard to seeds. Larry Cassis rescued us often from computer rage.

Matthew Benson was indispensable for his beautiful images and his generosity with professional advice. For the few photos not taken at our farm, we thank Deborah Wiggs, Phil Norris, Abbie and Mike McMillen, Chip Wadsworth, Kathy Long, and the late Helen Nearing for allowing us to shoot in their gardens.

Finally, we thank our friends, especially Sherry Streeter, Jon Wilson, Mia Kanazawa, Mark Kindschi, Chip Wadsworth, Tom Hoey, Jeannie Gaudette, and Peter Diemond, all of whom kept us in good spirits as this "quick little project" grew to four years. Akiwaba!

BARBARA AND ELIOT

TABLE OF CONTENTS

The Kitchen

After washing up we fix a simple supper, much
of it harvested moments before,
still alive and flavorful.
We feel like the luckiest people on earth.

Why Grow Your Own Food?

THE DAY HAS BEGUN TO COOL, so we reach for the sun-warmed shirts we'd shed earlier when we began cultivating the garden. The beds now look clean and tidy, the earth a dark background against which the plants stand out in rich colors. The deep green of the spinach and the bluish cast of the broccoli leaves tell us we've fed these plants well, and that they'll feed us well in return. We pull up some carrots for supper, pick a few cucumbers, dig a handful or two of potatoes, and add a head of lettuce and fresh herbs to the basket. Standing up, we stretch our backs, feeling a pleasant kind of tiredness. After washing up we fix a simple meal, much of it harvested moments

> *Everything about the act of growing plants seems like a custom-made antidote to the stresses and deprivations we experience in modern life.*

before, still alive and flavorful. We feel like the luckiest people on earth.

Does this sound romantic? If so, it's only because people seldom feed themselves from their gardens anymore. Yet for much of human history, it was the normal way to live. It was something everyone needed to know how to do. Then, in the twentieth century, gardening turned into a hobby.

Granted, it's a well-loved hobby. Life has many simple sensory pleasures, but few activities yield them as easily and dependably as gardening. Everything about the act of growing plants seems like a custom-made antidote to the stresses and deprivations we experience in modern life—just being outdoors is a mood lifter. Even a brightly lit room provides 200 to 300 times less light than outdoor sunlight, and 20 to 30 times less than outdoor light on a cloudy day.

Work in the garden tends to strike a good balance between aerobic tasks (such as digging) and more gentle but prolonged motion (such as cultivating and weeding). Many a pound has been lost and many a muscle has been toned there.

Much of gardening is calming work. Weeding, especially, is often described as meditative. It is work that connects you with the rest of the natural world. You are never oblivious to the weather or the seasons. You're on intimate terms with the sun, the rain, the soil under your feet. Creatures that work alongside you in the garden, from toads to beetles to birds, make you feel part of a large mysterious project, even when some of those companions hinder your work. Most help.

All this might equally be said of raising roses and petunias, but there is an extra dimension to gardening when you're growing food. Because vegetables and fruits begin to decline in both flavor and vitamin content as soon as they are picked, the difference between those that have traveled a long way to get to your plate and those you grow and pick is enormous. Most people know that a vine-ripened garden tomato tastes better than a supermarket one, bred for ease of shipping, not flavor, and artificially ripened after harvest. But this is just as true of a new potato or a basketful of spinach. What's more, you know exactly how your tomato and spinach were grown. Since eating is one of the most important things we do, it is life-changing to regain control over it. If you have a local farmstand or CSA nearby (Community Supported Agriculture—a subscription farm from which you prepurchase a weekly share of the harvest), you may have experienced on a regular basis the pleasure of eating fresh, wholesome food.

But when it is yours to pick, a few steps away from the kitchen, it is even fresher. And priceless.

FROM GARDENER TO COOK

EATING FROM THE garden will turn you into a cook, even if you aren't one already. Putting delicious food on the table is something everybody can do, because delicious food does not need to be fancy. In fact, one of the first things you discover about homegrown produce is that you don't want to mess with it too much. Lively flavors beg not to be masked, over-seasoned, over-sauced, over-dressed, and above all, over-cooked. The best chefs have always known this, and kitchen gardeners soon learn to let their produce call the shots. In the second half of this book, we share some of the recipes we've created from our own harvests.

Gardening as a hobby is associated in some minds with leisure—something people do when they have time, when their children have grown, when they have retired, when they own a place with a big yard. It is certainly a pastime that makes good times better. But food gardening is most popular when times are hard. Americans took up their shovels and planted "war gardens" during World War I and "victory gardens" in World War II, when there were food shortages and fewer wage-earning men at home. Depressions, recessions, and times of high unemployment are also times in which a packet of seeds seems like the best stimulus package a dollar or two can buy. And as we'll show throughout this book, it takes very little money to grow food,

sometimes none at all. If you have a garden there will always be something to eat. It's good to know that.

For many people, time is the issue. Jobs, commuting, child-rearing, care of parents—these are all limiting factors. But people with scarce time can often fit a garden in if they use efficient methods. On weekends, and during those golden hours in summer when the sun sets late, the garden can give you a way to unwind after a day of work. And usually when a family gardens, everyone gets involved to some degree, especially when kids are introduced to it at a young age. Even the oldest relatives can have their place, lightly cultivating a row or shelling peas. Some of the tools we'll introduce will make garden tasks surprisingly easy. Of the two of us, Eliot came to gardening in his late twenties, as an adventure. Barbara's family always loved growing food, especially her busy father, who felt that it lightened his load.

As our country becomes more and more urbanized, the possibility of gardening often seems remote. But most suburban yards permit at least a modest veggie plot. Towns, and even big cities,

have more arable land in them than people think. It's just masquerading as lawn. Look around the place you live and imagine what open spaces might house community food gardens. Hospitals? School grounds? Parks? Even where there is only pavement, city gardens are being planted in plastic milk crates lined with landscaping fabric and filled with soil. Such gardens are also portable, since the crates can be moved to another location if they need to be. And urban gardening is gaining ground. Community gardens, in which each gardener has a plot, have waiting lists, so clearly we need more of them. And these are great places to learn. Veteran gardeners are supportive of newcomers, and willing to share their enthusiasm and expertise.

We have both been growing food for over 45 years. In addition to our home garden, we operate a small organic farm on the coast of Maine, begun in 1968. We've always favored using the simplest possible methods, which we're passing along to you. We'll show you how to apply them if you are just starting out, or have limited time and space for a garden. But this book is also about possibilities. We'll show you how to take the garden a step further, should you so desire, and make it a major sustaining force in your lives. Here's a brief guide to the chapters in our book.

PART ONE: THE GARDEN

1. THE SOIL. We begin by explaining the most important thing you need to know about gardening—starting with good soil—and we introduce you to our gardening philosophy.

2. THE LAYOUT. Armed with an understanding of good soil, it's time to decide what and where your garden should be, and plan it out ahead of time. This allows you to get the most out of your garden each year, whether it's large or small.

3. THE CROPS: WHAT TO GROW. What should you grow? We help you decide based on what kind of garden you'd like to have, whether it's a small salad garden or one that will provide the most food possible, whatever may happen. We explain which crops give you the best return for the space they take up, which crops (and techniques) will provide a year-round supply, and we highlight some irresistible ones we grow just for their superb flavor. We show you how to become self-sufficient by saving your own seeds.

4. THE CROPS: HOW TO GROW. We give you essential details about growing and cooking each crop.

5. MAKING IT EASY. We share our bag of tricks for making the work of gardening easier and more satisfying.

PART TWO: THE KITCHEN

6. APPETIZERS AND SANDWICHES. Tasty meal starters to sharpen the appetite and light open-faced sandwiches to enjoy at lunchtime or for a late-night snack.

7. **SOUPS.** Some long simmered, others ready in under an hour; some hearty and filling, others light and refreshing; all garden fresh and inviting.

8. **SALADS AND DRESSINGS.** Tossed or composed, salads show off garden produce at its best. Greens, tomatoes, cucumbers, peppers, and radishes look as beautiful as they taste when set out in a bowl or plate.

9. **EGG DISHES.** Much more than a breakfast staple, eggs are pleasurable any meal of the day, so enjoy them in a savory custard or bread pudding, an open-faced omelet or a quiche.

10. **PASTA, GRAINS, AND LEGUMES.** Let the many grains, legumes, and pastas that are available act as a background to a mix of fresh and flavorful vegetables straight from your garden.

11. **SUMMER VEGETABLES.** Who doesn't await corn so fresh you can eat it raw or tomatoes, ripe and rich with juice? It's tempting to leave them as is, but try using these glorious vegetables to create some outstanding dishes.

12. **COOKING GREENS.** Tender and leafy, sautéed, steamed, or stir-fried, greens are so good, you can't help but feel healthier after a plateful.

13. **EARTHY VEGETABLES.** Reliable keepers such as carrots, potatoes, and onions are the basis of some of our favorite meals. Properly stored, they are a treasure trove to be enjoyed year-round.

14. **MEAT AND SEAFOOD DISHES.** Combined with vegetables from the garden, meat and seafood play a major role in the dishes in this chapter.

15. **DESSERTS.** Seasonal fruit takes center stage in many of the desserts we serve at our house. Fresh berries, just-picked apples, peaches and plums—irresistible as is or in cobblers, tarts, pies, and custards.

NOTE: Part One of this book is a joint effort. Part Two is by Barbara.

THE BEST FERTILIZER we can offer a new gardener is encouragement. It isn't about having a green thumb. In fact, it isn't even about you. It's about the generosity of the natural world. Given a few basic skills, there is very little you can't accomplish in the garden if you trust the systems that are already in place. Plants want to grow, and despite what you might have heard, there are not armies of pests, plagues, and other misfortunes lying in wait, poised to thwart your efforts. So let's get started! ☀

PART ONE

The Garden

The Soil

ANYONE CAN RECOGNIZE A FERTILE SOIL. Its color is dark brown to black, with a moist look; its texture spongy; its smell earthy, redolent of spring, musky and wholesome. It looks alive. Our awareness of soil is instinctive, from knowledge acquired in ages past, then wired into our DNA and connected to our sense of well-being. We trust fertile soil to grow the quality of food we want to eat. Seeds sown in it spring to life and grow vigorous plants, with vibrant colors. They produce food bountifully. And we know that when we eat that food our bodies will be nourished as they were meant to be.

Few soils a gardener begins with are fertile enough to fulfill that promise, but all of them can be made so. The process is simple—it's a lot like cooking.

THE NATURE OF SOIL

TO UNDERSTAND SOIL BETTER, let's start with the popular parable "Stone Soup." This is a simple tale of soldiers returning from the Napoleonic Wars. As they passed through a poor peasant village they were able to get a meal by telling the inhabitants they would feed them stone soup. After placing a stone in a large kettle of water over a fire, and claiming that was sufficient for the meal to come, they proceeded to hint that maybe a pinch of parsley, some carrots, a few potatoes and such would make the stone soup taste just that much better. Little by little, the initially reluctant villagers volunteered to donate one or another of the suggested "extra" ingredients. The result was a delicious communal meal enjoyed by all.

WHAT SOIL IS MADE OF

BUILDING FERTILE SOIL is a little like making stone soup, because every soil started out as stone or rock. Whether the soil particles in your backyard are now the size of sand (the largest) or silt (smaller) or clay (the smallest), or, as is usually the case, a mixture of the three, they were all originally, and still are, rock. Over passing millennia the rocks have been slowly reduced to their present particle size through the effects of freezing and thawing, the erosive action of wind and water, and the grinding of glaciers. The type of rock the particles originally came from influences their eventual size and determines their mineral content.

Those particles by themselves won't do much for the garden, but add the second key ingredient in soil—water—and the process begins. Not too much water, as with a real soup, but just enough to keep the rock particles consistently moist. Excessive water keeps air from being able to enter the small spaces between the particles, and it's important for air to enter. Air is the third key ingredient in soil. With those three—rock particles, water, and air—soil formation is off and running. For the earliest living organisms on our planet, that was enough, for they were able to survive by extracting mineral nutrients from rock. But as they died and decomposed, their remains began to add a fourth key ingredient: organic matter.

And that's the living earth under your feet. It is tempting to refer to soil as having four *simple* components. But just as with making soup, even a few additions, when combined, become something greater than their sum, a complex blend of flavors. Luckily, you can enjoy that soup without knowing what chemical reactions make it smell and taste so good.

The same goes for soil. As long as you concentrate on adding more of that essential fourth ingredient, organic matter, to the stone, water, and air you started with, you can create a fertile soil without even knowing how it happens. The whole range of benefits you get from the organic matter in the soil is only just beginning to be understood and fully appreciated by agricultural science. But we do know that if we amplify organic matter, plants will thrive. This is true for recent additions of organic matter, such as the roots of the lettuce you just picked, which were

Building fertile soil is a little like making stone soup, because every soil started out as stone or rock.

left behind in the soil and are starting to break down. It's also true for the older, biologically stable, well-decomposed organic material we call *humus*.

SOIL IS ALIVE

THE STORY GETS EVEN BETTER. In your garden there is a fifth component that arises out of all these parts, the most important one of all: soil life. It's not an ingredient like rock particles, water, air, and organic matter, it is the *force* that ties them all together. A marvelous living world exists under your feet and it makes the living world aboveground seem almost empty by comparison. The British scientist J.B.S. Haldane is reported to have said, jokingly, "If one could conclude as to the nature of the Creator from a study of creation it would appear that God has an inordinate fondness for stars and beetles." Beetles are, in fact, 20 percent of all known living organisms. And once you begin to learn about life in the soil, you wonder if Haldane might have better noted a million-fold greater fondness for soil dwellers in general. It has been said that if you include both the ones we can see with the naked eye (such as earthworms, ants, and beetles) and those that are only visible under a microscope (like bacteria and fungi), there are more living creatures in one cup of fertile soil than in the whole of the world above ground.

The sheer mass of soil creatures is as impressive as their numbers. An acre of rich pasture land, the produce of which is sufficient to feed a 2,000-pound steer grazing aboveground for one entire year, harbors a weight of creatures belowground equal to that of the steer

THE LIFE IN A HEALTHY SOIL: Because the soil in which the bean plant grows is rich in organic matter, it's teeming with creatures that give it fertility, aerate it, decompose wastes, make nutrients available to plants, and maintain a loose, crumbly structure. Most are invisible to the naked eye, but life on earth wouldn't be possible without them.

itself. The life processes of those soil creatures within the matrix created by our four original soil ingredients are what provide the fertility to grow the grass that feeds the steer. Soil microbiologists spend their careers identifying, counting, and categorizing these organisms into family, genus, and species, and observing how they interact with one another and with plants. But the home gardener can benefit from all this underground activity without that level of scientific expertise. All you need to know is that soil creatures work best and are most productive in creating fertile soil if you give them three things: a soil that is not too acidic, an adequate level of moisture, and plenty of organic matter.

SOIL PH

MANY GARDEN SOILS are too acidic, or tend to become more so over time. Soil acidity does not promote a mellow environment for most soil creatures, just as stomach acidity is not pleasant if you overindulge. In both cases an antacid helps to return the chemical reaction back to neutral. The antacid for soils is called lime and comes as finely ground particles of limestone, a calcium-containing rock. Most soil creatures are happiest when the soil is neutral to just *slightly* acid. Think of the soil inhabitants as your soil fertility staff. They work for free, so your responsibility is to give them a pleasant work environment by making sure the soil pH (the scale for measuring soil acidity) is between 6 and 7.

The best way to determine your soil pH is to have a soil test done. There are simple home kits that test for pH, but one done by a soil lab will give you information about your soil's mineral content as well. Your local Extension Service or state university will do this for a modest fee, and will usually send you instructions on how to collect the soil sample properly, as well as a mailer in which to submit it. The basics are also shown in the photo at left. (In case you'd like a more detailed report than your state office supplies, it can probably recommend a competent private soil-test lab.) After you send in your sample you'll get back not only an analysis of your soil, but also advice on how to remedy any soil deficiencies. Ask for organic recommendations when you fill out the form.

In general, it takes 5 to 10 pounds of lime per 100 square feet of soil to raise the soil's pH one interval on the scale—say, from 5.5 to 6.5. It takes more lime to raise the pH of clay than it does that of sand, so if

Soil Test

TAKE A SAMPLE. For a pure sample, use stainless steel implements and avoid touching the soil with your fingers. Dig samples from at least 12 places from a depth of 6 to 8 inches.

SEND IT OFF. Mix the soil thoroughly and fill the box or bag provided. Fill out the form the lab gives you, label the container, mail it, and await the results.

your soil is sandy add 5 pounds, and if it's clay add 10. (See the chart on page 17 to find out which you've got.) Bags of lime are available at farm and garden supply stores. If you know you're going to need to raise your soil's pH, you'll want to have enough lime on hand when it's time to start spreading it and other soil amendments on the ground as you begin your new garden. Thereafter, pH may not be much of an issue, because as more organic matter is added to the garden, year by year, it tends to buffer the effects of pH. Most gardeners, however, do add lime every four years because limestone contains calcium, an important plant nutrient.

NOURISHING THE SOIL

ONCE YOU'VE PROVIDED all those soil inhabitants with a great working environment, your second responsibility is to feed them. It couldn't be easier. Their food is organic matter of all kinds, and includes anything that was once alive and growing: the leaves on the forest floor, the dead grass stems in a field, the fallen fruit under a wild apple tree, the wilted flowers in a vase, the celery leaves you discarded when making dinner. This is the basis of Mother Nature's soil fertility system, a fact known since the earliest days of agriculture. The Greek philosopher Anaximander wrote 2,500 years ago, "Everything that forms in Nature incurs a debt which it must repay by dissolving so that other things may form." In other words, everything that once grew eventually rotted back down to provide growing conditions and nutrients for future plants and animals. And best yet, the process is cumulative. In undisturbed conditions, organic matter in the soil increases, and so does soil fertility.

Your job as a gardener is to make sure that a natural increase in fertility is a part of your plan. To do that you have to embrace the idea that all this life in the soil is good—all those bacteria and grubs and spiders are important and helpful to you. Although our society seems to have a passion for sterilizing everything, that is not desirable for your soil. When conditions are favorable, the good bacteria run the system.

Some things, such as the weather, you can't do anything about. Normal amounts of sunshine, rain, and benign temperatures are obviously beneficial to plant growth, and usually you at least have an idea of what to expect in the climate where you live. Things that you *can* control, such as the air, moisture, pH, and organic matter in the soil, are up to you. Gardening is a lot like raising a puppy, and instinct will tell you what to do. Warmth, air, light, food, care, and space to romp are all qualities that vegetables need just as much as puppies do. And soil creatures need them too. The world of soil, plants, and gardens is a wholly connected, heart-beating, pulse-pounding, interacting community of separate parts working in harmony with one goal: life. Under the conditions of the average home garden, maintained with lime and organic matter, the system is on your side.

WHERE TO BEGIN

THE MOST FERTILE SOILS exist in those parts of the world where nature's processes, such as wind and flowing water, have caused extra rock particles and organic matter to be deposited. River-bottom land, where erosion upstream has swept down particles that are left behind after floods, is one example. Areas of very deep fertile soil known as *loess,* formed by soil particles carried by the wind, are another. Soils downwind of active volcanoes may have benefited from the accumulation of volcanic ash—newly created rock particles that often have excellent inherent fertility. Soils that were once lake or sea bottoms before being raised by the earth's geologic activities retain the layers of nutrients deposited in their formative years. *Muck soils* are ones that have accumulated abundant organic material under swamplike conditions and become extremely fertile ground when the excess moisture is drained. Growers lucky enough to garden on river-bottom land, or loess soil, or drained muck have a head start on making the soil fertile, thanks to nature's generosity.

It could be, however, that the originally good soil in your backyard no longer resembles the gift of nature it once was. It may have been left open to erosion, or doused with chemicals, as so many of today's lawns are. It may have been removed during construction or, if it's former farmland, exploited for harvests year after year, with no thought given to maintaining levels of organic matter and minerals. Fortunately, these momentary defects can be fixed. As Tuisco Greiner, a 19th-century garden writer said in the delightful prose of his day, "But it is with soils as it is with people when they get into a bad way. If the foundation—the texture, the quality, the character—is good, they can be redeemed very easily." There's work to be done on such soils, but it is not difficult.

Gardeners in the less-favored areas will have to work a little harder. Where we live, on the Maine coast, another geologic process, glaciation, scraped away most of our soil and left us large stones and occasional patches of bedrock that have not changed much in the 10,000 years since the glaciers receded. But a determined gardener can do what nature has not had time to do yet by following the same principles that created all those naturally fertile soils. One of the classic examples of determined soil-building concerns the Aran Islands off the coast of Ireland. There, over centuries, the inhabitants created acres of fertile earth by layering sand from the beach with seaweed from the ocean, on top of bare limestone bedrock. The 1934 film *Man of*

The world of soil, plants, and gardens is a wholly connected, heart-beating, pulse-pounding, interacting community of separate parts working in harmony with one goal: life.

Aran celebrated both the farmers' efforts at soil creation and the self-sufficient lifestyle that arose as a result. Resolute gardeners everywhere have been inspired by their example to realize that all soils can be made fertile and productive (or just plain "made") with whatever rock particles and organic matter are available.

But isn't the process of overcoming poor soil conditions and creating a garden expensive? Isn't it necessary to buy a lot of stuff? What about all those gardening stories about adding up the costs and ending up with a $100 tomato? True, the $100 tomato is certainly possible if you spread expensive amendments on your garden in hopes that fertile soil might develop a bit sooner. But by understanding the natural soil-creation process we've described, and thinking in terms of inputs of management and knowledge rather than inputs of purchased goods, you can create a rich garden soil without a rich man's budget.

When soil particles flow down a river to be deposited on the floodplain or are carried by wind to fall on the soil surface, the result is an incrementally deeper, thicker layer of good soil—the topsoil. By digging a hole with a shovel and looking at the soil profile on the wall of the hole, you can see how deep the topsoil goes in your garden. It's the darker brown layer at the surface. Many studies have shown that simply making the topsoil deeper can result in better growing conditions for garden vegetables. So part of the soil improvement efforts in our own garden were aimed at increasing the inadequate 3 inches of topsoil nature had given us. Eventually we ended up with 10 inches of beautiful dark, rich, fluffy soil, created almost entirely from resources available on our property.

There were a number of steps to the process. First, we simply collected topsoil that we dug from other parts of the yard where it wasn't needed, such as the site of a new tool shed and the place where we laid a stone patio, and added that to the surface of the garden. Next we took a good look at the nature of our soil.

SOIL TEXTURE

THE TEXTURE of your backyard soil—whether it's fine particle clay, coarse particle sand, or the more friendly silts that lie between—will be an important consideration when trying to build fertile earth. That texture is the result of massive forces such as retreating glaciers, up-thrusting mountains, the depositing of water-carried or wind-carried soil particles, and erosion in general. It could also be the result of bulldozers and backhoes excavating the land on which your home stands. Fortunately, there is one solution to all the problems that your soil texture might cause you: making and spreading organic matter, especially in the form of compost. Whether the dominant particles are sand, silt, clay, or that ideal combination of all three known as *loam,* organic matter improves them all.

Clay soil takes many forms. The red clay found in parts of the South is a familiar sight but clay soils can also be gray, brown, greenish, bluish, yellow, or nearly black. Clay soil tends to be fertile. It holds on to moisture in times of drought. The fine particles provide a huge surface on which plant roots can find minerals. But clay soil can also be very sticky and tends to clump up when it's wet.

The sandy soil in our coastal garden was at the opposite end of the spectrum. It didn't clump. It was well aerated and easy to dig. It emerged from mud season in good shape, draining and warming up quickly when the sun shone. But it didn't hold on to nutrients and moisture well. When we dug a pond on our farm and found heavy blue clay during the excavation, we spread some on our garden and tilled it in. That mixture changed the texture in a most positive way. Maybe one gardener's curse is another's buried treasure.

If you have a really heavy clay soil, you might think that the reverse of what we did would work, and decide to amend the clay with sand. But because of the proportions involved (you'd need an awful lot of sand, and it would have to be very coarse), it wouldn't be as effective as our adding a small percentage of clay. You'd do far better by adding as much organic matter as possible to the soil instead. (For more about improving clay soil, see page 25.)

SOIL STRUCTURE

THE SPONGELIKE QUALITY of organic matter allows it to absorb excess moisture from clay, and hold on to scarce moisture from sand. The action of bacteria breaking down organic matter and digesting it produces *glomalin,* a sticky substance that makes soil particles clump like cookie crumbs to create the aerated structure that plant roots love. In fact, if we hadn't come upon that little bonus in the bottom of our pond, we could have improved the garden with organic matter alone. So the next thing we did, before we even started tilling up the soil, is the single most important thing you can do as a gardener. If you just do this one thing, you're pretty much

Fertile soil rich in organic matter looks like crumbs of chocolate cake.

SOIL TYPES

SOILS ARE COMPOSED of a mixture of particles of varying sizes, and are classified according to which sizes predominate. There are a number of subcategories within the major ones listed below, as defined by the USDA, but these are the ones most frequently used by gardeners in describing their soil.

	CLAY SOIL	LOAM	SANDY SOIL
WHAT IT'S LIKE	• Large percentage of fine particles (less than .002 mm; soil with particles between .002 mm and .05 mm is known as *silt*). • Particles remain tightly clumped together when the soil is squeezed while moist.	• Balanced combination of small and large particles. • Particles remain clumped together moderately well when the soil is squeezed while moist.	• Large percentage of coarse particles (between .05 mm and 2.0 mm). • Particles don't remain clumped together when the soil is squeezed while moist.
BENEFITS	• Retains nutrients. • Slow to dry out in drought.	• Holds on to moisture well in drought. • Drains well in wet weather. • Adequate retention of nutrients.	• Drains well in wet weather. • Resists compaction. • Warms up quickly in spring.
DRAWBACKS	• Hard to work: sticky when wet, hard when dry. • Easily compacted. • Less aeration. • Drains slowly in wet weather. • Slow to warm up in spring.	None.	• Dries out quickly in drought. • Doesn't retain nutrients well.
HOW TO IMPROVE IT	• Add organic matter to increase fertility and produce crumbly structure. Aerate frequently with broadfork or spading fork. • Add lime to raise pH if soil test indicates. Lime also helps to counteract stickiness. • Protect the biological life of the soil by avoiding chemical fertilizers.	• Add organic matter to improve fertility and produce crumbly structure. • Add lime to raise pH if soil test indicates. • Protect the biological life of the soil by avoiding chemical fertilizers.	• Add organic matter to improve fertility and produce crumbly structure. Add clay if available. Add lime to raise pH if soil test indicates. • Protect the biological life of the soil by avoiding chemical fertilizers.

guaranteed success in growing plants because it makes your soil fertile as well as improving its structure. We started a compost heap. In other words, we created our own organic matter factory at home.

"Now wait a minute," you might say. "It's spring and I want to put in a garden right now!" That's fine. You can do it with purchased organic soil improvers (see page 24). But at the same time, you'll want to begin your career as a compost maker— if you expect to garden economically and get the best possible food from your organic garden, year after year. ☼

COMPOST

THE BEST WAY TO ADD FERTILITY in all soils, whether they started out good, were once good but have deteriorated, or were never greatly blessed by nature's hand, is to make and spread compost. Compost is decomposed organic matter, well on its way to becoming the stable humus of the forest floor. It is the remains of once-living things that have been broken down by soil bacteria to a dark brown, crumbly state where their nutrients are ready to be used again by a new generation of plants. It has the sweet aroma of good earth. Adding compost will maintain and increase the crucial organic matter component of your soil, and hence its fertility. Best of all, good compost—the world's best fertilizer—can be made at no cost, right next to your vegetable plot, from the plant waste you'll find in your yard and garden.

HOW COMPOST WORKS

TO CONTINUE OUR stone soup metaphor, think of your compost heap as that iron soup pot, and your compost's ingredients as the vegetables donated to that soup. Just as a soup's flavor is improved by more than one ingredient, so is the quality of compost. The more varied the waste organic matter added to your heap, the more nutritious the finished product is for your plants. But unlike the soup, with its kale, onions, carrots, and potatoes, the compost heap might contain their discarded parts: kale stems, onion skins, carrot tops, and potato vines.

At its simplest the compost heap can be just that: a heap. You can pile up your garden and kitchen wastes in a corner of the yard, and over time (six months to a year and a half) they'll have broken down to a brown to black substance, resulting from the partial decay of plant and animal matter. The creation of compost is a biological process and is the job of all those creatures in the soil who know their roles, and will complete the job. You, the gardener, can help the process along by providing them with ideal working conditions.

Compost heaps heat up through bacterial action as decomposition proceeds. As bacteria break down a pile of organic matter, they create an exothermic reaction—that is, they give off heat. You might help insure the presence of numerous bacteria by sprinkling some soil onto the vegetable waste from time to time to inoculate a new heap with microbes, worms, and other creatures; but usually these come in on their own or with the soil on the roots of weeds or old crops you've pulled. Once the heap starts "working," you can feel its warmth by reaching your hand down into its center. If you take a garden fork and dig in, you'll see moist clouds of steam rising.

TOP: A wire mesh compost bin.
BOTTOM: A bin made of hay bales.

HOW TO CONTAIN COMPOST

AS WE MENTIONED ABOVE, you can just assemble and pile up organic wastes somewhere and compost will happen. But using some sort of container for the compost will make the operation look tidier and may also enhance decomposition. There are many styles, both homemade and purchased, and we have tried a number of them. Here are the two that we have found the easiest to create and use, and the most effective at breaking down organic material.

WIRE MESH. For the average yard, we recommend a 3-foot-high wire mesh enclosure. In our garden we do this by making a 6-sided bin out of the same heavy-duty, 1-inch wire mesh that's used to construct lobster traps in Maine. We purchase it as pre-made panels that are easily linked together, then removed individually for access to the materials inside (see page 453 for a source). An enclosure made from just four panels would be adequate for a small garden. This style is ideal for a climate with average moisture, or one with somewhat more-than-average moisture such as ours. Having walls around the compost helps to raise up the ingredients, especially wet, matted ones, for better aeration. And the fact that they are open mesh also helps let in air.

Air is an important ingredient in successful composting (just as it is in the soil) because all the microorganisms involved use oxygen. There is a simple rule that if the heap has a bad odor, it's too wet. It means that the bad-smelling putrefying bacteria, which do not need air,

Fresh materials added at the top will eventually break down to form compost.

have become dominant. You can cure this by taking your garden fork and mixing the too-wet ingredients with the drier ones to aerate them. On the other hand, aeration can be overdone if too much air movement causes the ingredients to dry out. The old formula holds that for best results, the materials in your compost heap should be as moist as a squeezed-out sponge.

HAY OR STRAW BALES. The other style we like is a compost pile enclosed by walls of hay bales or straw bales. Where either is available this is a great system. And in a cold climate like ours, or during fall, winter, and spring, these insulating walls will aid the process by keeping all those soil bacteria warm, comfortable, and active for as long as possible. (The activities of soil organisms slow way down when the temperature is below 42 degrees Fahrenheit.) Once the bale walls themselves begin to decompose after a year or two, they become an ideal ingredient

Compost, like good cheese and good wine, just takes time.

for future heaps, so we get double use out of them. At our farm operation we make long compost bins this way, but we also use smaller versions next to our home garden. They take up more room than the wire mesh ones do, and are not quite as tidy, but many gardeners find it satisfying to use a natural, biodegradable material. This is also a good system for drier climates, because the bales help keep the heap moist all the way to the edges. Sprinkling your heap with a hose in dry weather will also help keep decomposition going.

You'll find many commercially available "compost makers" on the market. They're usually made of plastic and advertise some novel feature, such as a handle to turn, to entice the buyer. These gadgets are tidy and discreet, for those with fastidious urban neighbors, but some are flimsy and don't deliver all that they promise. They're too small for the amount of compost you'll want to be making, and they don't offer any great benefit. Remember, the process of compost making is as natural as it gets. The fertility of both field and forest is continually maintained by the slow breakdown of organic matter that has fallen on the ground, be it leaves, stems, tree trunks, or buffalo droppings. Perhaps you can speed up the composting process by the extra aeration and turning provided by one of these gadgets, but the end product won't be any better and the cost will be considerable. Once you get ahead of the game and have your first mature compost, you'll always have a ready supply if you keep on making more. It's as if you tried to speed up wine making or cheese aging. Compost, like good cheese and good wine, just takes time.

WHERE SHOULD THE COMPOST HEAP GO?

PEOPLE SOMETIMES TALK ABOUT the compost heap as if it were a trash pile. We suggest you think of it as a member of the family that needs to be fed; if you feed it, it will feed you in soil fertility. So the compost area should be close to and easily reached from the garden, because you'll be making many trips back and forth, both to get garden residues to the compost heap and to bring finished compost to spread on the beds. You'll also want to get your harvest ready for the kitchen without leaving a mess of stems, outer leaves, and tops all over the garden.

To keep peace between kitchen and garden it's always wise to bring in clean vegetables, so any trimming or washing is taken care of before the garden bounty is brought indoors. When we harvest crops, we take them to an outdoor prep area with a sturdy old table right next to our compost heap. With this work area we can shuck the sweet corn, cut off the onion tops, and peel away the outer cabbage leaves directly onto the heap. For preparing root crops, it helps to have a water source nearby so you can easily hose the soil off the carrots and beets. You'll avoid clogging up the kitchen sink, and the food will look much more appetizing when it comes in the door.

On our vegetable farm we use recycled 16- by 24-inch hard-plastic bulb trays for harvesting. Dutch growers ship wholesale bulbs to the U.S. in them, and they're sometimes available from plant nurseries that offer spring bulbs. These trays are handy because the harvested crops can be hosed off right in them. Plastic milk-bottle crates are smaller but work fine for home

From Garden to Kitchen

WASH. A rugged metal table is great for washing soil off newly harvested vegetables, especially root crops.

TRIM. Cut off unusable tops and roots, so they never have to come indoors.

COMPOST. Toss waste right on the compost pile, to become a soil amendment for next year's harvest.

gardeners, as do wire baskets like those used for gathering eggs, or the garden hods that are made with sturdy wire mesh (see page 453 for a source).

FINDING COMPOST INGREDIENTS

SINCE COMPOST IS THE KEY to making your garden work well, you want to make as much of it as possible, and you might need more compost ingredients than your own garden, yard, and kitchen can produce. But once you start looking, you'll be amazed at how much usable organic matter is around. Some enthusiastic gardeners carry a plastic trash can in their car, and make a habit of picking up organic matter that other people don't want. You might begin with your neighbors' yards. Maybe someone keeps rabbits, or a horse. Very often those people have no further use for the manure and will happily contribute it to your garden's fertility. Whether you acquire your neighbors' autumn leaves, hedge trimmings, lawn clippings, or kitchen wastes, you'll want to make sure that whatever you bring home is free from chemical contamination. It's always worth asking about potential contaminants: Some lawn-care companies use products so toxic that they can seriously harm growing plants even after the grass clippings have been thoroughly composted. But for the

Whether you acquire your neighbors' autumn leaves, hedge trimmings, lawn clippings, or kitchen wastes, you'll want to make sure that whatever you bring home is free from chemical contamination.

most part, local organic waste will be a wonderful addition to your compost heap. After all, nature itself has no waste products and nothing is thrown away. The natural world is a cyclical system, and the waste product of one part of that system is the raw material for the next. That is just what Anaximander was talking about, and it's what gardeners have known for thousands of years.

Think about layering, lasagna-style, the organic matter you put into the heap. We divide our ingredients into two categories. The dry brown, high-carbon ingredients such as old cornstalks, dried pea or bean vines, and straw, which are slow to break down, are like the noodles in the lasagna. The moist, often green, high-nitrogen ingredients such as outer lettuce leaves, lawn clippings, kitchen scraps, and farm animal manure, which stimulate rapid breakdown, are the filling. Just as you make the best lasagna by alternating the two categories, so you can make the most effective compost heap. The dry ingredients, which are the fuel for this biological fire, do not pack easily together and thus allow the all-important air to enter more easily through that layer. The moist green ingredients are the fire itself, because they heat up quickly. They tend to mat down and exclude air if used in too thick a layer, but that tendency is easily overcome when a thin layer of the moist green stuff alternates with a thin layer of the dry brown. If you aren't sure which category an ingredient belongs to, just alternate it with other things and all will be well.

Some gardening books suggest using either sawdust or wood shavings as the dry brown ingredient in compost. But

there is scientific evidence that compost is less effective if it contains inadequately decomposed wood particles. That is usually the case when wood products are added to home compost heaps because they are not continually turned, the way compost is in commercial operations. If you want the very best type of dry brown ingredient for your home compost heap, use straw. Straw bales are available at your local farm and garden supply store. But you may find that your yard and garden provide sufficient amounts of dry brown ingredients. Some gardeners consider autumn leaves as a dry brown ingredient, and in small amounts they can be used in that way; but if you have access to large quantities of leaves, they're better placed in a separate pile on their own.

COMPOSTING AUTUMN LEAVES

WHERE LOTS OF autumn leaves are available, collect as many as you can every fall. In order for them to contribute to your garden's fertility, you'll first have to place them in a large pile by themselves and wait a few years—much longer than for a more diversified heap. But the resulting product, called leaf mold, is a long-treasured benefit to garden soils. The simplest way to go about this is to enclose an area with a circle of stiff wire fencing about 3 feet high. Make this leaf mold playpen as wide as you can get leaves to fill it. When you first dump the leaves in they may be so fluffy that the pile fills quickly. They will eventually settle down, but you can assure getting your bin as full as possible if you also jump in and stomp them down. Kids love doing this. If the leaves are very dry, bring over the hose and add moisture to the pile. The decomposition of autumn leaves takes place principally by virtue of *fungal* rather than bacterial action. Thus the extra moisture and the stomped-down condition do not hinder the making of leaf mold the way they would a bacterially powered compost heap.

If you make a new pile every year, you'll have a continual supply of leaf mold to lighten the soil and improve its fertility for both fruits and vegetables. The best way to use leaf mold is to mix it into the soil at the end of the gardening season and let it finish its decomposition and blend in with your soil particles over the winter. Natural soil tillers such as earthworms will lend a hand.

OTHER MATERIALS TO EXCLUDE

ALTHOUGH FARM ANIMAL manures make fine additions, either in the heap itself or—if well-decomposed—tilled directly into the soil, it is important not to use droppings from dogs or cats. These share too many parasites with humans. Many gardeners also avoid putting in meat scraps for fear of attracting rodents. Living in the country as we do, with all sorts of creatures scurrying and flying about our yard, we don't pay much attention to this. But if you or your neighbors would find them offensive, meat is best avoided.

WHEN IS IT "DONE"?

COMPOST IS CONSIDERED MATURE when its original ingredients are no longer recognizable. It just looks like beautiful,

Leaf mold is a beautiful crumbly substance, good for lightening and enriching garden soil.

dark, rich, crumbly soil. And as we said, if you do nothing to your compost pile but let it sit there, it will turn into this "black gold" that gardeners crave—usually in about a year. However, you can speed things up if you turn your compost once during the process. Take a fork like a digging fork or a manure fork, and mix the materials up so that the least completely decomposed areas (on top of the pile and around the edges) are placed where the action is (at the center and bottom). You can do this either by forking the material into an adjacent empty bin, or by forking it onto the ground and then back into the original container. Do this in fall, and a summer's worth of waste will usually be ready to use on the garden by the following spring.

If you live in a climate where the soil freezes in winter, you might consider adding the compost to the garden in fall, even if it is not fully mature, and letting it break down the rest of the way in the soil. With frozen ground there will be no danger of the nutrients being leached away before they are used. However, if you live where there are excessive fall and winter rains, and no freezing of the ground, it's better to wait until spring. ☀

OTHER SOURCES OF ORGANIC MATTER

CHANCES ARE THAT the compost you make will be all the organic matter your garden needs, but if you're just starting a garden on new ground, especially if the soil's structure needs help (as ours did), there are some initial steps to take while your compost pile is cooking.

GREEN MANURES. One time-honored technique is to plant a green manure. This is a crop you grow not for harvest but rather for improving the soil. There are many such crops to choose from, but the clovers are especially beneficial. As with all members of the legume family, nodules form on clovers' roots that help make nitrogen in the air available to plants—including those that might later be planted in the same place. When they are tilled under, their aboveground parts add fertility to the soil as well. The taller clovers such as sweet clover require farm equipment to mow and till them, but white clover (and red clover, too, if cut early in the season) can be mowed with a lawn mower and then turned under with a home rotary tiller, also known as a rototiller, or even a garden spade. It's important to wait at least three weeks before sowing or transplanting a garden crop into the bed, to allow the tilled or turned-under material to sufficiently decompose.

Another way to manage green manures is to plant ones that will be killed by winter cold, so that all you have to do is rake up the residue in spring and compost it, leaving the root residue in the ground. In our climate these might include legumes such as common vetch and field peas, or grasses such as oats and barley. In a climate with milder winters (below zone 6), you'd need plants like cowpeas or crotolaria, which are even more sensitive to cold.

Green manures also serve as placeholders when there is bare ground you're not ready to plant; they shade the soil, deter weeds, and prevent erosion. When used this way, without the chief goal of soil-improvement, they are referred to as cover crops, but they improve the soil nevertheless. They are all easy to sow simply by broadcasting the seeds over the area, raking them in, tamping the soil, then watering—just as you would if you were seeding a lawn.

BULK COMPOST. The other thing you can do in the absence of abundant compost is to find a bulk source of organic matter. Commercial compost can be purchased by the truckload or in bags, although the ingredients in it are often hard to determine and the quality varies. If you locate a convenient and available source of aged animal manure to till in, you're in luck!

PEAT MOSS. Another option is to spread a 2-inch layer of peat moss and till that in. Peat is the partially decomposed remains of plants that underwent their decomposition in a water-saturated environment in the absence of oxygen. Without oxygen the decomposition can proceed only so far. Peat, therefore, maintains a much more fibrous structure than that of compost due to a higher percentage of incompletely broken down *lignin,* the major structural component of mature plants. That fibrous quality

A good supply of well-made compost is a gardener's wealth.

improves the physical condition of the soil, lightening heavy clay soils by letting in air. In fact, adding peat to clay transforms it better than anything else you can do. It improves sandy soils as well, making them more able to absorb and retain water and nutrients.

Whereas compost can be made for free, peat has to be purchased, usually at garden centers in large, plastic-wrapped bales. Fall is a good time to shop for it. For most people the gardening season is over, so the garden center will no longer be selling many summer products. If they have lots of peat bales left, offer to take them at a discount. They might like to avoid moving and storing them for the winter.

Some authorities recommend adding an additional inch of peat every few years if you have clay soil, but in most cases plenty of compost will answer your soil's needs in years to come. Keep in mind that although peat improves soil structure, it does not add to soil fertility. Yearly applications of compost, rotted manure, or leaf mold—or all three—will bring you closer and closer to the ideal garden soil. In every case, the life in the soil, those billions of soil organisms large and small that feed on the organic matter, will come to your aid loosening, aerating, and producing fertility. They are your invaluable allies in working the soil you were dealt. ☀

Planting a crop of clover is especially beneficial for improving the soil.

MINERALS IN THE SOIL

ANOTHER THING we did before setting a single plant in the ground was to refer to our soil test (see page 12). It's nice to think that compost and perhaps some leaf mold can be the only yearly soil amendments your garden needs, and in many cases they can be! But if the soil you started with, from which much of your compost ingredients were created, is deficient in some important mineral, that mineral will not be created out of thin air by alchemy, and will have to be imported. The best assessment of that deficiency will come from your soil test.

Soil tests don't always tell the whole story. If you send samples to two or three labs that follow different testing philosophies, the results won't match perfectly. It's a little like the old saying that a man with one watch knows what time it is, but the man with two watches is never sure. Besides, there are many factors in soil fertility, including the quality and quantity of the compost you've been adding each year. But that initial soil test will give you a general idea of your soil's mineral status, as a baseline for making decisions.

PHOSPHORUS AND POTASSIUM. The two minerals that are most important here are phosphorus (P) and potassium (K). They are the P and K of the N-P-K trio on bags of mixed organic fertilizers for sale at your local garden center. (N stands for nitrogen.) The manufacturers have tried to come up with a reasonable balance between them in order to benefit particular crops, such as lawns, roses, or vegetables. But those percentages are just an approximation of what your plants might need, when all aspects of your garden's soil are taken into account.

In our gardening we have long followed what we consider the most experienced opinion on soil fertility, that of Mother Nature. Because all the mineral particles in the soil started out as rocks, and it's the interaction of soil organic matter, soil creatures, and plant roots that liberate nutrients from those rocks, we prefer to add any missing minerals in their natural rock form. Not as boulders, of course, but as finely ground rock powder (see below) similar to the soil particles themselves. By bringing into our garden only those mineral sources that were laid down in the geologic past, we don't have to worry about whether they contain chemical contamination from the modern world. Many of the commercial organic fertilizers available, such as bonemeal (which has been found to be high in lead) or feather meal and leather dust (which come from industry), don't seem as desirable so we prefer not to use most of them.

To add phosphorus, we use rock phosphate, a powder ground from rock deposits high in phosphorus. There are many brands on the market. Rock containing up to 12 percent potassium is found in some granite quarries, and bags of granite dust and other rock powders high in potassium are also sold. A useful product called greensand (glauconite) is mined from petrified seaweed deposits. In addition to potassium, greensand contains a whole range of trace elements, also called micronutrients, which are minor minerals like iron, sulfur, zinc, copper, and boron. We call them minor because they are only needed in small amounts by plants, but they are nonetheless vital to plant health and vigor. Many rock-based soil amendments, with various mineral ratios, are also sold. But rock phosphate and greensand, readily available, have done well by our garden over the years, as dependable and effective sources of P and K, and as a micronutrient insurance policy (see page 453 for sources). Fertilizers made from sustainably harvested seaweed and from fish or crustaceans also contain a range of micronutrients. Certain manures can also be a good source. Since the diets of cattle and sheep are often supplemented with trace minerals to keep the animals healthy, adding their manures to your compost heap will contribute these elements, in addition to being excellent sources of potassium.

Rock phosphate and greensand can be spread on the soil using a hand scoop in early spring or late fall at the recommended rate. If you have no such recommendation, we suggest 10 pounds per 100 square feet for your first application. Next year's soil test will tell you if you need more. After spreading, mix them in. A rotary tiller (see pages 40) is excellent for that initial mixing in a new garden since these rock particles work best if dispersed throughout the top 6

A hand scoop, available at a hardware or feed store, is a handy implement for sprinkling on rock powders such as greensand (left) and rock phosphate (right).

inches of your soil, as if they were members of your soil's original rock particle collection.

CALCIUM AND MAGNESIUM. Two other elements worth considering are calcium and magnesium. If you've spread limestone on your soil to make it less acidic, you've already added calcium, the principal mineral constituent of limestone. Limestone rocks contain varying levels of magnesium as well, so in most cases you've added that too. Different types of limestone are recommended in different parts of the country. If the soils in your area respond to a high-magnesium limestone, you should be able to learn that from the Extension Service, your soil test, or the local garden center.

NITROGEN. As for nitrogen, a very important element for plant growth, your compost applications should provide an ideal amount. If you do think extra nitrogen would help at the start, or if you're short on compost, there is a very natural product we can recommend from experience: alfalfa meal. Alfalfa is a deep-rooted, highly nourishing forage crop that is fed extensively to livestock. Alfalfa meal is made from alfalfa that was heat-dried after harvest to preserve all its nutrients. It is normally mixed into poultry rations, and pelleted forms are available for horses. Gardeners have found it to be a nice supplementary fertilizer for fast-growing green leafy crops like spinach. You can buy it from feed stores and from garden centers that stock organic fertilizers.

Just because you're using "natural" ingredients, don't assume you can't overdo it. Certain "organic" fertilizers like dried blood (a slaughterhouse byproduct available at most garden centers), if overused, can imbalance your soil system with excessive nitrogen in the same detrimental way that chemicals can, producing abundant but weak growth in plants and making them more susceptible to disease. Dumping on too much phosphate rock, although it is not water soluble like the chemical fertilizer superphosphate, can push plant growth without a corresponding consumption of nutritious trace elements. Wood ashes from woodstoves and fireplaces, although a popular organic fertilizer, contain both calcium and potassium in extremely soluble forms, and we know of many cases where using the garden as a disposal area for wood ashes has raised the pH too high and created an excess of potassium, which replaces other valuable nutrients. Most of this is common sense. If you get the occasional soil test for guidance, you'll steer a sensible course toward good soil. ☀

This colorful salad of mixed ingredients—lettuce, baby beet greens, curly endive, claytonia, and spinach—is like a multivitamin in a bowl.

NOURISHING THE GARDENER

THERE IS ANOTHER REASON to pay close attention to all the things that produce a fertile soil. You're not just interested in your horticultural triumphs, you also care about how well the vegetables you grow will feed you and your family. This means not only providing food, but providing *exceptionally nutritious* food. In

Eating these spring dandelion greens helped give our chickens' eggs their rich orange yolks. A salad made from both gives us a nutritional boost.

If we do right by the natural world, it will do right by us.

other words, is this carrot a good carrot, or what we'd call a "real" carrot?

Food isn't what it used to be. In recent decades researchers have analyzed vegetables for their mineral content and found that those grown today are far lower in key minerals than those that were tested in the 1940s and 50s. Regarding our diet, phrases such as "hidden hunger" and "the dilution effect" have come into common use. Why are vegetables less nutritious now? It has a lot to do with how they are being grown. Here are some of the causes given:

✦ New varieties bred solely for high yield rather than high nutrition.

✦ The declining availability of minerals in soils worn out by overuse of chemical fertilizers, without maintenance of the all-important organic matter.

✦ Pesticide residues that have been absorbed by plant roots in toxic soils.

✦ The forcing of plants into unnaturally fast growth by using high doses of soluble chemical fertilizers.

For most of us who've long been involved in organic agriculture, none of this is surprising. It has always seemed obvious that using exceptionally soluble forms of a limited number of nutrients to force plant growth might in turn make the plants' nutrient content unbalanced, and hence make them less nutritious for us to eat. And, we reasoned, if soil organic matter is as important as the scientific literature has always told us it is, how could anyone expect to grow good food in worn-out soil where organic matter is lacking?

We concluded years ago that if we wanted to eat the finest quality

vegetables containing everything they should contain, we'd need to grow them ourselves. If we paid attention to mineral balance, soil aeration, and organic matter levels we would return food to its former wholesomeness. But we could also go beyond that. Today's organic gardeners have access to tools and techniques that were not easily available in the early days of farming. To give just a few examples, small rotary tillers can mix mineral-rich rock powders throughout the soil more effectively. For weed control, today's gardeners can use a properly angled hoe that works shallowly, sparing the root systems of crops so they can take up enough important minerals (see photo at right). And today's composting techniques draw from all the discoveries of research into the importance of organic matter.

As we gain a clearer picture of nature's systems, we understand how important it is to follow them rather than replace them. This is as true on the livestock farm as it is in the garden. The cattle that provide us with meat and milk were designed by nature to eat grass. But for many decades they have been fed on concentrated grain diets consisting of mostly corn and soybeans—to push them toward faster and fatter growth. Just as with plants, this forcing makes them ill, and compromises the quality of the food we derive from them. Up-to-date studies now show that meat and milk from grain-fed cattle have far lower levels of certain important nutrients than meat and milk from grass-fed cattle. Hens raised outdoors on fresh carotene-rich greenery lay eggs with deep orange, carotene-rich yolks, whereas confined hens are fed a dye to achieve a pretense of that color.

There are nutritional benefits, beyond what agricultural science can even test for at the moment, to be found in food produced in alignment with natural principles. After studying the patterns of plant growth in field and forest, we have modeled our garden practices on these realities of the natural world. We consider that the only way to garden. ☀

What is an Organic Gardener?

EVERYONE IS FAMILIAR with the basic idea of organic gardening—that it avoids using pesticides and chemical fertilizers. Pesticides leave poisonous residue on vegetables and in the soil, and they harm wildlife. Runoff from chemical fertilizers pollutes rivers, streams, and drinking water. Neither pesticides nor chemicals make logical sense since food can be grown so successfully without them. But there's much more going on in an organic garden than just the absence of the negatives—the things you don't do, the practices you don't use. The real benefit comes from the presence of the positives— the things you *do,* the soil-building practices you employ.

If we do right by the natural world, it will do right by us. As organic gardeners we acknowledge the wisdom of what we see in nature as a pattern for our actions. We try to maintain soil fertility and plant health by imitating and enhancing natural processes:

✦ Adding compost made from garden leftovers mimics the annual deposit of organic matter from dead leaves, stems, fruits, and animal wastes that created the planet's fertile virgin soils.

✦ Additions of finely ground rock minerals augment the soil's nutrient supplies in their original form.

✦ Crop rotations correspond to the natural successions through which plants in field and forest pass over the years.

✦ Cover crops and mulches duplicate nature's system of soil protection against hot sun and pounding rains.

✦ Having a wide variety of plants in both the garden and surrounding areas approximates some of the diversity of an undisturbed ecosystem.

✦ Gently loosening the soil in a garden of annual plants duplicates the aeration that would normally be provided by perennial roots, and it supplements that which is provided by soil creatures.

✦ The sprinkler mimics a gentle rain.

✦ When you think about it, the only thing we do differently is reduce the randomness of what crops dominate others, favoring our choice of vegetables and flowers by spacing them appropriately and eliminating weed competition with a sharp hoe.

In short, nature's systems are impeccably designed. The more we understand and plug into them, the simpler it becomes to achieve gardening success. ☀

The angle of this collinear hoe keeps it parallel to the soil surface, and allows it to skim the soil shallowly, destroying weeds but sparing the roots of crop plants.

The Layout

GARDENS TODAY are different from the country gardens of a hundred years ago, when people had plenty of room for them. They were like miniature farm fields, laid out row by row with wide paths in between, as if a tractor—or a horse—would be by any minute to cultivate those rows for you, hill up the potatoes in them, and plow them under after they had fed you well. Now it's just you and your spade, rake, and hoe, and the space your great-grandfather allotted for his pea patch might be bigger than your whole garden. That's where careful planning comes in.

THE OVERALL PICTURE

YOU'RE OFF TO A GOOD START with a sound philosophy of gardening and a focus on the importance of soil. You've got a spade in your hand and you're ready to go. But first you'll need to make a few basic decisions about time and space.

HOW BIG SHOULD THE GARDEN BE?

LET'S IMAGINE two gardening households. One is eager to till up half the yard and plant every crop that looks great in the seed catalog. The other is timid about the whole idea of food gardening, not to mention the time or work it might take, so those folks are opting for a small (or even tiny) garden. With both families the outcomes will depend on how well they have judged their abilities, time constraints, and needs. We've seen complete beginners produce large, fabulous gardens on the first go and others—even veteran gardeners—who overestimate the amount of upkeep they'll be able to do. We've also seen novices with small gardens explode with ambition by season's end, as they realize how satisfying their new pastime is, and how it has whetted their palates for even more homegrown chow. And that's the great thing about gardens made up of annual food crops. You start over again each year, and can so easily expand or contract the garden's size (as we'll see on page 40), as well as choose what crops to grow.

Take a look at your dining table. Is that the size garden you'd like to have? It could be. The plan for the Salad Garden on page 65 might be just right for your first step, with a half dozen different crops to try. If that doesn't sound like the cornucopia you had in mind, take a look at the room the table is in. Is that more like it? In a 12-foot-square garden like the one in the plan on the opposite page, you could add some cooking greens to the fresh ones, plus some other favorites like tomatoes, peppers, zucchini, peas, beans, scallions, herbs, and even a few root crops like carrots and beets—just enough to spark up your summer and fall meals. (Later on we'll show you how to make that 144 square feet behave like even more, by planting succession crops.) Ramping it up a bit with

We love using fresh herbs. Our herb garden is right outside the kitchen.

a 12-FOOT BY 12-FOOT GARDEN

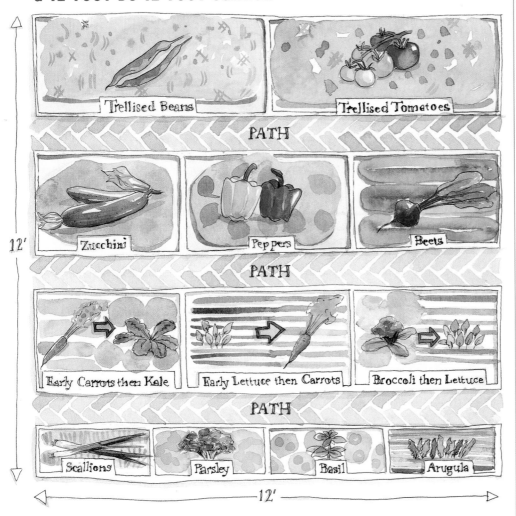

Trellised Beans

Trellised Tomatoes

PATH

Zucchini

Peppers

Beets

PATH

Early Carrots then Kale

Early Lettuce then Carrots

Broccoli then Lettuce

PATH

Scallions

Parsley

Basil

Arugula

12'

12'

Even a 12-foot by 12-foot garden can take you from spring to fall with lettuce, scallions, arugula, beans, carrots, tomatoes, peppers, zucchini, broccoli, beets, kale, and herbs like basil and parsley.

a 24-foot-square garden (576 square feet), you'll find that you don't go to the produce market nearly as much as you used to.

So let's say you have decided to feed your family as much as you can from your own yard, whether from necessity, love of food (or food gardening), or just the challenge of it. What would it take to do that?

Here's some data. A figure used by the wartime garden programs mentioned on page 3 suggested that 1,000 square feet was adequate to grow all the vegetables to feed one person for a year. Multiplied out to feed a family of four, that area would amount to 4,000 square feet, which you can visualize as a square approximately 64 feet on each side. But with today's

The perennial garden gives us fresh flowers all season, and attracts helpful insect pollinators.

more productive varieties and more intensive planting techniques, the goal can be achieved on less land, especially in warm areas where the season is longer. Our present home garden encompasses 2,500 square feet for the vegetables plus an additional 2,500 square feet for fruit trees, berry crops, a grape trellis, and a bit of extra just for new projects. For example, we have a small plot we call "Barbara's test garden," where unfamiliar varieties and unusual cooking ingredients are tried out. We delight in having enough space to grow new crops, in being able to feed visitors generously, and in having extra to share with neighbors and friends.

We'll be using the plan of our garden, shown on the opposite page, to illustrate our techniques for making the garden extra productive, and to show you what it would actually take to supply a household

with the produce it needs—all from the garden. You may not want to grow one that size, at least not initially. You can easily scale our plan down by omitting crops that don't interest you, and by cutting down on the number of beds assigned for each. Or you can add crops and add beds if the project is for a large family, or for a special project like a school garden.

HOW MUCH TIME WILL THE GARDEN TAKE?

WHAT IS A REASONABLE INVESTMENT of time in your garden? Is it really possible to make this part of an everyday modern lifestyle? One answer to that question can be arrived at by a simple mathematical calculation. According to government statistics, the average American spends about 10 percent of

OVERALL PLAN OF OUR FOOD GARDEN

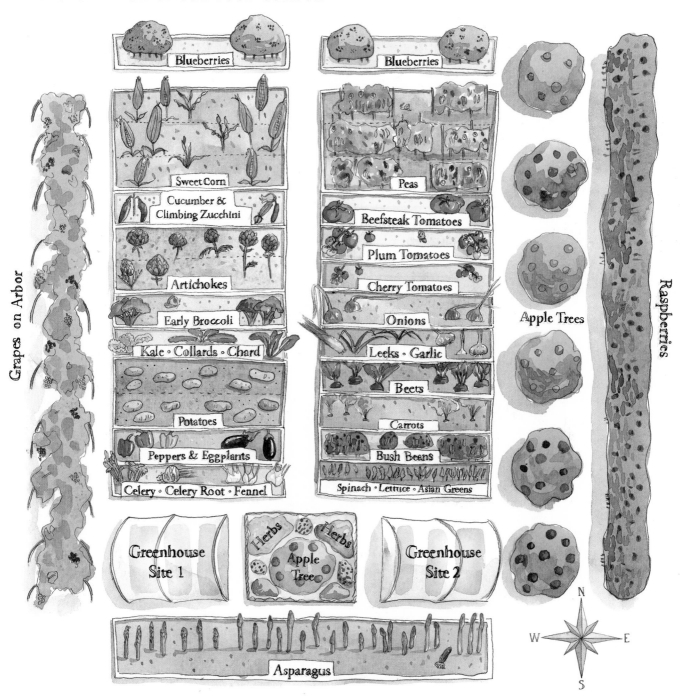

Grapes on Arbor

Blueberries

Blueberries

Sweet Corn

Cucumber & Climbing Zucchini

Artichokes

Early Broccoli

Kale · Collards · Chard

Potatoes

Peppers & Eggplants

Celery · Celery Root · Fennel

Peas

Beefsteak Tomatoes

Plum Tomatoes

Cherry Tomatoes

Onions

Leeks · Garlic

Beets

Carrots

Bush Beans

Spinach · Lettuce · Asian Greens

Apple Trees

Raspberries

Greenhouse Site 1

Herbs

Herbs

Apple Tree

Greenhouse Site 2

Asparagus

N
W   E
S

his or her income on food. Using that 10 percent figure, we calculate that you spend half a day of a five-day workweek paying for your purchased food. Obviously, the home garden isn't going to supply all of your food, even if you're a vegetarian, but this at least gives you a place to start in figuring the garden's economics.

One half-day per week is more than generous for getting the work done. On average over the course of the year we spend far less than that on our home garden. We're not counting the harvesting, which cancels out the time spent shopping for produce; we're talking about the actual hours spent preparing, planting, and tending the garden. We haven't subtracted that half-day from our regular workweek. We have added it on weekends or in the evenings because it's an enjoyable activity and a practical source of exercise. Short periods of digging, lifting, forking, wheeling, and bending are good for the body if you do these things regularly, pacing yourself to avoid strain; and they're a great way to unwind if you have a sedentary, indoor job. Besides, a garden is not something we take lightly. The quality of our

The quality of our family's food is crucial to us, so it's worth spending some time to assure it.

family's food is crucial to us, so it's worth spending some time to assure it.

After-work gardening has an interesting history. The introduction of daylight saving time in March of 1918, when the First World War was at its height and rationing was common, was due to the lobbying efforts of the National War Garden Commission. The commission was the power behind the original war garden program and had argued that setting the clock ahead every spring would result in the production of more food in home gardens, since it would give gardeners an extra hour of light after work every day. In materials published after the war, the commission proudly stressed how effective that extra hour of light during the gardening season had been. By multiplying all those extra hours over the course of the year by the number of war gardeners (more than five million by their estimate), they came up with the stupendous total of 900 million hours of gardening gained every year thanks to daylight saving time.

The victory gardens during World War II were even more productive, with some 20 million gardens planted, and an estimated total of vegetables grown that was equal to the whole of the country's commercial farm production. In fact, the victory gardens were so important that in 1946, when government encouragement ended and the number of gardens dropped way off, there was a major shortage of vegetables because commercial output had not recovered back to prewar levels. Today, it's estimated that there are as many acres of lawns in the U.S. as there are acres growing the huge U.S. corn crop—lawns

that could be enlisted in the service of our own food supply. So if you set aside a small plot of your land and spend an hour at the end of those long summer days growing food, you can feel a kinship with the many patriotic gardeners of years past.

WHERE SHOULD THE GARDEN GO?

THE BEST SITE FOR YOUR GARDEN will partly depend on its size, but the most important consideration will be sunlight. Yes, there are some vegetables that will put up with part shade (the leafy ones), and yes, there are some times when part shade might be a good thing (growing lettuce in midsummer), but for the most part full sun is what food plants need. Much as we love our own trees, we have occasionally cut one down in order to let the sun shine on a garden. (If you do have to remove a tree, try to plant a young one somewhere else on your property as a replacement.)

The ideal garden is accessible. You want to be able to easily enter and exit the area, move around in it.

Sunlight powers photosynthesis and photosynthesis creates vegetables, so choose a site that gets at least six hours of full sun. If there is no big sunny spot, it's better to divide your crops among several smaller sunny areas than to struggle with too much shade.

The ideal garden is accessible. You want to be able to easily enter and exit the area, and move around in it. If the garden is fenced, the gates need to be pleasant to open and shut, and there should be enough of them to give access to well-traveled routes. If you need to pass by or under trees on the way to the garden, don't hesitate to prune a spreading or low-hanging branch so you don't have to walk around it or risk bumping your head. If there's a main path to the garden, think about giving it an all-weather surface, like slate pavers or gravel, to avoid slogging through mud in the wet season. And since you'll probably want to deliver bulky materials such as manure or straw bales to the garden, it's helpful to have nearby access for a vehicle.

There is a tendency to think of a garden as something tucked away at the back of the property. An out-of-sight location may have been common in the past but in today's food-conscious world, that attitude is changing. Not only does it make sense to place the garden close to the kitchen for quick access, but many modern gardeners, especially those with limited space, have taken the bold step of putting the vegetable garden in the front yard. A well-managed vegetable garden can easily be the prettiest part of the property, so why *not* put it out where everyone can enjoy it? Just keep in mind that wherever you place the garden, easy access to a hose spigot for irrigation will make your life easier.

Choosing a site with good soil is another consideration that is often mentioned in gardening literature, but it's not next on our list. Beautiful deep, fertile soil is unlikely to be found in most backyards. We've both seen successful gardens on marginal sites that would logically have been passed over because they were too wet or too rocky. That experience has taught us to connect luxurious soil with the determined activities of the gardener rather than a fortunate chance of geography. An overly wet soil can be drained, and if that's not possible, the garden can be elevated above the water table by creating a raised growing area. Rocks can be removed. If they're too numerous or too large or are actually solid ledge, they can be covered with soil. Twelve inches of soil is sufficient height above a wet spot or a rock ledge to successfully grow most garden plants. Gardeners have created productive gardens in unlikely places for thousands of years out of the necessity of growing food. Think of those lovely *National Geographic* pictures of steep hillsides terraced into small fields in the Andes or Southeast Asia, and you'll realize that in most cases the average backyard presents far fewer challenges. Just follow the soil fertility guidelines in the preceding chapter and you can make any backyard produce vegetables. ☀

The bright red flowers of Scarlet Runner bean vines are followed by edible beans.

The first-year garden often shows extra vigorous growth. Maybe it's just nature's way of encouraging you to keep gardening.

DIGGING IN

NOW THAT YOU KNOW MORE about what you are doing, let's put that spade to work.

PREPARING THE SITE

HERE'S A TYPICAL SCENARIO: A part of your lawn is about to become a vegetable garden. We're all in favor of that, and not just because food is a more interesting and valuable thing to grow. The grasses and clovers that grow in lawns are very much like the grasses and clovers in the pastures of a farm. Even though a lawn mower rather than a large herbivore eats your "pasture," the same fertility-creating process is at work. The root mass of the grasses and clovers spreads fiber throughout the soil and the leafy residue adds organic matter to the surface. These processes are time-honored soil improvers. They created the deep fertile soils of the Great Plains.

The other promising thought is that there is often what we call a beneficial "x-factor" the first year on new land. We have never seen a scientific explanation, but perhaps because there have been no vegetables on that land previously, or because the residual fertility gives a nice boost, the first-year garden often shows extra vigorous growth. Maybe it's just Mother Nature's way of encouraging you to keep gardening.

Nevertheless, you'll still need to add the amendments we spoke of in Chapter 1, especially if your lawn has been chemically fed and struggles on thin, compacted soil. So in go the organic materials such as compost, well-rotted manure, leaf mold, and peat moss—plus lime, and rock powders as needed. That part is quite simple. You just mark out your garden with stakes and string, squaring the corners, and spread your amendments. For a large garden a mechanical spreader is handy for the powdery stuff, but it can also be broadcast

A rototiller is useful for putting in a new garden.

by hand. Compost, manure, and peat moss can be spread using a wheelbarrow or cart, and a shovel. Then you'll need to till them in, along with the grass sod on which they rest. Since you want to incorporate them very thoroughly to get the garden off to a healthy start, this is usually a job for a rototiller, even though you may never need to use one again. One can be borrowed, rented, shared with neighbors, or just brought over by someone you hire to do the job for you. If it's a small garden you may be able, armed with a good sharp spade, to dig the soil by hand, mixing in your additions and chopping up the sod as you go. In either case, you want the soil to be loosened and the amendments incorporated to a depth of 6 inches.

The best time to do all this is fall because it gives the sod plenty of time to decompose over the winter, giving you a decent seedbed. But if you're reading this in spring and are eager to get going, that's fine, as long as you wait till the soil is no longer soggy when you till, as this can ruin its structure. If you get too late a start for spring-planted crops, just put in a garden in summer and plan for a bountiful harvest in the fall months.

A stout mattock turns you into a "human rototiller."

In future years, if you want to expand the garden, just repeat this procedure in a plot marked out next to the existing one. To make the garden smaller, sow part of it back to grass and clover. Their fertility-enhancing powers will get right to work, and the area will be all ready for you if you change your mind again and want that part of the garden back. Some annual weeds may germinate along with the lawn seeds, but they'll be done in the first time you mow the new lawn.

On the other hand, not all new gardens will have the benefit of following fertile grassland that can be tilled up. Our present garden was woods when we began, and even after a backhoe removed the tree stumps, the soil was not ready to be tilled. So we began with mattocks, the classic rough soil-working tool. A mattock looks like an axe but with the blade turned at a right angle. Moving across the area chop by chop, like a couple of human rototillers, we set wheelbarrows next to us into which we could throw the rocks and tree roots we removed as we went along. That sounds daunting, but we found the key to success was to set a reasonable target—say, 200 square feet—each time we worked. We would get an area de-rooted and de-rocked and then till in lime, rock powders, and composted manure. It's amazing how much one can accomplish bit by bit over time, and it's all the more satisfying a garden because of the sweat that went into it.

MAKING A PLAN

NOW THAT YOUR PLOT IS TILLED and amended, you have a blank brown canvas on which to sketch out your garden. It's a good idea to do this on paper before you do it with garden tools. You want it to be productive, beautiful, and easy to maintain. Here are some things to think about: Take a look at the drawing of our garden's plan on page 35. We've always divided our garden into beds that are 30 inches wide, with 12-inch paths between them. The main access path through the garden runs on a north/south axis, with our growing beds and their paths extending off to either side of it, and perpendicular to it. (In a much smaller garden, a center path might not be needed.) That layout fulfills several needs.

Orientation

IT'S IMPORTANT TO ORIENT the garden so that you can take best advantage of your sunlight and get the most use out of your soil. We grow the taller crops in the beds to the back (north) of the garden, where they won't deny sunshine to the shorter vegetables in front. In addition to naturally tall crops like sweet corn and artichokes, we can grow any crops we wish to train vertically on a trellis, like tomatoes, cucumbers, peas, pole beans, and climbing zucchini. Trellised crops use vertical space rather than horizontal space, and thereby give us a bigger yield per square foot of garden. (For more about the virtues and techniques of trellising vegetables, see pages 240 to 244.)

Paths

IT'S ALSO IMPORTANT that the garden area be a pleasant place with enough space for the gardener to move about comfortably. Some people might prefer

wider paths between the beds than the 12 inches we allow, so they should adjust them accordingly. If you plan on using a wheelbarrow or a cart, make sure the main garden path is *at least* 4 feet wide. That way you can easily deliver compost to the garden—and bring compost materials from the garden to the compost heap—without stumbling, tipping over the wheelbarrow, bumping into its handles, or inadvertently stepping on garden plants. A two-wheeled garden cart will be easier for some people to use than the classic wheelbarrow, since it won't tip over. But others prefer the classic one-wheeled type, which has better maneuverability. We like one that holds 6 cubic feet of material, but if your garden and yard are small you might find one that holds 4 cubic feet more convenient.

Bed Style

THE DIVISION OF A GARDEN into paths and beds is based on a simple elemental fact: Plants grow best in soil that is not compacted. In between are the places where the gardener walks. Even in the wild you see paths where large animals walk habitually and plants no longer grow, because both the soil and the wild plants have been trodden down. In large-scale agriculture, tractor wheels compress the soil as they proceed down the fields, allowing crops to grow in the loose soil between rows. In old engravings of garden scenes from 500 years ago, you'll see gardens divided into growing and walking areas, often with little hedges or fences for emphasis.

Gardeners sometimes make the distinction even clearer by raising the soil in beds above the normal level of the

Grow the taller crops in the beds to the back (north) of the garden, where they won't deny sun to the shorter vegetables in front.

land, either by mounding the earth up or by enclosing the edges of the growing areas with boards, and then filling them with amended soil. This too has a long tradition behind it. In our view, there are times when raised beds might be a good idea—when you need to create extra soil depth over rocky or wet areas, for example, or to bring the soil closer to someone gardening in a wheelchair. But for most gardeners we think it's an unnecessary effort and expense. Instead of building up with boards, we simply dig up a little soil—about an inch deep—from the paths between the beds and throw it onto the beds, in order to define the footpaths (see photo below left). Our beds might look slightly raised, but what you're really seeing is just the contrast between the fluffy soil of the growing areas and the trodden ground of the paths. We think the roots of our vegetables are happier if the

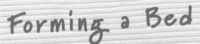

Forming a Bed

DEFINING THE BED. Mark the dimensions of the bed with stakes and string, then shovel out a little soil and add it to the bed, using the string as a guide.

MAKING IT LEVEL. Use a bed-forming rake to make the soil level and smooth it out.

FIRMING THE SOIL. Pound the soil with the back of the rake to firm it and prepare it for sowing or transplanting.

deep soil in which they grow is down in the earth rather than elevated. Plants in raised beds experience more extreme fluctuations between warm and cold or wet and dry. Whatever style you choose for your beds, it's important to keep the soil in them well aerated. You'll find more information on that on pages 223 to 225. ☀

These two types of wheelbarrows—a maneuverable one-wheel and a stable two-wheel—both have their uses. A garden cart takes care of bulky loads.

managing annual crops

ONE SATISFYING THING about growing annual vegetables is that they are only there for one growing season, and not always the whole season at that. This gives you a chance to move your crops strategically, like pieces on a chess board, in order to keep the plants as healthy as possible and increase the amount of food they'll produce.

ROTATING YOUR CROPS

CROP ROTATION refers to planting vegetables in a different spot in the garden each year, in a place where neither they nor their close relatives have recently grown. Since before the time of the ancient Romans, observant farmers and gardeners have noticed how much better a plant grows when this practice is followed and how much more free it is from pests and diseases. Crop rotation prevents the buildup of pest and disease problems particular to that plant in the spot where it grows, and it also avoids exhausting the nutrients in the soil that the plant most needs. Because plants in the same botanical family usually have similar disease

and pest problems and extract similar nutrients from the soil, they wouldn't be good choices to follow one another. This is one reason why gardeners so often talk about vegetables in terms of family relationships, as in the cabbage family (brassicas), the onion family, or the legumes (see page 44). The basic rule is to wait four years before growing the same crop, or a related crop, in the same place, so that a plant grown in year one would not appear there again until year five. In addition, studies on crop rotations over the years have shown that because the root systems of different plants have different effects on the soil, some plants grow better following certain plants than they do following others.

Here's an example of how it works. The pea is a legume. Leguminous crops like peas and beans have a symbiotic relationship with certain species of soil bacteria that allows them to take nitrogen from the air and store it in nodules on their roots for future use. They draw on that nitrogen when forming their seeds. Where you're harvesting the seeds at

Crop rotation prevents the buildup of pest and disease problems particular to a plant in the spot where it grows.

CHART OF VEGETABLE FAMILIES

THE CABBAGE FAMILY Cruciferae	cabbage, kale, collards, broccoli, Brussels sprouts, cauliflower, radishes, kohlrabi, turnip, rutabaga, arugula, Asian greens
THE ONION FAMILY Alliaceae	onions, leeks, garlic, scallions, shallots, chives, garlic chives
THE BEET FAMILY Amaranthaceae	beets, Swiss chard, spinach
THE CARROT FAMILY Apiaceae (Umbelliferae)	carrots, fennel, celery, celery root, parsnips, parsley, dill, cilantro, chervil, lovage
THE MINT FAMILY Lamiaceae (Labiatae)	mint, basil, oregano, marjoram, rosemary, sage, thyme, anise hyssop
THE MYRTLE FAMILY Myrtaceae	bay
THE VERBENA FAMILY Verbenaceae	lemon verbena
THE CUCUMBER FAMILY Cucurbitaceae	cucumbers, summer squash, winter squash, melons
THE TOMATO FAMILY Solanaceae	tomatoes, peppers, eggplants, tomatillos, potatoes
THE LEGUME FAMILY Leguminoseae (Fabaceae)	peas, beans
THE SUNFLOWER FAMILY Asteraceae (Compositae)	artichokes, sunchokes, lettuce, chicory, endive, escarole, radicchio, tarragon
THE VALERIAN FAMILY Valerianaceae	mâche
THE PURSLANE FAMILY Portulacaceae	claytonia
THE GRAIN FAMILY Poaceae (Graminaceae)	corn
THE ASPARAGUS FAMILY Asparagaceae	asparagus
THE BUCKWHEAT FAMILY Polygonaceae	sorrel, rhubarb
THE MORNING GLORY FAMILY Convolvulaceae	sweet potatoes

their immature green stage, as one does with peas, some of that nitrogen will be left over and can benefit a following crop. Since corn is a member of the grass family and the grasses benefit greatly from nitrogen, a traditional crop rotation is to have corn following a legume crop. Tomatoes and their relatives, in turn, do well when they follow corn, if the extensive organic matter from the remains of a corn crop has been turned into the soil the fall before.

Here's another example: Many old studies suggest that there are benefits to growing the onion family after light feeders like lettuce and squash, and then growing the cabbage family the year after the onion family. That's the type of information you might learn from a friend who is a veteran gardener, and eventually from your own observations—yet another case in which studying nature's own systems pays off.

Farmers rotate their crops all the time, and we're no exception. Carefully planned crop rotations have been crucial to our 40-plus years of success, growing 35 or so different healthy, high-yielding crops that need no propping up by chemical aids. But how necessary is crop rotation in the home garden? If you have good soil, replenished yearly with compost, you might get away planting everything in the same place each year without any disastrous problems. But since a vegetable garden is replanted each year anyway, why not give it the extra boost that this ancient practice confers?

Even just a two-year rotation is of benefit. To do this, you could divide your garden plan in two, then reverse the two sections each year. (If your garden is big enough to need a center path, you would grow each crop on one side of the path one year, and on the other side the next.) Longer rotations are more complicated both to plan and to carry out. But we've come to think of this as a game. In fact we've occasionally used crop rotation as a board game to lure city youngsters into the intriguing subtleties of a biologically based agriculture. The kids are given 3-by-5 cards, each written with the name of a crop. The game is to determine the best sequence for, say, 16 of them. We explain why crops are rotated, then give the "wait four years" rule, then a few "this grows well following that" rules. After each new rule, the cards have to be moved to incorporate the new information. We might then throw in a few more curve balls, such as doubling up on crops in a single bed, or following one crop with another during the same season and still obeying the rules of crop rotation. (These techniques are discussed below under "Succession Planting.") The winning plan is the one that comes closest to following all the guidelines. We say *closest* because no crop rotation is ever perfect, and even the best ones need to be fine-tuned in future years as crops are added or subtracted.

We don't believe in making the life of the gardener—especially the new gardener—more difficult. In the end, gardeners will pursue the intricacies of crop rotation only to the extent that their attention and patience allow. And while

(continued on page 48)

FACING PAGE (top to bottom):
Red cabbage.
Big Beef tomatoes.
Red and green kohlrabi.
Cheddar cauliflower.

Some plants grow better following certain plants than they do following others.

a four-year rotation of tall crops

YEAR 1

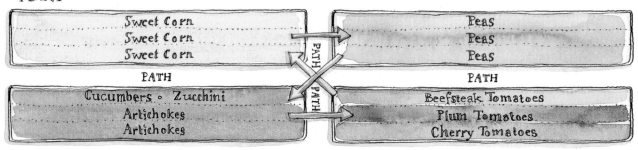

Sweet Corn	Peas
Sweet Corn	Peas
Sweet Corn	Peas
PATH	PATH
Cucumbers ∘ Zucchini	Beefsteak Tomatoes
Artichokes	Plum Tomatoes
Artichokes	Cherry Tomatoes

YEAR 2

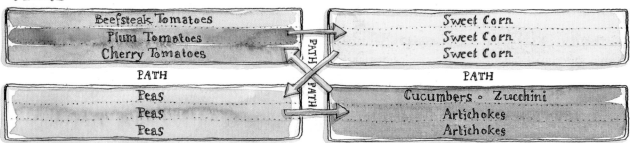

Beefsteak Tomatoes	Sweet Corn
Plum Tomatoes	Sweet Corn
Cherry Tomatoes	Sweet Corn
PATH	PATH
Peas	Cucumbers ∘ Zucchini
Peas	Artichokes
Peas	Artichokes

YEAR 3

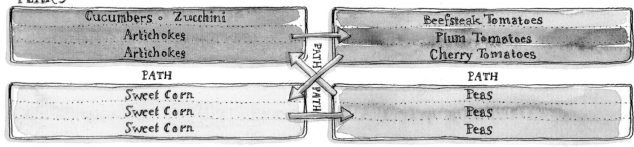

Cucumbers ∘ Zucchini	Beefsteak Tomatoes
Artichokes	Plum Tomatoes
Artichokes	Cherry Tomatoes
PATH	PATH
Sweet Corn	Peas
Sweet Corn	Peas
Sweet Corn	Peas

YEAR 4

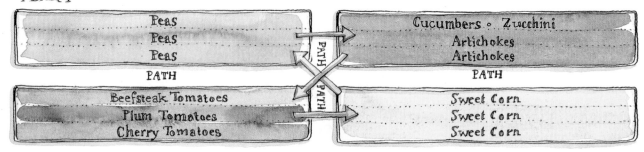

Peas	Cucumbers ∘ Zucchini
Peas	Artichokes
Peas	Artichokes
PATH	PATH
Beefsteak Tomatoes	Sweet Corn
Plum Tomatoes	Sweet Corn
Cherry Tomatoes	Sweet Corn

a FOUR-year ROTATION OF SHORTER CROPS

YEAR 1

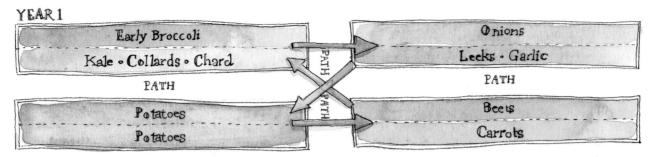

| Early Broccoli | Onions |
| Kale • Collards • Chard | Leeks • Garlic |

PATH   PATH

| Potatoes | Beets |
| Potatoes | Carrots |

YEAR 2

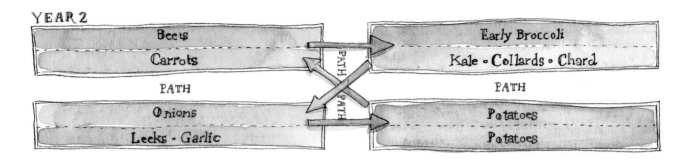

| Beets | Early Broccoli |
| Carrots | Kale • Collards • Chard |

PATH   PATH

| Onions | Potatoes |
| Leeks • Garlic | Potatoes |

YEAR 3

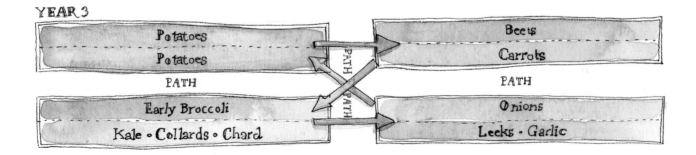

| Potatoes | Beets |
| Potatoes | Carrots |

PATH   PATH

| Early Broccoli | Onions |
| Kale • Collards • Chard | Leeks • Garlic |

YEAR 4

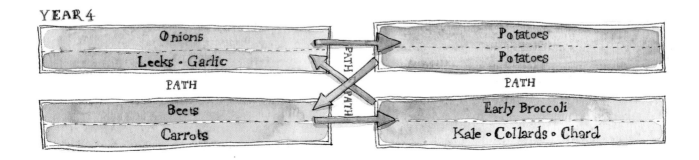

| Onions | Potatoes |
| Leeks • Garlic | Potatoes |

PATH   PATH

| Beets | Early Broccoli |
| Carrots | Kale • Collards • Chard |

a FOUR-YEAR ROTATION WITH FOUR BEDS

YEAR 1

| Peppers • Eggplant | Bush Beans |
| Celery • Celeriac • Fennel | Spinach • Lettuce • Asian Greens |

YEAR 2

| Spinach • Lettuce • Asian Greens | Peppers • Eggplant |
| Bush Beans | Celery • Celeriac • Fennel |

YEAR 3

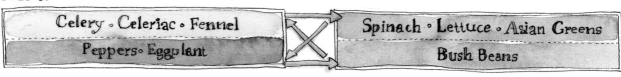

| Celery • Celeriac • Fennel | Spinach • Lettuce • Asian Greens |
| Peppers • Eggplant | Bush Beans |

YEAR 4

| Bush Beans | Celery • Celeriac • Fennel |
| Spinach • Lettuce • Asian Greens | Peppers • Eggplant |

(continued from page 45)

rotation does augment fertility and insure against pest and disease problems, you can do much to make up for an imperfect rotation by making sure plenty of organic matter is added to the soil each year. We find that if our crop rotation plan is simple and consistent, we're more apt to follow it. So in our garden we group the crops in sections, and then have them rotate within their section.

To show what we mean, take a look at the plan on page 46. The crops on both sides of the path, are all either naturally tall, like the corn and artichokes, or grown vertically on trellises, like the peas, tomatoes, cucumbers, and an Italian type of climbing zucchini we like to grow. So their positions can be switched around without shading one another. The three corn beds move as a group, the pea beds move as a group, the tomatoes move as a group, and the cucumbers, zucchini,

a mini-rotation within a single bed

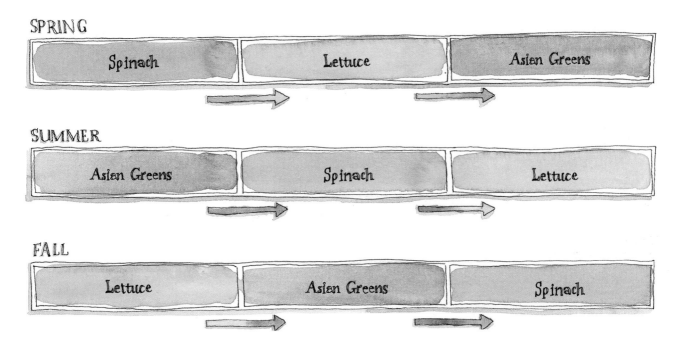

SPRING

| Spinach | Lettuce | Asian Greens |

SUMMER

| Asian Greens | Spinach | Lettuce |

FALL

| Lettuce | Asian Greens | Spinach |

and artichokes move as a group. So in the second year, the corn would grow where the peas were, the peas would grow where the cukes/zukes/chokes were. Those would move to where the tomatoes were, the tomatoes would replace the corn. The plan also shows the positions of all the crops in the first, second, third, and fourth years, until they go back to their original positions in the fifth. As each crop moves, it always replaces the same crop, moving right behind it, and always crossing the path as it goes, as shown by the directional arrows we've drawn to trace each crop's movement. Why cross the path? Because it puts a crop that much farther from where it grew the previous year. For the trellised crops, their movable trellises go with them (see Chapter 5).

The color is just for clarity. The directional arrows show the way each block of crops moves from one year to the next. Year 5 is exactly the same as year 1.

Let's see how it would work with the shorter crops in the southern part of the garden, as shown on page 47. Using the same pattern as the tall beds, three members of the cabbage family (broccoli, kale, and collards) move together along with chard. The onions, leeks, and garlic—closely related to one another—move together. And carrots and potatoes, each from an additional family, move singly. Here's some of the thinking that went into those decisions. Even though chard is not related to the others in its group, it is a leafy green that stays in the ground about the same length of time as they do, and would

Succession planting in action: When the large, mature heads of lettuce have been harvested, the smaller ones below them will be ready to eat.

mini-rotation. Since those are all short-duration crops, we can divide that bed into thirds and sow each different crop in succession after an earlier seeding of one of the others has finished. It would look like the plan on page 49.

That would work fine in New England; but in climates with hot summers, where the early cool-weather crops would need to take a break, the leafy crops could be replaced by a warm-weather green such as New Zealand spinach (unrelated to regular spinach) until cooler fall temperatures allow the others back in the mix.

Now we come to the really fun part, succession planting.

be perfect there. It *is* related to the beets on the other side of the path, but it will be two years before it moves to that bed, so we'll call that okay. Having the onion family follow potatoes was also a thought-out decision. Because we mulch our potato beds, the weeds there are very well controlled. And since the sparse, vertical foliage of onions and their relatives does not shade out weeds well, having them follow a crop that has kept weeds from seeding will make less work for the gardener.

The final section of our garden contains the vegetables that need less space, so there are only four beds in this rotation. The four beds rotate with the same movements we've discussed in the other sections.

Here again, it goes by family until you come to the bed with spinach, lettuce, and Asian greens. Those three are unrelated, both to one another and to all the others in the rotation. But this bed offers its own

SUCCESSION PLANTING

VEGETABLE GARDENERS are always looking for ways to get better yields from what they grow—not surprising in a time when both growing space and leisure time may be scarce. We think that finding these ways is one of the most fun and rewarding parts of the garden's design. As we'll see in the next chapter, much can be accomplished simply by choosing crops that produce bountifully over a long period of time, because they keep making either lots of fruits (like pole beans and cherry tomatoes), lots of matter in a small space (like storage beets and rutabagas), or new leaves as the old leaves are cut (like kale and spinach).

But there's yet another way to generate more food out of your modest plot, and that's succession planting. This can mean several different things. It could mean sowing the same crop several times. For instance, lovers of head lettuce find that after they've finished eating up all the heads in one bed, they need to have more of them, planted a few weeks later, to insure a steady supply. This could be a series of small plantings, lined up in the same bed, as in the photo on the opposite page. Or it could be staggered plantings of lettuce set out in various parts of the garden as empty spaces open up. Quick crops such as lettuce, radishes, and arugula play this game especially well. But you can also fill empty spaces—and hence increase your garden's bounty—by following one early crop with a later one. A bed of spring carrots, for example, might be followed by a fall crop of broccoli or, for that matter, spring broccoli followed by fall carrots. After a while you get a sense of how long each crop will bear and how much time you'll need to bring the following one to maturity before winter. You learn to use changes in the weather to your advantage, following cool-weather spring crops with summer ones, and summer ones with those that love the coolness of fall. You can even have successions year-round, as shown in The Winter Garden (see pages 97 to 101). By doing that you could effectively double or even triple the size of your garden's food production without changing its actual dimensions.

Yet another trick is to have two crops overlap in the same bed. Let's say you've just transplanted some Brussels sprout seedlings into the garden in spring. Since they will eventually be big plants, you've spaced them 18 inches apart in a single row, and they look pretty lonely in the bed. You could easily plant one of the early quick crops—baby butterhead lettuces, scallions, mustard greens, baby carrots—on either side of them, to be harvested before the Brussels sprouts get big enough to crowd them. This is called *interplanting*. When the smaller, earlier crop blankets the soil around the larger, later plant, it is called *underplanting*. The photo of pepper plants underplanted with arugula on this page is an example. In addition to being a tasty crop, arugula has helped shade out the weeds that normally colonize bare soil. You can also grow two crops together with the *same* growing period if they occupy different levels of the soil, as in the photo of lettuce and scallions together on page 52. The roots of the scallions are shallow; those of the lettuce go deeper.

The great thing about all these little maneuvers is that they are so visually obvious. You see an emptied bed. You see bare soil. And you ask yourself, "What could I plant there?" A garden is more beautiful and satisfying to look at when it is full, even if the placeholder is a green manure or a cover crop (see page 24). These make nutritional contributions too. But why not grow more food? You'll need to add nutrients to the soil after planting a succeeding crop, but this is easily taken care of (see page 223).

RECONCILING SUCCESSIONS WITH CROP ROTATION

ALL OF THIS GETS A LITTLE TRICKY when you realize that if you're suddenly bringing in a lot of new crops partway through the season, your tidy yearly rotations will unavoidably be disrupted. So you'll want to take note of what was the previous year's occupant of that

Peppers underplanted with arugula.

Lettuce and scallions interplanted together.

bed you just added an extra crop to, and what is destined to be in it the following year. At that point you might feel you've headed down one of the "expert" trails on the horticultural ski mountain, and it's a slippery slope. But just do your best and try to keep the rotation plan in the back of your mind. If there is a crop that you have had pest or disease problems with, or one that struggles a bit and might need the boost of an ideal preceding crop, let that influence the course you take. You learn to choose your battles and let some of the others go.

Here are a few examples of how this might work out:

The peas in the rotation plan on page 46 are an early crop and there's plenty of time after they mature to grow something else there. Corn would ripen, but corn is following peas in that bed next year. So we want to find a crop (or crops) unrelated to corn and to the other crops in this rotation, and one that can be planted in midsummer for a fall harvest. Members of the cabbage family are likely candidates, since they'll thrive in the cool weather to come. In fact they're doubly ideal if the stems of the spent pea vines have been cut off at soil level rather than being pulled out (leaving the nitrogen nodules in the soil), because the new cabbage family crops will greatly benefit from that nutrient.

But wait a minute. Isn't the corn slated for next year supposed to benefit from that? Yes, but if food production is our goal, then getting a whole extra harvest from the ground this year seems like a worthwhile trade-off. We can always make it up to next year's corn with a little extra compost or an application of a general-purpose nitrogen-containing fertilizer like alfalfa meal, which is dried alfalfa, sold in bags. (See page 223 for more on adding amendments to established gardens.)

We mentioned how the tomato family next year would thrive on the residue of last year's corn stalks. But if we clear the ground of our earliest maturing corn variety by pulling out those corn stalks and adding them to the compost heap rather than turning them under (the same as we did with the pea vines), there's still time to grow a cool-season crop in that area. Corn is a heavy feeder, so following corn we will first want to add more compost plus some alfalfa meal, and mix it in well. Then we can consider our options. Both arugula and the numerous Asian greens are short-duration cool-season crops. They would be good, but if we're trying to have a perfect four-year crop rotation here they aren't ideal because they are members of the cabbage family. Another choice—one that is acceptably unrelated in this rotation—could be Swiss chard or beets for their greens, but we'd want to have either of them started a few weeks ahead to transplant in as seedlings, because it might be a bit late in the season for direct-seeded beets or chard to attain full growth. Fall lettuce would seem an ideal choice here, either transplanted for full-size heads, or direct-seeded even if a bit late, because if planted thickly it can be very productive when cut as baby leaves. The cucumber/zucchini, the artichokes, and the tomatoes should keep producing all season and thus do not offer an opportunity for succession planting.

Those are the sorts of little decisions the productive gardener is continually making. The specific crops depend on what you particularly want to grow. ❋

PERMANENT CROPS

AS YOU CAN SEE from the overall plan of the garden on page 35, we've set apart permanent plantings that don't rotate from year to year the way the vegetables do, but rather stay in one spot. They are still right in the immediate vicinity though, and within full view of the house so they don't get neglected. See Chapter 4 for advice on growing them.

Asparagus

THE SOUTH EDGE was a good place to put our asparagus bed. Since the sun comes from the south in the Northern Hemisphere, we wouldn't want a planting on the southern edge to block sunlight. But asparagus is an ideal crop in that respect because it casts no shade in winter and spring. Once we end the harvesting in June and the asparagus fern (as its leaves and stems are called) begins to grow up, the sun is higher in the sky and its feathery shade does not fall on other crops. In fall when the fern is close to 6 feet tall and the sun is lower in the sky, the almost mature crops growing nearby appreciate the light shade. And finally, we love the asparagus foliage as a green backdrop for the garden in summer and a golden one in fall, against which all the other colors and textures of the garden are enhanced.

Herbs

AN HERB GARDEN separate from the vegetables but close to the kitchen door is handy for the home cook. It allows you to pop out the door and cut a bunch of chives or snip a sprig of tarragon the minute you need it. But just as with vegetables, how the various plants are arranged is important. Some of the herbs that cooks use a lot—like tarragon and chives—are perennials that require a permanent site. Others, such as basil and dill, are annuals that are replanted each year. We find that these two groups do best if grown in separate parts of the herb garden, because it's hard for newly planted annual seedlings to compete with established perennials. Annual herbs are

It's hard for annual herb seedlings to compete with established perennials. Best to separate them.

PLAN FOR AN HERB GARDEN

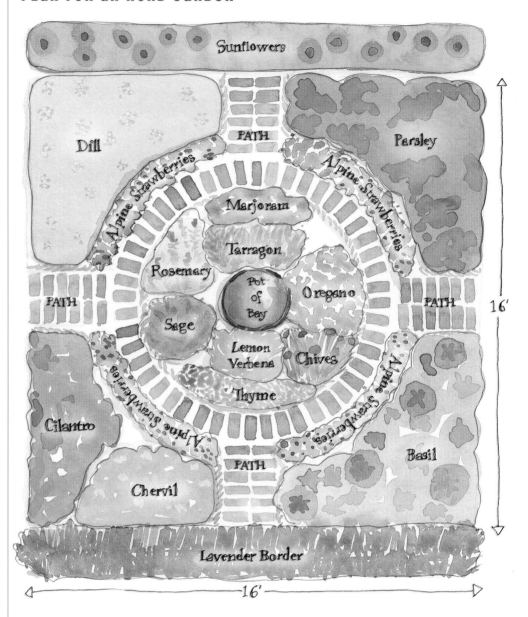

Pop out the kitchen door and cut a bunch of chives or snip a sprig of tarragon the minute you need it.

grown the way annual vegetables are, by amending their beds thoroughly with compost each season, and incorporating it into the soil. Perennial herbs can make do with a little surface dressing of compost from time to time, but most are very vigorous and need little help. In fact many are Mediterranean plants that do fine even with a lean soil. Our herb garden is also a place where we can be a little playful if we want to, and change the annual portion each year to include a stand of sunflowers, perhaps, or a few patches of edible flowers such as nasturtiums, borage, and calendulas.

In addition to this small dooryard herb plot, we make provision elsewhere for herbs we like to grow in larger quantities. Mint, which is wonderful to dry for tea, is best grown in an out-of-the-way spot, preferably a moist one. It is far too vigorous to grow alongside any other plants, which it will crowd out, so we've established it in a drainage ditch, where it thrives. Warm-season herbs like basil and lemon verbena can be started in a greenhouse to get a jump on the season. Extra basil for pesto can be grown as a succession crop in the main garden after the weather warms up, as can extra dill for preserving pickles and making "dilly beans." A small cold frame with an automatic venting mechanism, placed in a warm spot against the house, can extend the season for any herbs, both early and late (see pages 87 to 89).

Small Fruits

OF THE SWEET FRUITS we love to eat, few are annual crops. Melons are, and can be assigned to the vegetable garden, but they grow on vines and take up a lot of space. Closely related to cucumbers and squash, they share with these a love of warm weather. But unlike cucumbers, they bear fruits that are too heavy for trellising. One way around the problem is to grow them in a strip along the edge of the garden, so that their roots are in a well-fertilized bed but the vines themselves occupy an area where they can't overtake and smother other crops with their broad leaves (for more about melons see page 173). Strawberries, too, can be grown in an annual vegetable garden, even though they are, strictly speaking, perennial plants. Ours are grown commercially at the farm, or in Barbara's test garden, but we have sometimes worked them into the main home garden as well, following the two-year system described on page 210.

Grapes are decidedly a permanent part of our food landscape. We have a tunnel-shaped arbor along the west edge of our garden, covered with vines bearing seedless grapes. The grape leaves start to provide shade just as outdoor temperatures rise to the point where shade is appreciated. Once the grapes themselves begin to ripen (we grow several varieties for a progressive harvest), they can be plucked fresh from overhead as one rests underneath them.

Along the eastern edge of the garden, well separated from the vegetable area by a row of fruit trees, is a long row of berry fruits that include red raspberries (both standard and everbearing), black raspberries, and blackberries. Since all of them propagate by runners that spread quickly to whatever is planted next door, the vigorous growth of these plants can become a garden nuisance. In a previous garden, where we put the row of berry fruit alongside the vegetable area, we were continuously battling to keep the runners out. Their current location eliminates that problem.

Across the north edge of the garden, closest to the house, we've planted a hedge of blueberry bushes. At first, that was done because we thought they would look attractive, which they do. With its blazing

Grazing on strawberries.

The grape arbor over our terrace.

nearby herb garden because they are the first fruit to ripen where we live. Now there's a fruit paradise for little stomachs from the time the alpines appear till the last late-fall apples are harvested.

Tree Fruits

A BED WITH AN APPLE TREE, surrounded by perennial herbs, sits near the southern end of the garden. It makes a nice focal point, and a bench placed under the tree is a great place to take a little rest in the shade while you're gardening, or to shell a bowl of peas. At either side are beds where a little movable greenhouse sits, one year on the left and the following year on the right. (Those sites have their own cropping system, which is explained in Chapter 3, starting on page 97.)

Five more apple trees grow along the opposite side of the garden from the grape arbor. A few small, automatic-venting cold frames occupy the spaces between those fruit trees (see page 89). The leafless trees in early spring create very little shade for the early salads growing in the frames. When the trees leaf out and the sun is hotter, their shade is beneficial to the remaining salad greens. ☀

red foliage in fall, our native blueberry is one of the most underrated of landscape plants. We now realize that the location is handy as well, because it's close to the kitchen—for sprinkling the fruits on cereal in the morning, on fruit salad at noon, or over ice cream after dinner. But the best reason becomes apparent when grandchildren come to visit. They are barely out of the car before they scurry across the yard to feast on blueberries—and strawberries, raspberries, or blackberries, depending on the season. Their joy is such a delight for us that we maintain an extra bed of the little alpine strawberries toward the center of the

THE EDIBLE YARD

THE LAYOUT OF vegetables, herbs, and fruits described so far in this chapter is a self-contained unit, but the food we produce is not all confined to that plot. Above the terrace where we eat lunch in summer, ten grapevines provide welcome

shade and, come October, dangling bunches of ripe fruit. On warm fall days we reach up and pluck them for dessert. Each year, a talented neighbor turns some of them into a country-style wine. Along the driveway are filbert bushes where we collect nuts, and next to the parking area a row of elderberries, good for jam. Just over the rise behind the house is a small peach orchard. Often, when faced with the opportunity to plant something new for ornament, shade, visual screening, or to break the force of the wind, we ask ourselves, "Could it be something edible? Instead of an oak could we plant a hickory?"

We are not alone. These days the typical yard is smaller than it used to be, and it can be a challenge to find the space to grow more edibles. Our desires for food, beauty, and shade often seem to be at odds. They needn't be.

First of all, there's no reason why a vegetable garden should not be gorgeous. You can decorate it with patches of marigolds, of course, or a row of zinnias for cutting. There's nothing wrong with that. But we're convinced that a well-planned, well-tended vegetable plot contains its own beauty, and the same things that make it productive make it immensely attractive as well. If you create a tidy layout, the garden will have its own pleasing geometry. If you keep the beds full, with crops following others when beds become empty, the garden will always look bounteous. If you stake, prune, and train crops as needed, they will look orderly, not chaotic. If you cultivate often to keep weeds from emerging, the garden will look well cared for. Well-grown vegetables and fruits give off a glow of health, and are satisfying to look at. So is a rich, dark, well-conditioned soil. In fact, when all these efforts come together, a kitchen garden is pretty enough to put right in the front yard, visible from the street.

Once you've experienced the pleasures of growing your own food, you'll want to introduce edibles into the bigger picture. Nature, who makes no distinction between an edible and an ornamental plant, would approve. There are, however, natural distinctions between annual and perennial plants, and between plants that spread aggressively and those that do not. It's important to keep these distinctions in mind if you're tempted to mix veggies and flowers together in the same bed. For instance, if you introduce annual vegetables such as kale or corn into an established garden of perennial flowers, they might look quite striking. But they will not produce as much food as they would in a vegetable row, where

The red cabbages and storage carrots in front will not be harvested until fall. Meanwhile, their show goes on just as handsomely as the flowers behind them.

every effort is made to pamper them with all the root space they need during their relatively short season of growth. You must also consider how often the picture changes with most vegetables. Parsley makes a fine edging for a flower bed, because you're just picking a bit at a time. But a lettuce edging will be marred each time you cut a head for supper.

The easiest way to expand the menu in your yard, beyond the veggie garden, is to grow food-bearing shrubs and trees. Most popular fruits, such as apples, pears, plums, peaches, and cherries, grow on small trees well suited to today's properties, and have a wide distribution. The citrus types are bountiful and divinely fragrant in regions where they will survive and bear. Each climate has its own range of choices, including wonderful native fruits such as pawpaws and American persimmons. When you're looking for a larger tree, for majesty or shade, consider one that bears nuts, such as pecans in the South, hickories in the North, and the native nut-bearing pines of the Southwest.

For any landscaping challenge there's likely to be an edible solution. In a warmer climate, our arbor might have borne passion fruit instead of grapes. An unsightly chain link or stockade fence might be clothed with kiwi vines. Instead of a humdrum hedge of privet or yew, how about a mixed hedgerow filled with berry plants such as blueberries, currants, and beach plums? There'll be plenty of fruits to share with the birds as well. Even brambleberries, as raspberries and blackberries are sometimes called, work fine as a hedge, though they're too aggressive to mix well with other species. We've even created edible summer groundcovers out of pumpkin and sweet potato vines. Their foliage rambles over unplanted ground and keeps weeds from staking out the territory. ☼

CREATING PARADISE

THROUGHOUT RECORDED HISTORY there has been a close association between the garden and the concept of a paradise. The ancient Persian root of the word *paradise* (*pairi-daeza,* or "walled garden") affirms that connection. Rather than thinking of paradise as a myth or an exotic faraway place, we've always strived to create our own version of it right where we live. Paradise is the place where existence is positive, harmonious, and timeless. In a paradise crops should grow beautifully and that's what we aim for. The compost heap, the rock minerals, the well-aerated soil, the sprinkler are all part of our program for creating this ideal world for plants. But sometimes people are bemused by our sunny attitude toward our garden. "How can you create it without pesticides?" they ask. "What happens when all the bugs show up? Do poisons have a place in paradise?"

When we began gardening years ago, the spirit of Rachel Carson's *Silent Spring* was still very much alive. Toxic sprays were an obvious abomination, but what was a gardener to do? For us the idea of trying to grow nutritious food crops while at the same time covering them with insecticides during the growing process was too ridiculous to consider. It was clear that there had to be another answer. Books from the early writers on organic agriculture stressed that poor soil conditions made plants vulnerable to pests and diseases. They contended that if plants were healthy they wouldn't be bothered by pests, and that the sine qua non for growing healthy plants was an ideally fertile soil. Both ideas resonated with our understanding of the natural world and thus began our lifelong interest in determining whether those statements could be true—and if they were true, figuring out how to make it all happen. The idea that healthy plants resist pests can be traced back as far as agricultural practices have been recorded. But it is the more recent pre-pesticide period that is most interesting. What did our 18th- and 19th-century ancestors think and do?

In a letter to his daughter in 1793, Thomas Jefferson wrote, "I suspect that the insects which have harassed you have been encouraged by the feebleness of your plants and that has been produced by the lean state of the soil." A professional market gardener in Paris in the 1870s remarked: "One does not see pest problems in Parisian market gardens wherever copious compost use and rational crop rotations are practiced by the growers." By the close of the 19th century, many researchers had concluded that plants must be "predisposed" or weakened before a pest or disease could successfully attack them.

But all of this intelligent cultural control of pests through soil quality, which seems to have worked for our forebears, was either ignored or forgotten during the rush to pesticides in the 20th century. One must ask oneself: If modern pesticides are as essential as the manufacturers claim them to be, how did humans manage to feed themselves before the modern era? To our minds, the cultural approach that worked for gardeners in the 19th century should work for us. And work it does when we have done right by the soil. Doing right includes all those soil-fertility-improving practices stressed in the preceding chapter.

Grape vines give welcome summer shade.

Since 19th-century gardeners noticed that there were far fewer pests when the soil was in top shape, and since they had no easy recourse to pesticides anyway, they worked to create ideal growing conditions with the intent of preventing pests rather than battling them. A popular garden book from the 1830s said it simply: "The preventive operations are those of the best culture. . . . Vegetables which are vigorous and thrifty are not apt to be injured by worms, flies, bugs, etc." All the old garden books stress the vital role of adding lots of organic matter from manure, compost, or leaf mold. They also put great value on crop rotation, soil aeration, adequate irrigation, and selecting appropriate vegetable varieties for the specific soil or climate.

Advances in agricultural biology beginning in the mid-19th century (now overshadowed in the public mind by the propaganda of the chemical industries) began to unlock mysteries that make today's organic gardening as intellectually stimulating and valid as any other scientific pursuit. Though beyond the scope of this book, here are just some of the roads down which a gardener with a naturally curious bent might wander:

- ✦ **SOIL MICROBIOLOGY.** There's an amazing world down there under the soil.

- ✦ **NITROGEN FIXATION.** The ways in which legumes take nitrogen from the air and make it available to plants.

- ✦ **SYMBIOTIC RELATIONSHIPS.** Such as the mutually beneficial partnerships (micorrhizae) between certain fungi and plant roots.

- ✦ **ALLELOPATHY.** The chemical inhibition of one plant by another.

- ✦ **WEED ECOLOGY.** Controlling weeds by modifying soil conditions. (An example would be liming the soil to inhibit acid-loving pest plants such as wild sorrel.)

- ✦ **SYSTEMIC ACQUIRED RESISTANCE.** The means by which compost enhances plants' resistance to pests.

All of these are mind expanding, but here's the best part. They all illuminate the intuitive brilliance of age-old practices like crop rotation, green manures, mulching, and making compost.

In 1800 Erasmus Darwin (Charles Darwin's grandfather) wrote that whereas chemistry and physics could be considered as having achieved the status of sciences, agriculture (the growing of plants) remained an art. It still does. This art requires subtle judgment calls such as adding just enough limestone, finding just the proper depth at which

There's no reason why a vegetable garden should not be gorgeous.

to till, knowing when compost is mature and, most important, involving one's mind in all aspects of the biological world of the soil. None of this work is dull or unskilled, and it is driven, above all, by the power of observation. Working with the biology of the garden is fascinating, challenging, and also inspiring, since skill grows with practice. The result is a garden of vigorous healthy plants, a clean environment, and the satisfaction of taking part in a truly sustainable horticulture that can feed the human population in perpetuity.

Paradise to us includes not just the delicious products of a garden but also the way in which they are produced. In a true paradise the crops would approach perfection. So we've learned to pay attention to the natural world and how it works in improving life. Look around the woods and fields and what you see is mostly healthy vegetation. In the natural world the plants that survive natural selection are those that are best suited to the conditions of the site in which they grow. Since we want a vegetable paradise, we obviously need to create conditions best suited to the plants we wish to grow, so all of our efforts are aimed in that direction. Healthy plants are something the gardener has to work toward because conditions are never ideal.

Yes. A few pests may show up in your garden—say, some Colorado potato beetles on your potatoes. You can then go out every morning and knock them off into a jar filled with soapy water. But let's be clear: This is not an act of war. It isn't even a solution. It's an "oops" moment, a learning moment. It is a signal to ask yourself whether the soil in that potato row is up to snuff, and whether a hay mulch might keep the soil more cool and moist, thus relieving the plants (as research has shown) of summer heat stress. Depending on the soil and local conditions, it takes between three and five years to get the soil right. But if you've begun the soil-building instructions in Chapter 1, we guarantee you'll get there. ☀

CHAPTER 3

The Crops:
What to Grow

DECIDING WHAT VEGETABLES TO GROW should be easy, right? You just plant the ones that you love to eat. But it isn't quite that simple. In this chapter, we'll have you thinking more deeply about plant choices from a variety of perspectives—and getting more satisfaction out of your garden as a result.

New gardeners often choose just a few of the most popular standards, such as tomatoes, lettuce, and peppers, and it's easy to see why: Those are the ones offered as plants or seeds at all the garden centers, and they clearly reflect the taste of the American table.

Some gardeners go a step further and choose the crops whose flavor is most notably lacking in supermarket varieties. Tomatoes make that list again, as might strawberries, cucumbers, and melons. There are also gardeners with a passion for ethnic cooking, who can't find certain ingredients where they live, or want to use them fresh. They might specialize in exotic Thai eggplants or Peruvian chiles. And then there are those overenthusiastic beginners who, enthralled by seed-catalog prose, try to grow everything listed for sale. They often end up overwhelmed, exhausted, and wondering how to possibly use all that radicchio, and where to store six varieties of heirloom pumpkins.

In addition to what foods you like, you'll want to consider how much space you have and what goals you have for the garden. You might start small but end up expanding your garden as a resource in the years to come, whether by increasing its size and output, extending it through the cold season, storing the harvest, saving your own seeds, or experimenting with exciting and unusual foods. The techniques you need to learn will differ depending on these goals, and so will the crops you choose—even down to the specific varieties of a given crop. As we consider each of these perspectives, the overarching aim will always be to make the most of the garden, both in quality and quantity.

So which are the most versatile and dependable crops, the ones that offer the best return for your efforts? We present our suggestions below, as six concept gardens. Each one serves a different objective you might have in growing your own food. Some of these may seem especially important to you, or you may find, as we do, that they all have a place in your planning. ☀

THE SALAD GARDEN

WE'RE VERY FAMILIAR with the laments of gardenless gardeners. They have no yard, or the yard is tiny. The yard is big, but only a tiny piece of it gets sun. The yard is a stone terrace, a balcony, a fire escape, a rooftop, or a sunny window, where the only soil is in pots and window boxes. Sometimes we look at our dining table, which measures 3 feet by 6 feet, and ask ourselves what we would do if we wanted to grow food for that table but had no more space than the size of the table itself. Immediately, we think "salads."

Salad crops give you the most variety in a garden of limited size. Yes, you could devote the whole thing to potatoes, and if that little plot were all that stood between you and starvation, potatoes would be a fine choice. But under normal circumstances a fresh-picked salad, as a regular part of the average diet, delivers a great nutrient boost and is always a tasty addition to a meal. Many salad ingredients need very little space in which to grow, and together they can put quite a bit of diversity on your plate. In fact, if there were ever a symbol of what the home garden can give you that the

Salad crops give you the most variety in a garden of limited size.

PLAN FOR A SALAD GARDEN

6'

3'

Cherry Tomatoes

Chives

Tarragon

Thyme

Lettuce Mix

Spicy Greens Mix

Asian Greens Mix

Basil

Dill

Radishes

Scallions

LETTUCE MIX: Allstar Gourmet Lettuce Mix. Bright colors, unique leaf shapes, exceptional eating.

SPICY GREENS MIX: Ovation Greens Mix. A mixture of the mild, the spicy, and the decorative.

ASIAN GREENS MIX: Johnny's Selected Seeds' Braising Mix. For a salad with a little more bite.

CHERRY TOMATO: Sun Gold. Always praised for great flavor.

ONION SET: Forum. Simple and dependable.

RED RADISH: Cherriette. The classic round red radish.

WHITE RADISH: White Icicle. Unique and delicious.

FRENCH BREAKFAST RADISH: D'Avignon. The tenderest and most beautiful of all the radishes.

BASIL: Genovese. Authentic Italian flavor and slow to bolt.

PARSLEY: Titan. The most dependable flat-leaf parsley.

CILANTRO: Santo. Extra slow bolting.

DILL: Bouquet. The best variety for greens rather than seeds.

SWISS CHARD: Fordhook Giant. The best salad chard.

CUCUMBER: Tasty Jade. Easy to grow, seedless, with great flavor.

TOP: Scallions.
BOTTOM: Radishes.

supermarket can't, it would be a salad bowl full of just-picked ingredients—raw, tasty, and fresh.

When most people think of salads they think of lettuce, and when they think of lettuce they think of large, round heads. Nice as those are, most of them take up at least a square foot of garden space, and once you harvest one and eat it, it's gone. For our little table-size garden it would make more sense to plant a cut-and-come-again salad mix. The wonderful thing about such a mix is that you can let it grow quickly to about 3 inches tall, then cut it and let it regrow. The harvest can often go on for many weeks. Some salad mixes are composed of lettuces alone, with different colors and textures. Others include more pungent ingredients such as arugula, chicories, and mustards. Often mixes are composed wholly or in part of Asian greens. We suggest you plant successions of these mixes—say, a lettuce mix for spring, followed by a slightly more heat-tolerant Asian mix, followed in fall by a more spicy mix, or more lettuces. (See pages 50 to 52 for more on succession planting.)

For many people it wouldn't be a garden—or a salad—without tomatoes. All you may need is one tomato plant, especially if it bears cherry tomatoes. It will grow vigorously and continuously deliver bowlfuls of little fruit. Whether round, pear-shaped, or grape-shaped, they're a great salad addition. Grow beefsteak tomatoes if they are dear to your heart, but they will not give you such abundance. Stake or cage any tomatoes you grow (see page 176) to save room.

Growing scallions is a good way to add an oniony flavor to the bowl. Scallions, which are skinny, bulbless onions, are usually grown from seeds, but for this little table-size garden a simpler plan would be to grow them from onion sets, bought in spring (see page 140). Rather than letting them grow to full onion size, harvest them at a young age when they're small and *look* like scallions. (You can eat both the tiny bulb and the green foliage.) Save a handful of sets from your spring purchase (they'll keep fine in the bag, in a cool room), and plant another succession or two so you'll always have some young, tender green onion tops. Any older plants left in the ground can grow to full-size onions.

Radishes, the ultimate small-space crop, will add color and zing. They don't last long in the garden before they get pithy and start to go to seed, so plant successions of them too. It's easy to quickly tuck in a row wherever there's a bit of space. Even just a foot or two of closely planted radishes is useful.

Still have a little room left over? Grow some of your favorite herbs: an annual such as basil, parsley, cilantro, or dill, and one or two perennials that can nestle permanently into a corner, such as tarragon, chives, or thyme.

Let's say you have a little bigger space for the garden—perhaps the size of a 5-by-8 rug. Put in some Swiss chard as well, either from direct-sown seeds or from transplants. Leaves picked anywhere from 3 inches long to the size of your hand are tender enough for salad use, and chard is more heat tolerant than lettuce. If you keep cutting it back, it will send up young leaves for you all summer long. And okay, add one cucumber plant. Staked or trellised, just like your one tomato, it will have a tiny footprint but may well yield all you'll need. ☀

THE PRACTICAL GARDEN

LET'S SAY YOUR little salad garden was a great success and you'd like to grow much more of your own food. You're wishing that *all* the produce your family ate tasted that good, and you'd like to make a bigger dent in the food budget as well. Plus, the time you spent on the project was relaxing, in a sweaty sort of way, and fun. So you're ready to expand the garden and grow more crops. With all the choices in that bulging seed catalog, which ones will give you the highest return in terms of space allotted and time spent?

Let's return for a moment to the Stone Soup metaphor to help you decide. The fire is burning, the water is boiling, the stone's in the pot. Now what's the first ingredient you hope will be available? You'd obviously want it to taste good, have great vitamin and mineral value, and be easy to grow. Ideally it would also yield bountifully and dependably over many months, and could be eaten in a number of different ways. So the first thing we'd put in the soup pot, the vegetable with the best bang for the buck, would be in the dark leafy green category. Down South that might be collards or turnip greens. Up North it might be kale. But remember, you want your family to be eager to eat what your garden has produced, so flavor is just as important as healthfulness.

For us the perfect "first vegetable" would be the Italian-bred Tuscan kale, also known as *cavolo nero* or dinosaur kale. It shares the vitamin and mineral load of other dark green leaves but avoids the "eat me just because I'm good for you" burden that most kales and other tougher greens

carry. It's not one of those scratchy kales; it's a super-tender one, with a mild flavor. We've been told that's because it's a cross between kale and savoy cabbage. But whatever its provenance, it meets all our criteria. Even in our cool climate, we can begin picking it in June from an early sowing, and still be picking it in December. In addition, it's so attractive that it's often planted in display gardens for its looks alone. Growing 2 to 3 feet tall, the dark bluish green leaves with their rounded, pebbly texture are striking against any background. Visitors to our garden, rarely familiar with the plant, ask about it right away. And it's good not only in soups but also as a side dish, in casseroles, and even in raw salad when the leaves are young.

Let's pick another ingredient for the soup, one that meets all our criteria just as well. That would be the onion. Like Tuscan kale, onions don't mind heat or cold in the garden, and best yet, they can be used at almost any stage of growth. A few tops can be harvested as scallions, and bulbs may be stolen from the row for cooking while they're still developing. Finally, when mature, they keep for a long time in storage, and even when stored ones start to sprout in late spring, the sprouted tops can be used like green onions or scallions until the new crop is ready. Some onions such as multiplying onions are even perennial, saving you from having to purchase new seeds every year. Most cooks can't imagine cooking without onions, and there's hardly a dish that doesn't benefit from their presence.

TOP: Tuscan kale.
MIDDLE: Onions.
BOTTOM: Potatoes.

Varieties for the Practical Garden

ARUGULA: Astro. An exceedingly tasty variety.

BASIL: Genovese. The classic big-leaved Italian basil.

BEANS: Garden of Eden. Great at any stage.

BEANS: Red Ace. The best variety for both roots and greens.

BROCCOLI: Belstar. A widely adapted broccoli, with good side-shoot production for a longer harvest.

BRUSSELS SPROUTS: Churchill. Easy to grow, early and vigorous.

CABBAGE: Caraflex. A small, very tasty multiple-use cabbage.

CARROTS: Nelson. Early, heat resistant, and very flavorful.

CILANTRO: Santo. Slower to go to seed than some.

COLLARDS: Flash. Harvestable over a long period.

CORN: Too many to list. Best to find one well adapted to your area.

CUCUMBER: Diva. Thin-skinned, non-bitter, great tasting.

DILL: Ducat. Great flavor, lush, slow to go to seed.

EGGPLANT: Orient Express. Does well in both cool and hot weather.

GARLIC: German Extra Hardy. The easiest to grow, with large cloves.

KALE: Toscano. A kale your children will eat.

LETTUCE: Buttercrunch. An easy-to-grow and delicious old-timer.

MELON: Gold Star. The best-tasting northern melon. **Ambrosia.** A winner in many climates.

ONION: Forum. A truly superior onion set variety.

PARSLEY: Any good flat-leaf variety.

PEA: Green Arrow. Medium-size vines; heavy, reliable production.

PEPPER: Red Knight. Has good disease resistance and turns red early.

POTATO: Kennebec. The classic, all-purpose Maine-bred potato.

SPINACH: Tyee. An excellent bolt-resistant, upright, savoy type.

SQUASH, WINTER: Metro. A small-size butternut type with good disease resistance.

SQUASH, YELLOW SUMMER: Gentry. Well adapted and problem-free.

SQUASH, ZUCCHINI: Plato. A spineless, open-form plant for easy harvest.

TOMATO: Big Beef. Our favorite garden beefsteak tomato.

For earliest eating, you can sneak a few baby new potatoes out from under a potato plant once it begins flowering, a technique called grabbling.

Our Stone Soup now has a nice broth and depth of flavor, but it needs body, so let's make our next choice the carrot. Carrots at the baby size are popular snacks for children. Mature carrots, in addition to their vitamin content, are delicious in countless recipes. They're available all summer from a planting in early spring, and can be stored all winter. Three crops, and we're already eating very well.

By expanding the garden a little, we'll make room for the next dietary staple: some sort of easily grown and storable bulk carbohydrate. Because this is a home garden, our choice would be the potato rather than a grain like wheat, oats, or barley. Although small-scale grain growing has been common in the U. S. throughout its history and is now undergoing a revival, potatoes will yield about ten times as many bushels on the same-size plot as will wheat. And it's possible to eat home-grown potatoes every day of the year. For earliest eating, you can sneak a few baby new potatoes out from under a potato plant once it begins flowering, a technique called *grabbling*. When the potatoes have matured, they can be left in the ground until just before fall temperatures approach serious freezing, then dug and stored over the winter in a

cool, moist location until the "baby news" are ready again.

As we continue to add crops to this garden, we will use the criteria we've established—nutrition, dependability, ease of cultivation, and length of season— to guide our choices. In the following pages, the essential crop groups are listed in order of priority, based on our many years of feeding ourselves a dependable homegrown diet. Of course you'll make your selection based on your family's tastes and the climate you live in. Some variations are obvious. Gardeners in southern climates, for example, may grow more sweet potatoes than white potatoes; gardeners whose tastes run to Mediterranean cuisine might move eggplants and cucumbers higher up the list. But you should note the reasons for our choices in the descriptions below.

Leafy Greens

IN OUR VIEW, every backyard kitchen garden needs at least one robust cooking green. In addition to the kale, collards, and turnip greens mentioned, you might consider Swiss chard, mustard greens, and the many Asian greens such as tatsoi, mizuna, and bok choy (pac choi). All leafy

FACING PAGE (top to bottom):
Astro arugula.
Nelson carrots.
Caraflex cabbage.
Gold Star melon.

greens are nutritional powerhouses. For example, an average serving of kale, according to USDA data, gives you 200 percent of the Recommended Daily Allowance of vitamin A, 130 percent of Vitamin C, 10 percent of calcium, and it's filled with protective phytonutrients.

The Onion Family

PRACTICALLY EVERY CUISINE relies on onions and their relatives. Garlic, which takes little space to grow, has a place of honor in our kitchen. Leeks are also easy to fit in, and are so winter-hardy that they can survive outdoors year-round in all but the harshest climates. If you plant enough of them you can eat them all winter and still dig them fresh in spring.

The Carrot Family

CARROTS GROWN IN compost-enriched soil are among the most succulent of vegetables. They also have one of the longest seasons. We sow our first carrots as early in the spring as possible, and sometimes we're still finishing up the last stored ones in our root cellar just as the first new ones are coming along. The best type of carrot for the practical garden is one that matures early and withstands summer heat so it can be succession planted during the summer.

Celery is another member of the carrot family, but it's often a difficult crop for the home gardener to grow well because it needs extremely rich soil and a lot of extra moisture, so it is probably best postponed until you have a few years' experience. Celery's close relative, celery root (celeriac), on the other hand, is much

more forgiving. Though it doesn't mature until fall, it is great in soups and stews for winter eating.

Potatoes

BEFORE THE YEARS when the potato blight created such misery for the Irish, the potato was their major food staple in the countryside and many families survived quite well on a diet of milk, kale, and potatoes. The milk provided calcium, protein, and fat; the kale provided carotene, fiber, and the other benefits of a green leafy vegetable; and the potatoes supplied the carbohydrates and vitamin C. Potatoes are a well-known staple in the Andean diets of South America, and are the fourth most important food crop in the world. (The other three are corn, rice, and wheat.) Potatoes have more protein than corn and nearly twice the calcium.

Legumes

PEAS AND BEANS are next in line for our practical garden. They don't have the high production per square foot of our previous choices, but they add protein and variety to the diet, and are just plain delicious. We plant a large pea patch every year despite the short season for fresh green peas, the diligent attention necessary to keep them harvested promptly, and the time it takes to shell them. To make harvesting more efficient, we erect simple trellises for the vines to grow up (see page 243). We think there's no other vegetable whose taste is so dramatically better when fresh-picked as compared with store-bought. For a higher-yielding pea, plant the sugar snap

Grasp a potato plant's stems and pull. Up comes buried treasure.

type, which is eaten pod and all, and prized for its sweetness and crunch.

Snap beans (aka string beans or green beans) also belong in this garden, but the short bush types whose pods ripen all at once are less practical than the vining, pole bean types that yield continuously over a long period. The pole bean we like best, a variety called Garden of Eden, is not only long-producing but is also tasty at any stage. Even after the pods are very large and the seeds are fully rounded within, they keep their flavor and become tender with cooking. We even snack on them raw in the garden!

There's another way in which legumes like peas and beans justify the space they take up in the garden. Since they're able to extract some of their own nitrogen fertility needs from the air (see page 24), they leave the soil better than they found it. This greatly benefits the yield of any vegetables that follow them.

Salad Crops

NOW THAT WE have a dependable source of nutritious meals from our practical garden, the time has come to create additional growing space and add the salad crops. A case might be made for moving them up on the list, since fresh succulent salad crops like lettuce and spinach obviously suffer more from long storage and transportation than those sturdier crops we've listed ahead of them. But we're talking about the greatest nutritional return for garden space and time invested.

We recommend keeping things simple at the start by growing just lettuce and spinach. Most types of spinach are pretty similar, but there are many options of color and texture in the lettuce palette. The easiest lettuce for pure beginners is a classic leaf type like Black-Seeded Simpson. It grows well when started early because it's so cold tolerant. After that you might add a butterhead/Bibb type with enough heat tolerance to succeed for as much of the rest of the season as possible. These have deep green leaves enclosing a blanched heart and thus lend themselves to most any way of serving lettuce, but you might also add a planting of romaine for fall.

Spinach is a good crop for the practical garden in the sense that it does double duty: You can cook it the way you would kale and collards, or, while it's young and tender, use it raw in salads. It's a little trickier to grow than kale because it's very quick to bolt (go to seed) when the weather warms. On the other hand, it is very winter hardy and in most climates you can grow it as a spring, fall, and winter crop. And you can pick the outer leaves, letting new ones grow from the center, thus giving you a longer harvest.

If you like things a little spicy you might tuck in some arugula as well. Although best limited, like spinach, to cool temperatures (it bolts and becomes a bit *too* zingy in hot weather), arugula is a fast-growing and very nutritious salad ingredient. Best cut at about 4 inches tall as a cut-and-come-again crop, it provides a continual harvest spring, fall, and even winter with some protection. Asian greens (see page 137), grown either from direct-seeding or from transplants, can enliven a salad of mild lettuces—or be enjoyed on their own. Radishes, too, are easy to tuck into this garden.

If you like things a little spicy, you might tuck in some arugula.

Herbs

IN THE SALAD GARDEN section we noted how easy it is to sneak a few herbs into even the tiniest garden. In a larger one you could add more of the annual herbs, especially basil, which is useful to have in bulk for making pesto sauce (see page 320). Dill, parsley, and cilantro are also good to have in quantity if you use them a lot. The same goes for favorite perennial herbs, which require little care except for cutting them back in spring or fall, and sometimes curtailing their spreading tendencies.

Cucumbers and Summer Squash

CUCUMBERS, GROWING AS they do on long vines, do create a space issue. But if you choose a cucumber variety that can be trained to grow up a trellis (see page 243), you can get enormous production in a small garden area. The summer squashes, which grow as a more compact "bush," definitely deserve a place in this garden. They may not be dense in nutrients, but they are unstoppable and produce a lot of food from a single plant. A couple of zucchini or yellow summer squash plants are probably all that a family needs in their garden, unless they're planning to put some up in the freezer.

Tomatoes, Peppers, and Eggplant

GIVEN THE STAR status of tomatoes in home gardens, it may seem odd to find them this far down in our Practical

TOP TO BOTTOM:
Basil, red peppers, cherry tomatoes.

Garden priorities. We know many gardeners will ignore this advice entirely, but remember this is our bang-for-the-buck list. Tomatoes need warm weather, a location with full sun, and an early start—well ahead of outdoor planting time—in order to mature in most climates. They contain a lot of water and do not rank high on the basis of nutrients per square foot of garden space invested. But they can be trellised (see page 243), a point in their favor, and those who freeze or can vegetables find that the plum types earn their keep.

Peppers bear heavily on relatively small plants, and are a valuable source of vitamin C. Hot pepper varieties, especially the small bush types, can be tucked in odd corners of the garden for good space efficiency. Eggplants require the warmest growing conditions of this closely related trio, and are the least productive per square foot.

The Cabbage Family

THESE PLANTS ARE real peasant fare, especially the cabbage itself. They are all sturdy, nutritious foods that do well in the cool weather of fall, and many (including the abovementioned kale) can last well past frost. Cauliflower is the least productive, since it has a one-cut head as compared to the continuous production of secondary shoots that broccoli keeps growing after its main head is picked. (We choose broccoli varieties with this feature in mind.) A spring-grown cabbage will actually do something similar, and produce four small cabbages by later in the summer at the top of its cut stem, if you leave the stem and roots in the soil after cutting off the head. These mini cabbages look like baseball-size Brussels sprouts, and are particularly tender and delicious. They sprout from the upper leaf nodes on the stem, and you can encourage them to appear by cutting a shallow ✕ in the cut surface of the stem with a sharp knife. The real Brussels sprouts are a dependable fall crop that can be harvested as late as any other vegetable. When grown well and harvested fresh in cold weather, they are much better tasting than the wilted supermarket examples you may have experienced; and that, for us, justifies the long time the crop stays in the ground.

Red cabbage.

Other Root Crops

WE HAVE ALWAYS been beet lovers. We enjoy both the baby new beets of early spring with a little butter on them—and their greens—as well as the large storage beets of winter, baked and served cold as an ingredient in a hearty salad. But we remember futile efforts to convince young people to at least sample our finest beet dishes. Nevertheless, for those who like them, beets are an extremely practical crop because both their roots and tops can be enjoyed over a long period.

Turnips and rutabagas, especially as storage crops, give enormous return on garden space. But since they are usually an even harder sell than beets, they fall this far down on the list. And they are great hearty foods! Give some a try and you might give them a big thumbs-up.

More Vine Crops

THUS FAR WE'VE been making fairly modest scale increases to the size of the garden as each new vegetable crop is added, but if you're considering more vine crops we need to talk about a seriously larger garden. Pumpkins and winter squashes that are too heavy to trellis, or tie to a garden fence, need room for their vines to sprawl. There are bush varieties of winter squashes but we have never thought they had the eating quality of the old-time vining sorts.

Melons grow on a more compact plant, not needing as much space. What they do need, however, is lots of warm weather. For many gardeners who, like us, live in the northern states, a successful melon crop usually means some sort of plastic-covered protection: either black plastic to warm the soil, or row covers on supports over the plants, or both. Depending on the time and effort you have to put into your garden, that extra work for just one crop may not be considered "practical."

Sweet Corn

AND WHY IS sweet corn, that classic summer vegetable, way down here at the bottom of the list? From our experience as commercial vegetable growers, we know that sweet corn has the least return per square foot of all the crops we grow. Now admittedly, that is financial return, not pleasure-in-eating return, but still this is a very space-demanding crop that is usually available in quantity at every farmers' market. If you do grow sweet corn, you'll want to spread out your harvest over a period of time. With another crop we might suggest succession plantings of a quick-maturing variety; but since corn occupies the ground for quite a while, it's simpler to extend your harvest by planting a number of varieties all at the same time, each with a different maturity date. Also, many of the later maturing varieties are better eating than some of the earlies.

Remember, one of the criteria of this Practical Garden is to grow crops with a long season of availability so you get a lot of eating from one sowing. But some vegetables, like lettuce and spinach for example, are short-duration cool-climate crops that grow best at either end of the season. In that case you need a partner crop to be grown in that same location after they've been harvested or, if they're planned as a fall crop, to occupy the ground before they'll be planted. That double use of space is an excellent way to fit an early sweet corn variety into your garden, either after the spring lettuce or before the fall-planted spinach.

Special Crops

WHETHER A CROP is 100 percent practical should not necessarily limit you, or deter you from growing something you love to eat or are curious about. At one time or another we've grown countless specialty crops, without much regard to their practicality. That keeps our diet varied, and it is one of the things that have made gardening fun and exciting for us. Some, such as saltwort and cardoons, have proved interesting and worth growing, but not every year. For more along this train of thought, see the Savory Garden on page 116.

The named varieties selected for this Practical Garden and for the other gardens to follow have been selected with the intention of each garden in mind. The vegetable-seed world offers a huge range of choices, and we are always trying new ones. Often we grow more than one variety in a given season. For the list on page 68 we chose varieties that are simple to grow, undemanding of culture, and consistently productive. This is our "if you can grow only one variety" list. In seed catalogs, varieties such as these are often marked with a symbol or color indicating that they are the "best bets" for beginners, or they do better in one season than another, or they are best suited to a particular region. And of course, those judgments may change from one year to the next. But that's part of the fun.

If you're going to put effort into creating your first garden and providing your family with good food, you can count on the fact that this selection of crops and varieties will do pretty well by you. However, people have not always had the privilege of deciding whether or not to grow their own food. Sometimes the need to do so has been forced on them by circumstances beyond their control. It's interesting to speculate what specific crops might come to the fore under those conditions. ☼

THe HaRD TimeS GaRDeN

BACK DURING THE Great Depression, scores of one-time country dwellers who had left their rural roots many years before found that the city no longer offered them a means of earning their keep. So they returned to their old farms, mainly so that they could once again grow their own food. They were not attracted by the frills of the seed catalogs. They were not interested in garden subtleties. They aimed to raise enough of the staple foods to guarantee their families an adequate year-round diet for survival.

When you read some of the old stories written by Depression-era gardeners, it's fascinating how successful they were in providing their own sustenance. Many spoke of how they wished they had realized, before they left the farm, before they decided to quit struggling with agricultural prices, that their rural home was just as important for growing one's own food as it was for growing food to sell. Many people never went back to the city once the Depression ended, and the stories of their experience after returning to the farm justified that decision in a number of interesting ways. The good life, in their minds, was not growing commodity crops for a low-paying wholesale market but rather simply growing food for their family's needs and selling the excess fruits or vegetables or eggs for a little money.

Many felt this "maintenance farming," as they called it, was so desirable that they never wanted to return to commercial farming again. An economist might refer to this situation as "production for use" as opposed to "production for exchange," but whatever it's called, it results in a lifestyle that is more secure in times of unstable markets. Despite the modern prejudice against the life of the peasant farmer, the independence, sufficiency, abundance, and land stewardship inherent in these age-old low-technology systems has much to offer when things are tough.

The crops you'd grow for survival might have virtues that go beyond necessity, such as good flavor, or their importance in traditional recipes. But they also command a new respect when you view them as life-sustaining. In times when the food supply might be at risk, two groups of crops stand out as the ones to grow.

Corn, beans, and squash are often grown as the first crops on newly prepared garden soil.

VARIETIES FOR THE HARD TIMES GARDEN

The Hard Times Garden is a collection of the most dependable crops and the most dependable varieties of those crops that we know. It is also a garden with balanced protein (corn and beans) and plenty of vegetable variety. Furthermore, this is a garden that can provide winter salads without a greenhouse. The crops in this list will feed you dependably, no matter what else might be going on in the world.

BEANS: Soldier.
A basic, old-time New England dry bean with beautiful red markings; easy to grow, harvest, and thresh.

BEETS: Lutz Winter Keeper. This large, sweet storage beet does as its name implies. If you grow enough there will still be edible beets in the root cellar through July.

BRUSSELS SPROUTS: Diablo. A tall, late-season plant with solid sprouts and great leaf coverage.

CABBAGE: Storage No. 4. This has all the best qualities you'd want in a cabbage: tasty, easy to grow, stores well, and makes a full-flavored sauerkraut.

CARROTS: Bolero.
Thick, blunt-ended roots and superior disease resistance in storage.

CELERY ROOT: Brilliant. A delicious celery root that's easy to grow and long-keeping.

CORN: Nothstine Dent.
There's no better choice than this grinding corn, which matures early for successful field-drying and makes an exceptionally flavorful cornmeal.

GARLIC: Russian Red.
One of the most dependable varieties of garlic, and one of the easiest to grow.

KALE: Winterbor.
A curly kale with exceptional cold resistance that regrows vigorously after harvest.

KOHLRABI: Kossack.
The most tender and tastiest of the giant kohlrabi varieties, productive and easy to grow.

ONION: Patterson.
A nice large onion with early maturity and small necks that cure down easily for long storage.

PARSLEY ROOT: Fakir.
Good flavoring for soups and easy to force for winter parsley.

PARSNIP: Andover.
Its more cylindrical shape means higher yields, and the rounded tops are easier to clean.

POTATO: Superior.
This is about as dependable and long-storing a potato as we know. It's resistant to scab and lends itself to any type of cooking.

RUTABAGA: Helenor.
A rutabaga with great storage ability and a round, easy-to-clean shape.

SQUASH: Blue Hubbard.
This New England classic is the largest, most productive winter squash, and also the best storing, thanks to its rock-hard skin. Try a smaller, more user-friendly version of Blue Hubbard if the size intimidates you, or a butternut type such as **Waltham.**

THE THREE SISTERS

FIRST COME THE chief native North American crops: corn, beans, and squash, or "the three sisters" as they are traditionally known. These reliable producers, which tolerate a wide range of growing conditions, are adapted to our continent. They were staples in the diet of early American pioneers who learned to grow them from Native Americans, and they were staples for Depression-era gardeners. Corn, beans, and squash are often grown as the first crops on newly prepared garden soil because not only do they grow well on rough new land, but they also help to improve it. The large leaves of winter squash smother out weeds. The enormous amount of organic matter produced in corn stalks can be incorporated into the soil at the end of the season to begin increasing that all-important soil constituent. And beans, being legumes, give as much back to the soil as they take (see page 24).

When you're trying to grow all your food, there are some new considerations beyond those of the small backyard vegetable garden. Much as we dote on just-picked sweet corn and fresh snap beans, we'd need to grow field corn (for corn meal) and dry beans that store well if our goal is survival. These crops must be allowed to mature and dry down in the garden before being harvested. So not only do they take up a lot of space, but they also must be left in the ground longer than corn and beans would be if they were grown just for fresh eating, and there would be fewer options for following them with later crops growing in the same place.

> The Hard Times Garden is a collection of the most dependable crops and the most dependable varieties of those crops that we know.

Winter squash and pumpkins are easy crops, though these too take up a lot of room; they must be left in the garden until fully mature, and not picked until there's danger of a frost. For more on growing, harvesting, and storing all of the three sisters crops, see Chapter 4.

OLD WORLD ROOT CROPS

SECOND IN LINE for a secure food supply after the traditional American crops are the old-time European root crops, many of which were brought to North America by the earliest settlers. Roots are not flashy but they are truly dependable, hiding the part you eat safely in the soil while it's being grown. The potato is a most obvious candidate for this garden, a classic hard-times food. Another is the cold-resistant parsnip because the best way to store it is to leave it in the ground and dig it first thing in the spring, when new foods are treasured. Other logical choices are carrots, beets, parsley root, celery root, rutabagas, and turnips—although if we had to choose between turnips and rutabagas, the latter would win because

FACING PAGE (Top to bottom):
Celery root.
Brussels sprouts.
Rutabaga.
Blue Hubbard squash.

of their greater storability. Rutabagas are also easier to grow than turnips and their golden flesh has more nutrients than the typical American white turnip.

It may be surprising to people unfamiliar with food storage that cabbage, normally thought of as a green leafy vegetable, was traditionally considered a root crop because it can be stored all winter in the same underground conditions and the same underground space that successfully preserves the other crops just listed above: the root cellar.

Root Storage

THE KEY TO the Hard Times Garden, as it was for our pioneer ancestors, is to be able to store vegetable crops to carry you over the months when the garden is not producing. A root cellar is the time-tested way of doing that. The root crops mentioned above all need cool, moist, dark conditions for successful storage. Nothing could be easier, because cool, moist, dark—and frost-free—are the natural conditions of a hole in the ground. And that's basically what a root cellar is, a hole in the ground

in which you can keep vegetables edible all winter. Obviously that hole needs to have some structure to it, such as walls, ceiling, and floor, but it is the cool underground climate that sustains it.

The best old-time farm cellar was either a concrete room dug into a hillside or an insulated corner of the basement under the farmhouse. That level of protection is necessary in cold climates where root crops need to be well insulated from the frigid outside weather in order to prevent them from freezing. You can control temperatures by having an air inlet that will bring in cold air, when you're cooling the cellar down to storage temperature, and vent warm air out as needed. Those outlets should be partially closed up in really cold weather. Moisture levels are maintained by sprinkling water on the floor each time you go to the cellar. The closer you can come to achieving temperatures in the mid-30s and a humidity level close to 90 percent, the better your crops will store.

You can create a decent root cellar in any concrete or stone basement by separating off the corner farthest from a heat source. The best way to do that is by building a concrete block wall with an insulated door for access. Glue sheets of 2-inch-thick foam insulation to the cellar side of the block wall for better temperature control. Site the root cellar with access to at least one basement window. That's your cold-air inlet and warm-air outlet. Because the cool, moist environment that's ideal for vegetable storage will cause wood to rot, you should avoid wood for shelves or containers in the cellar. In fact, we have no shelves at all in ours. Hard plastic boxes or stacking crates,

An underground root cellar is the gold standard for keeping winter storage crops.

such as milk crates, make ideal cellar containers for both root crops and canning jars. They can sometimes be bought, used, from dairies.

When preparing roots for storage, you need to trim the greens off to within a half-inch of the top of the root, since the fresh succulent green parts would rot and get mucky in storage. Cutting them short removes that problem. We don't wash the root crops but put them directly into storage as we dig them. If the air in your cellar isn't moist enough, you can help keep roots from drying out by burying them in damp sand on the floor of the cellar. See page 128 for tips on cellar storage for cabbages.

Storing Roots Without a Cellar

IN MILDER CLIMATES where the storage period is shorter, much simpler structures will suffice for keeping root crops. Metal barrels or old refrigerators can be buried in the ground just deep enough to protect stored foods from freezing. We have used two simple options ourselves even though we live in a climate where winter temperatures can dip to 20 degrees below zero. The first was to dig a hole in the dirt floor of an old garden shed so we could bury a metal garbage can up to its top edge, with a piece of foam insulation glued to the underside of the lid. After harvest we put root crops into that can and placed the lid on top. A few bales of hay on top of the lid in really cold weather added extra insurance. That double layer of protection, first the shed and then the buried can, moderated the temperature enough to keep the roots from freezing.

We found that the idea works equally well in a greenhouse. We dug a deep hole in the soil at one end of a greenhouse and buried three garbage cans to make access to specific crops easier. One can was for potatoes, one for the other assorted root crops, and the third for cabbages. Again, we filled those cans with the crops and covered them with insulated lids, and again, because of the double protection, all the crops stored without a hitch. The nice thing about using a greenhouse as the outbuilding over the storage containers is that it's also the source of fresh winter green food (see pages 91 to 101). So with everything in the same place, one trip to the greenhouse yields all the produce for a winter meal.

Sprouting Root Crops Indoors

HERE'S A LITTLE trick by which you can enjoy fresh green food in winter even without a greenhouse. First, the science behind it: The plants we call "root crops" aren't storing nutrients in their roots to feed *us,* they're storing them to feed their own reproduction. They are biennials, which means they use those stored nutrients in the spring of their second year to grow the new leaves and then the flowering seed stalk that will produce seeds for future generations of that plant. So if you bring roots up from the storage area and place them in a sunny, warm, and moist environment in winter, they'll think spring has come and start sprouting the green leaves that precede their seed stalk. You can do that easily by setting pots or buckets of damp sand in front of a sunny window and replanting the stored root crops in the sand. They will soon begin growing new feeding roots to anchor themselves in the sand and will start drawing on their stored nutrition to grow leaves. Of course you're sacrificing the root itself, but that's a small price to pay for the pleasure of fresh green food in winter.

If you do this with beets you get beet greens; carrots yield carrot tops, not normally eaten but tasty when young, and good for flavoring soups and stocks. Rutabagas and turnips grow their characteristic greens, parsley root provides a rustic fresh green parsley, and celery root yields delicious leafy celery stems for soups or flavoring. (*Do not* do this with potatoes, as their greens are poisonous.) You can even grow fresh green cabbage shoots in winter if you've stored your cabbages with the roots on (see photo below). After cutting off the head of the cabbage for the kitchen, replant the stem and roots in a bucket of damp sand and place it in front of a window. New cabbage foliage grows from each of the leaf scar nodes along the stem, and it is a delicious fresh green winter food—good both raw and cooked. With a red cabbage the new leaves are a beautiful blue with red ribs, followed by contrasting yellow blossoms.

If you want to grow the popular sprouted European Belgian endive (sometimes called witloof), you can place the trimmed roots, grown the summer before, in a bucket of damp sand. You'll need to blanch them to make them edible. Blanching means allowing them to grow in complete darkness so that any new growth emerges white, tender, and mild-tasting, with no hint of the bitterness that often characterizes endive. You do this by forcing them into growth in a lightless place, such as under the kitchen sink or in a closet. Put a heavy black plastic bag over them as well, to exclude all light. (You might try forcing and blanching the roots of dandelions and salsify the same way, for winter variety.)

Sprouting Root Crops

WINDOWSILL GARDEN. Some crops can be resprouted by pulling them up and replanting them in pots of soil mix. The foliage of root parsley (left) and celery root (right) make fine winter seasonings. Cabbage stems (center) minus their heads yield leaves tender enough for a mixed salad.

Wild Greens from the Garden

CHICKWEED. This cool-weather plant might be a pest in the greenhouse, but it will brighten up a winter salad.

PURSLANE. A weed of warm weather, purslane makes mats in the summer garden. Its mild, succulent foliage gives salads a pleasant crunch.

SHEPHERD'S PURSE. This highly nutritious garden weed is prized by Korean cooks, who steam it.

WILD SORREL. The place to find wild sorrel is in the acid soil of our blueberry patch. Its sharp flavor is great in salad.

DANDELION. Gather the tender young plants for an early spring treat, either sautéed or in salad.

LAMB'S QUARTERS. Harvest it before it grows tall and goes to seed. Cook it like spinach.

We mentioned that in order to grow the sprouted root salads described above you have to sacrifice the root itself, but if you can be satisfied with somewhat less leaf production per root, there is a way to have your greens and eat the root, too. Take a beet as an example. When preparing to cook a beet, cut a ½-inch slice off the top of the beet and place that cut-side-down in a shallow saucer. Pour in a little water and add more occasionally so the beet top doesn't dry out. The top of a root is where the growing tip is located, and that growing tip will produce a nice snippet of leaves even without the support of the rest of the root.

OTHER STORAGE CROPS

WHEREAS ROOT CELLAR CROPS are best placed directly into the cellar after being dug and having their tops cut off, onions and garlic, although thought of as root crops, are treated differently. They do not store well in the moist conditions of a root cellar, and like winter squash, they need to be cured and dried in warm, dry, sunny conditions for a few weeks after harvest before they can be stored. For more on curing and storing these crops see Chapter 4.

There are four other crops we would include in the Hard Times Garden. The first is kohlrabi, a seldom grown and unique looking member of the cabbage family. Kohlrabi grows a hard round ball with leaves sticking out of it on narrow stems—sort of like a turnip growing just aboveground. It tastes something like a mild turnip and it has the delightful texture of a water chestnut when raw. If you're truly trying to survive from the garden, choose one of the giant types that reach 8 inches in diameter and can store for up to five or six months. They taste good, despite their large size.

Another good root cellar crop that adds a unique flavor component is winter radish. Unlike the small, round red varieties so commonly available, winter radishes are larger (up to 4 inches in

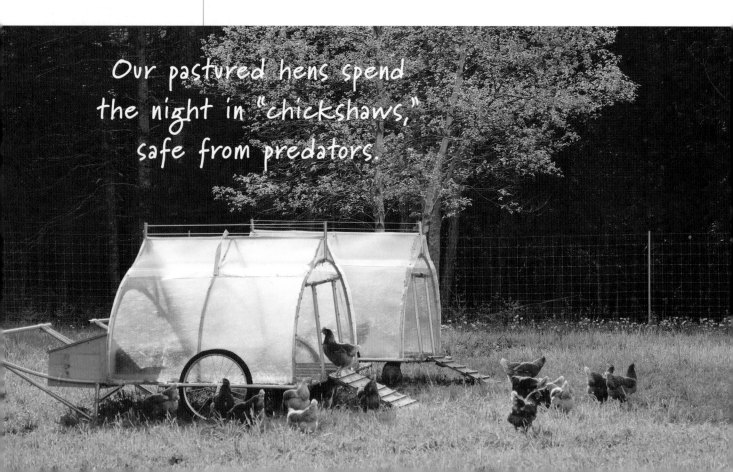

Our pastured hens spend the night in "chickshaws," safe from predators.

diameter for the round varieties and 16 inches long for the daikon types) and have either black or white skin. The round black Spanish radish we store has more bite than conventional radishes, to give the sometimes bland winter diet some zing. The long white oriental daikon radishes have milder, very crisp flesh, and can be stored either fresh or as pickles.

Kale and Brussels sprouts are real troopers when it comes to long-season outdoor production. They'll give you fresh nutritious greenery late into the fall and even into early winter when snow is on the ground. The leaves of Brussels sprouts start drooping down in cold fall weather and wrap protectively around the sprouts growing on the stem underneath like an insulating cover. Every winter we are pleasantly surprised by how long they remain edible. Kale, too, will sustain you in the fall, keeping through a number of hard frosts. The indoor storage technique described on page 130 will preserve it even longer.

Sprouting Belgian Endive

STORING. After a long season of growth outdoors, dig up the roots and cut off the leafy tops an inch above the root. Trim the roots to a uniform 9 inches and store in a dark cellar in buckets of moist sand.

FORCING. Bring them up one bucket at a time to grow in the warm temperatures of the house. Keep in a closed cupboard, covered with a black plastic bag, to exclude all light. This ensures tender, mild little heads to use in salads.

A FEW GARDEN COMPANIONS

THERE IS ANOTHER food source that was a traditional part of rural food sufficiency—almost every family kept poultry to supply fresh eggs. Both chickens and ducks are productive egg layers, and even though ducks are less commonly raised, they actually lay more eggs over the course of the year than chickens do. Ducks also don't make noise when they lay eggs and the male ducks (drakes) don't crow. That's something to consider if you have neighbors who might not appreciate the barnyard cacophony of chickens.

In order to be productive, the poultry that supply you with fresh eggs need to be fed well, just like the soil in which you grow your vegetables. Fortunately, feeding them can be as straightforward as feeding the garden. The key here is not to think of "poultry feed," a product that you have to buy, but rather think of "feeding poultry," which can be done with many of the foods you'd be growing for your own meals. It's a misconception that livestock food always has to be a special formula from the feed store. For example, the most important food for sheep and cattle is grass, which grows naturally in fields and pastures. Similarly, the purchase of special poultry food, which obviously benefits the feed company, will reduce the amount you save by raising animals. We've found that with a little ingenuity, the feed for poultry can be found in a wide range of what would otherwise be waste products.

It's also important to get the birds out of the poultry house for as much of the year as possible, and to revise your idea of what a poultry house looks like. On our commercial farm the chicken flock spends seven months of the year living outdoors on pasture. (This could be even longer in warmer climates.) They are sheltered at night by inexpensive, homemade 6-by-6-foot-wide, 3-foot-tall, lightweight structures on garden-cart wheels, which we call "chickshaws" because they can be wheeled about. Each can house up to 50 birds.

There are two reasons for providing shelter only at night. The first is that the poultry house can be made so much smaller if it's only for sleeping. Nighttime predator-safe roosting space requires only about half a square foot per bird, although we give them more than that. The second reason is that we want the birds to be outside all day feeding themselves as much as possible from weed seeds, grasses, clovers, worms, insects, and so forth, which they know very well how to do. In rainy weather or under blazing sun they shelter inside or underneath the chickshaw, which is well ventilated. Our direct involvement in feeding them means adding enough other foods to what they get for free to give them a well-rounded diet. For our commercial chicken flock we purchase whole grains and seeds, in addition to feeds we grow for them on the farm, to supplement what they get on pasture. But a small home poultry flock's diet can be pretty much rounded out with just leftovers and waste food from the garden and kitchen.

For instance, chickens think those overgrown zucchini, which every gardener has in abundance, are the finest of summertime snacks. Cut them in half to provide access to the immature seeds and soft insides, and they'll eat them right up. Poultry love tasty green stuff like the leaves of broccoli, cauliflower, and Brussels sprouts, which we don't generally eat, and kale, Swiss chard, and lettuce leaves, which we do. Overmature peas, beans, and sweet corn, or immature thinnings and young weeds, make great poultry food, so we feed them all of those throughout the season as they're available. The kitchen supplies such year-round treats as stale bread, curdled milk, leftover baked beans, uneaten breakfast cereal, excess fat from a

Your overgrown zucchini is a chicken's feast.

steak (suet), and leftover mashed potatoes. In our experience the nutritional balance in the diet we eat seems fine for poultry, supplemented with a sprinkling of nutritional yeast flakes, and it's a pail of scraps that would normally go on the compost heap every day. We exclude items they don't like, such as citrus rinds, and also raw egg or egg shells, so as to not give them a taste for eating eggs. The sight of that pail sends them stampeding toward us with the gentle thunder of their feet, and it's satisfying to watch them devour every kitchen and garden scrap we give them.

During the summer, chickens should have full-time access to an area of short grass and clover. That alone can cover up to 40 percent of their food needs. For extra green feed in winter, we make what we call "poultry hay" every time we mow the lawn in summer. Short clippings of young grasses and clovers are very nourishing for poultry. You just need to time your lawn mowing for when there will be a couple of sunny days to dry the clippings. When dry they can be raked up, stuffed into burlap sacks, and stored in a shed. (If they get moldy, it indicates you did not let the clippings get dry enough.) We've also fed wheat berries, sprouted for a couple of days, as a vitamin supplement. Another winter treat in which they take great delight is the giant kohlrabi pictured on page 86. If you cut one in half, the chickens will peck out every morsel of flesh down to the skin. We give them seaweed from the nearby Maine coast as their salt and mineral supplement, and we recommend a dried seaweed product for those not near the ocean. We also feed

a little freshly cracked corn year-round if we're short on scraps. Our birds' rate of egg production will drop off without proper food, so we gauge our success in meeting their needs by keeping track of how many eggs we get. We haven't been disappointed yet.

Since we presently raise chickens at the farm, we keep ducks in our home yard. Ducks are easier on the yard than chickens are. They don't scratch like chickens, and so do little or no damage to lawns and ornamental gardens. They spend a lot of their time pursuing their favorite food, slugs, and if you garden where slugs are a problem, you'll find no better solution than a few hungry ducks. Our home duck flock spends the night in a wheeled shelter similar to the chickshaw but smaller. It can hold four to six birds and is nicknamed Duckingham Palace.

During the gardening season we set up an 18-inch-high lightweight plastic mesh fence (the material shown on page 245) to keep the ducks out of the vegetable garden. Once all crops are mature or protected by cold frames, we give them the run of the garden in addition to the lawns and flower borders they've roamed all summer. Our preferred duck breed is the Indian Runner because they cause so little trouble, don't try to escape, and are excellent layers. Like all ducks, they appreciate the occasional sprinkler bath on hot, dry days but do not need water for swimming. If we had chickens in our yard instead of ducks, we would choose one of the older breeds such as Wyandottes or Barred Rocks because they are good foragers. In that case we would need to

Raise a flock of ducks for delicious eggs and a home team slug patrol.

Giant kohlrabi.

keep them in some simple bottomless cage, with shade at one end, that could be moved around the lawn daily in order to manage their scratching activities. If you don't want to build your own chicken pen, there are many ingeniously designed small-poultry containment units to be found on the web.

Housing for poultry during the winter months can be similar to what we suggest for vegetables in the next section of this chapter: a greenhouse. On our commercial farm the layer flock spends the winter in a large, movable, plastic-covered hoop house equipped with hanging feeders, built-in roosting bars, and laying boxes. We call it the "hoop coop." You could house a small flock in one of the small movable greenhouses described on pages 93 to 95, and the expense would be much less that that of building a separate poultry shed. Furthermore, when their winter home is a greenhouse, the birds get all the possible light available and we've seen no need for supplemental lighting to keep them laying in winter as we would have if they were in a building.

There's one other type of poultry that has been a dependable, low-input peasant food for hundreds of years: geese. If you have a large lawn area you can benefit from that tradition. Geese are grazers and, from three weeks of age on, can gain all their support from a mowed lawn. They thrive on short grasses, clovers, and broad-leaved weeds like dandelions as long as they have access to drinking water, grit (small stones for grinding food in their crop), and a calcium supplement like crushed oyster shells. They'll also thrive on almost any vegetable leftovers from the garden. If you're not sure of the quality of your lawn for grazing, a supplement of a pound or so of commercial pellets or grain per week per bird should cover any deficits. (Ask your local feed store for pellets suitable for geese.) Geese fatten best in cold weather; they should be fed whole grains or pellets, free choice, for a month in the fall. They'll put on enough extra weight to make a tasty meal for your holiday feasts.

In whatever way you choose to manage them, backyard poultry will be a valuable complement to your homegrown diet.

Although we've called this the Hard Times Garden, it's easy to see how nature's resources, coupled with a little experience in the choice of crops, can make for some very good times—and some mighty fine eating—even when the going gets tough! And with a root cellar, you get to enjoy some of your garden's bounty all through the winter as well. But why not take that idea further and have freshly harvested vegetables from the garden in addition to stored ones? You'll notice that in this book we don't focus much on canning and freezing. We appreciate—and sometimes take part in—those activities, but they are very time-consuming. We've taken another route instead, and are always looking for ever-more-simple ways of extending the fresh harvest. ☀

THE WINTER GARDEN

GARDENERS THROUGH THE AGES have tried to extend summer, and inventive minds have worked hard to find ways to keep fresh food forever on the table. A sheltered area that protects plants from cold and wind can often take them past their normal season. A south-facing stone or brick wall will absorb enough heat from the sun's rays, even in winter, to create what is called a microclimate at its base. At night the heat radiated from the stones creates warmer conditions for anything growing alongside. In fact, placing vegetable growing areas against the south wall of any structure will have that effect. Even the south side of a board fence or a thick hedge, blocking the cold north winds, will provide a slightly more benign climate. Old-time gardeners learned to take advantage of these warm and sheltered spots in order to keep the fresh harvest going as long as they could.

THE COLD FRAME

THE NEXT STEP beyond a warm and sheltered spot is a low glass- or plastic-covered structure such as a cold frame. It's just a four-sided, bottomless box that sits on the soil, with a transparent lid that can be opened. It operates like a greenhouse during the day, and in addition, heat absorbed from the sun is retained in the frame at night, when temperatures drop, instead of being radiated back into the surrounding air. Since the 16th century, cold frames have been used for winter plant protection.

Large commercial vegetable farms using acres of cold frames were common near cities in the 19th century. They provided out-of-season produce with a minimum of expense. Home gardeners embraced the technology too, and we have had many years' experience using cold frames to grow out-of-season crops. Although we now grow most of those crops under quick hoops (page 90) and in greenhouses (page 93), we still consider the cold frame a very useful structure, not only for growing food in early spring, late fall, and winter, but also for seed-starting, as shown on pages 227 to 229.

Our cold frames have always been made 12 inches high at the back (north) side and 8 inches high at the front (south). The end boards, connecting front to back, are cut on a diagonal from 12 inches at one end to 8 inches at the other. The dimensions (length and width) of this low box are determined by the size of the available glass frame to cover the top, most often a secondhand storm window.

If old storm windows are not easily available, you can make your own cold frame covers from sheets of any translucent material by enclosing it in a simple wooden frame. Because glass is heavy and easily breakable and plastic film is light and hard to secure, one of the glass substitutes like Plexiglas or double-walled polycarbonate would be the best choice. Since polycarbonate is less expensive than Plexiglas and is designed for greenhouse use, that's the material we choose. We build our polycarbonate-covered frames 4 feet long and 4 feet front-to-back. Those

Cut-and-come-again salad crops withstand winter if protected by a cold frame.

HARDY VEGETABLE VARIETIES FOR THE WINTER GARDEN

ARUGULA: Sylvetta. A wild arugula relative, the hardiest type to grow. Of the standard arugula varieties, **Even Star** is the hardiest but still may not survive everywhere.

CARROT: Napoli. Cold soil storage makes these the best tasting carrots you'll ever eat.

CLAYTONIA: There are few named cultivars. Seeds are available in most northern catalogs.

ENDIVE: Clodia. Endive may get beaten up in the worst of winter's cold, but it will regrow to provide a classic winter salad ingredient. This one is a frisée type.

BEET GREENS: Bull's Blood. Great as baby leaf greens in winter. The cold turns them deep crimson.

KALE: Dwarf Siberian. An extra-hardy variety, because its growing tip is closer to the ground than with most kale types.

LETTUCE: Oak Leaf. Lettuce leaves are hardiest when young, and the oak leaf type lettuces hold up well against freezing temperatures. Or you could sow one of the greenhouse lettuce mixes that are designed to be cut as baby leaves.

MÂCHE: Vit. A very popular winter salad crop in Europe, mâche is the cold-hardiest of all the greens.

MIZUNA: A dependable Asian green that keeps producing feathery leaves for salads or stir-fries throughout the winter.

PARSLEY: Forest Green. The curly parsleys are hardier than the flat-leaf types.

SCALLION: Evergreen Hardy White. Extra-hardy perennial variety.

SPINACH: Space. Spinach is the most popularly grown and universally productive of all the winter salad crops.

SWISS CHARD: Argentata. This old-time green variety is hardier than those with colored stems.

TATSOI: Yukina Savoy. Hardy and delicious. Sow in mid-September.

dimensions fit well with the standard dimensions of lumber and polycarbonate sheets.

To frame the polycarbonate for our cold frame covers we use 1½- inch by 1-inch cedar boards with a ½-inch slot cut into them where the polycarbonate is inserted. The slot is cut by running the boards through a table saw a few times until the slot is wide enough to fit over the polycarbonate. Those 1½-inch slotted boards fit around three sides of the polycarbonate, and the fourth side is a 1-inch board on which the polycarbonate rests. A small wooden stop keeps it from sliding out. The covers are placed on the frame with that edge down so rainwater can drain off.

The back (north side) of our frame and the end walls are made of 2-by-12 planks. For the front (south side), we frame out a piece of polycarbonate 4 feet long and 8 inches tall as we did for the covers. We like the polycarbonate front wall because light can enter and there is consequently much less shaded area when the sun is low in the sky than there is with the traditional solid piece of wood used as a front wall.

Except in the depths of winter, that valuable sunshine can overheat the cold frame and it must be opened whenever the inside temperature might get higher than 75 degrees. We keep a thermometer (shaded from the direct rays of the sun) inside the frame. If you're not sure about the weather or are going to be away during the day, it's always best to err on the side of venting. Too cool is nowhere near as dangerous as too hot, and the inside of a cold frame can overheat very quickly on a sunny day, even a cold one. Many gardeners have "cooked" their greens by forgetting to vent the frame in time. We have successfully managed this problem with the use of notched sticks, opening the frame every morning and shutting it at night or during bad weather. But the best solution is to have a frame with a lid light enough to be lifted by an automatic venting arm, well worth its modest price.

If you're not quite ready to build your own, you can purchase a modern cold frame of this design as your entry-level introduction to out-of-season harvesting. We recommend purchasing the automatic venting arm as well. (See page 453 for sources of both.)

A 4- by 4-foot cold frame, even a wooden one, can easily be moved to wherever you want it. Let's say that instead of growing seedlings, you used the frame to protect a bed of spinach so you could harvest it all winter. (An excellent choice, actually, since spinach is one of the most dependable winter harvest crops.) However, now it's spring and the spinach is still producing but no longer needs protection. You'd like to get an early lettuce sowing off to a great start but don't want to pull up the spinach. Simply pick up the frame and move it to where you wish to grow the lettuce. Later, once the lettuce is up and growing and spring has advanced enough that the lettuce can survive without protection, move the frame to another spot and set out extra-early cucumber transplants or any other warm-weather crop that would benefit from the cold frame protection.

FACING PAGE (top to bottom):
Dwarf Siberian kale.
Scallions.
Sylvetta arugula.
Tatsoi.

Here's an example of a 4- by 4-foot wooden cold frame, which can easily be moved to wherever you want it.

QUICK HOOPS

HARVESTING WINTER FARE is so satisfying that once you try it you'll probably want to extend your repertoire. But adding more cold frames to the garden means more time or money spent acquiring them. That's why we came up with an even simpler, lighter, and less expensive structure we call the quick hoop. It's just a sheet of clear plastic or row cover material (see below) supported by 10-foot lengths of pipe, bent into half circles and poked into the ground. It looks like a 3-foot-tall mini-greenhouse.

There are two types of pipe material you can use. One is plastic electrical conduit, which is cheap, lightweight, and easy to bend by hand. It's fine in parts of the country where no more than a few inches of snowfall can be expected. But to support the amount of snow that we get in Maine, we found that we needed ½-inch galvanized metal conduit, sold as "EMT" at any box store such as Home Depot. In addition to its strength, the advantage of EMT is that, once bent, it holds that shape permanently and is therefore easier to work with.

To give EMT pipe a curved shape, you need to bend it around a quick-hoop bending form, which is inexpensive and easy to use. (See pages 453 for sources.) The bending form is bolted to the top of a large flat surface such as a workbench or a sturdy picnic table. You just insert one end of the pipe, pull it against the curved surface of the form, slide it in farther, and pull again until you achieve the desired shape. The form itself is reasonably priced and could even be purchased by a garden club or a group of friends and made available for everyone's use.

If you take a 10-foot length of EMT and bend it into a half-circle bow, it will have a 6-foot diameter. That 6-foot width will cover two of our 30-inch-wide beds with a 1-foot path between them. We make 10-inch-deep holes with an iron bar on either side of the two beds, and insert the ends of the conduit into them, placing one of these conduit bows every 5 feet along the beds. That means just three bows will cover a 10-foot-long area. Then we drape a 10-foot-wide piece of floating row cover material over the bows. This spun-bonded white polyester fabric lets in water and light, conveys up to 4 degrees of frost protection, and excludes insect pests. (For sources see pages 453.) We cut it long enough so that it can drape down to the ground, plus about 2 feet at the ends of the structure. We then secure the edges of the row cover around the perimeter of the structure with sand bags. These can be recycled plastic bags filled with soil, or you can purchase sand bags and fill them with sand or gravel. Be gentle with the fabric, but try to secure it without any slack so the wind is less likely to catch it and blow it around.

Clearly, you can plant up much more ground under quick hoops than under a cold frame, and you can also grow and protect taller crops. You might start seedlings with the potting-soil-on-the-surface technique (see page 227) in one covered bed, and grow early salads in another. Since the spun-bonded floating row cover material is self-venting, there's no need for automatic arms to prevent overheating. And the row cover lets in both sunlight and water. Access to the crops is achieved by removing the sand bags and folding back the cover.

Another quick hoop trick is to add a layer of clear plastic over the row cover for extra protection when the weather gets very cold. With it in place you can overwinter crops such as spinach, lettuce, and onions, without worrying about the snow load, which can rip the row cover fabric. The plastic layer can be held down with sand bags along the perimeter and ends, just as with the row cover. But since we live in a windy area we also use form-fitting plastic clips that handily secure the plastic to the bowed pipes (for sources see page 453). At the point in spring when the temperature inside the quick hoop can rise to 75, you'll need to vent the plastic by opening the ends, or remove it entirely, so that only the row cover material remains.

WOULD A GREENHOUSE BE EVEN BETTER?

WE THINK THERE'S a step beyond the cold frame and the quick hoop that's just as simple for the home gardener: a small, inexpensive modular greenhouse. At first this might seem like a *big* step. But we've found that you can build a very practical 10-foot by 12-foot home greenhouse for less money than you'd spend on the

This small glass home greenhouse is giving tomatoes an early boost.

purchased 4-foot by 4-foot cold frame described above.

Even gardeners in warm or moderate climates can benefit from a greenhouse. South of the Mason-Dixon Line you can grow many crops in winter with no protection at all. But surprisingly, many people do not. Perhaps it's the common notion that spring is the planting season, and that's that. We enthusiastically suggest that a greenhouse will give you much more variety in your winter fare, wherever you live, and also make the experience of growing it more pleasant. Like the cold frame or the quick hoop, a greenhouse provides that warm and sheltered spot for plants. But since you can stand up inside, it also shelters you, the gardener. Just think about going out with your harvest basket

FACING PAGE (top to bottom):
Installing quick hoops over two beds.
Clear plastic over a quick hoop, weighted with sandbags.
Overwintering onions inside a quick hoop.
A small movable greenhouse is another simple protective device.

and not having a cold winter shower trickle down your neck.

Like the cold frame, the simple greenhouse merely captures the sun's heat and eliminates the drying, chilling effects of wind. Often a gardener's first thought will be: "Wouldn't it be nice to grow warm-weather crops, such as tomatoes, during the winter?" But that means providing some sort of artificial heat, and suddenly the home greenhouse becomes a big expense. Here's the great part: You don't need to heat the greenhouse in winter if you choose hardy crops that *like* to grow in cool weather. Then follow them with spring crops and finally even those warm-weather tomatoes, planted earlier than you could outdoors, for extra-early ripening.

How Big Should the Greenhouse Be?

TO DO THIS right and feed your family all year round, you need a real greenhouse, not a toy. With so many small greenhouses advertised in the garden magazines with dimensions of 6 by 6 feet or 6 by 8 feet, those must be popular sizes. They're sold to people who "don't want anything too big." But the trouble is that they are so small, you can't actually grow much in them, and they're expensive for the amount of ground they cover. They are basically potting sheds, fine for a little seed starting but not for growing. A real greenhouse, one large enough to make a significant contribution to feeding your

In winter, even an unheated greenhouse can protect a variety of greens, and root crops like carrots. Early spring flower bulbs are a bonus.

family year-round, should be at least 10 by 12 feet. So our basic greenhouse is just that, and can be doubled or even tripled in length just by adding on modules of the same size.

The Greenhouse Structure

PRECURSORS OF THE modern greenhouse date back as far as ancient Pompeii, where thin sheets of mica were used instead of glass. In the 19th century, advances in the making of window glass took the sheltering of plants a quantum leap forward, and palatial greenhouses were built that only the wealthy could afford. Since then, the idea of the home greenhouse is still associated with luxury in many people's minds. But in the mid-1950s, once sheets of plastic became easily available, the picture changed for greenhouse construction. This thin, translucent material, which lets light in and keeps cold winds out, is far less expensive than glass, and it makes the everyman's greenhouse possible, just as it has saved dollars for commercial growers.

The frame of a plastic-covered greenhouse—the structural surface against which the plastic rests—can be made of a far wider range of materials than the frame of a glasshouse can be. We've seen them made of bowed saplings from the woods. We've seen greenhouse frames made from curved sections of concrete reinforcing wire panels. We've seen greenhouses made where a few leaning poles held the plastic sheet out from the south wall of a building, to make one of those warm and sheltered spots even warmer. All of these simple structures grew plants, and we applaud the creativity with which gardeners come up with their own structures for winter growing.

In the standard commercial greenhouse, bowed metal hoops forming a pipe frame support the plastic sheet. This is what is described by the phrase "hoop house," and it's the style on which we modeled our little home greenhouse. But we added a trick to make our greenhouse even more productive: It moves.

The Movable Greenhouse

IF YOU CAN move a greenhouse from one place to another, that eases the seasonal transition from winter to summer and back to winter in the greenhouse. You can leave it over the summer crops to protect them from fall frosts and keep crops like tomatoes, peppers, and basil producing longer. Then you can move the greenhouse to protect hardy winter crops that have been planted nearby. These don't mind early frosts—in fact they prefer to be making their growth in the increasingly cool days of fall.

When a greenhouse can be moved to where you want it, when you want it, a whole new world opens up. You get the positives of greenhouse growing, such as cold protection, while eliminating the negatives, such as the pest and disease buildup that can occur in continuously covered soil. It's not a new idea. The first movable greenhouses for commercial use were constructed toward the end of the 19th century. But the concept was all but abandoned in the mid-20th century because toxic chemical products for sterilizing the soil were pushed as an easier way to avoid pest and disease buildup. Now organic growers—both

Even gardeners in warm or moderate climates can benefit from a greenhouse.

home gardeners and small-scale vegetable farmers—who believe toxic chemicals have no place in the soil, are reviving the movable greenhouse. Exposing the soil to the outdoor world takes care of most problems. And as a bonus, growers increase the number of crops that can be protected by one greenhouse by covering them only when they need protection. It's a simple solution that we've used for years.

To make a greenhouse mobile, all that's required is a slight modification in its construction. Normally, the standard pipe-frame plastic-covered greenhouses are erected on a foundation of pipes driven into the ground. The far more expensive glass ones are usually erected on a concrete foundation. Ours is firmly attached to the ground when it's in place, but can be detached for moving before being anchored again. Our goals in designing it were that it be simple to build with off-the-shelf parts, easy to move, easy to anchor, and inexpensive.

The frame of our backyard greenhouse consists of three half circles of metal pipe attached to structural cross pieces. A 10-foot length of pipe is easily bent into a quarter circle, and two of them make a half-circle hoop. We bend them the same way we do to make the quick hoops on page 90, but we use a bender designed for high tunnels instead of low ones, sold by the same company that offers the quick hoop one, and for the same price. For pipe we use the 10-foot-long and 1-inch-diameter pipes used for electrical conduit and known as "1-inch EMT." They are sold in the electrical department of your local home-improvement store.

Leeks and Dwarf Siberian kale overwintering in a movable greenhouse.

For the foundation of the greenhouse, instead of inserting the bottom end of the hoops into larger diameter pipes driven into the ground, as with standard hoophouses, we attach the bottom of the hoops perpendicularly to a length of the same 1-inch EMT lying horizontally on the ground. In this way all the parts of the 10-foot-long by 12-foot-wide greenhouse module are connected as a single unit rather than having each rib individually attached to its own ground post. The greenhouse is thus like a metal pipe birdcage that can be picked up and moved to wherever you want it. When the greenhouse is in place we attach it to anchors to hold it in place. (They're easily dis-attached for moving.) The plastic is held on with the same clips we used to winterize the quick hoops. All of this works smoothly and keeps the price extremely low.

The weight of the pipes, the connecting parts, and the plastic for this modular greenhouse add up to a total of about 100 pounds. Thus the "picked up and moved" part above is doable for two reasonably fit gardeners. The two of us have moved this greenhouse design many times with no problems, and because the greenhouse does not have to be dragged into place as it moves, you can put it on a site more distant from its original position. If that seems beyond you, just find a helper or two on moving day. In our garden the greenhouse is moved once a year across the garden path from one side of the garden to the other. The next year it moves back. (For construction details see our website, fourseasonfarm.com.)

Barbara totes the greenhouse, with Eliot on the other side.

What Crops to Grow

THE WINTER INHABITANTS of your greenhouse will be cold-hardy crops. There are lots of vegetables that withstand cold weather and actually taste better because of it. A few frosts have a way of sweetening both leaf crops and root crops. Arugula, for example, is a crop that tastes too strong for some palates, but the cold makes it milder. Carrots and spinach become downright sugary.

Some of the cold-season crops such as spinach, scallions, and Swiss chard are familiar, others are much less so. Mâche, also known as corn salad, is a popular European winter salad green. Claytonia, also known as miner's lettuce, is a cultivated weed from the mountains of California. Tatsoi is a dark green, highly nutritious Asian vegetable. What they all have in common is an amazing tolerance of freezing

Two people can move a lightweight homemade greenhouse from one place to another.

CROPS FOR THE SPRING & SUMMER GREENHOUSE

ARUGULA: Astro. An early variety with broad leaves and high production that is both heat and cold tolerant.

BASIL: Aroma. A Genovese type that is well adapted to growing in a greenhouse.

BEANS: Jade. A gourmet quality bean that does well under both cool and warm conditions.

BEET: Merlin. An early beet with small tops and exceptional flavor.

CARROT: Mokum. This early bunching carrot is very sweet and tolerates both heat and cold.

CUCUMBER: Rocky. A greenhouse variety that starts producing seedless baby cucumbers in only 46 days.

EGGPLANT: Orient Express. This attractive, slender early eggplant does well in both cool and hot conditions.

LETTUCE: Black-Seeded Simpson. This earliest-of-all lettuces has delicious, juicy light green leaves and is adapted to greenhouse growing.

PEPPER: Ace. This extra-early pepper variety establishes well under the cooler conditions of early spring.

POTATO: Rose Gold. Of all the potatoes we've grown, this has worked best for early greenhouse production.

TOMATO: Big Beef. This wonderful large and tasty tomato is as successful in the early greenhouse as it is in the field, but if you have a proven variety that has done well for you, use it. **New Girl** is a good greenhouse variety for extra-early tomatoes.

temperatures as long as they are protected from cold, dry winter winds.

In most of the country, these crops are harvestable during the winter months as long as they have the minimum amount of protection from the outdoor weather that a single layer of plastic can give them. That one layer effectively moves the covered area to a climate about 500 miles to the south here on the East Coast. In very cold climates, such as where we live, a second layer of protection inside the greenhouse will double the value of a greenhouse alone. For that second layer we choose the same spun-bonded row cover we use for the quick hoops described above. It is held a foot above the soil by wire wickets (see photo at right) and held in place by clothespins. Since the cover lets in light and irrigation water, there is no need to remove it except for harvesting, or an occasional weeding, and then it is simply unclipped and pulled aside. (During the coldest months, little or no weeding or watering may be needed.) The second layer effectively moves the area under it an *additional* 500

miles farther south, and will assure winter harvests even in climates where the outdoor temperatures drop to minus 20 or lower.

We've kept temperature records for years, and here on the Maine coast our simple greenhouse alone creates a New Jersey winter climate and the inner layer moves the area under it to Georgia. When it's 15 below zero outside in Maine, it's 18 above zero under the inner layer. The cold-hardy winter crops don't mind that at all. And although we've been using these techniques for some 30 years, the thrill has not worn off. We're still as delighted as children by the wide range of crops we can harvest every day from our greenhouse winter garden.

The Plan

AS IN ALL the greenhouses we have built, this one is designed for growing plants directly in the ground, not on the waist-high benches that some hobby greenhouses feature. Following the same layout suggested in Chapter 2, there are four beds with 12-inch paths between them. The two center beds are 30 inches wide, just like our garden beds in Chapter 2. The two edge beds can be 24 inches wide because we will only be reaching into them from one side. These four beds, side by side, cover the 12-foot width. A worm's-eye view of them looks like the drawing at right:

Since we need some room to move about in the greenhouse, we've left a little space (12 inches) at either end. (If we put two of these basic modules together to form a 12-foot-wide by 20-foot-long house, we'd also leave a center cross path for easier access.) The bird's-eye view looks like the plan on page 98.

We now have four beds, each 8 feet long. The next step is to use this space to grow as much fresh food as possible during the colder months. Over the years we've experimented with some 30 different vegetables in our Winter Garden: arugula, beet greens, broccoli raab, carrots, chard, chicory, claytonia, collards, dandelion, endive, escarole, garlic greens, kale, kohlrabi, leeks, lettuce, mâche, mizuna, mustard greens, bok choy (pac choi), parsley, radicchio, radish, scallions, sorrel, spinach, tatsoi, turnips, and watercress. (See Chapter 4 for specific advice about growing most of these crops.) They've all been successful to some degree. The favorites in our household are spinach, carrots, tatsoi, Swiss chard, and kale. Of course you'll replace the ones we grow, depending on your preferences. Personal experience with your favorite crops, in your own climate, will be the best teacher as to what sowing dates and what rotational sequence work best, but the following account of our own plan offers a place from which to start.

The Planting Scheme

LET'S TAKE A simple greenhouse layout and show how productive it can be, just by planting something new every time an empty space becomes available, as we did in the outdoor home garden described in Chapter 2. The two winter crops most popular with our family—carrots and spinach—each get a large bed all their own (#2 and #3; see page 98). Tatsoi and chard share bed #1. Kale grows in bed #4.

Remember, these crops are being planted outdoors and we will be moving a greenhouse over them. For the kale we'll use one of the Siberian varieties (*Brassica napus*) because it is extra-hardy and will sprout new leaves continuously through late winter and spring. For chard we use the variety Argentata, which is the hardiest chard in our experience. We sow both by August first and plan on two rows to the bed. The carrots are sown before mid-August at six rows per bed. We sow the tatsoi and spinach on September 15, the tatsoi at three rows to the bed and the spinach at five.

A floating row cover, supported by #9 gauge wire wickets and held in place with clothespins, lets in sunlight and rain, and is easily pulled aside for weeding or harvesting.

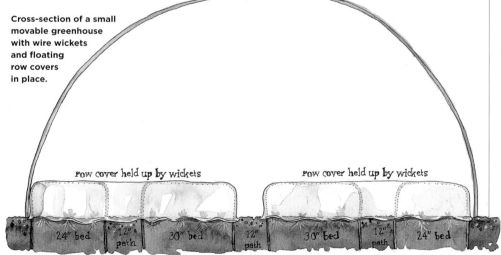

Cross-section of a small movable greenhouse with wire wickets and floating row covers in place.

row cover held up by wickets   row cover held up by wickets

24" bed   12" path   30" bed   12" path   30" bed   12" path   24" bed

Once everything is up and growing, our bird's-eye view would look like the plan below.

None of these cold-hardy crops will mind the first frosts. That means we can leave the movable greenhouse where it has been all summer, protecting summer crops. We usually move it over the winter crops about mid-October, and plan to start eating those crops about mid-November, just when the last of the outdoor garden crops have pretty much had their day.

The spinach in bed #3 is the most productive crop and will be harvested all winter long. Once it begins to go to seed in spring, the bed can be cleared, re-composted, and replanted with early tomatoes. (We store enough compost for early bed preparation in plastic garbage cans in our tool shed.) We can put tomatoes in about six weeks before our last spring frost date, because the protection provided by both the greenhouse and the inner layer will keep them from freezing. The carrots in bed #2 are harvested progressively all winter, as we need them. If planted by the middle of August, they're ready for their harvest to begin around mid-November, about the time the outdoor carrots are finished. (For more information on planting and harvesting times, see page 456.)

We harvest starting at one end, and can sow short rows of arugula crosswise, at any time space is available. It seems amazing, but even midwinter sowings of arugula will germinate and grow in this protected environment. For best flavor, the last of the carrots should be harvested at least by early March, before they make

FIRST WINTER

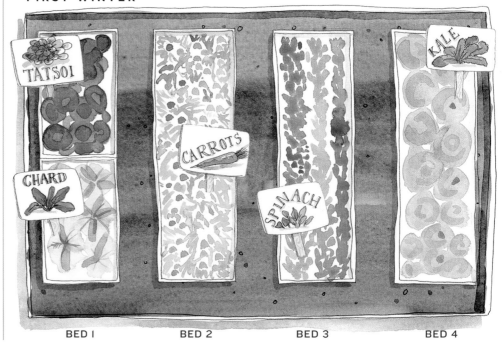

TATSOI

CHARD

CARROTS

SPINACH

KALE

BED 1   BED 2   BED 3   BED 4

We can put tomatoes in about six weeks before our last spring frost date, because the protection provided by both the greenhouse and the inner layer will keep them from freezing.

too much new growth. (Since they are biennials, they will start to go to seed and begin to lose their sweetness as days lengthen.) The ideal spring crop in this bed, after the carrots and arugula are gone, is early potatoes. We re-prepare the soil by spreading an inch of compost. For quicker growth we've pre-sprouted the potatoes by setting them out in a tray in a warm room on February 15. We plant them on

March 15. This schedule gives us baby new potatoes to eat by the second half of May. We follow the potatoes with a row of green beans for summer.

When the kale in bed #4 is finished, we can re-prepare the bed with more compost and some alfalfa meal to get it ready for cucumbers. Three-week-old cucumber transplants, which we have started ahead in a sunny window of the house, can be set

SUMMER

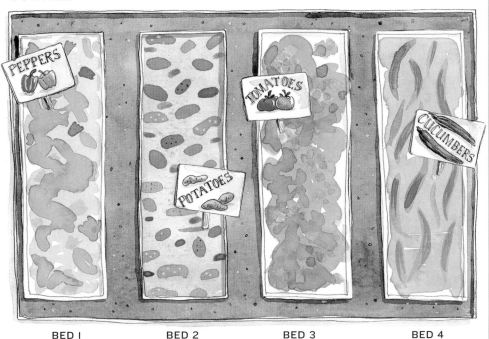

BED 1   BED 2   BED 3   BED 4

out three weeks before the average last frost date in spring, as long as they are protected by an inner cover.

The tatsoi and the chard in bed #1 have fed us all winter. Once they start to go to seed and are removed, the soil in the bed is re-prepared and we set out pepper transplants about four weeks before our last frost date. Once things get a little warmer, we might tuck in basil and other annual herbs here and there.

By early summer the bird's-eye view of the greenhouse looks like the plan on page 99.

Our summer crops will have a great head start, and in this temperate climate they will keep producing all summer as long as the greenhouse is well vented. The doors at either end—we call them scissor doors— used for both access and ventilation, allow for complete air flow when tied in the fully open position. That works for us, and should work almost anywhere to keep the house from overheating (see bottom photo on page 89). However, if you live where summers get very hot, too hot for even a well-vented greenhouse, there are other options. For one, you can uncover the greenhouse by taking off the plastic once it has given the early crops a head start but before they're going to bake in there. It's easiest if you unclip it from one side and both ends. Then you can roll up the plastic and still leave it attached to the final side, so it's right where you want it when the time comes to re-cover crops in the fall. If you protect the rolled-up plastic with an opaque cover (like black plastic) to exclude light, you'll get an extra few years of use out of it by having sheltered it from the fierce summer sun. If you prefer to leave the greenhouse covered, you can add a layer of shade cloth over the plastic to decrease the heat buildup. Shade cloths comes in different levels of shade (from 30 to 60 percent) and are made of many different materials. A 40 percent shade cloth made of a reflective material is a good bet for the backyard greenhouse. See pages 453 for a source.

Another summer option is to use that excess heat to your advantage. In this case you would clean out all the early greenhouse crops once the outdoor garden starts producing. Then you would irrigate the greenhouse thoroughly, lay a sheet of clear plastic over the soil inside, and shut the doors. Those two layers of plastic (the greenhouse itself and the plastic over the soil) will trap enough of the summer sun's heat to kill weed seeds and plant disease organisms down to at least four inches deep in the soil. This process is known as solarization and is used very effectively by commercial growers in the South to control weeds and soil pests.

Even in the heat of summer though, next winter should always be in the back of your mind. The alternate site of the movable greenhouse needs to be gotten ready for its late summer and early fall planting dates. That way the progression of crops from the greenhouse will always be there for you. As you move the greenhouse back and forth every year, it's also worth thinking in terms of crop rotation, so the layout of the winter crop beds might look like the illustration on the facing page for the next time the greenhouse winters on that same plot.

Here all the winter crops are growing in different bed locations from where they grew before, and their succession crops will be similarly rotated, just as garden crops were in Chapter 2. Rotating crops in a greenhouse is even more important than it is in the outdoor garden, due to the more intense conditions of growth. With a little bit of imagination, you can move your crops around like pieces on a chessboard, so the same pattern does not repeat for many years.

If you'd rather have more instant gratification from salad-type vegetables than wait for tomatoes, peppers, etc., to mature, another winter-into-spring planting scheme might look like the following:

Bed #1 is planted to both beets and spinach. Bed #2 has potatoes as before since early baby new potatoes are one of the finest greenhouse treats. Bed #3 has lettuce with a few scallions at one end (most easily planted from onion sets), and bed #4 has spring carrots. The beets, spinach, lettuce, scallions, and carrots can be planted anytime in the spring as soon as the space can be cleared from the winter crop. Of course, you could always have all of these in addition to the early tomatoes, etc., if you built a second greenhouse. We're betting that you probably will.

The varieties we've chosen for the seed lists in this chapter are based on our experience over the years, growing gardens under many different conditions. It seems so simple and straightforward nowadays to specify the ones we prefer, and then note the companies that sell them. But obtaining seeds was not always that easy. The first seed catalogs, as we know them, didn't appear until around the 1830s. Before that, people saved and exchanged their own seeds. The next section answers the question: "What would you do if new seeds were not easily available?'"

SECOND WINTER

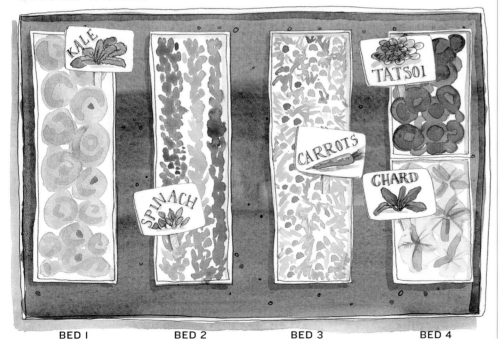

BED 1   BED 2   BED 3   BED 4

THE SELF-RELIANT GARDEN

ONE EVENING WHILE we were thinking about different garden scenarios, we speculated about how well we could eat from our home garden if we were as isolated from the world as were the early American pioneers, homesteading at the far edge of the frontier. What would it take for a home garden to be so dependable that you could count on ample and varied produce, even if there were no garden centers or seed catalogs from which to buy new seeds and plants each year? How possible would it be to grow the varied gardens, with all the crops we have selected, if we had to produce all our own seeds? Obviously, we'd need to know something about seed saving. But how would that change our choice of crops or varieties?

WHY SAVE SEEDS?

AS AN AVERAGE home gardener you may never *need* to save your own seeds. But there is a security in knowing that—even in a remote place, or in a time of unreliable supplies of food, plants, and seeds—the home garden could still be a most dependable source of varied nourishment, and roll out that bounty on its own, year after year. In addition, some knowledge of the process will help you to better understand the broad resources of the plant kingdom and the functional design of its members.

Another thing worth remembering about the old days is that people not only saved the seed they grew from year to year, but also passed their own family strains down from one generation to the next.

That is how so many fine old varieties have survived, and together they make up a highly diverse gene pool for vegetable crops. Although we may think of seed-planting in those days as constrained by limited choices, it had much that is missing today. Saving and planting a variety over many years and many harvests adapts it to your climate. It cements family bonds. And it fosters a community of growers, as one neighbor shares seeds with another. Just as the seeds we save are worth preserving for their special qualities, and to help maintain the genetic diversity of the planet, these traditions also enrich our gardening lives.

Saving your own seeds is also a way of improving the crops you grow. When you gather seeds to save, you don't just collect them randomly; you take them from the best plants in the row, the ones that are the healthiest, the most vigorous, and the most productive. Which pepper plant has the most fruits on it? Do the melons on a particular vine taste extra-flavorful and sweet? Think about traits you're particularly interested in—for example, a spinach plant that lasts the longest without bolting, or a tomato plant that bears the earliest red-ripe tomato, or the squash that lasts the longest in storage. Save seeds from those winners. The next year you do the same thing again, choosing the best. Year after year, you will be shaping your own strain of the crop, the one that has been selected to do well in your particular climate and your particular soil.

It's easy to save seed from this Italian heirloom pepper, a gift from a friend.

HYBRID VS. OPEN-POLLINATED VARIETIES

WHEN YOU CONSIDER saving your own seeds, you begin to understand the importance of "open-pollinated" (OP) varieties of vegetables and why that concept is of such interest to gardeners. The seeds for "hybrid" varieties of vegetables (the ones that have the symbol "F1" after their name in the seed catalogs) are created through crossing two (usually inbred) parent lines of that vegetable. When the ideal parents are crossed, the result is a new variety with what is called "hybrid vigor," which you can think of as a one-generation burst of extra growing energy. Whatever the horticultural benefit of hybrid crops, one virtue is certainly economic. Only the originator of the cross knows which cultivars were crossed to get there. That proprietary knowledge is valuable. But if you save seeds from a hybrid variety, the plants will not be uniform like the hybrid parent, but rather a mishmash of traits from each parent. Thus no one else can produce that variety for sale without knowledge of the original cross and, consequently, the seed company

that developed it has a built-in exclusive on it. There are many wonderful modern hybrids that produce fine plants. But for a seed saver they are a dead end.

The development of commercially available hybrid varieties began with field corn in the 1920s and subsequently spread to vegetables and flowers. Before 1920 all seed varieties were open-pollinated, as all seeds had been since they evolved. When seed stalks emerge and flowers open in the natural world, they pollinate with others of their kind or self-pollinate and produce seeds that grow plants like themselves next year. (Unless of course they cross-pollinate with a variety of a related crop, but we'll get to that shortly.) Named OP varieties result from crosses, but they have been stabilized over the years to the point that you know what to expect when you save and plant their seeds. In this particular garden, your choices will be limited to these OP varieties of vegetables rather than the hybrids. Yes, that constrains your options slightly, but not to any great detriment. The passion for seed saving and OP varieties since the 1970s has resulted in the breeding of new ones, and the renewed availability of many classic varieties that

Even in a remote place, or in a time of unreliable supplies of food, plants, and seeds, the home garden can still be a most dependable source of varied nourishment.

OPEN-POLLINATED VEGETABLE VARIETIES FOR THE SELF-RELIANT GARDEN

ARTICHOKE: Green Globe. The standard artichoke variety.

ARUGULA: Astro. Broad leaved, very productive.

ASPARAGUS: Mary Washington. A dependable heirloom.

BASIL: Genovese. A classic, productive basil.

BEANS: Provider. The standard green bean. **Yellow Eye.** Good dry bean variety for baked beans.

BEET: Detroit Dark Red. Deep color, great beet flavor.

CABBAGE: Premium Late Flat Dutch. Excellent for storage.

CARROT: Scarlet Nantes. Tender, coreless, old-time carrot flavor.

CELERY ROOT: Giant Prague. Large, very white roots.

SWISS CHARD: Fordhook. The standard, reliable green chard.

CHIVES: Purly. Upright plant with straight leaves.

CORN: Bloody Butcher. For both sweet corn and cornmeal.

CUCUMBER: Marketmore 76. Very popular OP variety.

EGGPLANT: Diamond. Ukrainian heirloom variety.

GARLIC: Music. Hardy and vigorous.

KALE: Dwarf Siberian. Hardy enough to survive winter.

LETTUCE: Winter Density. Vigorous, multiple-use lettuce.

LEEK: Bandit. Very winter hardy.

MÂCHE: Vit. Best overwintering mâche variety.

MELON: Hale's Best. Use **Delicious 51** for short-season climates.

ONION: Southport Red Globe. Or use a multiplier onion.

PARSLEY: Moss Curled. Vigorous and uniform.

PARSNIP: Lancer. Very sweet, good winter survival.

PEAS: Laxton's Progress. Large podded, hardy, non-staking.

PEPPER: Yankee Bell. Strongly branched plants, with good leaf cover to prevent sunscald.

POTATO: Butte. Rugged and reliable.

SCALLION: Evergreen. Divide clumps in spring for new crop.

SHALLOT: Pikant. Makes large bulbs that store well.

SORREL: Profusion. Can be productive all year long.

SPINACH: Bloomsdale. Savoyed (crinkled) leaves, fine quality, slow to bolt.

SQUASH: Buttercup. Deep orange flesh, sweet flavor. **Waltham Butternut.** Long meaty neck, small seed cavity.

TOMATO: Stupice (earlier) or **Rose** (later). Both are vigorous, healthy, indeterminate varieties with good taste.

WATERCRESS: No named varieties in most catalogs.

ZUCCHINI: Black Beauty. Heirloom prizewinner.

were starting to disappear due to the sales pressure of the hybrids.

If, however, there is a hybrid variety of which you are particularly fond, there is a way to breed it back over time. Assuming the gardener has the space to grow a population of the plant large enough to select from (that is, save seed from a number of the best plants), after a few generations of selection work uniformity will be approached and the new variety will be adapted to the gardener's environment. Think of it this way: A plant breeder has already made the cross of two elite parent lines—a great start for enthusiasts to develop one or more nice new varieties of their own.

How do you get seeds from the plants you grow? Sometimes it's very simple and obvious; sometimes it involves a few extra gardening steps. Here are the six logical categories into which to divide our vegetable crops when we think about perpetuating them from year to year.

PERENNIAL CROPS THAT COME BACK EVERY YEAR

THE PERENNIAL CROPS are, of course, no problem for the isolated gardener once they've been planted, because they regrow each year on their own. Usually it is not necessary to save seed from them, although doing so is added insurance against the crop's decline. Here are some perennials that are especially well adapted for vegetable gardeners.

Asparagus comes back reliably every spring, as long as you only cut the spears for six weeks, so as not to exhaust the bed. However, production may start to decline after 12 to 15 years or so. Asparagus produces plants of both sexes, with the females bearing tiny red berries. As long as you grow an open-pollinated variety, you can save seed from your female plants in order to start a brand-new bed. This also means avoiding the modern hybrids that produce all-male plants for greater productivity—but of course no berries. You might need to use bird netting to protect the berries, which are harvested before they fall. To save the seeds, crush the berries and process them by the same method as tomatoes, shown on page 111.

Watercress will often regrow each year when planted on the banks of streams and ponds with clear, clean water and nonacidic soil. You can start it originally from seed or transplants. We grow ours in a bed we established in the outflow from a small pond, and we eat a lot when it's at its best, in spring and fall.

Dandelions are a wonderfully nutritious and dependable crop that provides leaves to eat, buds to eat, roots to roast (as a coffee substitute), and blossoms to turn into dandelion wine. Garden dandelions are at their best eating in the spring.

Perennial herbs such as tarragon, oregano, sage, thyme, and chives will remain in place, and can be propagated by taking cuttings or by dividing the plant. Some, such as sage and thyme, are ideal candidates for layering. Notice how a sage branch will send down roots where it touches the ground. To make this happen intentionally, just bury a section of branch in the soil, weight it with a stone, and then sever it from the mother plant when the roots have taken hold. You can then replant it anywhere or bring it indoors in a pot.

Watercress thrives in shallow water at the edge of our pond.

Semi-hardy herbs such as rosemary are often brought indoors for the winter. Chive seeds are easily saved, but there is little need since they self-sow in the garden.

Certain extra-hardy scallions, such as Evergreen, can function as perennials because they multiply; you plant them for fall, have them winter over, then divide the clumps and replant individually. Sorrel yields leaves from spring through fall and, additionally, through the winter if it's transplanted into a greenhouse.

Globe artichokes are an easy perennial in climates where the winter temperatures don't go below 10 degrees. In our cold climate we usually grow them from seed every year as annuals, but we have also maintained them as perennials by digging up the roots in fall and storing them over the winter in a cellar, as one does with dahlia bulbs. They can then be divided before replanting in the spring. Each root usually provides between three and five new young plants after dividing. These methods are much easier than collecting seeds.

Sunchokes (aka Jerusalem artichokes) are tall, sunflower-like plants whose roots are small, knobby, nutty-tasting tubers. These tubers multiply rapidly and are easy to grow. Since any seeds produced are usually sterile, tubers are a reliable means of propagating the crop. If you need to keep them in the root cellar over the winter, store them in plastic bags to keep them from drying out.

Fruits, both small and large, also belong in the perennial category, as do horseradish and rhubarb. There are great numbers of other perennial crops that have been used for food (good King Henry, Egyptian onion, groundnut, sea kale, and wood nettle, to name a few), but they are hardly household words. Their obscurity might point to a lack of culinary appeal— or just to our lack of imagination. In any case, it is wise to keep a healthy curiosity about them, since they have helped sustain populations throughout history, and could lend that much more variety to a self-sufficient diet.

CROPS IN WHICH THE VEGETATIVE PARTS YOU EAT ARE WHAT YOU PLANT

MANY CROPS ARE reproduced not from seed but vegetatively, which means that a part of this year's plant is saved and planted in the soil the following year. Some popular vegetables such as potatoes, sweet potatoes, sunchokes, garlic, and shallots are easy for the self-sufficient gardener, since you basically plant the part you eat in order to get more of it. (These parts are often referred to as "seed"—as in "seed potatoes" and "seed garlic"—because they grow new plants, even though they are not literally seeds.)

For example, all those little eyes on the potato skin are the sites where the new sprouts emerge that turn into new potato plants, so if you plant a potato in the soil, you'll have more potatoes at the end of the season. We pre-sprout ours for a few weeks before planting to make sure they are well on their way to growth when we drop them into the cool spring soil.

The fact that you're taking food that could have been eaten and saving it for planting gives a particular dimension to seed saving. At numerous times in human history, people in need have had to make sure they did not eat their "seed corn," so to speak. There is a scene in the classic New England novel *Come Spring* by Ben Ames Williams when one of the characters, having planted his seed potatoes and then realized how little stored food was left for his family, returned to the garden, dug up all the tubers and cut away the potato flesh except directly around each eye, before he replanted what were basically just potato eyes. The new potato crop still grew from the eyes (though probably with not quite the early vigor that would have come from feeding on the starchy potato), and the potato flesh he dug up and salvaged made at least a few more meals possible.

As with any seed-saving effort, you want to be selective about what you replant. With potatoes you should choose your seed for next year's crop when you harvest your potatoes. That way you'll be able to judge which are the healthiest, most productive plants and can choose tubers from among them. Seed potatoes of a size somewhere between a golf ball and a jumbo chicken egg are the most economical and efficient. If your yields

go down after a few years, you may have a disease problem and need to start over again with new seed potatoes. If, however, there is plenty of compost in your soil, and you rotate your crops, potato disease may never be a problem.

You can plant sweet potatoes that you have saved directly in the garden too, but the most economical way is to pre-spout them and plant the sprouts individually as "slips." You can grow the slips by covering a few tubers with moist potting mix in a tray and setting them in a warm place, or you can just submerge a tuber partway in a glass of water, with the pointiest end down. (Maybe you did this for fun as a child.) In either case, lots of long stems will emerge. When they are at least 6 inches long you can gently pull these off and plant them, just as you would the purchased slips described on page 206. Very long vines can be cut into sections and planted. That's how easily sweet potato shoots root in any moist environment, including the soil! But you can hasten progress and ensure success by placing their ends in a glass of water first, until substantial roots form.

A garlic clove planted in fall will give you a garlic bulb the following July. A fall-planted shallot turns into a clump of shallots the next summer. With garlic and shallots you want to select the largest, most vigorous specimens for replanting. They obviously are the ones that are best adapted to your soil and your growing conditions.

If you have a reasonably short winter, sunchokes can be saved and replanted in spring, though this is rarely necessary since they spread so successfully on their own. Choose small, round, evenly shaped tubers.

TOP: Eliot sets seed potatoes out for sprouting.
BOTTOM: The sprouts begin to emerge.

CROPS IN WHICH THE SEEDS YOU EAT ARE WHAT YOU PLANT

PROBABLY THE EASIEST seeds to save for planting again next year are dry beans. They're likely the most popular crop among seed-saving enthusiasts. Bean collections have run into the hundreds of varieties because of the varied colors, shapes, sizes, and flavors available with this crop. It's a good beginner seed to save because the dried beans stored in your kitchen cupboard for your next baked bean dish are the exact same beans that you'll plant to get more dried beans for next year. They're also easy to handle, and simple to extract from their pods. The process is described on page 188, and is the same technique you'd use for dried peas—for making pea soup—and any other legume as well. We once got some children interested in gardening by having them plant all the different seeds (garbanzo beans, lentils, barley, and so on) in a package of dried minestrone soup mix from the health-food store. Amazingly, they all grew!

In the same way, you can save the seeds of beans and peas that are grown for fresh eating, as long as they are open-pollinated varieties. Although the fresh types can also be dried for winter eating, the main purpose of saving them is for planting next year, so as to enjoy them in their green state. Just remember to earmark some of the healthiest, most vigorous plants from which to gather seeds, and let their pods dry in the garden.

Corn is in this same category. You simply select a sufficient number of the nicest, healthiest plants, and save some of the kernels for next year's crop (see pages 203 to 204).

The introduction of corn brings up a new consideration—crossing— that has not been a factor up till now. (As we'll show later on, crossing must be considered for other crops as well, besides corn.) Peas and beans are self-pollinating. But if you plant more than one variety of sweet corn or one sweet corn and one grinding corn, they'll cross-pollinate unless you space them at least 1,000 feet apart, or plant one early and one late, for maturity separation. If two do cross-

Saving Pea Seeds

DRY ON THE VINE. Let the vines and pods dry right on their trellis until crisp and brown.

RELEASE FROM THE PODS. Stuff the vines in a large bag or feed sack, as in the photo on page 114. Beat it or stomp on it, and the peas will fall neatly to the bottom.

pollinate, you will not end up with corn that is identical to what you planted. Thus, it's probably safest to just grow only one type, to keep seed-saving simple. Fortunately, there are varieties that are tasty as sweet corn when young, and then mature into a perfectly acceptable grinding corn.

CROPS IN WHICH THE SEEDS YOU PLANT ARE IN WHAT YOU EAT

MANY PLANTS SUCH as tomatoes, peppers, winter squash, and melons contain mature seeds in the part you eat. So it's easy to set some of the seeds aside for saving. In some cases you'll have to deal with cross-pollination issues. And the means by which you process the seeds for drying also varies from crop to crop. But the following are well within the ability of the novice.

Tomatoes, peppers, and eggplants are all members of the Solanaceae family (see page 44) but they do not cross with each other. Peppers will sometimes cross with other peppers (as we noted with corn, above) unless you separate varieties by 100 feet, so you might need to limit your Self-Reliant Garden to one pepper variety (or perhaps join with a neighbor—she grows the hot ones and you the sweet). The seeds are very easy to save. Take several extra-nice peppers from a few extra-healthy, extra-vigorous plants and cut them open. (If it's close to frost time, and your peppers have not completely ripened, it's okay to ripen them indoors in a warm room.) Pick the seeds off the ribs of each fruit, wearing gloves if they are a very hot type. Then mix the seeds together and dry them thoroughly on a screen or a plate, keeping them out of direct sunlight.

The amazing diversity of bean seeds. Varieties include Scarlet Runner (top row, center); Jacob's Cattle (middle row, left); flageolet type (middle row, center); cannellini (bottom row, left); Black Turtle (bottom row, center); and Tiger Eye (bottom row, right).

Tomatoes are self-pollinating and won't cross with one another, so it is not difficult to save more than one variety. The fruits are selected ripe, just the way peppers are, but the seeds must be fermented in order to remove the jellylike coating on them that keeps them from germinating too soon. Just follow the simple steps on page 111.

Eggplant varieties will seldom cross, but obtaining the seed is a bit of a production. The stage at which we eat eggplants is not the ripe one, and you must wait until they are brownish in color and almost starting to rot before the seeds are mature. You use the same technique as with tomatoes except that there is no seed coating that needs to be fermented. There is, however, a lot of squishing of pulp and rewashing before the seeds all sink to the bottom of the container. You also need to sacrifice a large number of fruits to get a good genetic selection, so this is not the easiest crop for seed saving at home.

The squashes, the cucumbers, and the

A historic partnership between human and plant lies behind these beautiful ears of field corn, good for corn meal.

melons are all members of the cucurbit family (page 44) but they do not cross with one another. Within the squash category there are a number of different species, and while those of the same species will cross, those of different species almost never do. So since two of our favorite winter squashes, Butternut (*Cucurbita moschata*) and Buttercup (*C. maxima*), belong to different species, and summer squash such as zucchini (*C. pepo*) belongs to a third, all of them can be grown for seed saving in the same garden. But do check the species of any you intend to save. Acorn squash, for example, even though it is a winter squash, is *C. pepo* and would therefore cross with zucchini.

Select well-grown, nicely shaped specimens of winter squash and save seed from the ones that have lasted longest in storage. For summer squash, let a few of them go beyond the tender edible stage until they are big and hard, like a winter squash. To prepare the seeds for saving you just cut open the squash, pull out the seeds, and work off as much of the pulp as you can with your fingers. Washing them helps. They do not need to be fermented, nor do the viable ones sink in liquid. As you dry them, on screens or plates, try to separate them and clean off any remaining pulp with your fingers.

Cucumbers (*Cucumis sativus*) and melons (*C. melo*) are related but not of the same species, so they too can coexist in a seed-saving garden. With cucumbers, as with eggplants and summer squash, you need to let some fruits grow beyond the traditional fresh-eating stage so the seeds can mature. (Mark the selected ones in some way to keep them from being picked.) They will have softened

and, depending on the variety, will be colored anywhere from pale yellow to orange when fully ripe. Soak and ferment the seeds just like tomatoes (see opposite page), making sure they no longer have a slippery feel to them. As with squash, mature seeds don't sink, but any immature or hollow ones, together with bits of debris, can be winnowed with a fan as with the kale seeds on page 115.

Melons all cross with one another, so you'll need to pick one favorite. But its seeds will be a joy to save, because the ones in a ripe melon are at the perfect seed stage. So you can eat your melon and save it too. Process the seeds the same way as you would for cucumbers.

ANNUALS WHOSE SEEDS ARE NOT PART OF WHAT YOU EAT

THIS CATEGORY IS composed of major salad crops such as spinach, lettuce, arugula, radishes, Asian greens, and herbs such as basil and dill. All are annuals that can reproduce themselves in only one year of growth. (Broccoli, unlike most of its close relatives, will also go to seed in the same year it is planted.) The crops described in the preceding three sections do this too. But the difference here is that these crops produce seeds not as part of what we eat but *following* their production of the part we eat. So seed saving with these crops is a separate step, and one that requires a little more attention. It involves letting a plant go to seed, when normally you would harvest and eat the plant before that happened.

This means leaving the crop (or at least some of it) in the ground longer

Saving Tomato Seeds

CUT A RIPE TOMATO in half and squeeze the pulp and seeds into a glass of water. Eat the rest.

ALLOW A RAFT OF FOAM and mold to form on the surface. The coating of the seeds ferments and the heavy seeds themselves sink to the bottom.

STIR THE GLASS occasionally, pour off everything but the seeds, and replenish the water.

WHEN ALL VIABLE SEEDS have sunk (discard the floaters), put them in a strainer and rinse them in cold water.

SPREAD THEM on a sturdy paper plate, labeled with the variety. When they are ABSOLUTELY dry, store them in airtight containers, away from heat or light.

Tomato Brandywine

Lettuce in bloom.

When saving seeds you want your lettuce and collards to bolt!

than usual. Another way to go about it, if you have the space, is to set aside a dedicated area for annual and biennial seed production. The area should be large enough to grow at least ten specimens of each vegetable to maintain crop variability. Plan on making an early sowing of spinach, lettuce, arugula, radishes, mâche, and Asian greens in your seed garden so the seeds will have plenty of time to mature and dry. Save seed from those plants that remain green and edible the longest before they "run to seed." Although running to seed is not usually looked upon favorably by gardeners (who normally wish the production season from a sowing of spinach or lettuce would continue longer), in this case it enables future sowings to be made. With spinach, which has both male and female plants that cannot be distinguished until seed stalks form (only the females have them), you need to leave at least 25 plants so you'll be sure to end up with at least two males and four females for genetic diversity.

Cross-pollination is not much of a concern with lettuce varieties. Spinach varieties will cross-pollinate each other, as will radishes. Chinese cabbages and mustards will cross-pollinate, but not with the regular cabbage relatives such as broccoli and kale.

To collect seeds from a plant, you let it bloom, then harvest the seeds that follow when they're mature and dry. It's interesting to watch the process unfold. With lettuce, for example, the seed stalk emerges from the center of the plant. (With head lettuces that make a firm ball, you might need to cut an X in the center, or peel back some of the leaves, to enable the stem to rise.) This may look comical

at first, but the flowers that form on top are often colorful and quite lovely. After they take on a feathery appearance, it's time to poke them into a paper bag while they're still on the plant, and shake them to make the seeds fall to the bottom. Use the same technique for other seeds that shatter (drop from the plant easily), such as dill, cutting off the seed heads and bagging them before the seeds have a chance to drop. All plants will drop their seeds eventually—that's how they sow themselves. But with some there is more leeway. Keep an eye on things to see what the seeds are doing. Ideally you'll want the seeds to be fully mature, and if you're used to handling purchased seed in packets, you'll know what they should look like. With most plants it's fine to cut the stems and let the plants finish drying indoors, especially if frost or a long stretch of rain threatens. Those that don't shatter can be hung upside down from, say, the rafters of a dry shed or the ceiling of the garage until they are fully dry. If you're not sure, stack them flat on newspaper or a piece of cloth, out of direct sun.

Some seeds can easily be shaken, slipped, or pried out of their pods, capsules, or seed heads, but many others, such as spinach, and brassicas like arugula, radishes, and broccoli, take a little effort to thresh. Usually this is a simple matter of putting them in a sturdy cloth or plastic bag and stomping or beating on it to release the seeds. Some you'll need to winnow to separate the seed from the chaff, that is, the material that once covered them and any other debris from the plant. The proper way to do this is to first put them through a screen called a scalper, which has openings just a bit bigger than the seeds, so that they fall through and the debris doesn't. Then you place them on another screen called a sieve, which lets any uncollected debris fall through but not the seeds. After that you can just blow on the seeds gently, or pour them from bowl to bowl in a mild breeze, or next to a fan, to waft away any remaining dust as shown on page 115. Use your judgment as to how much air movement you can use without blowing away seeds, which vary in weight.

With many seeds, you can both thresh and winnow by picking them out with your fingers, especially if you're saving only a small quantity. On the other hand, if you get very involved with seed saving you might want to pick up some winnowing screens from the source on page 453. That can be expensive though, and gardeners can sometimes amass a collection of screens or winnowing baskets from flea markets in just the right sizes for the seeds they commonly save.

BIENNIALS WHOSE SEEDS ARE NOT PART OF WHAT YOU EAT

THE LAST CATEGORY, biennials, also produce seed separate from the part we eat, but biennials wait until their second year to do this. This makes them a challenge for the seed saver, who must find a way to get them through the winter. Many biennials—such as carrots, beets, rutabagas, celery root, and cabbages—can be stored in a root cellar over the winter. Then you can plant some of them back out the following spring to complete their biennial growth pattern and produce seed. In warm or moderate climates

biennials can overwinter in the ground but need to be protected from voles, deer, and other critters. Parsnips are so hardy that they're traditionally left in the garden and harvested the following spring. Onions and leeks do not cross with each other, so both can be part of a seed-saving garden. (If it's too cold to overwinter leeks in the ground where you live, you'll need to store some in a root cellar with their roots buried in damp sand, to make sure they'll still be alive for replanting next spring.) In most cases, just setting out 12 to 20 roots of each plant type and allowing them to go to seed is all you need to do, but some experts recommend setting out up to 40 carrots to maintain a broad genetic base. This prevents inbreeding, which would result in an irreversible weakening of the variety.

The leafy biennials—like kale, collards, and Swiss chard—are hardy enough to survive over the winter to produce seed the following year, which is a good thing because there would be no easy way to store them. In the coldest climates they could either be protected with a cold frame, or a super-hardy variety like Winterbor kale or Argentata chard could be grown. You'll have to make a choice between beets and chard since they cross readily. Beets are the logical choice since both their greens and roots are edible.

If you plan to save cabbage seeds (*Brassica oleracea*) you wouldn't want to grow regular kale (also *B. oleracea*), which would cross with it. Fortunately, Nature's larder is generous, and Siberian kale (*B. napus*) does not cross and is an excellent and very hardy alternative. However, since rutabagas are also *B. napus*, you'd have to decide which of those

To collect seeds from a plant, you let it bloom, then harvest the seeds that follow when they're mature and dry.

Saving Seed from Overwintered Kale

ALLOW PLANTS TO GROW. Let flowers form. These plants were grown in our small unheated greenhouse.

SEEDPODS WILL FORM. Note the thread-like seed pods that emerge after the flowers.

STAKE THE PLANTS. Now taller and covered with green pods, they require 4-foot grade stakes and strong twine for support.

LET THEM DRY. Check pods frequently so they don't shatter. As soon as they are brown and the seeds inside have darkened, stuff them into a pillowcase or bag.

TIE OR HOLD THE BAG closed and beat it on a hard surface (or stomp it with your feet).

THIS WILL BREAK UP THE PODS, so that the seeds will fall out and collect at the bottom of the bag.

two to grow. The other cross-pollination concern is with carrots. The ubiquitous wild Queen Anne's lace is actually a wild carrot, which you'll realize when you see the similar flowers and seed heads on your carrot seed crop. But if you do get crossing, it's easy to tell. The white root color of Queen Anne's lace is dominant, so you simply wouldn't save any white roots for your next generation of seed production—thereby eliminating the Queen Anne's lace.

There are ways to get around all these cross-pollinating problems. Separation by distance is one, but home gardeners rarely have the space to do this. There are also sophisticated techniques such as hand pollination and caging flowers on alternate days, practiced by professional seed growers and by experienced home gardeners who have taken the trouble to learn these methods. But for the average home grower the simplest answer is often just to save each vegetable from a competing pair (broccoli and cabbage, beets and chard, Siberian kale and rutabagas) on alternate years.

STORING YOUR SEEDS

THE BEST PLACE to store all these seeds is somewhere cool and dry. To do the job correctly from the start, be sure that the seeds you have collected are dry *before* you store them. The storage containers should be either glass or metal with airtight lids. Canning jars with their rubber-sealed lids are an excellent choice. Save the lids used for food storage (as long as they're not bent or misshapen), and you can get an extra year of use out of them. Look for a cool, dark place where the temperature does not fluctuate. It is a general rule that the sum of the relative humidity and the temperature in degrees Fahrenheit should add up to less than 100, but you want to do even better than that. The more carefully seeds are stored, the longer they will retain the vigor you want them to have when you next plant them. Humidity meters can be found at most hardware stores. Well-dried seeds can also be kept in tightly sealed jars in the freezer or refrigerator. But let the containers come back to room temperature before opening them, lest condensation occur.

Seeds vary as to how long they can be stored and still remain viable. For this reason, it's best to take them out and grow them at least every three years, and save new ones from that crop. (Some short-lived seeds such as parsley and cilantro must be grown out every year.)

As you can see, saving seeds is a complex topic. Beginners usually start by saving a few of the easiest crops such as potatoes, beans, and corn. If your appetite has been whetted by the idea, we recommend two sources that go into more detail than this chapter can afford: *Growing Garden Seeds* by Robert Johnston, Jr., and *Seed to Seed* by Suzanne Ashworth (see page 454).

Our choices of varieties for this garden (see page 104) are all sure-fire open-pollinated ones with qualities that make them worth perpetuating. ✺

Winnowing Kale Seed

SIFT by putting the seeds and chaff on a coarse screen, over a bowl, and rubbing to make the seeds fall through.

POUR the seeds from one bowl to another in front of a fan. Repeat until all the chaff has blown away.

COLLECT the seed, making sure it is fully dry. Store in an airtight container.

THE SAVORY GARDEN

OUR HOPE IS always to weave together the virtues of all the gardens portrayed above, and get us closer to the ideal we strive for when we grow food. A garden wants to be practical so that it makes economic sense. A garden wants to be dependable, even if the hard times never come, because once you experience the pleasures of fresh food on your doorstep you will rely on it. A garden will certainly want to include extending the season, both early and late, not only for the year-round fresh food but also for the fun of succeeding at something considered impossible. And a garden wants to be self-reliant, for the secure feeling it gives you when you're part of the natural cycle of the garden: from seed to harvest and back to seed. But let's also have a garden built on centuries of aspiring toward exceptional food. Eating well makes life more pleasurable.

Sometimes we hear "eating well" talked about as if it only applied to expensive, fancy, or "gourmet" fare. To us it's strange that something as basic as a great homegrown, home-cooked meal should be considered a luxury, something that no one has time for anymore. It's become a performance put on by a well-paid TV chef. But we'd like to point out that even the most talented chefs who've become famous by practicing the culinary arts are not creating them but inheriting them. These arts (as with the gardening arts) were devised over many years by people who were feeding themselves and their families with the foods available in their parts of the world. The planet's great cuisines are built on peasant food. They result from harvests, bountiful or not, and the occasional lack of this or that ingredient has inspired many a new combination, and new ways of preparing what was at hand.

The quality of the food on your table depends on both the skill of the cook and the quality of the ingredients. If you grew those ingredients, choices you made can exert a great influence on the quality of the meal. Certain growing techniques and planting dates can shape the results. If you're paying attention to the soil-building principles explained in Chapter 1, and your irrigation system is doing its job, that part of the good-food equation should be well taken care of. The other part is following the natural curiosity of your senses, to select the most luscious varieties to grow and to search out the most exciting tastes to try: some modern, some old. Not all vegetable varieties are created equal. Certain ones have more potential for flavor and tenderness than others.

REACHING FOR FLAVOR

LET'S TAKE A few examples, starting with one of the yummiest things you can eat, the strawberry. There are many strawberry varieties on the market. Most of them produce just one heavy crop per year, but some are everbearing varieties, which means they bear smaller amounts continuously from June through October. Most modern varieties have been bred to produce very large, bright red berries that speak to your eyes more than your taste buds. Fortunately, there are some wonderful exceptions. In our garden we have grown for many years a French everbearing strawberry variety called Mara des Bois. Plants for this variety are, at present, hard to find and there are only a few suppliers (see page 452). Unlike other berries, Mara des Bois has been bred to be as flavorful as a wild strawberry. People who eat wild strawberries often comment on the unmatched flavor and aroma of those tiny fruits. Well, Mara des Bois comes pretty close to that standard and, in addition, the berries are the size of a regular garden strawberry.

If Mara des Bois seems a bit too esoteric for you, just try the alpine strawberries instead. These are varieties of wild strawberries, available in many catalogs, that you can grow from seed. If you start the seeds toward the end of the winter, the alpines will bear the first year, and since they're perennials, they'll come back vigorously each year after that to yield a small but intensely flavorful crop. Their taste is complex, like a good wine. As with any berry, you have to be patient and let them ripen thoroughly before harvest; if their undersides are pale, the taste will be also, and they won't be sweet. Since alpine strawberries don't make runners, they're perfect for edging beds in an herb garden. Don't expect to find baskets of these in a market because they are small, fragile, and take a long time to pick. But hey, when it's your home garden and you're growing for your own personal pleasure, these little beauties are worth the effort.

There are so many similar taste delights unknown to the supermarket shopper. The first one people think of is the tomato. Most commercial tomatoes are picked green so they can be shipped long distances, and then they're artificially ripened in an atmosphere of ethylene gas. Not only does this practice make them taste bland, it severely restricts the food value as well. The more subtle flavors and nutritional components form during the final stages of natural ripening on the plant, and simply do not exist in artificially ripened fruits picked many days before they're ready. Some shoppers don't even know there is a difference. But once they begin to grow their own and let them ripen on the vine, a whole new world opens up.

Currently there's an enormous interest in heirloom tomato varieties. These are the old-time tomatoes that were popular in seed catalogs up to 150 years ago, before suitability for long-distance shipping and adaptability to artificial ripening became the criteria for variety selection. Many of the heirlooms found in specialist tomato catalogs offer new options of color, texture, and taste beyond the experience of even the confirmed tomato lover.

(continued on page 120)

Don't expect to find baskets of alpine strawberries in a market because they are small, fragile, and take a long time to pick.

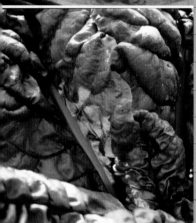

OUR FAVORITE VARIETIES FOR THE SAVORY GARDEN

ARTICHOKE: Imperial Star. Even if you never imagined growing artichokes, this dependable annual producer is the one to start with. **Opera** is a purple artichoke with striking color, great flavor, and a long production season.

ARUGULA: Astro. Arugula tastes best in fall, winter, and spring, but this heat-tolerant variety can extend the season into the warmer months for arugula fanatics.

ASPARAGUS: Mary Washington. Newer varieties may yield more, but they don't have the eating quality of this wonderful heirloom.

BASIL: Genovese. Traditional Italian basil that is easy to grow and has everything we want in authentic basil flavor.

BEANS: Maxibel. Nothing beats the French filet beans for eating pleasure. Pick them small and pick them at least every other day. **Garden of Eden.** This heirloom pole bean is edible from filet size through large flat pods. After that it is tasty as a shell bean.

BEETS: Chioggia Guardsmark. A wonderful candy-striped beet that is amazingly sweet when cut into very thin slices and eaten raw. **Badger Gold.** The new standard for golden beet lovers. **Forono.** Uniform slices for cooking or pickling from an elongated beet. **Merlin.** Our favorite for sweet, round red beets.

BROCCOLI: Piracicaba. Bred in Brazil for excellent heat tolerance, but it also withstands cold weather.

BRUSSELS SPROUTS: Diablo. Pick fresh from your fall garden for an idea of just how good a Brussels sprout can be.

CABBAGE: Caraflex. Small, cone-shaped heads with rich flavor and very tender leaves.

CARROTS: Mokum. The sweetest early baby carrot. **Napoli.** The fall-planted, overwintered wonder.

CAULIFLOWER: Cheddar. Orange color brightens when cooked. **Graffiti.** A spectacular purple cauliflower for fall harvest. **Veronica.** This lime green Romanesco type will delight the eye as well as the palate.

CELERY: Tango. Everything you want in a great celery.

CELERY ROOT: Mars. A refined, easy to grow celeriac.

CHARD: Bright Lights. Lovely stem colors, excellent eating quality.

CORN: Golden Bantam, Double Standard, and **Country Gentleman** are some of the best old-time open-pollinated sweet corns with the real corn flavor that is lacking in the new super-sweets.

CUCUMBER: Diva. Thin-skinned, non-bitter, great tasting. **Sultan.** A Middle Eastern trellising type for the home garden.

EGGPLANT: Orient Express. Does well in both cool and hot weather. **Hansel.** This

TOP TO BOTTOM:
Imperial Star artichoke; Cheddar cauliflower; Bright Lights Swiss chard; Quadrato di Asti peppers.

mini-eggplant is perfect for grilling.

ESCAROLE: Natacha. Easy to blanch and wonderful for fall salads.

FENNEL: Orion. An easy to grow, very crisp variety for salads, grilling, and soups.

GARLIC: We grow a nameless heirloom from an Italian neighbor because it has adapted so well to our soil.

KALE: Toscano. This is the best tasting type of kale.

LEEK: Upton. A three-season leek that is easy to blanch. **Bandit.** An extremely winter-hardy leek with thick shafts.

LETTUCE: Adriana. Tasty green leaves with a soft, blanched heart.

MELON: Savor. An improved Charentais type for the home garden.

ONION: Red Long of Tropea. Tall, elongated red bulbs. **Walla Walla**

Sweet. Mild, sweet, overwintering type. **Purplette.** Delicate mini, perfect for creamed onions.

PARSLEY: Titan. A full-flavored flat-leaf variety.

PEAS: Lincoln. The best for eating fresh from the garden and excellent for freezing. **Sugar Snap.** Vigorous vines, 6 feet or taller, covered with the sweetest sugar snap peas.

PEPPER: Tiburon. An ancho for roasting or chili powder. **Quadrato di Asti.** Large Italian red or yellow bell. Superb.

PERENNIAL HERBS: Grow the essentials such as common sage, chives, and French tarragon, but also try some specialties such as Lemon Verbena.

POTATO: Charlotte. We think there is no better potato than this for winter storage and winter eating. **Russian Banana.** A late, long-storing fingerling that is a favorite of chefs.

RADICCHIO: Indigo. Reliable header with great radicchio flavor.

RADISH: D'Avignon. This small French Breakfast radish is a real delight in spring and fall.

SCALLION: Nabechan. Complex flavor. No bulbing.

SHALLOT: French Gray. Positively the finest ever.

SPINACH: Space. Smooth look, great taste.

TOMATO: Brandy Boy. This hybrid has the same awesome flavor as the heirloom Brandywine, but is much more productive. **Sapho.** A wonderfully flavored salad tomato. **Matt's Wild Cherry.** Tiny gems of the finest tomato flavor.

TURNIP: Hakurei. Consistently superior to all of the other small, sweet turnips.

WINTER SQUASH: Waltham Butternut. The standard for flavor and still the best.

ZUCCHINI: Costata Romanesco. Best flavor and texture of all.

TOP TO BOTTOM:
Orion fennel; Indigo radicchio; D'Avignon radishes; Hakurei turnips.

Piracicaba broccoli.

We like Piracicaba broccoli for its wonderful taste and for its brushlike ability to pick up lots of dip when we serve it raw on a platter of crudités.

(continued from page 117)

Not just red and yellow but pink, green, dark purple, striped, and white varieties are available. There are large succulent fruits with a convoluted shape and there are tiny, intensely flavored pea-size ones to be eaten as snacks or added to salads. Some of the large heirloom varieties like Brandywine have such depth of flavor that once you've tasted them there's no going back. No other vegetable can so quickly make you a confirmed home gardener.

Even the common green bean will delight if you grow the delicate French filet beans. These tiny, elegant, stringless beans don't lend themselves to machine picking and thus are available only from specialty farms or home gardens. They're at their best when ⅛ to ¼ inch in diameter and should be picked frequently, at least every other day, to enjoy them at their best.

The common beet also offers surprising pleasures. Chioggia beets, with red and white concentric circles in their flesh, add visual delight to dishes as well as intense beet flavor. We think their leaves, when young, make the best baby beet greens. Another beet variety, the golden beet, offers the home cook a color that doesn't run. And *all* beets can be made

to grow and taste better when there are adequate trace elements, such as boron, in the soil.

Even the earthy cabbage and its relatives have crossed new frontiers. Did you know that there are both round and pointed cabbages? And that you can make them grow smaller by planting them closer together? There's also a very early and unusual broccoli from Brazil called Piracicaba. It produces numerous small heads with a more open structure than regular broccoli. We like it for its wonderful taste and for its brushlike ability to pick up lots of dip when we serve it raw on a platter of crudités.

Finger-size carrots are the perfect snack, but you won't see real ones in the supermarket. What they sell as baby carrots are actually large mature carrots, cut in half, and then tumbled to round the edges. They're known as "grinders" in the trade. But you can pick any size you wish from your home garden. You might grow one of the small round "Parisian market" varieties that, while not quite as sweet, are cute enough to entice children. Carrots now come in many colors, too, although not with any real improvement in flavor. Our favorite carrots are the result of a growing technique: We plant them outdoors in mid-August, then protect them in late October with a cold frame, low plastic-covered tunnel, or movable greenhouse. When carrots are left in the cold soil like that with their roots intact, the cold temperatures make them sweeter—so much so that our children always referred to them as "candy carrots" and could never get enough.

New colors add interest to a wide range of vegetables. The colors of Swiss chard stems have expanded beyond white and red to almost every color in the rainbow. The adventurous gardener can grow eggplants in many sizes, shapes, and colors, in addition to special types for grilling and a wide range of taste choices. If you're in a cool climate, as we are, the early-maturing Asian eggplant varieties will allow you to enjoy this vegetable just as much as if you lived in a warmer climate.

Lettuce is no longer just green and round. What with green leaf, red leaf, Lollo, oakleaf, romaine, butterhead, Bibb, and summer crisp, the variety in lettuce colors, textures, and taste is extremely broad. Cauliflowers are no longer just white. Green, purple, and golden-headed cauliflowers expand the versatility of this classic vegetable and increase its nutritional value, with anthocyanins in the purple and carotene in the gold. The spiraled, lime green heads of the Romanesco cauliflowers are beautiful, tasty, and a great geometry lesson. If you study the heads closely, you'll see that they offer an edible display of fractals, the self-similar, replicating shapes so fascinating to mathematicians—also seen in frost crystals, fern leaves, and corals.

As with cabbages and broccoli, you can create smaller cauliflower heads by closer planting. But the real key to cauliflower enjoyment is to limit their harvest to the cool-weather months of the year, since the stress of maturing in hot weather can result in low-quality heads. Another vote for the much-underestimated cool season.

Brussels sprouts, yes, Brussels sprouts, are another surprise gourmet vegetable when done right. This is another case where time of harvest affects the flavor of the vegetable. The cold-wet-freeze-thaw treatment provided by Mother Nature as fall turns into winter is just what this crop needs to bring out its very best. Always plan on growing enough Brussels sprouts to harvest them as late into the fall and winter as your climate can possibly allow—often much later than you'd think.

Sometimes new developments in vegetables are not to our taste. Take super-sweet corn. There is far more to corn than just sweetness, but sadly, that is all the new super-sweet types seem to offer. The wonderful old corn flavor is missing. Fortunately, the real corn essence lives on in the classic open-pollinated varieties like Golden Bantam. (Many other OP varieties are still sold, though you have to prowl the seed catalogs to find them.) This is another crop where the home garden excels because you won't find these varieties in the market.

With cucumbers, however, we've been happy to see them improved. What the seed catalogs call Middle Eastern breeding (also known as Beit Alpha) has given us seedless cucumbers, with thin skin and unprecedented good flavor, that can easily be grown at home. For pickling,

Romanesco cauliflower.

Anelli beans, sometimes called anellini, are charmingly curly (the name means "rings" in Italian). We like to grow a mix of varieties.

the smaller European types and the classic blocky American varieties are still the first choice. But it bears repeating that any succulent vegetable will only be at its best when grown in a soil with adequate organic matter, balanced mineral levels, and a constant supply of moisture.

If you have ever visited France in summer you may have returned, like many travelers, enthusing about the flavor and aroma of the intensely aromatic Charentais melons sold in all French markets. We grow these in our home garden, as you can in yours, and the seeds are not hard to find. Are they better than the standard ones you've been growing? Since you'll rarely find them in markets here, there's only one way to find out!

Another of our flavor adventures took us in pursuit of superior onions. Onion flavors run from the sweet Spanish types, mild enough to eat like an apple, through the little pungent/sweet Italian Cipollinis, to the more intense hard storage onions. But the ones everybody gushes about are the Vidalias. Vidalia onions are not a special variety but rather a normal short-day onion (see page 139) grown on a specific low-sulfur, calcium-rich soil in Georgia. We have grown them during the short days of winter in a minimally heated greenhouse (adding a little extra limestone to the soil) with truly flavorful results. We purchased Texas-grown seedlings, transplanted them in late December, and achieved the same early-May harvest date as the growers in Georgia.

Not all peas are created equal and many of the old-time varieties, especially the ones with tall vines that are no longer grown commercially, offer a real fresh eating bonus. In addition, if you grow them in your home garden you can pick them at their peak of ripeness and sweetness. Thanks to the work of heirloom vegetable enthusiasts, seeds of such classics as Alderman (also called Tall Telephone) and Lincoln are still available and definitely worth the extra trouble of trellising them.

The palette of peppers that can be grown, from the very hot to the very mild, always excites home gardeners who appreciate southwestern, Asian, or African food. By growing just one plant each of a wide number of pepper varieties, you'd be able to travel the world without leaving your kitchen. And this is true for so many foods, as you can see by looking through the crops profiled in Chapter 4. Think of the varied shapes, sizes, and colors available in winter squashes alone. The unique texture of spaghetti squash continues to inspire cooks' imaginations. And the newer varieties of naked-seeded pumpkins (that is, ones without hulls) are much more successful than their predecessors, so that you can now make your own roasted and salted pumpkin seed snacks.

GOING FURTHER

KNOWING THAT YOU can grow all of these delights if you care to, it's fun (and mouthwatering) to think about what else might be possible. Beyond just the outstandingly flavorful versions of your usual garden crops, think about what boundaries you might push with the Winter Garden techniques discussed on pages 87 to 101. For example, we love to eat fresh figs but have always lived in climates where fig trees won't survive. We'd read about heroic efforts by other fig lovers as far north as Boston who either thoroughly wrap their trees with tar paper over thick insulation, heel them over and bury them, or have them planted in tubs to be moved indoors for the winter. We gratified our fig passion by planting an Italian Honey fig tree in an unheated greenhouse where we would wrap it every fall in four layers of used row cover material. It bore in late summer, and when the fruits were ripe, they dripped sweet syrup. We'd try to pick them at the moment of perfect ripeness, when just a slight touch made them fall, heavy with juice, into a cupped hand. Our favorite ways to eat them were just as is, or in a bowl with chopped walnuts and cream (no sugar needed), or in what we called figgy pudding. Not the kind in the wassail song, which is a dense, daunting fruitcake, but one along the lines of the Plum Custard recipe on page 443, substituting figs for plums.

But a fig has a vigorous, greedy root system that will spread throughout the soil of a greenhouse and compete unfairly with any winter greens and root crops that may also be growing there. Some day we would love to grow fig trees in a movable greenhouse all their own. The greenhouse would be moved over the figs in fall to protect them from the cold, then moved to an adjacent plot where we would use it to grow a warm-weather crop during our cool coastal summer.

Perhaps that crop could be pawpaw trees! These extraordinary native fruits can be grown just about anywhere in America—except mid-coastal Maine. They would survive our winters fine, but our summers are too short and cool to ripen them. In the wild, they grow in thickets of small, shrubby trees, and a number of horticultural varieties have been developed over the years.

Despite its hardiness, there is something tropical-seeming about the pawpaw, which should not be confused with the papaya, a true warm-climate plant. The fruits are the size of avocados, with sweet yellow, custard-like flesh. Easily bruised, with a brief shelf life, they're difficult to ship, which may explain why they are so little known. Although there are many ways to use them in cooking, such as in puddings and pies, it is hard to imagine anything better than a pawpaw sliced in half and set on a plate. You simply spoon the delicious flesh out of the skin, spitting out the large, smooth black seeds as you go.

And how about citrus? We currently grow lemon and calamondin trees outdoors in pots, moving them into the house in winter, but they're not fond of the winter heat thrown off by our woodstove, and would prefer a cool, sunny room. One winter we kept them in a cool greenhouse, heated to just above freezing. With their roots in the ground, they exploded in fragrant flowers, followed by buckets of fruit. Because fuel prices have since pushed even a minimally heated home greenhouse beyond our budget, our citrus are back to the indoor/outdoor shuttle. But we know there's a better solution, so we'll work on it until we find it. ☼

TOP: Our Meyer lemon tree makes its peace with winter indoors in a pot. BOTTOM: Our potted calamondin tree, with its tart little fruits, thrives.

The Crops: How to Grow

WHEN YOU START OUT AS A GARDENER, it might seem daunting to learn that there are dozens of different plants you'll learn to grow. And it is true that each one looks different, tastes different, and may have its own little quirks. But the learning curve will seem much less steep if you get to know them on a family basis. As you can see from the chart on page 44, most garden vegetables fall into just a few major botanical families. Botanists have given Latin names to these families, but gardeners find it helpful to let one popular member represent its clan, hence "the cabbage family" or "the onion family."

Conveniently, much of the advice about growing one vegetable applies equally well to its cousins. Plant relatives might

Though the color may vary from yellow to white, this flower shape is found in cabbage family vegetables.

seem dissimilar, especially if one is grown for its leaves and another for its storage root, but their kinship is evident—and useful—when considering their preferences in fertility, moisture, temperature, and susceptibility to certain pests. As we've seen in Chapter 2, family groupings are very important in planning how to rotate the crops in your garden from year to year. And thinking in terms of families may also help you to prioritize in deciding what to grow. A garden that combines food plants from a number of different families will give you a well-balanced diet. In this chapter we've grouped the crops by families to simplify the advice we offer on growing them. As a result, much of this information is contained in the introductions to each plant family, with specifics added under individual vegetables. Within a family, we've tended to start with the most indispensable and have sometimes clustered those whose culture is closely allied. For planting times and plant spacing, see the charts on pages 456 to 459.

This chapter also tells you how and when to pick food crops and how to handle them when they come in from the garden, from peeling and trimming in the kitchen to thinking of ways to cook them. As a general principle, it's best to get into the habit of picking what you eat just before you need it for a meal. Fill your basket, hose off your vegetables outdoors (see page 21), then bring them indoors and prepare them for the table. Use the garden as your crisper drawer. Think how much space you'll save in the fridge!

Complete recipes follow in the second section of this book, starting on page 250.

THE CABBAGE FAMILY

- CABBAGE
- KALE
- COLLARDS
- BROCCOLI
- BRUSSELS SPROUTS
- CAULIFLOWER
- RADISHES
- KOHLRABI
- TURNIPS & RUTABAGAS
- ARUGULA
- ASIAN GREENS

YOU'LL SOMETIMES HEAR this large and important group referred to as the crucifers (Cruciferae), which means "cross-bearing." Botanists classify most of the plants we grow according to the structure of their flowers, and you'll notice that when the cabbage relatives go to seed their flowers are always cross-shaped, with four symmetrical petals. They are even more often called brassicas because most of the cabbage family are species within the genus *Brassica*.

Cabbage family members need a fertile soil with plenty of organic matter, and they all benefit from a good supply of available nitrogen, especially when they are making their initial growth. We've found that one of the best ways to achieve this is to incorporate that most common of free fertilizers—autumn leaves—into the soil the fall before. If you've composted your autumn leaves to make leaf mold (see page 22), that's even better. We spread garden lime on the surface at the rate of 1 pound per 20 square feet, and then spread on a 2-inch layer of autumn leaves, tilling these amendments in or chopping them in with a hoe or spade. We till or chop the area again as soon as the soil can be worked the following spring and then sow the seeds or set out transplants. Autumn leaves carry a lot of built-in nutrients but are slightly acid. The lime helps to get them well started on decomposition. With that extra stirring in the spring, they're ready to liberate those nutrients at just the rate the cabbage family plants seem to appreciate.

Another way to boost fertility for these vegetables is to grow a leguminous green manure crop such as clover the summer before, then till it under a few weeks before you set out your brassicas. Preceding them with a crop in the onion family will set up the soil too. If you've done none of these things, a good nitrogen source is dehydrated alfalfa applied at the rate of 1 quart per 25 square feet, and scratched into the top 2 or 3 inches of the soil.

Any of these maneuvers will help strengthen your cabbage family members against a couple of pests to which they are susceptible, and that make them less dependable than other choices for the beginner's garden. These are root maggots and cabbageworms. Root maggots spoil brassica crops by tunnelling into the roots. Cabbageworms, which chew on the leaves, are the larvae of the little white butterflies you see hovering about the garden in summer. Over time, once your garden soil matures and gains real fertility, these pests become much less of a problem, but at the start new gardeners can become discouraged and disappointed. In addition to the fertility boosters described above, the most successful solution is to cover newly sown or transplanted seedlings with lightweight, spun-bonded row cover material. You can either lay it directly over the crop, in which case the crop lifts the fabric as it grows, or it can be held above the crop with supports such as wickets made of #9 wire (as shown on page 97). The edges of the fabric can be held down with soil or with sandbags around the perimeter.

Another pest that bothers many crops, but the cabbage family especially, is the cutworm. This fat off-white creature feeds at night, usually by felling a seedling as if it were a little tree. Some cutworms also climb. Drawn to soil rich in organic matter (like your garden), they're worse in some years than others. The classic remedy is to make a collar out of cardboard and surround the plant stem. This does help, if you poke the collar a half-inch or so beneath the soil surface so the cutworms can't crawl under it. We use plastic or paper cups with the bottoms cut out, or toothpicks poked into the soil on either side of the plant stems (the worms think these are stems, and too tough to chew). Another trick is to go out in the morning and wiggle your finger around in the soil near the plants until you find the culprits. They'll be near the felled seedlings, just beneath the soil surface, curled up like the letter "C." Squish them.

Except for the few noted below, we grow our brassicas from transplants, and we've found that they do best if they're not allowed to grow too large before setting

Use the garden as your crisper drawer. Think how much space you'll save in the fridge!

Cabbage is a great old-fashioned vegetable and it's not hard to grow.

out. Ideally, we transplant them into their permanent beds when they are three weeks old. In general, these are cool-weather crops that can be set out early in the season. They need an average amount of water, and will benefit from a mulch in dry climates to keep the soil evenly moist.

Some members of this family have a tendency to go to seed prematurely, although this can be controlled by timing plantings according to expected temperatures, as explained with individual crops below. But as all gardeners know, neither plant growth nor the weather are always predictable, and from time to time, despite your efforts to keep up with the picking, you'll reap an unexpected bounty of yellow or white cross-shaped flowers instead of broccoli heads or lush, tasty greens. If an entire planting bolts like this and food production has stopped, try to enjoy these blooms for a little while, until the long, slender seedpods form. The flowers are manna for bees and other pollinators—as well as pretty to look at, both in the garden and as an edible garnish on your plate.

For the brassicas that are storage crops, it's important to choose sowing dates that will give you plants at the ideal stage for storing in fall. The chart on page 457 will guide you, but you may need to experiment with different dates to see what works best in your climate or location.

Cabbage

THE PHRASE "BOILED CABBAGE" has done little to enhance cabbage's reputation, but it's a great old-fashioned vegetable when treated with finesse, and it's not hard to grow.

GROW. Early cabbages can be set out as transplants three or four weeks before the last average frost date for a summer crop, then set out again in early to mid summer for a fall or—in mild climates—a winter crop. If you've had pest problems in past years, try using a more powerful organic fertilizer like dried blood for extra nitrogen.

HARVEST. Wait for the cabbage to "head up," that is, develop a firm center. Then remove just the round head by cutting it above the huge outer leaves, which tend to be tough. See page 72 for producing regrowth in the garden from spring sowings, and page 80 for forcing the stems indoors.

STORE. Even though they are an aboveground crop, cabbages bred for storage can be treated the way you would treat root crops. Thanks to their dense heads they'll keep for months, whether they are in a root cellar or just in the fridge. Even the early cabbages and the savoys will still last for weeks if kept cool. A great trick for root-cellar storage is to pull up the plants, roots and all, with the heads intact, and replant them in damp sand in the root cellar, either directly on the floor or in a container.

COOK. It doesn't take long to slice up a cabbage, steam it, and butter it for a side dish. A well-grown cabbage is mild tasting and can be seasoned with a favorite herb, such as dill or caraway, or a spice, such as cumin. You can also simmer cabbage in vegetable stock, or a meaty broth, perhaps stirring in a dollop of sour cream at the end. And of course it's great in hearty soups such as the borscht on page 272, or cooked and then mixed with mashed potatoes for an Irish colcannon. Dribble some brown butter over that!

We usually cut cabbage into quarters from top to bottom with a large knife, cut out the core pieces, then slice crosswise, the thinner the better if it's going into a coleslaw or a salad. Even a few slivers of red cabbage are enough to make a green salad more festive. Red and green cabbages have the same texture, unless the green one is a savoy. Those have more loosely wrapped, frilled leaves, and are very light textured and tender. They require less cooking. While they do not keep as well as the firm ball cabbages, they are a great delicacy and well worth growing. Baby cabbages are excellent too, especially for small families. These include actual baby varieties and the small cabbages that resprout from a cut stem base. If you cut either in half and bake them, cut-side-down, in an oiled dish, they are delectable.

Kale

KALE IS TRUE SURVIVAL FOOD—such a traditional mainstay in Scotland that the word *kail* stands in for dinner itself, and *kail-yard* for a garden. Long before fiber, minerals, and beta-carotene caught the attention of the health-conscious, kale was known as a plant of substance that could keep you strong, even if all you had were kale, oats, and the family cow. It helps that kale is so winter hardy. Unless your summers are blistering, or your winters frigid, it's possible to have it in the garden throughout the year. But survival food does not have to bring up thoughts of

Most varieties of kale can survive outdoors through the winter in all but the most extreme climates.

hardship. Kale is tasty in winter when few other outdoor plants have stayed green. Brush off the snow and you'll find its leaves sweetened by the cold.

The colors of kale varieties range from the blue-gray of Vates to the deep maroon of Redbor, or the stunning carmine-veined Red Russian. The anthocyanins responsible for these red hues leach out in cooking, but sautéing kale rather than boiling it will help capture these and other nutrients.

Some kales have three-dimensional leaves with dramatically curled margins; others have leaves that are flat and smooth. Tuscan kale, which also goes by the names black kale (*cavolo nero*), dinosaur kale, and lacinato, is very distinctive. It grows in an upright vase shape, its leaves narrow and pebble-textured. These vary in color, even within a single plant, from dark blue-gray to a very deep forest green. It's our favorite, tender in texture and mild in flavor. But do try several types to see which you like best, and which respond best to your growing conditions.

GROW. An early and a late crop can be grown, just as with cabbage, but kale is even hardier, and most varieties can survive outdoors through the winter in all but the most extreme climates. For winter kale in Maine, grown with some

Tender young leaves emerge perpetually from the center of a kale plant as the plant grows.

Curly kale.

protection (page 94), we sow seeds in mid-July. Some varieties, such as the Tuscan ones, have stems that elongate as successive leaves are produced, so that you eventually have a big tuft of leaves atop a tall stalk. The ones that grow lower to the ground, such as the stemless Dwarf Siberian, which sprouts leaves from a low heart, often remain sound throughout the winter because they are less exposed.

HARVEST. Picking kale leaves from the perimeter of the plant will encourage new leaves to grow at the center, but the outermost ones should be left if they are tough and worn. We usually take medium-size leaves from several different plants in the row. Individual leaves will sometimes turn yellow and can be easily pulled off to keep the plot looking tidy.

STORE. Kale will keep for a week or so in the fridge but is best picked fresh as needed. In fall, store it on the plant, in the garden, as long as possible. In climates where severe ice and snow prevail, you can cut off the center parts of the heads and store them, often for up to several months, in a large black plastic bag in an unheated garage or shed. It's okay if they freeze. Check frequently and remove any yellowed or rotting leaves.

COOK. Unless the leaves are very small and tender, you'll need to pull the tender parts away from the stems, which are then discarded. Another way to do this is to fold the leaf so that the underside (where the stem is most prominent) faces outward, then slice lengthwise next to the stem to remove it.

We frequently cook up some chopped kale as a side dish, either steamed or sautéed with olive oil and garlic. We'll also toss it into a soup to create a whole-meal dish. It makes a great healthy component to a big protein breakfast, and the sight of a cast iron pan in which bacon, sausage, or pork chops have been cooked will usually send us out to the garden for some kale to toss in.

Although it's rare to see any kale used raw, the Tuscan kind can be soft enough for that role. Our chef friend Joshua McFadden makes a knockout salad out of it, with pecorino cheese, garlic, lemon, hot pepper, and breadcrumbs. We sometimes include raw kale in robust winter salads, or slice up thin ribbons of it to give light-colored lettuce salads a wonderful deep green accent, and a bit more substance.

Collards

BEST KNOWN BELOW THE MASON-DIXON LINE where they are a popular winter crop, collards (also called collard greens) are tall, large-leaved plants that form a loose rosette. They taste best in cold weather.

GROW. Grow collards the same way you would kale, above.

HARVEST. Cut individual leaves from the bottom part of the stalk, passing up any that look tough or blemished. Remove the stems before cooking the same way you would for kale.

STORE. Keep the leaves on the plant as long as possible. They will store well for up to a week in the fridge.

The leaves of this heirloom red-stemmed collard have striking red ribs in the blue-green leaves.

COOK. Traditionally, collards are boiled or simmered for an hour or more with a flavorful piece of pork. Knowing that the discarded "pot likker," or cooking liquid, contains nutrients, you can rescue it and use it as a fortifying broth or soup base after the greens are drained. But although collard greens are firm-textured, they don't necessarily need this degree of tenderizing to taste good, and those who love them appreciate their strong flavor. A good compromise is to make a soup of the whole business: the greens, the pork, the collard broth and some potatoes, onions, and herbs. Or cook them in a long-simmered soup of beans or black-eyed peas. They're also great cooked in a skillet with pork fat, as in the turnip greens recipe on page 383.

Broccoli

BROCCOLI GROWS LIKE ANY BRASSICA except that it's been bred to develop an edible central head of tiny, tightly closed buds. Side shoots form lower on the stem after the central head is cut, and these make smaller heads. All varieties will do this, but some have better side-shoot production than others.

GROW. It's best to grow broccoli as a cool-weather crop, in early summer and then again in fall, but we have also managed summer crops by planting them in quick succession and harvesting the heads promptly before they go to seed. The plants don't mind mild frosts and are good up until the first hard freeze and sometimes beyond.

Another type of broccoli called broccoli raab (or *broccoli di rapa* in Italy, where it is popular) never forms heads at all, but just small upright shoots that are eaten stem, leaves, buds, and all. We find it a little too bitter, but it does have many ardent fans. We prefer a variety called Happy Rich, which is a cross between broccoli and an Asian brassica called gai lan. Its blue-green stems, leaves, and small shoots are very mild and sweet-tasting, and if it does finally bolt from lack of cutting, the gorgeous white flowers will win your heart.

HARVEST. A head of broccoli, left to grow, will quickly erupt in a bouquet of yellow flowers. If there are tiny yellow buds or even open flowers, the broccoli will still taste fine but it will look brownish when cooked, and not as appetizing. Better to pick the head before its tightly closed green buds open, even if it means giving extra to your friends. If it has started to bloom, cut it off right away and compost it, since doing this will encourage side shoots to form on the plant. The best way to cut broccoli is with a sharp knife. Try to cut above any new little heads that might be forming lower on the stem. There is no need to remove any broccoli leaves that remain on board; in fact, broccoli foliage by itself is quite tasty and nutritious as a cooked green!

STORE. Broccoli stores for a few days if wrapped up and kept cool, but is much better picked fresh.

COOK. Before cooking broccoli it's a good idea to check for little green cabbage worms that might be hiding in it. Swishing the heads in a sink full of cold salted water will usually kill them, and they'll float to

The central head formed by a broccoli plant.

the bottom. You can also just check for them after cooking when they have turned white and are easier to see. If accidentally eaten, they will do you no harm.

Broccoli will cook more uniformly if the heads are cut into individual spears. It's fine to leave the spears fairly large, with several inches of stem, but these will cook more uniformly if you split the ends with a knife. Otherwise the buds will cook much faster than the stems, and start to fall apart before the stems are tender. If you're serving broccoli as a side dish, a simple bowl of it, steamed and buttered, is hard to beat. For added richness, spoon over warm hollandaise, or a cream sauce sparked with cheese.

When adding broccoli to a quiche, pasta, bread pudding, or some such dish, it's best to use just the florets, with most of the central stem removed. But the remaining stems can be used for other purposes. If they're not too tough you can chill and salt them for fresh nibbling or dipping, just as you would carrot sticks. For this purpose we like the Happy Rich variety mentioned above. For dipping raw or lightly blanched spears with the florets attached, we like Piracicaba (page 120), a broccoli variety with a large bead. This means the buds in its clusters are larger and more open, rather than small and tightly compressed.

Brussels Sprouts

WHEN COOL WEATHER SETTLES IN and we've had a few frosts, we start looking forward to the first meal of Brussels sprouts, and the colder it gets, the sweeter they taste.

Brussels sprouts.

GROW. This heroic brassica needs little care during its long tenure in your garden. Keep it weeded and thoroughly watered and it will come into its own after frost, when many other crops have succumbed to the cold. Although it does occupy quite a bit of space in the garden, and for a long time, you can easily interplant it with some smaller and earlier non-brassica crop such as spring lettuce or baby carrots (see page 51). We prefer to grow it from transplants, but you can also direct-sow outdoors, even in warm weather in climates with a long growing season. The seeds germinate well in temperatures up to 86 degrees.

HARVEST. The sprouts, which look like tiny cabbages, appear on the stout stem from the ground up. Pick the fat ones on the bottom first and those on top will continue to grow. Commercial growers pinch off the top of the stem when the lower sprouts are about dime-size to make all the sprouts mature together for one big picking. You can do this too if your goal is to freeze them all at once. Otherwise, take advantage of the fact that they mature gradually, for small, repeated harvests over a longer season.

To pick the sprouts, snap them sideways as if you were flipping a switch, and they'll come right off. This leaves a bit of stub left on the sprout. In the kitchen cutting off this stub will also release the outer layer of leaves, which sometimes look a bit scruffy, especially if they've been on the plant a long time.

STORE. Keep the sprouts on the stem as long as possible in fall to keep them fresh and to let them sweeten up. They will take repeated frosts, although eventually they'll turn mushy in cold climates. We always try to have some Brussels sprouts for Christmas dinner, even if it means picking an entire stem and putting it in the root cellar or in the refrigerator if severe winter weather has set in by then. It will keep for several weeks that way.

COOK. In cooking, the outer layers will tenderize more quickly than the hard little inner core. Cutting an ✕ in the hard bottom of the sprout with a knife will ensure that the leaves and core cook at the same rate. Since their form is so appealing, we usually don't chop the sprouts, but leave them whole, either as a side dish or distributed around a roast. (If the sizes are mixed, cut any jumbo ones in half.) They are perfect just steamed and buttered. When tender, plunge them into cold water to preserve their bright green color, then reheat them in a skillet with butter. Their strong, faintly bitter flavor marries well with sweet fall vegetables such as carrots, onions, and fennel.

Cauliflower

CAULIFLOWER POSSESSES that familial cabbagey flavor, but in a less assertive, more refined way. It is distinguished by its mysterious solitary white heads which can, in rich soil, attain great size—a foot across or more. Colored cauliflowers are a great addition to the repertoire. The deep purple ones turn green when cooked, but are striking if cut up and served raw on a mixed crudité platter. There are also lime-green varieties, and gorgeous gold-colored, carotene-rich ones whose color intensifies with cooking. Most spectacular

of all is the chartreuse Romanesco type. Its head is a spiral made up of self-replicating smaller spirals, which, in turn, are made up of even smaller spirals—and so on until frost or senescence ends this amazing fractal display.

GROW. For the beginning gardener, cauliflower is a little trickier to grow than the other brassicas. Transplants shouldn't be any older than three weeks when set out, or their growth will stop. The young plants will take some frost but not a hard freeze. When the heads are forming, cauliflowers are traditionally blanched by tying the big leaves over the developing heads to exclude light, thereby keeping them a pristine white. Today we have self-blanching varieties, but even these look nicer if a leaf is bent over the head, breaking the rib so that it stays in place. If you like cauliflower as much as we do, and want to try your hand at growing it, start with a fall crop, transplanted out in time to mature before hard frost. The cool weather of early fall will help it to form nice heads.

HARVEST. You can harvest a cauliflower before it reaches full size, but not after its peak of maturity, when its surface will soon start to look dingy. Cut it with a sharp knife at the base of the head, removing any attached leaves, which are normally not eaten.

STORE. Rugged as a cauliflower head might seem, its surface is fragile and prone to decay. Since any discoloration will show up even more in cooking, it's best to pick the head when it looks great and eat it right away. Even refrigeration will only save it for a few days.

Cheddar cauliflower is a variety rich in carotene.

TOP TO BOTTOM:
Beauty Heart radishes.
Tinto radishes.
D'Avignon radishes.

COOK. You can puree cauliflower for dips, and make creamy soups with it, but it stands out best in dishes that highlight the fine, smooth texture of its large white head. Include it in vegetable medleys. Add it to curries and pasta dishes. Or just let it stand alone. A friend of mine once boiled a cauliflower, set it on a platter in the middle of the table, lovingly smeared a pat of butter over its top, then sliced it as if she were carving a crown roast. A little more butter, salt, and pepper and it was perfect. Try a head sliced, roasted in olive oil, then topped with a tasty gremolata dressing, as in the recipe on page 388. Most recipes make use of the florets, cut at a uniform size, but the lower base is perfectly edible too. Cauliflower flesh seems dense when raw, but it cooks faster than you might expect, so keep testing it with the tip of a knife until it's tender but not mushy.

Radishes

ON MOST AMERICAN TABLES, a radish is a dainty, zesty and colorful little bite, perfect for stimulating the appetite before a meal. Cylindrical ones such as White Icicle are elegant sliced lengthwise to scoop up dips. And our favorites are the French Breakfast types such as d'Avignon, which are red with white tips. Some might consider such a niche, though useful, to be limiting. Earlier in our country's history, the radish was an important sustaining root crop, as it remains in most parts of the world. More recent interest in Asian vegetables has broadened our repertoire to include many excellent ones, from the mighty daikon to the Beauty Heart varieties, suffused with red like a sunset when sliced crosswise.

GROW. Radishes share cultural traits with their cabbage family relatives. They grow and taste best in cool weather; in hot weather they quickly become hard and pithy. They are prone to root maggots, which can be controlled with floating row covers (page 90), but if they're given the soil fertility and moisture they need to make fast, healthy growth, they'll elude pests. Radishes are among the quickest of crops, especially the small ones, and can be tucked into any space in the garden in spring or fall (winter in mild climates), although it's best not to put them where other cabbage relatives have recently grown.

HARVEST. Pull radishes before they become overmature. If the leaves are young there's no reason to discard them, as they are quite edible.

STORE. If you have a nice crop that heat or frost is about to do in, you can store the radishes quite well in the fridge for weeks at a time. Placing them in cold water, changed often, will help keep them crisp. Storage radishes such as Black Spanish or Munchen Beir can be stored for several months in a winter root cellar.

COOK. Wonderful as radishes are raw, they are equally good in cooking. The red-skinned ones will lose their bright color, but those with red interiors will still glow. Heating removes both the radishes' crunch and their peppery bite; you can prevent that by adding them at the very end, in fried rice or in a stir-fry (see page 376). But sometimes heat's action is a good thing. If radishes have gone a little past their prime and are too hot or a bit fibrous, cooking them will mellow and tenderize them. The greens as well are good cooked while young, in a stir-fry or a soup. They can even spark up a raw salad before they grow larger and turn fuzzy. If your radishes have gone to seed and the rest of the plant is beyond redemption, try using the seedpods, either raw in salad or stir-fried. There is even a variety called Rat Tail, bred solely for this purpose, whose purplish pods have a slight radishy tang.

Kohlrabi

IN THE GARDEN, kohlrabi looks a bit like a space satellite: a smooth-skinned, baseball-size globe sitting on top of the soil, with rodlike stems protruding upright from its surface. Its greens, as edible as those from any brassica, are held well above the ground, but that round root (which is actually an enlarged stem base) is the part most often used in the kitchen. Its flavor is turnip-like but a lot milder and sweeter, especially after a few frosts. Some kohlrabi roots are pale green on the outside, others a vivid purple, a color not sustained in cooking. Varieties also differ in size. We have grown little tender ones, and enormous ones the size of soccer balls.

GROW. As a member of the cabbage family, kohlrabi thrives in the same soil conditions we have described for its relatives. It grows best as a late summer into fall crop and would fit in nicely if succession-planted after early potatoes.

HARVEST. You don't have to wait until it is mature to eat kohlrabi, but if you do it will keep for a long time in the bed, right up until the first hard freeze. Cut it off at the base with a sharp knife and slice off the stems. The leaves can be saved and cooked the way you would other brassica greens such as collards or kale.

STORE. If your climate is mild, or if you can put a cold frame or plastic greenhouse over it, just leave it in the ground during winter. Kohlrabi is a genuine storage crop, remaining tender, not pithy if kept cool, and stores for up to six months in the winter root cellar and in the fridge.

COOK. In soups, stews, stir-fries, and roast-vegetable medleys, it plays a more subtle role than that of a turnip, and is excellent mashed or blended, as in the Kohlrabi and Parsley Puree on page 391. Unlike the starchier potato, kohlrabi weeps a bit when pulverized; that is, the solid and liquid parts tend to separate. If this seems a defect to you, add a bit of potato to the dish to bind it, or make a roux with a little butter and flour to thicken it. Small young kohlrabis can be sliced and eaten raw in salads or as canapés topped with a savory spread. Unless they are very young, kohlrabis are generally peeled.

Turnips and Rutabagas

A BOWL OF STEAMING MASHED TURNIPS or rutabagas ("bashed neeps," the Scots call them) is a fine dish for a cold day. No wonder you find them at Thanksgiving tables, even in households where they're not commonly served. Mighty fine with turkey, they do well to usher in the winter season.

A rutabaga is larger than a turnip, with yellow flesh and skin, its foliage smooth and tinged with blue. Both vegetables are brassicas—that is, cabbage relatives—but

TOP TO BOTTOM:
Kohlrabi.
Purple Top turnips.
Rutabuga.

FACING PAGE (top to bottom):
Mei Qing Choi.
Tatsoi.
Mizuna.
Tokyo Bekana.

Arugula's flavor is not quite mustardy, but gives your tongue the same playful bite.

their flavors are distinct. Rutabagas are a little richer and sweeter and turnips sometimes have a trace of mustard's bite. But if you grow the small, white Asian types such as Hakurei, you'll discover how mild a turnip can be. We even love them raw. They need no peeling, as mature turnips and rutabagas do. This is also a good type to grow for turnip greens.

GROW. Turnips and rutabagas grow best in cool weather. Turnips, the quicker of the two, can be direct-sown as early as the soil can be worked in spring, then again in late summer for a fall crop. You can also grow a succession of baby turnips for winter harvest if your climate is mild or if you give them winter protection. We sow a storage crop of rutabagas after June 21 for fall harvest. Both rutabagas and turnips require a fertile soil with plenty of organic matter.

HARVEST. We pull baby Asian turnips when they are about golf-ball size, but they are still tasty if left to grow to two or three inches in diameter. When young the greens are especially good too. Fall turnips and rutabagas are left in the ground until just before the first hard freeze.

STORE. Baby turnips will keep for a few weeks in the fridge, but then start to become pithy. Storage turnips keep for months in the root cellar, but rutabagas are one of the best-keeping of all vegetables and will stay firm and delicious until spring, given the right conditions (page 78).

COOK. Baby Asian turnips have a huge moisture content and must be cooked carefully. Boiled and mashed, they become so watery that they almost disappear in the pan. A quick sauté with hot butter or oil works best. They can be tossed into stews toward the end of cooking, until just tender, and are also great added to stir-fries for a few minutes so that they cook but retain their crispness. Since turnips and rutabagas grown for storage are in your life for a long time, it's helpful to vary the way you cook them over the winter season. Both are wonderful roasted along with sweetly caramelized onions, and strewn around a platter of roasted pork. Use them in hearty vegetable soups, either chunky or pureed, as in the Creamy Fall Vegetable Soup on page 281. Steam them until soft but not breaking apart, then glaze with maple syrup and a favorite spice such as nutmeg, cinnamon, or cardamom. Or mash them along with potatoes. That would be "bashed neeps and tatties," if you're honoring the Scots poet Robert Burns on his birthday, January 25. The haggis is optional.

Arugula

ARUGULA'S FLAVOR IS not quite mustardy, but gives your tongue the same playful bite. We can grow it at almost any time of year, but we prefer it in cool weather when the leaves are milder and not stressed by heat. The standard arugula, *Eruca sativa,* is distinct from a similar plant called sylvetta or wild arugula (*Diplotaxis muralis*). The latter has deeply lobed foliage and is a lot more cold hardy.

GROW. You can grow arugula in rows, but there is no need to. Just scatter the seeds lightly over a small area, cover them with a sprinkling of compost, keep them moist until they germinate, and wait a few weeks before picking. In spring and fall we grow arugula as a cut-and-come-again crop, enjoying the regrowth we get after cutting it. In summer it works best to plant successions and cut once for a single harvest, as regrowth in warm weather can bolt easily. For winter in Maine, we start sowing the third week in September and do succession plantings every month, or plant a cut-and-come-again crop of the hardier sylvetta. Flea beetles, which make tiny holes in the leaves, are a problem with spring and summer crops and are best controlled by covering the arugula with floating row covers at planting time (page 90). Fall crops are not bothered, and sowings made inside a greenhouse are usually spared.

HARVEST. Using a small, sharp knife, we harvest the leaves when they are ideally about three inches tall, cutting the leaves near the soil level and leaving about half an inch in the ground for regrowth. If they have grown taller, cut just the top three inches, then pull out the rest and resow in another spot. Arugula leaves with long tail-like stems are awkward to eat.

STORE. Pick just before serving. You can keep the leaves refrigerated in a plastic bag for a few days, but they will soon start to turn limp and not taste as fresh.

COOK. True arugula lovers will eat whole bowlfuls, but most people prefer its heat tempered by mixing with other ingredients. Unlike a too-bitter, poorly grown chicory leaf, which can taint a whole salad, arugula blends right in,

lending a background kind of heat. It also has a flat, lobed leaf that benefits from the lift it gets from firmer, curlier salad leaves such as lettuce—unless you're using it as a bed on which to lay sliced vegetables or fruits, and then it is perfect alone. Since it is thin and soft-textured, it should not be dressed too heavily in a salad where lightness and loft is called for. Trim off any ungainly stems. Arugula is sometimes sautéed or tossed into cooked pasta dishes, but we find that much of the flavor is lost in cooking.

Asian Greens

THE FULL RANGE of greens used in Asian cooking is vast and at times perplexing, but a number of them have become common in western markets and popular with home gardeners and cooks. Most are members of the brassica family. Here are some with which we have had particular success.

Bok Choy

Also spelled pak choi and pac choi, this is a versatile, head-forming green with large, striking ribs. The beautiful wide, smooth leaves open up like a bouquet. Our favorite variety is Mei Qing Choi. We also like one simply called Red Choi (see photo on page 60), one of the most beautiful plants you can grow, its leaves maroon with bright lime-green ribs and veins.

Tatsoi

Most of the greens we eat grow upward. Tatsoi starts out that way, then spreads out into a flat rosette with dark green spoon-shaped leaves as the weather gets colder, hunkering down for the winter.

Mizuna

This green has upright, arching leaves that are finely dissected, giving them a feathery look. Its colors range from pale green to purple-tipped, with a pleasant, mild flavor.

Tokyo Bekana

This is an open-headed, loose-leaf plant with wavy, pale green leaves. It is heavenly picked at baby-leaf size, but also good if left to mature. We prefer it to the firm-headed Chinese cabbages, although these are very substantial and popular with some gardeners.

GROW. Most Asian varieties like the same conditions as our traditional cabbages and kales—cool weather, especially—whether they are greens such as tatsoi or root crops such as radishes and baby turnips. All can be either direct sown or transplanted. Of the Asian greens we've experimented with, tatsoi is the most cold hardy (perhaps because of its ground-hugging habit), and one of the mainstays of the winter greenhouse. We sow it in mid-September. Mizuna has also proved easy to grow, and can be direct-sown in fall and then right on through the winter in warm climates, and even in cold ones, given enough protection. Bok choy, Tokyo Bekana and the firm-headed Chinese cabbage can be grown in warm weather only in the cooler parts of the country, and even there it's best to seek out slow-bolting varieties for summer plantings. The heading types can also bolt if set out in spring before the danger of frost has passed.

All the Asian greens are susceptible to flea-beetle damage (indicated by small holes all over the leaves) in the early years of a garden, before the soil is truly fertile. That can be prevented by covering the bed right after sowing or transplanting with one of the lightweight floating row-cover materials that exclude pests without overheating the protected crops underneath. Another option is to grow them in the greenhouse, where they don't seem to mind the cold *or* the heat. In our experience, flea-beetle pressure there is much less intense.

HARVEST. Bok choy is sweet and tender when cut at about 8 inches tall, and even more exquisite when cut as a 4-inch mini. (You can have it both ways by thinning every other plant and letting the remaining ones double in size.) With bok choy we cut the whole heads, but with tatsoi we're more apt to pick individual leaves, which continue to grow all winter at the center of the plant until warm spring weather makes them bolt. In general, all these greens can be cut at both large size for cooking or baby-leaf size for salad use, except for the firm-headed Chinese cabbages, which are usually allowed to grow to maturity.

STORE. Since no fresh greens keep their quality for very long, we pick all these as needed. Heads of bok choy will keep all right in the fridge for several days, and the heading cabbages can be stored in a moist root cellar for about two months.

Since no fresh greens keep their quality for very long, we pick all these as needed.

COOK. Asian vegetables have a long history of careful breeding and are very versatile. Their use need not be restricted to Asian recipes.

Bok choy is the perfect stir-fry vegetable, best added to the pan or wok in two stages: first the firm stems, then the softer leaves. The stems are juicy and crunchy, the whole plant tender enough to use in salads. The red varieties are colorful in winter salads, and make a striking garnish for platters. Tatsoi, as well, is good both raw and cooked. Try stir-frying it or dropping it into a soup at the last minute. We find that both these vegetables taste good even after they've bolted, and do not take on a bitter taste.

Mizuna can be steamed or sautéed like spinach, and makes a nice textural contrast in salads if picked young. Slip it into a tuna fish sandwich.

Chinese cabbage of any type is good in a salad if young and tender. Otherwise, treat it the way you would a western cabbage (in the recipe on page 379 for example) but much more delicately. Brief cooking is best.

THE ONION FAMILY

• ONIONS	• SCALLIONS
• LEEKS	• SHALLOTS
• GARLIC	• CHIVES & GARLIC CHIVES

THE ALLIUMS (Alliaceae), or members of the onion family, grow best in as fertile a soil as you can create. That means growing them with plenty of compost in order to achieve a nutrient balance, and a full range of trace elements. They don't do well in an acid soil so it's important to make sure the pH is between 6 and 7 by liming if necessary. They also require adequate moisture and must be irrigated in dry weather. Some are grown for the green tops, others for the bulbs beneath, and even the bulb sorts can provide pungent greenery when it is needed. Any crop grown in soil following an onion relative will benefit from it, but the onion family tends not to do well following the cabbage family, which feeds heavily on the soil. Because of their strong flavors, onion relatives tend not to attract predators.

Onions

THE COMMON ONION needs little introduction. It comes in varying sizes, colored yellow, white, or red. Some are better keepers than others, so for long-term use you should look for a storage onion. The other thing to consider is that onion growth is affected by seasonal day length, which changes depending on where you live, so it's important to choose a variety adapted to your location. "Short-day" onions do well in the south, where the winter days are mild enough to allow them to begin bulb formation when the days are 10 to 12 hours long. "Long-day" onions need the 14- to 16-hour days you find up north to form their bulbs, and are also cold hardier, with better storage capability. Good seed catalogs specify the latitude range for each variety they list.

Baby onions such as the Italian-born cipolline varieties are also quite sweet and choice. But some cooks find these a bit laborious to peel because of their flattened, slightly convex ends. You can

Onions drying in the garden row where they have grown.

also just raid a regular onion row for "spring onions" when the bulbs are about ping-pong-ball size.

GROW. Onions can be started in several different ways. You can sow them directly in the garden. You can start seeds ahead and transplant the seedlings (or use purchased seedlings). And you can choose the easiest route, which is to grow onions from sets. These are small, dime-size onions that have been started ahead for you the previous season and can be found at your local garden center. Their only drawback is that they come in a very limited number of varieties. To plant onion sets, you just poke them an inch deep into the soil in the spring, at

a distance of 4 inches apart in the row. To plant onion seedlings, lay their roots into a shallow furrow made with a hoe and firm up the soil around them for support. They should be irrigated right after transplanting, and again on a daily basis for the next week until they are well established and growing new roots.

In addition to regular watering, you need to pay close attention to weeding after you've put in an onion crop. Onions are skinny plants that do a very poor job of shading weeds out, and it's so easy to lose sight of them completely as broadleaf weeds take hold. Mulching between rows will help with this problem, as well as conserving moisture. Another great trick is to plant onion seeds, seedlings, or sets in clusters (see page 234). This gives you more space around the plants to keep them hoed or mulched.

HARVEST. Wait to harvest storage onions until the tops fall over. Then pull them up and lay them on the ground for a day or two, right in the row, to dry out a bit in the sun. After that, cure them by laying them on a dry surface, foliage and all. This is an important step that extends their storage life. A screen supported by sawhorses and the floor of a sunny covered porch are both good places to cure onions. If the curing must be done outdoors and rain is predicted, cover the onions with a tarp to keep them dry. They're ready to store when the tops of the bulbs are tight and firm, the foliage dry and brown. Any green left in the stem will make the bulbs more prone to decay and premature sprouting. Cut off the tops, leaving an inch above the bulbs.

The brick floor we laid at one end of our former greenhouse made a good place to cure onions.

STORE. Net bags or plastic crates make good storage containers for onions. Look for a spot somewhere on your property that is cold and dry but does not freeze. This might be an unheated porch in a warmer climate or under the couch next to a north wall in a colder one.

COOK. An onion is a workhorse in the kitchen, and I'll bet half the things we cook have onions in them. They're always peeled before eating, and although only the papery skin is inedible, it's faster to strip off the first layer under that as well. If peeling onions turns you into a stinging, weepy-eyed mess, hold the onions under running water as you work; and if chopping is the next job, do it quickly with a good sharp knife. Some people love raw onions, but to our minds, a little raw onion in salads or sandwiches goes a long way. Grating it with a fine grater or a Microplane is a useful way to incorporate a small amount.

The best stand-alone onion dish we know is the simplest one: onions cut in half crosswise, salted, peppered, dotted with butter or drizzled with olive oil, and baked cut-side-up in the oven until caramelized. These can be served as a side dish, a garnish, or part of a room-temperature antipasto platter. Simpler still are onions sliced thin and cooked long and slowly in a saucepan until they turn into a sweet, dark, rich jam, seasoned with nothing but themselves. Even oil or butter is optional.

Leeks

A LEEK IS LIKE A TALL, FAT SCALLION, or an onion that doesn't form a bulb. And it's indispensable, not only for its kitchen versatility but also for the sheer beauty of its upright blue foliage, marching down the row. Rarely nibbled by anything, leeks sail dependably through spring, summer, fall, and beyond. Although leeks take up space in the garden for a long time, you can pull some early at a smaller size whenever you need them, leaving the rest to thicken up. Our garden always has two plantings, one a more green-colored leek that matures in summer, the other a winter variety, stouter and bluer in color, prized for its resistance to cold.

GROW. Leeks like deep, loose, fertile soil. While they can be direct-sown in early spring, we prefer to sow them indoors in flats in late winter, and then transplant them out into the garden when they are about pencil-size. One of the chief goals in leek-growing is to get a long, tender white shank—the part that wins the cook's heart. To do this you have to blanch the bottom of the plants by excluding light, and the normal way to do this is by gradually hilling them up with soil in the row. But instead, we transplant them by dropping them into 9-inch deep, 1-inch-diameter holes poked in the soil with a dibber and just leaving them there. At the start only an inch or so of their tops poke out of the soil, but gradually the holes fill up with soil as rain falls and the gardener plies her hoe. By the time the leek is tall and full

Leek Technique

USE A DIBBER. We made this dibber with a stop on it so it makes a consistent 9-inch hole in the soil.

DROP IN A SEEDLING. Just a bit of green protrudes from the leek seedling. We don't fill the hole. The action of rain and weeding will dribble soil in gradually over the course of the season, burying the leek's stem.

THE RESULT: beautiful long white shafts on the leeks, blanched by darkness.

grown, the bottom has been well covered and is snow-white. This is obviously easier than hilling up the surrounding soil, and it means you can plant your rows much closer together, to save room.

Leeks are so hardy that in most climates they can be left in the ground all winter long, best protected in the coldest months with an unheated greenhouse, cold frame, or a simple A-frame tent just tall enough to walk into.

HARVEST. If the soil is very loose you can just grasp a leek at soil level and give it a tug. If you find your plants are breaking off, gently pry the ground around them with a digging fork to loosen it, then pull. Unless you want some of the tops to flavor a stock, chop them off a few inches above where the white part ends and add them to the compost pile, as any dark-colored parts will be quite tough even after long cooking.

STORE. Although we prefer to store our leeks in the ground indefinitely, digging them as needed, it is possible to bring leeks into the root cellar where they will keep for a month or two. In time, whether in the ground, cellar, or fridge, the leeks will continue to elongate and will eventually form a thick, hard flower stalk in the center of the shank.

Leeks are among the best garden vegetables to feature in casseroles, gratins, bread puddings, and quiches.

COOK. Leeks are milder than onions—you might sniffle a bit while chopping them, but your eyes won't run with tears. Rarely eaten raw, they develop a creamy texture when cooked that adds body to any soup or stew. And a simple side dish of leeks simmered until tender in butter and a little water lends elegance to any meal.

Preparing leeks for cooking takes some extra care, whether you've dug them from your garden or purchased them at a market. After cutting off the tops, you'll need to clean the shanks, which are composed of tightly wrapped layers. Any that are tough, ratty, wrinkled, or streaked with brown should be discarded. Cut off the roots, leaving the firm, white basal plate just above them intact. Make sure the stem is bendable; if it has a hard, rigid core, this means that a seed stalk has formed, and it is not much use.

Even the most carefully grown leeks usually have some grit between the layers. Slicing the shanks lengthwise and sloshing them in a sink full of warm water is the easiest way to clean them. Leave the bottom intact to make the shank easier to grasp. If you want to cook the leeks whole, slice down one side only as far as you need to go. You can then reassemble them tidily in the cooking vessel with the cut side down.

How many leeks you need for a dish depends not only on the length and width of the shank, but also on how much it has been blanched. You'll notice that even inside a white shank, the leaves are varying degrees of green. The lighter green leaves will tenderize very nicely in cooking, and add color interest.

Dishes of whole leeks lined up like logs are very pretty, although I've noticed that some diners find them hard to cut, so I'm most apt to leave them whole only when they're small and very tender. Overcooking, on the other hand, will turn them mushy. Like onions, they have a high sugar content and so are apt to burn easily, so while sautéing or even simmering, keep a very watchful eye. They also can react strangely when braised in wine, taking on an odd pinkish color even if the wine is white. A meat or vegetable broth—or just water—works best.

Leeks have many uses in addition to those named above. They're famously paired with potatoes in soups, either cold, as in vichyssoise, or hot in the creamy soup on page 281. They are splendid steamed and added to salads, dressed with a mustardy vinaigrette, and are among the best garden vegetables to feature in casseroles, gratins, bread puddings, quiches, and the like. Try them sautéed as a luxurious bed on which to set fish. Grilled leeks are delectable, especially small ones, parboiled or steamed first in order to tenderize them.

Garlic

WE DON'T USUALLY THINK OF GARLIC as a seasonal treat, but it really does taste best when it's just been harvested in mid to late summer. Still, it's great that it keeps well for fall and winter use, even if it's a bit less succulent. Store-bought, garlic is apt to be the softneck type, whose heads are made up of many cloves that get progressively small and tedious to peel toward the center. The withered tops of softnecks can be braided together, and hung up as garlic braids. We grow the more cold-tolerant hardneck type, which does not keep quite as long but whose

heads form one circle of nice fat cloves, so much more efficient for the cook to handle. A third type, elephant garlic, which is closely related to leeks, has giant cloves with a milder flavor.

Cloves too small to bother with do, however, have a use. You'll want to save some of the fattest cloves you've grown for planting the next year's crop, but the small ones can be sown to produce garlic scallions, a great thing to have next spring and early summer while you're waiting for fresh garlic heads to come into season.

Another thrill along the way is the garlic scape, which is the flower stem that hardneck garlic sends up in summer, to form seed. It is rather firm and green, ending in a seed case with a pointed tail or "whisker." The stem and seed case are edible, the tough tail is not. Some garlic varieties, called rocamboles, have scapes that form fanciful loops and look delightful in gardens.

GROW. Garlic is grown by breaking apart some heads you saved from your previous harvest and poking the cloves into the ground, pointed end up, about an inch deep. Just the very tip of the clove will be visible at soil level. Plant them at the same time in the fall as you would plant tulip or daffodil bulbs in your area. It's that simple. Just as with a tulip, the idea is to plant while the bulb is dormant, leaving enough time for some roots to grow in cool fall weather, but not so early that the tops start to grow. That happens in very early spring. You can also plant garlic in the cool weather of spring. The cloves will be a little smaller, and the crop will mature about a month later, but it will also keep longer in storage, so you might

TOP: Garlic bulbs.
BOTTOM: Garlic scapes.

even consider growing both crops if you're a real garlic lover. Though garlic is very hardy, mulching in cold climates with a material such as straw or seaweed will keep the garlic from being heaved out of the ground during periods of freezing and thawing.

In summer, while the garlic is growing, provide plenty of moisture. There is some debate as to whether garlic scapes should be cut off when they appear, so that the plants will put all their energy into the bulbs. We find that with good soil fertility this isn't necessary, but we do it anyway in order to have the scapes for cooking (see below).

HARVEST. When the foliage starts to turn brown in midsummer, but there are still about six green leaves left, gently pry up the garlic heads, keeping their covering layers intact, and dry them on screens or some other surface in a cool, dry place. Don't forget to set aside the biggest and best for planting next year.

STORE. Softneck garlic can be hung with the tops bunched or braided. We store our hardnecks with the tops cut off an inch or two above the heads, in mesh bags, or with their long stems tied together and placed in the hard-plastic mesh trays that nurseries use to sell annual seedlings. We find a dry spot where they will stay as cold as possible without freezing.

COOK. For passionate garlic lovers, no amount of raw garlic in the pesto or hummus dip is too much. For others, either the palate or the stomach eventually calls a halt; and for some, only cooked garlic will do. How you deal with a garlic clove—

whether you slice it, dice it fine, press it in a garlic press, grate it with a Microplane, or mash it with coarse salt with the tip of a knife—is up to your preference. Roasted garlic, one of the simple triumphs of cookery, is accomplished by placing unpeeled garlic cloves in a medium oven. Twenty to 30 minutes later their unctuous flesh can be squeezed out of the papery skins onto bread or pizza, or added to a sauce, dip, soup, and countless other dishes. Garlic pulp (raw or cooked) spread beneath the skin of a chicken before roasting yields an earthy treat. Use garlic in mashed or scalloped potatoes. Press it into a basic vinaigrette dressing. When your cloves start to turn a little brown, soft, and bitter, with a green shoot beginning to emerge, it's time to discard them.

Garlic scapes pureed in a food processor are wonderful used raw or in a pesto sauce, or in various dips. We also love to cut them into pieces an inch or two long and add them to stir-fries, or combine them with other summer vegetables. Roasted in the oven in butter or olive oil, they become soft, slightly chewy, and caramelized, with a mild garlicky taste. Grilled, they are splendid. Picture a whole grilled fish, or a platter of grilled eggplants, surrounded by loopy garlic scapes. To me, that's reason enough to grow the plant.

Scallions

SCALLIONS, also called bunching onions, are a species of onion that does not form a bulb at the bottom. Some varieties, such as Evergreen Hardy White, are very cold tolerant and will overwinter. Breeders have also produced ones with red skins at the bottom, in addition to the usual snow-

These scallions were sown in clumps for easier weeding.

white. These make an especially colorful garnish. All have tasty green tops that are enormously useful for the cook.

Scallions grow best in cool weather and it's sometimes hard to keep a steady supply going in very hot weather, just when you need them for summer salads. But gardener-cooks learn to be on the prowl for scallion-like substitutes at any time of the year. These might start in late winter with the sprouting tops of storage onions, a bit firmer than a scallion but tasty, and a perfect size for snipping. (If they are pale in color, green them up on a sunny windowsill for a day or two.) These will tide you over until spring scallions start to bear. Rob the tops of regular summer or fall onions while they are still young and tender. A few leaves won't be missed. Do the same with shallot or garlic tops, which are delicious in their own distinct way. Plant up any leftover onions sets (page 140) just for their tops, and snip them until cool scallion-planting weather returns.

GROW. Sow seeds very early in spring for an early summer crop, then in mid to late summer for a fall harvest. In Maine we plant them in early August for a protected winter crop. They are easily direct-sown, but we sow them in clumps in 2-inch soil blocks (page 230), for efficiency and easy weeding. Give scallions fertile soil and plenty of moisture or the tops will turn brown.

HARVEST. Scallions are another very cold tolerant vegetable that can be harvested even when frozen, and still look normal once they have thawed. Generally they are harvested young, when the foliage is succulent and tender. Old scallions, both tops and bottoms, can be used in cooking if that is all you have, but we usually pull them out to make room for a more desirable crop.

STORE. You can keep scallions for several days in the fridge, but the tops will start to go bad pretty quickly. Better to go pull a few whenever you need them.

COOK. Though sometimes used whole, for dipping, scallions are more typically chopped with a knife or snipped with scissors for use in omelets, salads, stir-fries, Asian soups, and numerous other dishes, either raw or cooked. If ever a creation of yours looks boring, perk it up with a sprinkling of chopped scallions on top.

Shallots

WE WILL ALWAYS ASSOCIATE SHALLOTS with France, which for years cornered the export market. But now they're more available and less expensive, so any home gardener can grow them. Unfortunately, a bit has been lost along with progress. Shallots grown from sets (small individual bulbs) tend to be true to the original shallot form—small brown clustered bulbs, joined at the base, which are then pulled apart before peeling. They have a delicate, distinctive shallot flavor. Those grown from seed tend to look and taste like small brown onions, with nothing special but their size. Our favorites are the ones called French Gray shallots, which are grown from bulbs, not from seed, and are a delicacy indeed. These are small, hard to find, fussy to peel, and not very good keepers. But they are worth the effort from beginning to end. They taste the way real shallots should.

French Gray shallots.

GROW. You'll want to grow your shallots from sets, the way you grow garlic, with fall planting; the clumps of bulbs they form are more open, and not like a garlic's typical head. There is no hardneck form the way there is with garlic.

HARVEST. Dig gently in summer, when the foliage falls over and turns brown.

STORE. Keep in a cold, dry place, like garlic.

COOK. We use shallots to season sauces and salad dressing (page 316) and also for roasting whole, as in the Roasted Brussels Sprouts and Shallots on page 378. Peeled and roasted, they have a talent for absorbing butter, oil, or pan drippings, and are the ultimate garnish with which to surround a roast. You can also bake them unpeeled, the way you would garlic, then squeeze out the unctuous paste within. *Bon appétit.*

Chives and Garlic Chives

THESE ARE TWO DISTINCT SPECIES, each with their virtues. Regular chives are like very tiny scallions and grow in dense clumps. The grass-green tops have a mild oniony flavor and are a versatile garnish. Perennial, with a long season, they are there for you whenever a salad or some other dish needs to taste oniony. Snip, snip, and there you are. Garlic chives, also called Chinese chives or Chinese leeks, are similar but have a mild garlicky flavor instead, and their leaves are broader, flatter, and blue-green in color. Where regular chives have round purple-pink flower clusters the size of marbles in early summer, garlic chives' are white and bloom closer to summer's

Chives.

end. They start out like flat umbels, then gradually form spheres at least an inch across. In both cases, the flowers make a strong-tasting edible garnish.

GROW. Both types are very easy to grow from seed, and can also be purchased as started plants. They self-sow in rich garden soil, in a variety of climates, although for some reason our garlic chives are well behaved. But both are very winter hardy. Cutting chives back before the flowers form will encourage fresh new growth to spring up. (Let some bloom if you can't bear to miss the show, or want to please the bees.) Otherwise, the tips of the leaves turn yellow, making them tedious to pick and prepare for use. Once you have one clump, it's easy to propagate by dividing the clump in spring and replanting. Extend the season by tucking a clump into a cold frame or the corner of a greenhouse. Although they will go dormant in cool winters, new growth will emerge extra early in spring.

HARVEST. Pick as needed, snipping with scissors.

STORE. Chives lose their flavor when dried, but can be snipped and frozen in ice cubes.

COOK. Little chive snippings are the ubiquitous decoration for vichyssoise and numerous other soups, baked potatoes with sour cream, omelets or scrambled eggs, and a long list of dishes that need their elfin touch. They're best added at or near the end of cooking to preserve their flavor. You can always enliven a salad with them if there is a chive plant outside the kitchen door. Even if you've just cut it back to promote fresh growth, there's still enough foliage to introduce a note of onion-ness. Chive flowers are fine to strew over a salad but make an assertive mouthful. Individual florets are more subtle and look just as pretty.

When you do cut back your chives and have a sudden excess, put them into a blended soup such as Green Gazpacho (page 287) or make a green-tinted vichyssoise. Garlic chives can be used like regular chives, but since the leaves have more substance they have more potential for cooking. In Chinese cooking they are cut while in bud and simmered with other ingredients, stuffed into dumplings, or dropped into soups.

THE BEET FAMILY

- **BEETS**
- **SWISS CHARD**
- **SPINACH**

OFTEN CALLED THE AMARANTH FAMILY (Amaranthaceae) after that noble ancient grain, this group also includes some weeds that are especially bothersome for gardeners, such as lamb's quarters and redroot pigweed. But let's celebrate its inclusion of beets, Swiss chard, and spinach. What would we do without those?

All of these crops prefer cool weather, unlike the weedy cousins named above. If you have trouble growing any of them well, a seaweed-based fertilizer can often help. The simplest answer is to amend the soil with one of the many dried seaweed products available as fertilizers, which are rich in trace elements. As we mentioned in Chapter 1, trace elements have an important effect on plant growth despite being needed in only minute amounts. We've recommended using greensand, a slowly available fertilizer, as a sort of trace element insurance policy. If you check catalogs or the fertilizer shelves at your local garden store you'll find a lot of other products claiming to provide a wide range of trace elements. These products may not always be necessary, but it is wise to be aware of their existence in case you ever suspect you need them. On some soils beets, in particular, may benefit greatly from the addition of small amounts of the element boron. Ask your Extension Service whether boron deficiency is common in your area, what boron carrier they recommend, and how much. Usually you put on just a small amount, like a dusting of powdered sugar to top a cake.

The larvae of leaf miners, which make wandering tunnels in the leaves, can be a problem with all three of these crops if the infestation is severe. They are worse in the early part of the season, so one solution is to just grow a late crop. For early ones, floating row covers can be applied when the crop is first planted, to prevent the fly from laying the eggs from which the larvae hatch.

Beets

BEETS ARE SO GOOD TO EAT, and so versatile, it's a wonder they aren't part of everyone's weekly diet. Nutritionists praise this easy-to-grow vegetable for its fiber load, its rich antioxidants, and its reputation as a digestive tune-up, which goes back to Classical times. It

Red Ace beets.

Beet greens are tasty eaten raw if they're picked when only a few inches tall, and make a fine ingredient in a baby leaf salad mix.

TOP: Chioggia beets display a striking bull's-eye pattern when sliced. BOTTOM: Bull's Blood beets to be harvested in winter as baby leaf salad greens.

also does double duty, just as turnips do, by providing great-tasting greens atop that famously swollen taproot. So you get two crops for the price of one. Most beets are the classic crimson hue, but try growing golden beets sometime. They're a gorgeous orange color on the outside, bright yellow within. Since they don't bleed red, they're handy for use with light-colored foods you'd prefer not to stain. (We also like the cylindrical beets, which are so handy for slicing because they make such nice uniform rounds.) The Chioggia type, named for a town near Venice, is fun to grow. Cut crosswise, it sports a dramatic red-and-white bull's-eye pattern. It's also quite sugary, and gorgeous to serve, either cooked or as a raw, ultra-thin wafer.

GROW. Beets can be direct-sown after the ground has warmed up a little in spring, then in successive harvests all the way up to six weeks before the first frost. We often grow them from transplants to reduce the need for thinning (see pages 225 to 235).

Beets were originally a wild seacoast crop. If you're having trouble growing them well, the problem might be a lack of trace elements, and especially boron, in your soil.

Beet foliage sometimes gets a leaf-spot disease in summer, which can be discouraged somewhat by crop rotation (see pages 43 to 52). But because it mostly happens with mature leaves, which are generally eaten cooked, and since their taste is not affected, it's not a serious problem. Meadow voles, on the other hand, can be a more serious pest. They are fruit eaters by choice, so they go for those sugar-filled roots with gusto. It helps to leave enough space between rows that voles can't take cover easily, and are thereby exposed to predators. For trapping voles, see page 150.

HARVEST. Beets you are growing just for the greens can be pulled at any time. If you're taking them from a crop that you're also using for roots, just cut some of the good outer leaves, a few from each plant, so that you've left enough greenery to feed the roots. Be sure to cut the stems too, which are sweet and delicious. You can also steal little beet roots from the row, taking every other one and letting the ones on either side grow. This is a great thing to do when you're planning to cook baby beets together with their tops—a wonderful dish.

Beet greens are tasty eaten raw if they're picked when only a few inches tall, and make a fine ingredient in a baby leaf salad mix. Red-leaved varieties such as Bull's Blood or the red-veined Red Ace are especially attractive, sparking a salad with color.

STORE. Beets last a long time in storage, but of all the root crops they are the most demanding of high humidity. The refrigerator is usually moist enough—in fact, beets can sometimes turn moldy inside it—but in a root cellar that is not sufficiently damp, beets can get soft too quickly. It helps to go in and splash the floor and walls with a bucket of water every couple of days to maintain high humidity, spritz them with a hose, or even install a little low-volume mister, as we have done with great success. But having said that, don't give up on your beets if they do soften or shrivel a bit. Even after they've started to lose their firmness, they make acceptable eating and are fine for juicing.

Beet greens will keep longer in the fridge than, say, a butterhead lettuce, so it's okay to put them in a plastic bag if you're eating the roots and saving the tops for later. But after a week the tops will start to yellow and lose their goodness.

COOK. Since beets are so full of goodies, it's a shame to let any of their essence escape. You can tell by the color the water turns when you boil beets that something is lost in draining. One way to conserve the juices is to simmer beets in just enough water to evaporate while you are tenderizing them, or else reduce the simmering water afterward until it becomes a syrup, perhaps with a little butter. Add a little honey too if you like, but since beets are naturally sweet this is rarely necessary. Brand-new, marble-size beet roots can be simmered along with their greens in this manner. Grating beet roots into a soup, such as the Beef Borscht on page 272 is a wonderful way to use them as well.

If you go to Europe, or to a store that caters to an old-world clientele, you may see whole baked beets for sale. Their caramelized goodness came as such a pleasant surprise for us that baking them unpeeled soon became our favorite way to cook them. We try to keep some in the fridge at all times, either for heating up as a quick vegetable dish, or in a salad. (See the recipe on page 298 for baking instructions.) Raw, grated beets have become popular in salads as well. Beets are usually peeled unless they are small.

As for the fact that beets bleed when cut, use this to advantage. Juice made from them is a terrific food coloring. The recipe for Pink Applesauce on page 448 is one example. Use beets to make a red sauce a little redder, to create pink lemonade and pink champagne, or to turn a glass of white wine into a Kir, without that expensive bottle of Crème de Cassis.

And by the way, that pernicious pigweed we scorned above? Try it in a stir-fry. And cook the lamb's quarters and redroot pigweed the way you would creamed spinach. Both are edible, tasty, and as abundant as you could ever ask a crop to be.

Swiss Chard

SWISS CHARD AND BEETS are botanically the same vegetable, except that beets have been bred to produce large roots, and Swiss chard to produce large leaves with thick, juicy stems and ribs. In Britain it's called leaf beet, as opposed to beetroot. In Austalia it's silverbeet. At our place we just refer to it as chard, with all due respect to the Swiss.

Golden beets.

This narrow-stemmed chard, picked small, is tender enough to put in a salad.

Chard is a little more heat tolerant than other garden greens, and very cold tolerant as well. It is one of the few crops left standing as winter sets in, and sometimes regrows from its roots in spring, even here in Maine. And it has even taken on a bit of glamour, thanks to the edible landscaping movement. Beautiful red-ribbed chard varieties such as Ruby have been around for a long time, but now there are rainbow-hued mixes such as Bright Lights, selected from heirloom strains. View them with the late-afternoon sun shining behind them, and it's like having a stained glass window in your garden.

GROW. Like beet greens, chard can be sown thickly as a cut-and-come-again baby leaf green for fresh eating, or sown farther apart for larger cooking greens. In fact, directions for growing beets in general apply to chard as well. Voles attack the fleshy part of the lower stems and upper roots, which are apparently delicious to them. They know a beet when they see one.

We are especially fond of chard as a winter crop, sown in mid-July and transplanted into the greenhouse.

HARVEST. Whether the leaves are small, medium, or large, just keep picking them and they will regrow.

STORE. The more mature the chard leaf, the longer it will keep under refrigeration, but as with all leaf crops, just-picked is best.

COOK. Few greens are as versatile as chard, and I can't imagine planting a garden without it. If picked at baby-leaf size, about three inches tall, it's tender

Voles are a serious problem in our garden. We trap them with a simple wooden box containing unbaited mousetraps.

and mild in salads. A little later, when the leaves have grown to the size of your hand, they are more firm-textured, yet still salad worthy, sliced into thin ribbons and combined with softer greens such as lettuce. At this point they are especially good if briefly steamed; we refer to this stage as "butter chard," both for the tender, buttery texture and for the simple logic of topping them with butter and a little salt.

Once mature, chard is really two vegetables in one. The stems, which continue up the center of the leaves as ribs, need more cooking time than the leaves do. If serving them together, it's best to cut out the stalks and ribs, chop them, and start them cooking first, then add the leaves after about four minutes. The varieties with brilliant red, yellow, orange, or pink stems and ribs lose some of that coloring in cooking, especially the red pigments, which are water soluble. Those in the yellow to orange spectrum keep more of their brightness.

Chard leaves soften a bit more than kale leaves do when cooked, but not as much as spinach, nor do they absorb as much water. You can place a bed of them under fish without having them ooze their juice onto the plate. If cut into pieces they keep their shape fairly well when dropped into soups, stir-fries, and fried rice. The stems, sliced and sautéed, are great in those dishes too.

Spinach

OF ALL THE GREENS WE COOK, spinach is the most popular, with its smooth texture and rich green taste. Why is it so often the butt of jokes about children being forced to eat it, with a champion like Popeye needed to boost its appeal? Perhaps because there is a good spinach, grown well in its proper cool season, and its evil twin: spinach grown with too much nitrogen, too little calcium, or in weather that's too hot. Good spinach is both mellow and sprightly and you can taste the seasonal changes in the crop. Spring spinach has a tender freshness. Summer spinach, if you can grow it at all, is more harsh. Spinach grown in fall and winter is the best of all, sublimely sweet. Left in the ground until spring, the sweetness is soon lost and the flavor coarsens as it prepares to go to seed.

GROW. Spinach is a cool-weather green that does poorly in a climate where spring is brief, with the flame of summer heat licking at its heels. There it will quickly go to seed, urged on not only by warmth but also by lengthening days. Planting modern bolt-resistant or "long-standing" varieties such as Tyee will help, but in many areas it's best to limit the crop to fall and winter. Seeds should be sown just as the days are cooling off, but with enough time for the plants to mature before deep cold sets in. For that time of year a fast-growing variety such as Space is best. For our winter crop we sow in the unheated greenhouse the third week in September. We'll be eating spinach at Thanksgiving dinner, and the plants will keep producing until they start going to seed in late March. Gardeners may also have luck sowing a long-standing variety in time for the crop to germinate just before freezing weather, then letting it sit there and do its growing in the spring.

Spinach needs excellent drainage, and well-balanced fertility. Heavy applications of high-nitrate fertilizer lead to unhealthy nitrate levels for us, when we consume the leaves, and to accumulations of oxalic acid, which is also detrimental to humans. Adding well-aged manure or compost is a much safer bet, and some lime if your soil is acid or low in calcium.

HARVEST. Once a spinach patch gets going it's hard to keep up with the picking. With each cut, more will grow. Using a sharp little knife makes the job go quickly—in fact we have spinach races at our farm. The trick is to collect the harvested leaves with one hand while you cut the stems with a knife held in the other. When you have at least six leaves, you drop them quickly into a bucket or large bowl that is positioned close to the hand that collects the leaves. In fall the more you pick your spinach patch, the more productive it will be. In spring you'll get one enthusiastic flush of leaves before the weather gets too hot.

STORE. Spinach keeps better in a bag in the fridge than most greens, but even it will start to get slimy before too long.

COOK. How spinach is cooked makes as much difference as how it's grown. A soggy wad of it, with stems dangling down, will not tempt anyone, young or old. Chopping it before cooking will turn out a tidier mound, and removing the tougher stems will tame it as well. The moisture factor is a little harder to tackle. Unlike kale, spinach holds on to a lot of water, which can be squeezed or pressed out, but with some loss of nutrients. Often I will steam spinach for just a few minutes to wilt it, then press very gently to release a bit of the water. Another way is to toss it briefly in a large pan with a

Spinach grown in fall and winter is the best of all, sublimely sweet.

Spinach grown for baby leaf harvest.

bit of fat—such as butter, bacon fat, or olive oil—and garlic. A pair of tongs is a great tool for stirring it around until it has just wilted. It will not need draining, and can be served just as is, added to quiche fillings, casseroles, and open-faced omelets, or set under meat, fish, and eggs.

You'll need to pick a lot of spinach to feed a crowd, because it shrinks dramatically when cooked. Spinach is also used in hearty salads and will stand up well to heavy dressings with honey and mustard, or bacon. But personally I find spinach salads a bit too chewy unless baby spinach with leaves no longer than 2 inches long is used. It's tender and tasty enough to please us all.

THE CARROT FAMILY

• CARROTS	• HERBS IN THE CARROT FAMILY:
• FENNEL	
• CELERY	• Parsley
• CELERY ROOT	• Dill
• PARSNIPS	• Cilantro
	• Chervil

Nelson carrots.

FOR THIS GROUP two Latin names are commonly used, both referring to attributes of its members' flowers. One, Apiaceae, suggests their attractiveness to bees, and the other, Umbelliferae, their shape, which is that of a little umbrella. And in fact, the luring of beneficial insect pollinators and predators is one good reason to have these plants in your garden. If you are growing umbelliferous herbs for their tasty seeds (see below), or saving seeds from any of the carrot family crops for next year's planting, this attribute becomes very apparent as the bees

and other insects bustle around them, doing their work. All your other crops will benefit from the presence of these insect helpers in keeping your plants well pollinated and pest-free.

These plants send down a taproot, that is, one long central root from which smaller side roots eventually branch out. As such, they appreciate a deeply dug, reasonably light and stone-free soil, which that taproot can easily penetrate. Dense clay, rocky soil, or a hardpan layer will be obstacles to them. Most of them do best in cool weather. Seed germination, which is often difficult for members of this family, is especially hard in summer. The trick is to use fresh seed, have the soil on the surface very fine textured, and never let it dry out.

Carrots

CARROTS WERE BRED long ago from the common Queen Anne's lace plant. Dig up this familiar weed, with its lacy white flower heads, and you'll find a skinny, white taproot that's not much use in the kitchen. The horticultural carrot, on the other hand, is bursting with flavor and nutrients. Its orange color proclaims the presence of carotene, a powerful antioxidant.

It's fun to grow carrots in other shades besides orange. But we've never found the white or yellow ones as tasty as the orange. The bright red types, with boosted lycopene (another prized antioxidant), are better, at least when cooked. But as for the mottled purple-and-orange ones, well, I suppose their gaudiness would suit a special late-winter Mardi Gras dinner—if they grew at that time of year. But late winter and early spring are the only times we aren't likely to be harvesting carrots in our garden. Our spring harvest of them, in an unheated greenhouse, begins the second week in May. Later sowings get us through the summer and fall. And a mid-August sowing provides us with the best carrots of all: those that are sweetened by the frosts of late fall, and in winter with the protection of a greenhouse. These give us great eating all the way up until the ten-hour day returns in early February, and they start to send up flower stalks to make seed. As biennials, which grow one year and reproduce the next, they are doing what nature has programmed them to do. But their roots will lose their good flavor and sweetness.

GROW. If you have a clay soil, till in a couple inches of peat moss where the carrots will be grown. Aerating the soil deeply with a spading fork or broadfork (page 224) before sowing carrots is also a good practice.

Carrots are always direct-sown, not grown from transplants. It is crucial to keep the soil moist after sowing them, even if you have to sprinkle them lightly with a hose several times a day, so that the soil surface is always dark with moisture. If you can't do this when you're away at work, put a board over the row to keep it moist, and check it when you come home to see if they are up. Once you see those delicate little points of green you know they're going to be okay, and you can leave the board off. They'll still need lots of water, but you can be a little less obsessive about it. Your rows will need to be thinned if the seedlings are any closer than 2 inches apart, which is a tedious job but a

Starting with Vegetables

MIREPOIX. Onions, carrots, and celery are usually the first things to put on the counter when you set out to make a stock, a stew, and in many cases a soup, sauce, roasted meat dish, or braise. The mélange of these three, in roughly equal parts and finely chopped, give the dish a subtle extra depth. They can be added directly to the pot, or sautéed first in a pan, with butter, over medium-low heat. Try sweating them until tender by covering the pan; if you want the flavor more robust, uncover them toward the end and brown them slightly. Be sure to check the pan and stir frequently throughout, to avoid burning.

In France this would be called a *mirepoix.* In Italy it would be a *soffrito,* with finely chopped garlic and pancetta or bacon added. For Spanish or Louisiana-style dishes, peppers are often substituted for carrots.

necessary one. Keeping the bed weeded is important too, since carrots' feathery fronds do not shade out weeds well.

HARVEST. You can start to pull carrots as soon as they are fully colored—usually when they are finger-size—leaving the others in the row to grow. Although baby carrots are considered a delicacy, good flavor in carrots is less a matter of size than it is a matter of good soil, moisture, and cool temperatures. We've enjoyed meals of huge, lumpy storage carrots from the root cellar in midwinter that had excellent flavor; they just needed a little more cooking. If your soil is loose and fluffy you can often just grasp a carrot by its shoulders, just below the soil level, and extract it with a firm, upright tug. But to avoid breaking the roots, it helps to loosen the earth next to the row with a spading fork, giving it a gentle wiggle. Cut off the tops right away, leaving just an inch or two of green. Yes, the long, lacy fronds are pretty, but the evaporation on their leaf surfaces will draw moisture from the roots and make them limp. With young, freshly dug carrots, we often leave on the green sprig when we cook them; it's both pretty and edible. Some cooks even flavor soups with carrot tops, since you can taste something of their kinship with parsley. But on an older carrot, the top inch or so of the root is not tasty at all. The little tail at a carrot's end also has little to offer.

STORE. We hose down carrots before they are brought into the house to eat, but we leave the soil on those headed for the root cellar. There they will keep well until spring. After a while they will get a little fuzzy with side roots, but you can scrub those off and enjoy the last of the crop while you're waiting for the spring carrots to grow.

COOK. Like all root vegetables, carrots need a good scrubbing before they are kitchen-worthy, but it's not necessary to peel them unless they have blemishes you find unappetizing. Carrot skin is not tough, and it has food value.

Both the flavor and the nutrients in carrots hold up well in cooking, and can even be enhanced by it. The first little carrots in spring are tender and are great to combine with other early treasures such as asparagus, peas, baby turnips, scallions,

Fennel.

and eventually the first of the new potatoes. Just by themselves they're delectable, whether lightly steamed and buttered, or raw in a bowl on the table. Small fresh carrots are best steamed or sautéed to the point that they still have a bit of crunch. Older or larger carrots lend full flavor to long-simmered dishes. As such they are a mainstay in the culinary trinity called mirepoix: carrots, celery, and onions. You'll notice that these are the first things to set on the counter when you start to make many of the recipes in this book. Browning carrots, whether in a pan or in the oven, caramelizes their sugars wonderfully, though you need to watch them carefully so they don't burn. Roasted carrots, with or without other savory root vegetables, are delectable.

Fennel

IT'S A WONDER that fennel is not more widely grown in home gardens, with its long season and ease of cultivation. An Italian import enjoyed by Thomas Jefferson in his gardens at Monticello, it has become naturalized on the West Coast as a volunteer, but somehow the tradition of growing it lapsed elsewhere.

There are two types of fennel plants. The one called leaf fennel, grown as an herb, has tender stems, beautiful fernlike foliage, yellow flowers, and tasty seeds. The bulb type, generally called Florence fennel, has been bred to widen at the bottom into a swollen mass of overlapping stem bases. Bulb fennel will make flowers, too, but if you're just after the flowers and seeds for ornament and flavoring, it makes more sense to grow leaf fennel. In climates milder than ours it acts like a perennial, sending up new flowering shoots each year. A type called bronze fennel, with dark bronze foliage, is especially beautiful in the herb garden and we sometimes grow it as an annual in ours.

GROW. We enjoy fennel from early summer until frost and even beyond, if some of the last remaining bulbs are dug and stored for several weeks in the root cellar or refrigerator. Planting several successions of fennel ensures a full summer and fall's worth of eating, and by overlapping them we often have the choice of small tender bulbs and the larger ones as well. We've even found that baby fennel plants can resprout from roots left in the ground after harvest. For spring crops, grow a bolt-resistant variety.

Because of its taproot, fennel does not like to be transplanted, and may bolt. However, we have gotten away with transplants by starting it in soil blocks (page 230). When direct-sowing, sow thinly in a fine-textured seedbed and keep the soil consistently moist until germination, just the way you would for carrots. The best bulbs are produced in a fertile soil and in cool weather, so a fall crop is likely to be your best one.

HARVEST. It's best to harvest fennel before the bulbs become tough and woody. Cut them off at soil level with a sharp knife. Since an entire plant is quite large and unwieldy, we slice off the stems. Any stems we plan to use for cooking can be dealt with separately.

STORE. Mature fennel bulbs will keep at least a month in the root cellar in fall, or in a bag in the refrigerator.

> Mature fennel bulbs will keep at least a month in the root cellar in fall, or in a bag in the refrigerator.

COOK. Fennel has a mild, slightly sweet anise-like flavor, which is very pronounced when served raw, but much mellowed by cooking. For raw use in salads, small bulbs are best, but larger, older bulbs can also be used if the toughest outermost layers are removed, and the interior ones thinly sliced. (Wash them thoroughly, cutting out any brown parts as you go.) This is easy to do if you stack several of the curved layers, cupped together, grasp them at the top, and slice the bases thinly with a mandoline (see page 302). The mature ones are also delicious roasted, grilled, or braised. Fennel is one of those versatile vegetables that can enhance many dishes quite apart from those where it is featured alone. Add it to the *mirepoix* described on page 153—and it will add a subtle extra depth of flavor.

When you're cooking with fennel bulbs, save a few stalks and leafy fronds for future use. The fronds are especially useful chopped and sprinkled over a dish as an herbal garnish, or as a bed on which to lay fish. Tender stems and bulbs can be used for seasoning, snacked on raw like celery, or included in a crudité platter, with a dip. Try them with the Bagna Cauda recipe on page 261.

> While celery is growing you can steal a few of the outer stalks as needed for the kitchen.

Celery.

Celery

CELERY IS A Mediterranean marsh plant, grown by Thomas Jefferson at Monticello and later popularized by 19th-century Dutch farmers who settled around Kalamazoo, Michigan. Its first role was as a crisp, tasty snack, and for many people it still is—essentially an edible utensil designed to transport cream cheese or onion dip from plate to mouth. But cooks know how all-purpose it is, and always manage to have some in the refrigerator or, better yet, in the garden. As we said on page 70, celery is a fussy plant to grow, and not the first one you would urge a beginner to try. But we'd be remiss not to introduce you to its culture, to which any competent gardener might aspire, given a little patience. If you decide that growing stalk celery is too much trouble, you can replace it with cutting celery, which has the same flavor but is bred for its leaves, not its stem, and is a good plant for the herb garden. If you do well with celery, try a red variety such as Redventure, as well.

GROW. Normally, celery would be a late-July to mid-November crop on the coast of Maine. Frost will damage the outer stalks, but we can still harvest the inner ones for weeks thereafter. And with the protection of a greenhouse or cold frame we can enjoy it until Christmas. Milder climates, of course, can keep it going even longer and have a new crop in late spring. The key is to give it extravagantly fertile soil, well enriched with compost, and twice the amount of water you would give other crops. You will need to sow it indoors about ten weeks before the danger of frost has passed. The tiny seeds may take a long time to germinate. Wait until temperatures are above 50 degrees to transplant it outdoors. It is a biennial, and if it encounters an extended cold period it will think a winter has passed, and go to seed.

HARVEST. While celery is growing you can steal a few of the outer stalks as needed for the kitchen. After the heads are full and lush, harvest by cutting them off at soil level. Remove any blemished leaves. When celery is left in the ground the outer stems will begin to toughen. You'll be able to see this by slicing a cross-section of a lower stem. If its channels are hollow rather than filled with moisture, the stem will not be tender, although you could season a stock with it if need be. The heart of the plant, composed of newer stalks and protected by the outer ones, will be harvestable longer.

STORE. Celery will keep up to about a month in the root cellar or a spare fridge.

COOK. Home-grown celery is fresher and livelier. It's also topped with abundant foliage so good for the stock pot, or for seasoning a salad. And it's a vegetable that's great to keep on hand. You can't stuff a chicken without celery, or make chicken salad from the leftovers. In fact tuna salad, potato salad, or egg salad would be poor without it too. And of course it's one of the three essential parts of a mirepoix (see page 153).

Although used chiefly as a supporting player, there are ways to use celery front and center, as in the Celery Heart Salad on page 305. Make a cream of celery soup, or serve it sliced on the diagonal in a side dish with reduced cream, dill, and a grating of nutmeg. But try not to overcook it: With celery it's all about the crunch.

Celery Root

THIS KNOBBY VEGETABLE, also called celeriac and turnip-rooted celery, is not exactly a root but rather a celery plant bred to have an enlarged storage organ at the base of the stem. You can see it plainly in the garden, crowned by normal-looking celery foliage, and plain it is: a greenish-beige sphere, sitting at ground level. Dig it up and it is more homely yet, with tangled, tentacle-like roots dangling from its base. But once you discover its virtues you'll want to grow your own every year, since it is not commonly available in markets.

GROW. Celery root, like stem celery, must have soil of more-than-average fertility and plenty of water, although neither are quite as critical as with the stem crop. Celery root is not a quick crop to grow. It must be sown indoors at least six weeks before it is transplanted into the garden, and it can take three or four months to get roots of decent size. (We rob a few small ones here and there in the meantime, as they're just as flavorful as the large ones.) While you are waiting, the aboveground parts of the plant are handsome to look at, with bright green, healthy looking stems and swollen bottoms. The lower stems will start to bend over, and it's fine to pull these off; in fact it will make for smoother roots.

HARVEST. Before you bring the roots into the house, chop off their leaves and stems unless you need a few of them to lend celery flavor to a stock. (They were not bred for tenderness.) Then chop off the dangling roots as well, so that you're just left with the solid, round knobs. If you're using them right away, or keeping them in the refrigerator, hose them off, washing away as much of the embedded grit as you can. But it's not necessary to clean them if you're going to store them in the root cellar.

STORE. Celery root is a champion when it comes to storage, and will keep eight months or more in either a root cellar or refrigerator.

COOK. Even after an outdoor trim and prewash, you may have a ways to go with your knobs, cutting off protuberances and grit-filled crevices with a heavy sharp knife. Orbs that were softball-size will be baseball-size by the time you're done, and might lose up to half their weight in the process. If you're not using them right away, you can float them in a bowl of water acidified with a little lemon juice or vinegar to keep them from browning. But in most cooked dishes, a little discoloration is unimportant.

Europeans, who are more familiar with celeriac than they are with our stem celery, enjoy celery root raw. They'll grate, shred, or julienne the hard off-white flesh and marinate it in a salad dressing overnight. Whether a

Celery root.

vinaigrette, a mayonnaise, or a mustardy rémoulade—a favorite in France—it will be absorbed to tasty effect. A generous mound on a bed of fresh salad greens makes a substantial individual salad that can replace the starch in a meal. The flavor is like that of celery but milder, with a hint of parsley, a close relative. In Germany, celery root in a salad is more commonly cooked than raw.

Compared with potatoes, celery roots are a bit firmer and less starchy, but the two cook up beautifully together. One of our favorite dishes consists of potatoes and root celery combined in equal amounts, simmered until tender, and mashed (page 396). And a puree of celery root alone is exquisite, without any of the gumminess you get with pureed potatoes. We add it sliced to scalloped potatoes. A more unusual dish is the Celery Root Cutlet recipe on page 390. You'll also find celery root a wonderful addition to soups, stews, and medleys of roasted vegetables.

Parsnips

ROOT CROPS ARE RARELY GLAMOROUS, and the parsnip is no exception, with its off-white color and slightly lumpy shape, fat on top, skinny at the bottom. But like many fall vegetables, it is naturally sweet in cold weather: in this case almost dessert-sweet. After a long undramatic season of growth in the garden, from spring planting to late, frosty autumn, the roots are fat, sugary, and ready to dig. But in fall other roots crops can be dug as well, and since parsnips keep so well in the soil, many people save them for a spring treat, or a midwinter one if the ground is unfrozen.

GROW. Parsnips have a year-long lease on their garden row. In they go in early spring, direct-sown, and there they remain until spring comes the following year. Getting them off to a good start is important, since they are even more temperamental about germination than carrots are (see page 153). It also helps to mulch them to keep in moisture and cut down on weeding.

HARVEST. You'll probably need a spade or a spading fork to unearth these treasures. To avoid stabbing or breaking them, do it carefully, loosening the soil all around them and then pulling them up by the shoulders or by the stem, with your fingers.

STORE. Parsnips will keep fine refrigerated or cellared, but are even better when kept in the ground until it thaws.

COOK. Parsnips need a lot of scrubbing, and may need peeling, too, if the roots are discolored or if you want a very smooth puree. Most of the time we leave them unpeeled, and we haven't found the need to remove the core either, as some cooks do, even with very large ones. Just slice off the dark area at the top where the stem begins.

Butter and parsnips are made for each other, so for us it's parsnips sautéed in butter, roasted in butter, or boiled, drained, and pureed with butter and cream. Try them mixed with other root vegetables such as carrots and celery root, whether in a soup or stew, roasted, or combined in a mash. A puree of parsnips also makes a good foil for fatty meats such as pork or duck, taking the place of a sweet sauce or condiment.

Even in cold climates, parsnips can be left in the ground in wintertime, then dug whenever the soil has thawed.

Herbs in the Carrot Family

GARDEN HERBS are often lumped together because of the way they are used in cooking—generally in small amounts, as seasonings. (See "Cooking with Herbs and Flowers," page 166.) But they are not always grown the same way or in the same place, as we explain on page 53. Like the vegetables in this chapter they do clump together along family lines. With a few exceptions, treated under "Herbs in Other Families" on page 165, they belong to two major groups, the carrot family and the mint family.

GROW. The herbs in the carrot clan have some of the same traits as carrots, parsnips, and such—the umbrella-shaped flowers that attract beneficial insects, the taproot, the fussiness about germination. Most are annuals (with the towering, celery-like lovage a notable exception). Although they are often direct-sown, we have had good luck setting them out as transplants when we sow soil blocks. They do best in cool weather. Dill, cilantro, and chervil, especially, are quick to bolt in heat, so it's best to grow them in the cooler weather of spring, fall, and in some cases winter. If you absolutely must have them in summer, make frequent succession plantings. You may find that the plants do this for you by dropping their seeds. We often get two generations of dill and cilantro in a summer, and then more volunteers in spring.

As with other carrot relatives, moisture will benefit these herbs. Parsley is the most frost hardy, and sown in mid-July, it will survive Maine winters in a cold frame or unheated greenhouse, although its growth slows down when the cold is severe and light levels are low. Even when solidly frozen the leaves can be used as garnishes and seasoning in winter. Come spring, parsley soon goes to seed, so it's smart to have some transplants ready to go in as soon as the ground can be worked.

HARVEST. These herbs are best harvested as needed, although we sometimes cut them and put them in a glass of water in the kitchen, for a quick snip.

STORE. The foliage of these herbs loses most of its flavor when dried, but many of them have highly aromatic, flavorful seeds that can be collected when mature and stored for future use. None of the umbelliferous herbs do especially well when brought indoors for the winter. Repeated sowings made in containers indoors are worth trying if you're determined to use these herbs year-round, and have a particularly sunny window or a greenhouse.

COOK. Below are four of the most popular and useful of the bunch. (Others found in gardens include anise, caraway, cumin, and angelica.)

Parsley

The No. 1 restaurant cliché used to be the parsley sprig garnish on the edge of the plate. Now it's parsley flecks. But

Flat-leaf parsley.

Parsley is assertive but not overwhelming, so it's a seasoning you can use in abundance.

thankfully, cooks are starting to take parsley more seriously as a bona fide ingredient. You even see the occasional parsley soup, parsley salad, and parsley pesto—all good things. The parsley story became much more interesting when the flat-leaf Italian kind became as available as the more common curly one, to both gardeners and cooks. Its flavor is more pleasant and pronounced. It doesn't have the scratchy texture that curly parsley has, and it is much easier to chop. But curly parsley is still worth growing because it's more winter hardy, looks beautiful in bouquets, gives more loft to a salad, and can still be used for garnishing if you like that retro look. It also keeps longer in a glass of water without wilting.

Parsley is rich in iron and vitamin C. Its flavor is assertive but not overwhelming, so it's a seasoning you can use in abundance. As a result, it's great for greening food up. Handfuls of it will make a mayonnaise or a pale creamy soup seriously green. It will even override the army-green color that sorrel takes on when heated, in a soup or sauce. Sprinkle it on anything white or beige, such as boiled potatoes, scallops, flounder, parsnips, or rice for a quick color rescue.

Another type of parsley, called root parsley or Hamburg parsley, is grown for its long white, starchy root, which looks like a narrow parsnip, but has a mild parsley-like flavor. More popular in Europe, it is used in soups and purees and is best brightened up with—naturally—a green parsley garnish.

Dill

The spidery fronds that make up dill foliage, often called dill weed to distinguish it from dill seed, are pretty in the garden, especially the blue-green or bronze varieties bred for ornament but nonetheless tasty. No cook wants to be without dill in summer, for making cucumber salads and sandwiches, for dressing fish dishes (hot or cold), for garnishing smoked salmon canapés, and chopping into simple vegetable preparations. Any vegetable would be enhanced by a sprinkling of fresh dill. It pairs especially well with dairy products, and makes a fine addition to creamy favorites such as Swedish meatballs, creamy veal stews, yogurt or sour cream dips, and scalloped potatoes. Use it liberally in creamy soups. Toss fistfuls of it, roughly chopped, into salads. Put it in omelets, scrambled eggs, deviled eggs, egg salad. Make a shrimp cocktail without the red glop—just vinaigrette and plenty of dill.

Bolted dill produces beautiful, flat-topped yellow flowers that are also great in salads, or as a garnish. The seeds they bear are so flavorful in pickled vegetables that they are the operative word in dilly beans and dill pickles. Dill bread is another traditional use. You can dry dill successfully—it retains more green color when dried than most herbs do—but the strength of its flavor declines quickly. The seed, however can be added to stews, soups, and other cooked dishes for a more pronounced effect.

Cilantro

If you're a cilantro lover you tend to regard cilantro haters as a little pathetic, unwilling to try anything that's unusual, ethnic, or strong. But as it turns out, they experience cilantro's taste as soapy and unpleasant and they can't help it; they were born that way. They can sniff out cilantro even when it's mixed in with hot pepper and other power flavors, in chili or curry or black bean soup. A democratic host passes the delicious herb separately, in a bowl. When the bowl reaches you, stir it liberally into your crab salad, tuck it into your taco, blanket your salsa-topped seared tuna with it, and thank your lucky genes.

Cilantro subjected to long cooking will lose its force. It also dries and freezes poorly, although you can make a pesto or herb butter out of it, and freeze it that way. Its habit of bolting in summer is annoying and requires sequential sowings for a bounteous supply. However, you'll find that even the coarser basal foliage, thin stems, and flowers carry the flavor and can be blended into a guacamole. Bolting also produces seeds so tasty that they have their own name, coriander, which is considered a spice. When ground, it is one of the basic building blocks of curry powder, and imparts a spice note to cookies, cakes, and pumpkin pies.

Chervil

This dainty-leaved herb will offend no one. It has a bit of the anise flavor it shares with tarragon, but is more subtle and can be used in greater quantities. Tedious to mince, it can be loosely chopped before tossing into a salad, and even small whole sprigs are welcome as long as the stems are small and tender. Chervil is the perfect omelet herb, blending beautifully in a fines herbes mix or by itself. Stuff it into sandwiches. Garnish deviled eggs with it. If you have a lot, make a mild pesto sauce from it, or blend it into a creamy sauce to go over vegetables. Mince it and make a compound butter to melt over fish. But don't overcook,

or its delicate flavor will be lost. We love it added to vegetables such as carrots, peas, or asparagus, at the last minute, warmed just enough to wilt it a bit. Although it's possible to dry or freeze chervil, we never do because of its winter hardiness. Even in cold climates, a cold frame can give you fresh chervil well into the winter months.

THE MINT FAMILY

- **MINT**
- **BASIL**
- **OREGANO & MARJORAM**
- **ROSEMARY**
- **SAGE**
- **THYME**
- **ANISE HYSSOP**

THE MINT FAMILY, designated as the Lamiaceae or Labiatae, dominate the culinary herbs, thanks to their aromatic, flavorful leaves, rich in essential oils. In addition to the true mints (in the genus *Mentha*), the family includes such favorites as basil, oregano, marjoram, rosemary, sage, thyme, summer and winter savory, hyssop, anise hyssop, lemon balm, perilla, and lavender—the last treasured for its scent more than its culinary possibilities, though its flowers add much to a salad.

GROW. A few of these plants, such as basil, are very frost tender and hence grown as annuals in most gardens, but most are staunchly perennial and often woody and shrublike in habit. Even some of these have limits to their cold tolerance. Rosemary, for example, spends the winter in a pot in our living room, and not all thymes survive. (Lemon thyme, in a sheltered spot in our garden, has toughed it out so far.)

FACING PAGE (top to bottom):
Dill.
Cilantro.
Chervil.

We find that with these herbs the key is good drainage and finding the right level of moisture. Mint likes a very moist soil, but the rest are happiest with the Mediterranean ideal of a moist winter and a drier summer. Rocky slopes make them feel right at home. Beds edged with warm stones and gravel paths are their Garden of Eden. In swamps, sumps, gullies, and shady wooded places they will not grow. If you avoid cutting them back in winter, even their bare stems and the autumn leaves that catch in them will provide some insulation against the cold. But we cut most everything back in springtime and remove the leaves, especially flat ones that might mat down and cause the crowns to rot. This brings in air and sunlight to encourage fresh new growth.

Each of these herbs has its particular growth habit. Mint is a rampant plant that spreads by underground stems, especially in the moist soil it loves. Unless truly parched or starved it will take over a garden, and is best grown in an out-of-the way spot, all by itself. Ours is magnificent in a long drainage ditch.

Grow basil in its own bed, with loose rich soil and plenty of space so that it can grow lush and bushy. Pinching the tips will accomplish this as well. When it goes to flower, leaf production will decline, so it helps to have a new sowing ready.

The rest of these herbs need no particular care while growing outdoors, but rosemary needs daily watering if indoors in a pot. Sage, which forms a woody bush, can be brought indoors in a pot, but it can be quite productive if left outdoors in wintertime. The foliage at the branch tips stays green well into winter,

and even dried on the bush the leaves are usable in cooking. Old sage plants can be pruned each year in early spring to keep them tidy, and they'll live a long time, but putting in new ones each year does result in compact plants with better foliage. Anise hyssop self-sows with abandon, but the seedlings are not hard to weed out.

HARVEST. The oils that give herbs their flavor are strongest just before the plants bloom, and this is when you should harvest any you plan to dry. The rest of the time, cooks just pick what they need, when they want it. That's why herbs should always be close to the house. Many do best if picked frequently, even if you don't need more than a few snips. It encourages more fresh new growth, usually at the base of the plant.

STORE. These herbs keep in a plastic bag in cold storage for a while, or in a tall glass on a windowsill, but picking fresh is always a good habit to get into. You'll notice that mint rapidly starts to grow roots in the glass if you keep it there for a few days. This group, as a whole, lends itself very well to drying. There's no mystery to it—just go out on a dry day, cut a big bunch, secure the stems with a rubber band that will hold even when the stems shrink, then hang them upside down from a string. (If you're collecting the seeds, attach a paper bag for the seeds to fall into.) Don't have a picturesque rafter from which to suspend herbs? Anything will do, even a broom handle stretched from the top of one cabinet to another—as long as it's safe from wind, moisture, and direct sunlight. When they're thoroughly dry, put them away in a bag or strip the leaves into a jar, so they don't gather dust. Replace them next year, since their flavor will gradually decline.

Another way to preserve herbs is to freeze them in oil or butter, either in small jars or in cubes made with ice trays. We've also enjoyed tucking sprays of them into bottles of vinegar, to flavor it.

COOK. See "Cooking with Herbs and Flowers," page 166 for general advice.

Cooking with Mint Family Herbs

HERE ARE SOME specifics for the mint family.

Mint

If you have a corner where mint can wander without strangling other plants you're much the richer for it, especially in summertime. Few drinks are more refreshing than cold mint tea, made in advance by steeping mint and honey in a few cupfuls of hot water, then chilling it with lots of ice and enough cold water to fill a large pitcher. Quick summer desserts are easily made by cutting up fruit with mint and a little sugar or sweet liqueur—or just mint alone. Whole mint leaves sprinkled liberally through a salad give it a refreshing spark. Try them in yogurty raitas, both savory and sweet, and sauces for meat, especially lamb. It's great in all those Greek dishes with ground lamb, such as moussaka, or as a substitute for oregano in the Lamb-Stuffed Eggplant on page 364.

The subtle differences between apple mint, chocolate mint, and other such variations are fascinating, but perhaps not worth the effort of keeping different mint types from cross-pollinating, or entangling one another with their wayward roots. But the more common peppermint and spearmint do shine in different ways. Peppermint, as the name suggests, has the sharper, stronger flavor and makes mint tea really minty. Spearmint has a more subtle flavor, if you can call any mint subtle, and we think it's the best for cooking if you have to choose just one.

Mint is easily dried and sustains its flavor very well. Hot mint tea is restorative in cold weather or during sickness, especially the tummy kind. Eliot enjoys a cup of it after a long, indulgent meal.

Basil

Cooks love basil for its wonderful flavor, welcoming aroma, and the suave softness of its foliage. We often use large leaves whole in tossed salads, or tucked among sliced tomatoes. In winter, basil pesto we've frozen goes into pasta and omelets. (For Pesto Sauce see page 320.) In summer its cohorts are warm-weather fruiting vegetables like zucchini, eggplant, and peppers. It does not abide the cold. It doesn't even like the fridge, so I tend to pick it just before using, or keep a few fragrant sprigs in a jar of water on the counter for a quick little snip. Basil lovers tremble when they hear frost warnings and rush to gather armloads while there's still time.

I rarely mince basil; a coarse chop will do. Often I'll stack the big leaves and slice them very thinly to make ribbons. These are beautiful scattered on almost anything, whether the green type or a deep purple variety such as Red Rubin. Purple Ruffles has a less intense purple color

TOP: Mint.
BOTTOM: Basil.

and more crinkly texture, but it makes a nice garnish and is also good whole in salads. Basil lovers collect varieties with spicy flavors like cinnamon and clove, many of them wonderful in Asian food, especially Thai-inspired curries and vegetable dishes. Lemon basil, with small narrow leaves, is a lovely herb to cook with, and turns something as basic as buttered yellow crookneck squash into a celebration of summer.

Oregano and Marjoram

These two have similar, somewhat minty flavors, but marjoram is a little milder and sweeter. We like having both in the herb garden because of their attractive little rounded purple-and-pink flower clusters, great for bouquets and great for the bees; and both of them wind up in tomato sauces, on pizza, and in Greek dishes such as moussaka. They combine well with any of the summer fruiting vegetables, especially tomatoes and eggplant, but are also great in fall and winter dishes such as baked whole onions or squash soup. For this reason it's good to dry a few bunches of them for year-round use. For fresh use in salads, marjoram blends in best. That's also the one to reach for to enhance a number of cooked vegetable such as asparagus, summer squash, or leeks, when you want an herb with a bit more delicacy.

Rosemary

We would hate to cook without rosemary. In summer its stiff little branches are great for seasoning grilled meats and vegetables or sprinkling on the pizza

TOP TO BOTTOM:
Oregano.
Rosemary.
Sage.

we make in our outdoor oven. In fall it's essential with oven-roasted artichokes (page 359). In winter, we bring pots indoors where they struggle along, looking like little bonsai pines. But they keep us in sprigs big enough to poke under the skin of a chicken or snip into a dish of steamed carrots glazed with honey (page 386). When the light starts to return in late winter, the plant sends out fresh growth at the tips, which is so pleasantly soft in texture that it's graceful in salads, without any twigginess. Dried rosemary barely softens, even in cooking.

Rosemary, at our house, is snipped liberally into stews, bean dishes, and fish soups, especially ones that are Mediterranean in style. Any marinades or rubs we make for meat are apt to have rosemary in them. Lemon, garlic, and rosemary are frequent teammates. The only time it doesn't flavor our scalloped potatoes is when sage is used instead.

Sage

Sage is not just for making sausage, or turkey stuffing. Its beautiful gray-green leaves have crept into our kitchen for good. It started with little new potatoes, steamed in a covered pan with nothing more than their own moisture—plus butter and sage. Then sage became habitual in an otherwise classic fettuccine Alfredo, in spaghetti squash (page 398) and poked under the skin of roast chicken (page 421). It recurs in many of the recipes in this book. Our grilled cheese sandwiches have sage leaves tucked under the cheese. Frequently they're used whole, but they are easy to chop. Just stack a few on top of each other and slice thinly, crosswise, with a sharp little knife.

Thyme

Thyme is the ultimate all-purpose herb, equally good fresh or dried, although the uses are not interchangeable. Fresh thyme enhances a salad as is, but dried thyme is improved by the softening power of heat. In either case, its flavor seems to blend with almost anything. It's in every herb bouquet added to a stock or stew. It's in the flour used for dredging chops or veal scallops before frying. It's in marinades. The tiny leaves invariably enhance vegetable side dishes. And omelets. And garlic toast.

Ah, the tiny leaves. They are thyme's one big problem, apart from its iffy winter hardiness in the north. It's not possible to "strip the leaves from the stem" as writers always advise. The stems break, whether they are young or old, fresh or dried. You must pluck them off one by one. Fortunately, a little thyme goes a long way in most dishes. When making a stew or braising a large cut of meat, we wrap a few thyme sprigs in a bundle and tie it with string, then fish it out when the dish is ready to serve, a classic technique. You can also convey thyme's flavor by laying small branches of it atop a savory tart or gratin of summer vegetables, and it will impart its savor both to the dish itself and to the air around it when brought to table.

Anise Hyssop

Neither an anise nor a hyssop, this mint relative is so beautiful in the garden, with its purple flower spikes, that many gardeners plant it not knowing it has a place in the kitchen. The leaves are minty and quite sweet, with a touch of anise (a licorice-like herb). Anise hyssop can be used as a mint substitute, but you'll come to know it as a flavor in its own right. Leaves can be used whole in salads, and steeped in boiling water for a soothing tea. Its sweetness complements cooked carrots or parsnips, and is especially fine in fruit dishes, whether fresh medleys or pies, tarts, and sorbets. Add a sprig of it, flower and all, to your favorite rum drink in summertime.

HERBS IN OTHER FAMILIES

- **BAY**
- **LEMON VERBENA**

(For chives, see page 146; for tarragon see page 198.)

Bay

A LONER among the other herb clans, bay is a member of the myrtle family (Myrtaceae), largely populated by woody evergreen plants rich in essential oils. Also called bay laurel (as opposed to the mountain laurel that blooms in eastern woods in late spring), it was the herb used to crown poets in classical times, sacred to Apollo, and celebrated as a soother of stomachs. Rumors of its toxicity are false, though one needs to respect its powers. It is a uterine stimulant—not an herb to consume in large quantities while pregnant, although the token bay leaf in the stew is fine.

TOP TO BOTTOM:
Thyme.
Anise hyssop.
Bay.

GROW. In California we have worshipped at the feet of towering bay trees, stuffing branches into our suitcases to take home. Our own little potted bays, brought in for the winter, struggle. Bay is easily killed with kindness by overwatering. Give it well-draining soil, and never let it sit in water that has collected in the pot saucer. Wash its leaves with a sponge if you see the stickiness that indicates scale insects, or the webs made by spider mites. We find our plants put out fresh growth when fed a balanced liquid fertilizer or compost tea (compost steeped in water), and also in response to the lengthening days of late winter.

COOKING WITH HERBS AND FLOWERS

THERE IS NO hard and fast difference between an herb and a spice. As a botanical term, "herb" and the adjective "herbaceous" refer to plants with soft green stems, as opposed to hard woody ones. But this excludes several plants that cooks regard as herbs, such as rosemary, sage, and lavender. In culinary speech, herbs tend to be plants with intensely flavored and/or fragrant leaves or seeds. What we call spices usually come from plant parts other than foliage. Often these are the seeds, as with coriander, but sometimes the roots, as with ginger, or the bark, as with cinnamon. Mace is the covering around a nutmeg seed. Many popular spices are from tropical plants that cannot be grown in the temperate zone, although sometimes lovers of fresh food find a way. We've successfully grown ginger in our greenhouse.

The essential oils that give these plants their fragrance, flavor, and sometimes therapeutic effects are powerful chemicals that cooks learn to use with a controlled hand. People have their own preferences, and a flavor that's addictive for one might repel another. Cooks find their own middle ground between an amount that overpowers and one too timid to matter. You'll notice, for example, how a tossed salad can moderate quite a bit of an herb's flavor, just as it moderates the heat of arugula or the mustards. Go ahead—toss in handfuls of mint, parsley, basil, or even strong-flavored lovage if your diners are fans.

In our "occasional use" category are lovage, lemon balm, summer and winter savory. Ones we haven't yet tried to grow include lemon grass and epazote. But we'll get to them. It's an adventure to experiment with new herbs, even ones that might be tricky in one's climate. We're coming to realize how arbitrary the division is between sweet and savory dishes, especially when it comes to herbs. Why is it mint's job to represent the "sweet" category, when lemon verbena can shine there too? And delicious ice creams and sorbets can be made with lavender, tarragon, bay, basil, and thyme.

Many common ornamental flowers can add color and flavor as edible garnishes, and may even contain a drop of sweet nectar when picked. (*Caution:* Not all flowers are safe to eat and some, such as daphne, are highly toxic.)

The petals of nasturtium, bee balm, calendula, marigolds, roses, violets, and daylilies (sweet and crunchy!) are good choices. The vegetable garden also yields a few, such as the flavorful blossoms of bolted arugula—or any brassica for that matter—and the squash blossoms used for the fritters on page 262.

The herb garden itself is a treasure trove of flower garnishes, and herb blossoms often have seasoning power equal to that of their leaves or seeds. Tiny florets of lavender make a salad sparkle with their unmistakable taste and neon-blue color. Borage flowers (with their coarse, furry calyxes removed) add a brilliant true blue to a dessert. The entire mint family, which includes not only the true mints but also marjoram, oregano, basil, and anise hyssop, have flavorful flowers ranging from white to purple, as do the thymes. Umbelliferae such as dill, cilantro, chervil, and parsley, named for their umbrellas of tiny florets in shades of yellow, cream, or white, make tasty garnishes too.

When adding flowers to a salad, just remember to do it at the end, after arranging, dressing, and tossing. A blossom sodden with oil and vinegar has no allure.

HARVEST. Bay leaves can be picked whenever you need them, and this will also encourage new growth. Cooks are accustomed to using dried bay leaves, which keep their flavor well enough, but fresh young bay, in its strength and brightness, is much superior. It is bright green and pliable, though still not quite tender enough to munch on, so we generally remove it before serving a dish. If you live in bay country, harvest some fresh leaves and send them as gifts to friends who are northern gardeners.

STORE. Keep bay leaves in a cupboard, out of the light, and they will retain their color better. There is no need to refrigerate them.

COOK. That single bay leaf we drop into so many dishes has a rationale. It is treasured as an undertone seasoning, with a meaty umami quality that always lends just a bit of richness. But we love the flavor of bay so much that we often slip in one or two more. We'll even season something—a bean soup, for instance—just with bay, and tuck it into a baking potato or a simmering pot of rice. Though most uses of bay tend to involve long-cooked recipes, fresh bay can even be added to a quickly cooked dish and still imbue lots of flavor. And it can flavor marinades a bit without being cooked at all.

Lemon Verbena

THIS SOUTH AMERICAN PLANT is one we discovered late in our gardening lives, but it quickly became a favorite. A member of the family Verbenaceae, its long, slender bright green leaves have a slight lemony tang, but that's a side note to something much more mysterious, and quite unlike the flavor of any of the familiar Mediterranean herbs. Although its habit is a bit ungainly, with long, woody, arching stems that can straggle into a path, you'll find this a plus as you brush up against the slightly sticky leaves while walking, and catch a hint of their lovely scent. Lemon verbena originally came to Europe in the late 18th century as a perfume plant, and it's easy to see why.

GROW. Best grown from a purchased plant, not from seed, lemon verbena takes off like a shot and forms a fountain of greenery by midsummer. Snipping it often can give it a more compact shape. It's not happy in clay soil, but can easily be grown in a container filled with a lighter soil mix. Although it is cold tender, we have wintered it over in a minimally heated greenhouse in Maine, but it does die back to the ground. It may survive outdoors as far north as Washington, D.C., with a good mulch, but is evergreen only in very warm climates.

HARVEST. Pick branches or individual leaves as needed. Harvest all the foliage before frost for drying.

Lemon verbena.

> Lemon verbena came to Europe in the late 18th century as a perfume plant.

Herb measurements are intended as guidelines. The potency of an herb or spice lessens over time.

STORE. While it does dry very easily for winter tea and other uses, retaining lots of flavor, we especially love it fresh-picked and find the flavor is stronger when fresh.

COOK. Young, fresh leaves can be snipped and eaten in salads and fruit dishes. Both these and older ones can be used as a steeping herb in marinades, in oils and vinegars, in jellies, in ice cream, milk custard, or panna cotta, or in a sweet syrup to use with fruit. While we remove the leaves that have steeped, we might use some freshly picked ones as a garnish to rub between the fingers and sniff, to echo the taste of the dish. In addition to hot tea, the leaves make a beautiful iced tea in summer, either alone or combined with mint.

We love to toss in a small handful of young lemon verbena leaves when making brown butter (page 396), then pour it over boiled potatoes. The leaves will be crisp and the butter wonderfully flavored.

For chives, see the Onion Family, page 146.

For tarragon, see the Sunflower Family, page 198.

I take with a grain of salt any prescribed ratios of fresh to dried herbs, and even in these pages, herb measurements are intended as guidelines. The potency of an herb or spice lessens over time. Initially, a dried herb may be more intense than an equal measurement of the fresh leaves, simply because the relative volume of the leaves decreases in drying. But as the dried herb ages, the balance may shift, so that you'll need more rather than less. This is quite evident in the case of large-leaved herbs such as bay or lemon verbena, where you can easily compare a single fresh leaf with a dried one. As the final arbiters, your nose and your taste buds write the book.

THE CUCUMBER FAMILY

- CUCUMBERS
- SUMMER SQUASH
- WINTER SQUASH
- MELONS

THE CUCURBITACEAE, often called cucurbits for short, are warm-weather plants. Like that other summery clan, the tomato family, they are grown for their fruits, which require heat for ripening. Although breeders have developed compact "bush" varieties (most notably for the various summer squashes), they are inherently vine crops that can take up a lot of room in the garden. With some exceptions, such as the relatively small-fruited cucumbers, they bear fruits that are too heavy to train vertically, and so would strain the capacity of a small plot. But they are so valuable that many gardeners find a way, even if it means letting the vines ramble outside the garden's bounds.

These crops all respond positively to extra soil fertility. They will grow best with plenty of compost and a dependable moisture supply. A traditional technique for squash and pumpkins is to place low piles of compost (about the amount held by a five-gallon bucket) at an adequate spacing (about five feet apart each way) and sow the seeds directly into those fertile mounds. That will give the plants a rapid start and their leaves will soon cover the whole area.

Since cucurbits are very cold sensitive, it is helpful in cold climates to warm the soil ahead of time by spreading down a sheet of IRT (infrared-transmitting) plastic (see page 174). Direct-sowing is best done when the soil temperature has reached about 70 degrees. You can also speed things up by starting the plants indoors, but the timing of this is important. You'll need to transplant them out into the garden after the danger of frost has passed and the weather is likely to be in the 60s, and settled. Two to three weeks before that, sow the seeds in pots at least three inches in diameter, three seeds to a pot, then thin to the most vigorous seedling that comes up. Letting the seedlings get more than three weeks old would make transplanting difficult. Since our spring weather is iffy, we sow an extra set of transplants at the same time the first ones are set out, just for insurance.

If we lived in a warmer part of the country, we might mulch the cucurbits to control weeds and conserve moisture, but mulching keeps the soil cooler, which is not what we want for heat-loving crops in our cool climate.

Cucumbers

GETTING THE BEST flavor from your cucumbers starts with growing tasty varieties, not the American supermarket slicing type, which is bred to be thick-skinned for shipping. Small pickling cucumbers and any of the European, Asian, and Middle Eastern types tend to be more interesting, but there are also standard slicing types bred for thin skins, good flavor, and lack of seeds. Look for these traits in seed catalogs. You'll enjoy your cukes more, and spare yourself the job of peeling and seeding.

GROW. Cucumbers are vigorous growers that fill your harvest basket to overflowing in summer. You can let them sprawl on the ground but to manage them better, and to save space, we train them to grow upward to a support bar 6½ feet above the ground (see page 243).

A pest you need to watch out for is the cucumber beetle (yellow with black stripes east of the Rockies, spotted in the west). Not only can they damage the plants, but they also spread a serious bacterial wilt disease. Spreading floating row covers when you set out your plants will exclude this pest at the stage when the plants are the most vulnerable to it, but be sure to remove the row covers once the blossoms appear so that wild pollinators can do their job. (You would also need to take off the covers for trellising.) Pick off any beetles you find if they do appear. One handy way to do this is with a shop vacuum cleaner, using the slot attachment, which does the least damage to the foliage. This is best done in the early morning when the insects are

Cucumbers trellised on strings, held in place with plastic clips.

It's important to keep up with the picking, in order to keep the vines producing, even if this means feeding the extras to the compost pile.

sluggish and move more slowly. But having said that, we find that if we provide our cucumbers with plenty of fertility from lots of compost or aged manure, and an application of seaweed or greensand to insure a full spectrum of micronutrients, we do not experience serious pest or disease problems.

HARVEST. It's important to keep up with the picking, in order to keep the vines producing, even if this means feeding the extras to the compost pile. We cut them with a small sharp knife, being careful not to injure the vines, then place them gently in a bucket or basket. Cucumbers bred for pickling are harvested anywhere from tiny to fairly small. With the slicing type, avoid letting them get huge. You should be able to eat a cucumber, seeds and all, without finding it tough.

STORE. Cucumbers do not keep well. It is much better to pick them the day you are to eat them than to hoard them in the fridge, although chilling them before eating does enhance their refreshing crunch. Best to give away the extras, compost them, or make lots of pickles.

COOK. Fortunately there are many ways to enjoy cucumbers' abundance. Slice and toss them into salads, or create salads of cukes alone. They are fine dressed with a vinaigrette or lemony dressing. We often mix them with sour cream, yogurt (as in Cucumber Raita, page 361), or a mixture of the two, together with some finely sliced red onions. Although dill is the traditional herbal companion, cucumber is also tasty with mint, chervil, tarragon, fennel fronds, lovage, or celery leaves. One modest little cucumber classic is that staple of English teas: quartered cucumber sandwiches with watercress and mayonnaise. A flashier favorite is cold poached salmon decorated with thin, overlapping cucumber slices to represent scales. For a more informal version, just arrange cucumbers next to a nice piece of salmon or bluefish, hot or cold, with a dollop of Creamy Chervil Dressing (page 319) on the side.

Chopped cucumbers give a pleasant crunch to dishes such as tuna, chicken, or egg salad when you might otherwise use celery. Try cukes in rice salad, potato salad, and salsas, in which they're mixed with tomatoes, peppers, corn kernels, tomatillos, or sweet summer fruits. Because of their sheer abundance, they are also standard pickle fodder, whether sliced crosswise and sweetened as bread-and-butter pickles, or sliced vertically as garlicky dills.

Strangely, cooked cucumbers remain a rarity. They retain a surprising amount of their crispness when cooked. Try the Sautéed Cucumbers recipe on page 362, then blaze a few trails of your own.

Summer Squash

GARDENERS LOVE TO GROW summer squash because they're an easy crop and so productive. Most of them are bush types rather than vining ones, and can take their place in a plot where space is an issue. There are a number of different shapes, from good ol' striped green zucchini, to the classic yellow crooknecks, to the pattypans (like little flying saucers) and spherical ones like Ronde de Nice. The edible blossoms are great for stuffing (for a recipe see page 262).

GROW. These are grown like any of the cucurbits. Although less space-consuming than squash that grow on long vines, individual plants are somewhat large and sprawling and need to be planted three feet apart. As they mature and their central stems elongate, they tend to sprawl into the paths. This can be avoided by succession planting, with fresh new transplants ready to go in around midsummer. Though you'll need to weed around them at the start, the big leaves will eventually shade out most competing plants.

HARVEST. Success with summer squash, as with many summer crops, depends on a good harvesting program. This is the season of abundance, when plants and their fruits grow quickly. Turn your back on the zucchini patch for a week, and you'll find giant green submarines cruising beneath the broad leaves. I once tried stuffing one of these monsters with a rice and cheese concoction and yes, it was good eating, but not good enough to repeat often. Besides, big squash slow

Zucchini with blossoms still attached to the fruits.

down the production of the small, tender ones that cooks prefer. Summer squash are particularly tasty when picked small, but they don't have to be the dainty 2-inch babies you sometimes find on restaurant plates. Even a 10-inch zucchini or yellow crookneck tastes just fine, though we usually harvest our zucchini at no more than 6 inches long.

If you're picking the flowers for cooking, do so first thing in the morning while they are wide open. Choose the males, which grow on long, slender stems, if you want to maximize your squash yield. (We leave the stems on to use as handles when we're frying them.) If your goal is to practice squash birth control, harvest some of the female blossoms as well! They're ones with the little bump of squash-to-be at the base of the flower.

STORE. Kept cold, summer squash can last for at least a week if you're saving up a quantity of them for an event or a special dish. If they get ahead of you, eat the freshest ones and compost or give away the rest. With summer squash there will always be more coming along.

Zucchini and yellow summer squash.

COOK. Our favorite summer squash recipe is the simple quartet of zucchini, onions, butter, and herbs on page 371. Larger ones lend themselves to slicing into disks, which are then fried on both sides in butter or olive oil, and sprinkled with a little finely grated parmesan cheese. An Italian friend once taught my mother to stew them with onions and tomatoes. Add eggplant to that and it's a French ratatouille. Just about any summer medley might include them: pasta with vegetables, a quick stir-fry, or a soup such as the one on page 275. The only trick is to use a light touch in cooking them, whatever their shape. Their centers always cook a bit faster than the outer parts, and after too much cooking a squash slice loses its structural integrity. Best to leave the outside a bit firm than to let the center turn to watery mush.

Winter Squash

FOR A BOTANIST there is no hard and fast difference between a squash and a pumpkin, nor for the cook as well. Both are fruits with very firm flesh and hard skins. They ripen in warm summer weather, and then are stored for future use. Even their bright colors, inside or out, warm up cold winter days. Sometimes I'll keep a big, gorgeous red Rouge Vif d'Étampes squash on the kitchen counter just to enjoy the sight of it.

There is a wide variety of winter squash to choose from, in many shapes, sizes, and colors. An enormous Blue Hubbard squash is fine for a large family, or for canning, but might not be convenient otherwise. The dark-green-skinned acorn and buttercup types are popular in small

A collection of winter squash, with Sweet Dumpling at top, a pumpkin in the middle, and Butternut at bottom.

households because you can cut one in half to make two individual servings. Little Delicata and Sweet Dumpling squash are smaller still. For all-around use, the plain beige butternut type is the most practical, with its delectable flesh and its handy clublike shape. And don't hesitate to experiment with some of the heirloom squashes, in all their colorful variety. Pumpkins are divided into two general categories: the Halloween type, great for carving, but with watery, tasteless flesh; and the "pie" pumpkins, which are meaty and delicious for baking.

GROW. Squash can be sown directly or started ahead as transplants. In cold climates the latter is often wise, since they will need to mature before frost and some squash take quite a while to grow. A mulch can be helpful for keeping the fruits from rotting in moist weather, and for keeping the large expanse between plants weed-free. But weed removal can also be accomplished by hoeing, and before too long the leaves will blanket the ground.

If you're determined to grow winter squash but don't have enough room, there are a few creative solutions you can try. We've trellised the small ones such as buttercup by tying the stems to a lattice fence. We've planted a few in the compost pile and let the vines erupt there and trail down to the ground. And we've used the vines to cover a bare patch of ground where we would like to keep weeds from growing. If a squash vine escapes from the garden, you can always turn it around so that it heads back the way it came—or just let it take off through the fence and join the circus. As long as it's in an area you don't need to mow regularly, there's no harm in it.

As the season starts to wind down and you don't think the tips of the vines are going to form any more squash that will mature in time, you can snip off those ends so the plant will put its energy into ripening the ones that are well on their way.

HARVEST. Unlike summer squash, winter ones do not have superior flavor at "baby size," but rather after they have fully matured and developed their full complement of nutrients and flavor. Picked before frost, to escape cold damage, they usher in hearty fall and winter meals. Harvest them with a sharp knife after they've achieved their full coloration, leaving several inches of stem, but don't use the stem as a handle to pick them up by. Treat the fruits carefully. They might look sturdy, but nicks and bruises will impair their keeping qualities.

If a light first frost sneaks up on you and touches the vines it will usually not affect the fruits' keeping ability. If they are not fully mature, and you think a spell of weather warm enough to ripen them might follow, spread a tarp over the fruits, gathering them together with the vines intact, as needed. If this has happened to you often, you would do better with an earlier-ripening variety. On the other hand, if the fruits are ripe by first light frost, harvest them all and round up the vines for the compost pile. After picking, spread the squash out in a warm dry place to cure.

STORE. Not only do winter squashes store very well through the winter, but they do it without the need for a root cellar. A cool, dry room is all you need. A temperature of around 50 degrees is ideal. If a huge squash overwhelms you, share it with friends, or cook it up and mash it, then can or freeze it. I have even cut a big one into wedges and frozen them, as is. Freezing affects their texture, but they still make a good soup.

COOK. A winter squash has an interior cavity filled with seeds that are discarded—unless you choose to roast them with salt and butter or oil, for snacking. (There are "naked seed" pumpkins with delicious, hull-less seeds, but their flesh is useless, so you really need to love pumpkin seeds to take the trouble to grow this kind.)

The skin of a winter squash or pumpkin is hard to peel when raw, but easy to slip off after cooking. If left on, the skin often comes in handy, forming a serving vessel. Acorn and buttercup squash may be baked with butter, honey, and nuts in their cavities and eaten right out of the skins.

Squash flesh is often a bit stringy, which is not a defect, but if you prefer it smooth and nearly stringless, Butternut squash is the one for you. Its bright orange flesh is among the most flavorful, and makes beautiful, velvety soups when pureed (see page 281). I also like its long straight neck, perfect for slicing into disks for the Butternut Squash Rounds on page 400. And then there's the spaghetti squash, which makes a virtue of all those strings, each one attached to a seed. Discard the seeds, bake or boil the squash, and then fork out the spaghetti-like strands. They are crunchy, mild, and delicious.

Melons

ALTHOUGH MAINE IS NOT MELON COUNTRY, we do manage to grow some

If a squash vine escapes from the garden, you can always turn it around so that it heads back the way it came.

Goldstar melons.

exquisite ones and eagerly await their ripening each year. The scourge of flavorless hotel breakfast melons was surely sent just to make us appreciate that moment when a home-grown one is ripe. We find the standard cantaloupes (properly called muskmelons) the easiest to grow. For us, one called Goldstar does best, but every region has melons that perform well there, so ask at your garden center or local grower's. Though a bit more challenging, we often grow modern cultivars of the French Charentais type, which are small and greenish, with heavenly, fragrant flesh inside. And we have succeeded with small watermelons, which are a handier size for us, anyway. There are lots of other melons grown by melon fanciers, but the types mentioned above are our favorites.

GROW. To assure a melon harvest in the cooler parts of the country we recommend starting the seeds three weeks ahead and transplanting the seedlings under row covers. We've also grown them with a mulch of black IRT (infrared-transmitting) plastic, which is spread on the soil to prewarm it and also helps with weed control. We cut a small hole where each transplant should go. The seedlings need to be transplanted very carefully with as little root disturbance as possible; in long-season climates they can be direct-sown. If you're using row covers, be sure to remove them when the flowers start to open, so that bees can pollinate the flowers.

HARVEST. For most melons it's not just a matter of the fruits attaining the right color. Cantaloupes are picked when they are at "full slip," which means that nudging the end of the stem slightly with your thumb causes it to slip off the fruit. When in doubt we give the blossom end a sniff. A sensitive nose can usually pick up melony ripeness. Charentais melons are picked when the small leaf at the end of the stem turns tan in color. Small cracks often appear at their blossom end as well— not a flaw, but an acknowledged signal of intense sweetness and ripeness for melon aficionados.

STORE. Melons have fragile flesh and are best picked ripe and eaten right away. While an underripe melon will mature a little on the kitchen counter, its flavor will not be much improved. Depending on the type, melons can be kept in the refrigerator for one to two weeks, but their flavor may suffer a bit.

COOK. Although melons are generally too juicy to hold up in cooking, there are several classic ways you can serve them raw. Wrap cubes, balls, or slices of them in thin-sliced prosciutto, as an appetizer. For dessert, cut a melon in half and serve each half with a scoop of sorbet in the cavity, or a shot of Calvados, Port, or Madeira. Years ago my sister Eloise came back from the Peace Corps in Chile with a wonderfully simple recipe for a refreshing melon *ponche,* consisting of cubes of honeydew melon floating in white wine.

But most of the time we just gather an armful of ripe melons, picked that day, cut them into wedges, and spread them out on a big blue enamel platter or a cutting board for everyone to gorge on, messily, summer style.

THE TOMATO FAMILY

- TOMATOES
- PEPPERS
- EGGPLANTS
- TOMATILLOS
- POTATOES

THIS FAMILY IS KNOWN botanically as the Solanaceae. If you were to look closely at the five common garden plants listed above, you'd find many similarities among them in terms of the shapes of their flowers and the appearance of their leaves and seeds. That includes No. 5, the potato. (There is actually a category of tomato called "potato-leaved" because the somewhat crinkly leaves are so similar.) But the potato is the oddball of the group because it has been selected for its underground tubers, and the fruits that sometimes follow its flowers are of no culinary significance.

Although these are all tropical New World plants from the Southern Hemisphere, they have been embraced globally and are grown as annuals in any climate where there is frost. The plants are heat loving and, for the most part, moisture loving. Unlike the happy-go-lucky brassicas, which rejoice in cool weather, these princesses are usually started ahead indoors (see pages 229 to 231) and not put out until the soil is comfortably warm. (The case of potatoes is different.) You can try to protect them from frost once they are in the ground, but unless the soil has warmed to about 55 degrees and the weather has settled, they will tend to sulk, and ones transplanted later will soon catch up to them. These are the plants that gardeners are most likely to purchase at garden centers, especially if they lack a sunny enough spot to start them at home. Windowsill tomatoes, especially, are often leggy and spindly, reaching for the light.

Seedlings of the right size, and ready for planting at the right time for your area, are available at garden centers around the country every spring. When you buy them, look closely at two features: the size of the pot or container in which the seedlings are growing, and the condition of the seed leaves. The container is important because the larger the root space, the less stressed the growing conditions and the better the transplant. If they are all in small containers, choose younger plants from a later sowing date. They will catch up and exceed the stressed plants once you put them in your garden. Also, look for healthy seed leaves. The seed leaves are the first to emerge when the seed sprouts—the two long, thin leaves at the base of the plant. In a really healthy transplant they will still be green. If they are yellowed that is still acceptable, but if they are nonexistent, that plant has been stressed and will likely be less productive in your garden.

It is especially important to rotate the members of the tomato family to keep them free of certain pests and diseases that they're prone to, making sure they do not follow one another in the same spot. (See

Tomatoes will sit there and sulk if planted before the soil has warmed to about 55 degrees.

Even bush tomatoes can benefit from a wire cage for support.

pages 43 to 52 for crop rotation.) In many cases (especially with tomatoes) there may be resistant varieties you can grow if your problems recur. Once they've been assigned their beds, make sure the soil has been well amended. This will not only help the plants resist disease, but also, in the case of the fruiting species, give them the extra energy they need for fruit production. Sufficient water is also important. The need for plant support varies.

Tomatoes

WHEN WE OVERLOAD OUR PLATES

we have "eyes bigger than our stomachs," and when it comes to tomatoes most of us have eyes bigger than our gardens. How to set a limit when there are so many kinds? We want big beefsteaks, little salad types, cherry tomatoes, grape tomatoes, and of course mountains of meaty, plum-shaped paste types to turn into sauce. It was simpler when all most people knew about were red, round balls. Now there are yellows, oranges, and even whites, not to mention all those luscious, streaky heirloom bicolors: the yellow-and-reds,

Brandy Boy tomatoes.

the red-and-blacks, the striped yellow-and-greens. So what if the countertops overflow? Extra zucchini might go begging, but beautiful, ripe, homegrown tomatoes? Nobody turns them down.

GROW. Ideally, tomato plants are six to eight weeks old when you set them out in the garden. By then, ours have been moved up from a 2-inch soil block to a 5-inch plastic pot, so they have great root systems on them.

When it comes to growth habit, there are two kinds of tomatoes. The determinate types grow on a sprawling bush and all ripen together within a fairly short period of time. These are good to have when you're preserving the fruits and want to get it all done at once. But for a continuous harvest throughout the summer, you want the indeterminate types, which grow on long, trailing vines. So before you put any of your tomatoes in the ground you'll want to decide how to deal with their growth. The bush type can be left to sprawl on the ground if you like, spaced about 30 inches apart, but the indeterminates will soon become a jungle if not supported.

Our preferred way is to grow them on a trellis, as shown on page 243. Another is to use tomatoes cages, set 2 feet apart. These work great if they are sturdily built, but many of the ones sold in stores are flimsy. We make our own out of concrete reinforcing wire, which we buy in 5-foot-wide sheets from a building supply store. This sturdy mesh has 6-inch-square openings so you can easily reach the tomatoes for picking. Using bolt cutters, we cut sections big enough to form into cylinders 16 inches in diameter, secure them by bending the cut wires, and set one

> Your goal is to expose the fruits to the sun and to keep them clean and away from slugs, chipmunks, and any other critters that crave a bite of them.

over each young plant. An enthusiastic indeterminate tomato plant will weigh a lot, so it's a good idea to pound in a grade stake or metal T-post next to the cage, and secure it to keep the cage from tipping over.

As the plant grows, its branches will fill the enclosure and be supported by the mesh. But first we remove the suckers that emerge just above the seed leaves at the base of the plant. A sucker is a little shoot that appears in the angle made by the leaf branch and the main stem. Left to grow, these suckers would branch out rather than up, and get in the way. As summer goes on we might control growth by pinching off more suckers. We tuck fruiting branches in from time to time to keep them growing upward in the cage, and cut back any that are too hard to keep inside. We might also cut off the top of the main stem of the plant if it extends much beyond the top of the cage, or let it drape down the outside.

Your goal is to expose the fruits to the sun and to keep them clean and away from slugs, chipmunks, and any other critters that crave a bite of them. So you may want to cage even your short determinate tomatoes. We cut our 5-foot cages in half to make 2½-foot-tall ones, and they are just right.

HARVEST. Pick tomatoes when they are fully colored but before they start to get too soft on the bottom. The bottom of the tomato is the most flavorful part, so you don't want to let it go overripe. Small tomatoes, especially the little cherry type, can be picked very easily; in fact we often pop a few in our mouths as we pass by. With large tomatoes it's best to use a sharp knife or, better yet, a pair of scissors, so you can cut with one hand while you're cupping the tomato with the other. It would be a shame to drop one, because the tasty tomatoes that home gardeners grow are not tough-skinned like the ones shipped to markets.

It can be hard to let go of tomatoes as frost threatens, and people can be quite obsessive about ripening them indoors. True, any green tomato with even a touch of pink showing will turn red in time, but this doesn't mean they'll taste as good as the ones you've been enjoying all summer. Even vine-ripened tomatoes in late fall have diminished flavor, because there simply isn't enough good sun left to do the job right, so past October we don't bother. It's best to preserve some at their prime for winter use, then compost the rest, or feed them to the chickens.

STORE. We always make up a batch of pureed paste tomatoes in fall to put up in jars. This does not fall within our program of seasonal eating, but in this case it's a

To prune a tomato plant to a single stem, pinch out the suckers that appear in the forks where fruiting branches join the main stem.

Tricks with Frozen Tomatoes

FREEZING. Wash plum tomatoes and slice off just a bit of the stem end to make skinning easier later on. Freeze.

SKINNING. While still frozen, hold under hot water for a few seconds. The skins can be slipped right off. Use as is, or reduce.

REDUCING. Place the tomatoes in a colander over a pot or bowl, to thaw slowly. Water will drip through, leaving concentrated flesh for a fresh-tasting sauce.

rule we're happy to break, even if the process takes all day. We sometimes dry tomatoes as well, using a commercial food drier. We find it is best to turn it down quite low—about 115 degrees—so that the sugar in the tomatoes doesn't burn. We stop when they are no longer sticky, but still bendable, then store them in jars or plastic bags, in a dark cupboard.

Here's the quickest, simplest storage technique of all. Wash your plum tomatoes, remove the stem, and freeze them whole in gallon plastic freezer bags. Retrieve handfuls of them as needed, holding each one, still frozen, under warm running water for a few seconds so that you can slip off the skins. Even frozen, they chop easily with a large, heavy knife. Drop them right into a soup or any other dish where they would taste good. To make a lazy tomato sauce, place them in a colander over a bowl and let them drip-dry as they thaw. The almost colorless liquid collects in the bowl (you can use it in soups), leaving a thick, reduced sauce in the colander, with no long simmering required.

COOK. Tomatoes, like the other fruiting vegetables—such as peppers, eggplants, and squash—are their own serving dishes, handy for stuffing once their seedy innards are scraped out. They can be stuffed and baked, as on page 331, or stuffed cold with a savory rice salad like the one on page 314. Chop them into salsas, fold them into omelets, add them to an infinite variety of soups, curries, and stews.

Tomatoes eaten raw need no peeling, in my view, unless the skins have been toughened by dry weather and inadequate watering. But tomatoes you plan to cook are usually more appetizing if you remove the skins. This is easily done by popping them into a pan of boiling water for about ten seconds. The skins will slip right off.

You can make tomato sauce with any kind of tomato, but the kind referred to as plum or paste tomatoes—oval-shaped ones that range from the size of pecans to that of jumbo pears—are especially meaty, and require less reduction to get to that thick-sauce stage. They are first-rate for slow-roasting in the oven (page 370), one of the most delicious things you can do with a tomato, since it concentrates the flavor in such a sweet, mellow way. Put roasted tomatoes on slices of crusty French or Italian bread. Top salads with them. Add them to pasta.

Peppers

SWEET PEPPERS, so called to distinguish them from hot peppers, really are sweet when well grown. So are hot peppers, a fact sometimes lost on those whose mouths are aflame. Hot peppers, especially, are used all over the world, and each cuisine seems to have ones they particularly treasure. People's tolerance for pepper heat varies enormously too. We're fond of those in the medium-hot range, such as poblanos, pasillas, and jalapeños, because you can use plenty of them for flavor without causing extreme pain. Padron peppers, grilled whole with olive oil and eaten right off the stem, are another medium-hot treat. But whether hot or sweet, a red, yellow, or orange pepper is often all you need to make a dish sparkle. Chopped fine or sliced thin, a scattering of pepper enlivens the look of a salad, an omelet, a bowl of rice. We've never understood the popularity of green peppers, picked before they attain their mature color of red, orange, yellow, purple, cream, or brown. What a rainbow they have become! Only impatience would make us eat them green, to enjoy some pepper flavor and crunch before any in the garden have colored up.

GROW. Peppers are grown in much the same way as tomatoes, since they have a similar need for sun, heat, and moisture. Although we've done fine with them outdoors, even without a plastic mulch, we do like to extend their season as best we can and often use our home greenhouse for this purpose. Since they don't have long, trailing stems, peppers need not be trellised but may need some support when laden with fruits. One stout stake will usually do the trick, but we have also used the short tomato cages shown on page 176.

Plenty of soil fertility is important, but high-nitrogen fertilizers are best avoided since they will encourage leaf growth at the expense of fruit formation. Plentiful compost is the best way to go. Pinching off any little white flowers that form for a week after transplanting will also boost your eventual yield, since it directs the plant to create a more vigorous root system

on which to support production. If you insist on enjoying some extra-early fruits, leave a few of your plants unpinched. In general, peppers have few pest or disease problems, but they should still be in a crop rotation (pages 43 to 52).

HARVEST. Peppers can be picked at any time they taste good to you, and regular picking will keep production going. Use shears or a sharp knife. Wrenching off a fruit may damage the plant.

STORE. When frost threatens, pick the peppers and bring them indoors. They will ripen on the kitchen counter just as tomatoes do, but as with tomatoes, fall robs them of their summery taste. Better to dry some when they're in their prime, and no vegetable dries more easily than peppers, even in a chilly, foggy place like Maine. We may not have long, red ristras hanging on the wall of our barn in the hot sun, but a tray of peppers cut in quarters and set above the woodstove dries in just a few days. An electric or solar dehydrator also does the trick. And we have hung whole pepper plants upside down in a greenhouse where they dry quickly on sunny fall days. Dried peppers can be stored in plastic bags, in a dark cupboard, then crumbled into pieces and dropped into a cooking liquid to soften them. We also pulverize them in the blender for homemade paprika, both hot and sweet.

COOK. Like onions, peppers sweeten even more when they are cooked and the sugar in them caramelizes. (Celebrate this duo in the recipe on page 363.) As the process happens, a cook must keep an eye

This pepper plant is staked early in the season.

Later on, with heavy fruit dangling, the support is appreciated.

on them because anything with sugar in it is prone to burning. Roasted peppers develop a wonderful smoky sweetness, and are at their best in a simple bruschetta on toasted bread, or in the dip on page 258. You can also puree them after roasting for a deliciously simple sauce for meat, eggs, or fish.

When using peppers, cut away the stem, pull out the central core with all the seeds attached to it, then clap the open end to your palm to expel any stray seeds, which serve no culinary purpose. With hot peppers, the spongy ribs are the hottest part. When stuffing any pepper, these are removed to make a bigger cavity.

Eggplants

EGGPLANTS COME IN MANY SIZES, shapes, and colors, from the big, bulbous deep purple ones to the little round white ones. Some have striped or spattered patterns, and there is an aptly named magenta one called Neon that positively glows. There are even small white ones that resemble the eggs after which the plant is named. All are beautiful and tasty in their own way, although I find the deep purple, nearly black ones the most spectacular. We especially like the dark, slender, elegant Japanese ones such as Orient Express, because they mature early even in our cool weather.

GROW. Give eggplant the same sun and heat you give tomatoes and peppers. But you'll find them a bit less demanding of moisture, and a bit more intolerant of poor drainage. They'll need a good head start in cool climates and will do poorly if transplanted too early into cold soil. Flea beetles, which stipple the leaves with tiny holes and thereby weaken the plants, often afflict them early in the season when the beetles are hatching and the plants are small and defenseless, so you may have to make row covers a yearly habit for your transplants (page 90). This will also keep them warmer.

We often grow our eggplants in a greenhouse, for the extra heat, but it's a shame not to put some in the garden itself because they are so beautiful, their showy bright purple flowers luminous against the dark green leaves. More open in their habit and less bushy than peppers, they allow a good view of both flowers and fruits. They look great when grown in containers. Wherever you grow them, trellising or staking is sometimes necessary, to keep the plants from flopping over.

HARVEST. Eggplants can be picked young, but we prefer to let their flavor develop a little more. The fruits should be harvested while still glossy. A dulling of the skin and a darkening of the seeds are signs of overmaturity. Cut with scissors or a sharp knife, and keep up with the picking so that production will not slow down.

STORE. Eggplants will keep well for up to a week in the refrigerator, but will keep their flavor better if stored at room temperature. Handle them with some care: Their skins are quite protective but only if they aren't punctured.

COOK. Since eggplant is a warm-climate crop it is not surprising that it appears so often in Mediterranean dishes such as the Greek or Turkish moussaka, Provencal ratatouille, Italian

Eggplants trellised with strings.

eggplant parmigiana, Sicilian caponata and the ubiquitous Middle Eastern baba ganoush. But you will also find it in Asian countries, including China, Thailand, and Japan. We grow several sizes, for different purposes. The big ones are great for layered casseroles, and for grilling, brushed with olive oil, herbs, and spices. We also grill the long Japanese ones, or slice them lengthwise and fry them in olive oil. For stuffing eggplant see page 364.

Tomatillos

THEIR NAME SUGGESTS a "little tomato," and they are in fact distant cousins within the tomato family. But where tomatoes are soft and fragile, tomatillos are quite hard and firm. The closer you live to Mexico, the more likely that you've met and enjoyed them. And they're ridiculously easy to grow, offering up their little fruits abundantly, even in cold climates, and then going to seed wherever they might fall—including the compost pile.

GROW. Seeds can be direct-sown or started indoors, like tomatoes, then set out after all danger of frost has passed. The beautiful, lush plants grow very fast, then sport little, round green, papery husks, like Japanese lanterns. As these turn tan-colored, the hard, round green fruits begin to form inside, eventually bursting through their coverings. We love to grow them on an open lattice fence, gently nudging the fast-growing stems so that they weave in and out between the slats. Like tomatoes, the stems are vinelike, but don't really have any means of clinging to a support, unless you count their avid desire to sprint upward toward the sun. The leaves, yellow flowers, and the fruits are all very decorative and would earn their place on the fence for that reason alone.

HARVEST. When the husks turn pale gold (or purple, with some varieties) they are ready to pick, and will start dropping to the ground. Unlike other summer vegetables, they do not need immediate rescuing at that point. You can pick them up or pluck them off the vines at your leisure.

STORE. Tomatillos will keep for weeks sitting in a bowl on your kitchen counter. The flesh can also be canned or turned into jams.

COOK. Tomatillos are strongly associated with Mexican cooking. Although they have a distinctive flavor, their role in the kitchen is more of a supportive one. They make a fine thickening agent in sauces or soups, and are a key ingredient in the Mexican salsa verde, which also includes onions, chile peppers, cilantro, and sometimes lime. Although they are edible raw, I prefer tomatillos cooked, and especially roasted. Chicago chef Rick Bayless does them at 450 degrees on a baking sheet with sweet and hot peppers, garlic, and onions. The skin is edible, but I always discard it after squeezing out the soft flesh inside, which provides an optional ingredient for the Green Gazpacho on page 287.

Tomatillos, popular in Mexican cooking, can be green or purple depending on the variety.

TOP: Charlotte potatoes.
BOTTOM: Rose Gold potatoes.

Potatoes

RICH IN NUTRIENTS, potatoes rank with rice and wheat as survival foods, but unlike rice and wheat, they can be grown by any gardener. Sure, potatoes are inexpensive to buy, but growing your own is truly worth it. Many people have never tasted a freshly dug potato, and you don't often see the word fresh in the same sentence as this earthy brown tuber. But the flavor of a new potato is extraordinary, and even with large storage potatoes, well grown in an organic soil, you *can* taste the difference.

People sometimes think that a new potato is just a certain type, small and round, and in fact there are certain varieties commonly sold as "new." But true baby new potatoes are the ones you sneak out from under any potato plant when it has first started to flower. Their skins are delicate and start to peel off while you're washing them. But apart from the age issue, there are different types of potatoes grown for different purposes. Baking potatoes such as russets (sometimes called Idaho potatoes, whether they're from Idaho or not) are starchy, rather dry, and crumbly when cooked. Boiling potatoes, which can be either red- or brown-skinned and either round or finger-shaped, are lower in starch. They are moister, and hold their shape well when boiled. All-purpose potato varieties such as Kennebec fall between with regard to starch, and they're versatile.

GROW. Potatoes are planted by placing one of them (or in some cases, a piece of one that contains at least one "eye," or sprout) in the ground. Your seed potatoes should be spread out at room temperature about a month before planting time, to begin sprouting (see page 107). Place them in a single layer in a shallow container in a bright location but out of direct sunlight. This practice of pre-sprouting increases early yields and assures that the seed potatoes you plant are going to grow. (Any that don't produce sprouts are discarded.) In the garden, the seed potatoes are planted about three inches deep. If you have pre-sprouted them, plant two weeks before your last frost date. If you haven't, plant three weeks before.

After the shoots emerge, the plants should be mulched thickly or have soil hilled up around their stems to prevent any potatoes that grow near the soil surface from being exposed to sunlight. Exposure to light turns the potato skins green by forming a glycoalkaloid called solanine, which makes the skins poisonous. We prefer mulching to hilling; it's simpler, and the mulch is a great help in keeping the soil moist.

Moisture is very important for potatoes. In our experience it greatly reduces their susceptibility to the Colorado potato beetle, which can quickly devour all the leaves. In very rainy summers, we find, the crop isn't bothered by this pest at all. Growing the potatoes under row covers (page 90) is also a good insurance policy against the Colorado potato beetle. If your potato area is not huge, daily picking of the beetles keeps the numbers down. Also look for the red-orange patches of tiny eggs, usually on the underside of the leaves, and rub them out with your fingers. Next to appear are the fat pink, bloated larvae, then finally the striped yellow-and-black adult beetles. Take an empty quart-size yogurt container, fill it half full with water and a squirt of dish detergent, then hold it under the larvae or beetles and brush them in. Do this every day and you can save even a badly infested crop by reducing the pest's numbers.

A common defect in potatoes is a disease called scab, which causes small, rough, circular patches on the skin. It is mainly a cosmetic problem and not of great concern for the home gardener. We only mention it because it can be aggravated by too high a pH, as with over-liming, and the overuse of manure. There are also resistant varieties.

HARVEST. As soon as you see pretty white, pink, or lavender flowers on your potato plants, you know that there are small potatoes forming underground. At that point it's hard to resist sneaking out a few by clawing the soil around the edge of the plant with your fingers until you find some tubers—a time-honored piece of mischief known as *grabbling*. Later in the season the stems and foliage will start to turn brown and die back. The potatoes won't increase in either size or number after that, but it's fine to leave them right where they are until the first serious frost threatens. Then it's time to dig them up. If your soil is very loose and fluffy, with lots of organic matter, this can be accomplished just by pulling up the plant, taking any potatoes that still cling to the roots, then digging the rest up with your hands, making sure you explore widely and deeply to get them all. In most gardens you'll need to free some of them by gently lifting the soil near them with a spading fork, trying hard not to stab them with the tines. Any wounded ones should be eaten right away because they won't keep well.

STORE. Nothing gives a feeling of security like a good stash of spuds in the cellar as winter sets in. To keep their skins from greening up and becoming toxic, potatoes should be stored in complete darkness, in a cool place—but not the refrigerator, which is a bit too cool and can turn them too sweet. They're best stored with the dirt still clinging to them, and not overly moist. Check them frequently for signs of rot, since just one rotten potato can spread decay and a bad odor. For more on root crop storage see pages 77 to 79. For information on saving seed potatoes for next year see pages 106 to 107.

COOK. With new potatoes, all you need to do is steam them lightly, whole, add butter, salt, pepper, and maybe a sprinkling of parsley or dill, and you're in heaven. The baking type are best when baked at a high temperature (about 425 degrees) until their skins are crisp, their insides soft. You can judge both these criteria with the stab of a small knife. We also like them cut up and roasted with garlic and olive oil. Boiling potatoes, because of their moisture content, make perfect hash browns. But to tell the truth, we've cooked all types of potatoes in every way we know, and if they've been grown and stored well they're all fine for any purpose. In most gardens, the all-purpose potato is simply the one you've grown. You just have to be extra-careful not to cook the high-starch ones too long if you're making potato salad, lest they fall apart.

After you scrub potatoes, look for and remove any green spots, and remove any sprouted eyes as well. Potato leaves, stems, and blossoms are generally

As soon as you see pretty white, pink, or lavender flowers on your potato plants, you know that there are small potatoes forming underground.

considered unsafe to eat. Most of the things you can do with potatoes alone, such as mashing and frying, deserve to be as well known as they are, but potatoes truly shine as collaborators, when they turn meat, fish, and/or other vegetables into a one-pot meal, as in soups, stews, curries, chowders, or that great pub dish, Shepherd's Pie (see page 416). And a mash or a puree can do so much more than just sit there in a pile or puddle. Use it instead of a roux to thicken a creamy soup or to bind up a crab cake or a croquette.

THE LEGUME FAMILY

- **PEAS**
- **BEANS**

THE LEGUMES, or Leguminosae (also called Fabaceae), are a large and fascinating family that includes alfalfa, peanuts, mimosa trees, and licorice, in addition to the peas and beans we know and love. As we explained on page 24, legumes have the ability to extract some of their own nitrogen needs from the air. But nevertheless they will still grow best in a fertile soil, especially one high in organic matter. Soil organic matter is a constantly recurring theme in this book, and for good reason. It is the undisputed key to maintaining garden productivity. The yield from peas and beans, for example, although they can partially take care of themselves, will still be twice as large in a garden with well-tended soil. Since peas are a cool-season crop, their production period can be somewhat extended by mulching with old or spoiled

hay (no longer good for feeding livestock) or straw to keep the soil cooler around their roots.

Peas and beans bear large edible seeds. Both climb, although in different ways: Peas latch onto a support by means of threadlike tendrils attached to the main stem; climbing beans twine the entire main stem around and around the support. But there are dwarf versions of both that may need no supporting structure. Perhaps the most important difference between the two, from the gardener's standpoint, is that peas are a cool-weather crop and beans are a warm one.

Peas

THE SWELLING OF THE PEA PODS, pregnant with the first sweet garden peas, is a jubilant moment in a gardener's year, but for us it is a very quiet joy. Family members make a game of keeping their discovery a secret, hiding amid the tall, leafy vines and munching down the row, scattering pods in their wake. It's days before any of the harvest reaches the kitchen.

Although the traditional garden peas, also called green peas or English peas, are a must for us, many gardeners find that the edible pod types make the best use of garden space. They yield a higher volume since they are picked and eaten, shell and all. We love these as well, both the flat-podded Chinese types, usually referred to as snow peas, and the more rounded sugar snap types.

Southern peas are another thing altogether. Unlike the kinds grown in the north, they are a warm-weather crop, and cannot be sown until after the danger of frost has passed. We can't grow them at all on the cool Maine coast, but Barbara's Louisiana grandparents, Lucille and Asa Southern, sure could. In the afternoon, family members, neighbors, and drop-in friends would gather out on the lawn and shell these peas together. It was how they visited. There are a lot of types of southern peas, some brown such as Mississippi Silver, some pale in color such as cream peas, some with a dark spot, such as black-eyed peas. Most are small and round. Lucille and Asa favored a very small, sweet cream pea called a lady pea.

GROW. Garden peas are the first crop we sow in spring. We spread compost on the bed the previous fall, so it's all ready to go come spring. That way we won't have to work the soil while it is still a bit wet from the spring thaw. Seeds go into a pair of 1-inch-deep furrows, one on either side of a trellis with pea netting (see page 242). We make a point of spacing them accurately—between 1 and 2 inches apart—so they don't need to be thinned, and after the ground has warmed up we put down a hay mulch so they won't need to be weeded. Both thinning and weeding would disturb the fragile root systems, and we want to get them off to a good start. Most years we'll sow as many as four beds, each with its own trellis running down the center, and plant four varieties that mature in sequence to make the season longer. We sow snow peas and snap peas at the same time. In fall, when the weather is cool again, we look forward to a second crop that was sown in mid-July. The success of the fall crop is dependent on the weather, but when we have leftover seeds it's a risk we like to take.

Garden peas forming in their pods. They are picked when the pods are rounded but their skin is still bright green and smooth.

HARVEST. If you grow any of these types, you have a daily assignment in the pea patch—not an unpleasant one if you're a snacker. The moment of perfection for each pod lasts a day, although you can go two and still have a decent pea. Both garden peas and sugar snap peas should be picked when they are fat with the round seeds inside, but before the pods take on a rough texture. As soon as this happens they become rather tough, starchy, and no longer sweet. Snow peas are picked before the peas swell, when they are still tender.

Garden peas, of course, must be shelled before eating, by pressing on the round end opposite the stem, to pop it open. This is the job we'll often give to a visitor who wants to be useful. Some older varieties of sugar snaps have a tough

string running down the concave side of the pod, just like old-fashioned "string beans." These are easily removed by grasping them at the stem end and pulling the string down as if you were unzipping the pod. Modern ones are stringless.

STORE. Peas of any sort will keep a few days after picking if chilled right away, but they are best fresh. Shelled garden peas are among the very few vegetables we freeze for winter use, because we get such a large volume all at once, in a season that is all too short. But it's essential to pick only the sweet, tender ones and freeze them right away, or it is not worth the effort.

COOK. When the kitchen finally has a good supply of garden peas, they go into everything: stir-fries, pasta dishes, rice casseroles. I'll even sprinkle them onto salads raw, making the most of their fresh tenderness. And of course, it's hard to beat a simple bowl of shelled peas steamed five minutes or so and buttered.

Snow peas are perfectly suited to stir-fries, either in a vegetable mixture or just by themselves, with sesame oil, ginger, and a dash of soy sauce added at the end (see page 376). Sugar snaps too are best stir-fried or steamed briefly—or not at all. They are superb raw in salads, and I can think of few better or simpler appetizers than a bowl of them on the table for munching.

Southern peas can be eaten either fresh or dried, and are delicious cooked with pork or bacon. Grandmother Lucille cooked them until they were tender, then dressed them with a sweet tomato relish.

Beans

BEANS ARE among the most versatile plants you can grow. Not only are there both bush and climbing varieties, and many ways to cook them, but you can also use beans at every point in their growth cycle. Here are the major stages.

Snap Beans

Also known as green beans, despite the occasional variation in the color of their pods, this is the crop that most gardeners grow. If you plant the bush type, which all bear within the space of a few weeks, you may find yourself struggling to use them up in the kitchen. But this trait comes in handy if you want beans for freezing, or for putting up in jars as dilly beans, with garlic, vinegar, and fresh dill. On the other hand, if you prefer to have a long season of fresh eating, pole beans provide the most steady, manageable supply. As long as you keep up with the picking, they'll continue to bear until frost. When we were growing up, snap beans were called string beans, because they often had a tough string running down one side. This trait has been bred out of modern beans, but in some old varieties you must remove the string by grasping the bean's stem end and pulling the string downward.

Shell Beans

The next stage in a bean's life is the brief period when the seeds have swelled but have not yet dried, and are tender enough to be pierced with your fingernail. In most cases the pods are beyond eating at this point, but the seeds are very succulent after a brief simmer. This is one of those treats that you rarely experience without having a garden, because in American markets you

seldom find shell beans in their pods for sale. The only common one is the lima (also called butter bean), and it's home is usually the frozen food aisle. Beans traditionally celebrated at the shell-bean stage include fava beans, the pale green French flageolets, Italian cannellini beans (which resemble white kidney beans), and a number of types with red-streaked pods and red-mottled seeds, such as Vermont Cranberry, Tongues of Fire, Jacob's Cattle, the French horticultural beans, and the Italian borlotti beans. Most of those are bush varieties, selected for the ease with which the pods can be opened while green.

King of the Garden is a good pole lima for "shellies," but we are too far north to grow them well. So we experiment with just about any pole bean at the fresh shelling stage, even if opening the pods requires a knife. Pods of the classic old favorite Kentucky Wonder open without much trouble, and the whitish beans are tasty. Scarlet Runner beans, grown as a snap bean in England, and here for their bright red blossoms beloved by hummingbirds, have gorgeous seeds. As they grow, they progress from cream to rose to shocking pink; then a mottled navy-blue speckled pattern creeps over one side until the entire bean, at its dry, mature stage, is deep blue-black with magenta specks. Tracking their progress is like watching a sunset. Alas, all these colors fade to lavender-gray when the beans are cooked, but they are good to eat nonetheless.

Dried Beans

The diversity of beans you can grow is one of the wonders of the horticultural world, and to appreciate this you must look at the mature seeds. On a table at Maine's

It's a pleasure to see their various colors lined up on the pantry shelf, and to know that we have such an important food staple right at hand for the rest of the year.

Common Ground Country Fair, or in the pages of a catalog such as the Seed Savers Exchange, you'll find a kaleidoscope of colors, patterned with speckles, spots, stripes, and splotches, as beautiful as a display of ancient jewelry in a museum, and as tempting as jars of penny candy. This is because beans evolved over the centuries in a partnership between man and bean, the bean supplying sustenance in return for its perpetuation. So each bean has a story behind it, of the community of growers that kept it going by planting it each year. Though gardeners develop their favorites, there are always new ones to grow.

FACING PAGE (top to bottom):
Yellow snap beans.
Rattlesnake shell beans.
Italian anellini beans.

TOP: Eliot planting peas.
BOTTOM: Eliot weeding peas.

If you have the space to grow beans for drying, give a few varieties a try. Even varieties sold for snap or shell use can be left on the vine to become dry beans, if you grow too many and fall behind with the picking.

GROW. Unlike peas, beans must be planted after the ground has warmed up to 60 degrees. If they are the climbing, vining type, which are called "pole beans" for a reason, you must have something for them to climb on before you poke the first seed into the ground. Poles are fine, whether they are of milled lumber or saplings cut from the woods, but they must be sturdy enough to support the laden vines. Single poles should be spaced 3 feet apart with four seeds in a circle around the base of each pole. Arranging three or four poles to form a tepee, tying them securely together at the top, is even sturdier. Or you can use the trellis system explained on pages 242 to 243.

When we grow bush beans we make succession plantings so that there are always some more coming along, sowing 6 inches apart, with two rows to the bed.

HARVEST. With pole beans, pick promptly to keep production going. Most snap beans are at their tender best picked before you can feel the lumps of seeds in the pods. The skinny little French filet beans, which are small-seeded and a bit slower to size up, are picked when they are about ⅜ inch wide. They date back to the old string days, when you picked beans young and tender before strings formed. Now modern filet beans are stringless too. Although a cute and succulent gourmet treat, they're a bit tedious for the busy cook and will turn large, like any bean, if not picked. We prefer to grow a good all-purpose pole bean like Fortex and pick some of the pods when they are ¼ inch wide, whenever we want filets. At the opposite extreme are the flat, wide, Italian Romano type, unusual in that they taste good even after the seeds have begun to swell. You just have to cook them a little bit longer.

A bean crop for drying is left in the garden with its roots in the ground until the pods are turning brown and the beans inside have reached their mature coloration. The plants are then clipped off at soil level and brought indoors to dry further, discarding any with signs of mold or other diseases. One way to do this is to tie them in bunches of about six plants and hang them upside-down from the rafters of an outbuilding such as a garage or an airy shed. We set ours on window screens supported horizontally for air circulation, in our furnace room.

After the bean pods and seeds are thoroughly dry they can be threshed to release the seeds from their pods. There are several ways to do this: You can beat them against the inside of a metal garbage can, or stuff them into an old laundry bag, pillowcase, or feed sack and beat on them or stomp on them to break apart the pods. To winnow them, pour the resulting mixture of beans and pod pieces back and forth from one large bowl to another outdoors on a windy day, or in front of a fan, discarding any seeds that are immature or moldy. They can then be stored for eating and for planting the following spring.

STORE. When dried beans are *thoroughly* dry they can be stored out of the sunlight in glass jars. It's a pleasure to see their various colors lined up on the pantry shelf, and to know that we have such an important food staple right at hand for the rest of the year. As for snap and shell beans, they're all about fresh eating soon after harvest.

COOK. Snap beans are prepared for cooking by cutting off the stem ends; we usually snip off the tough little point on the blossom end as well. Overcooking green beans leads to loss of both nutrients and flavor, so we steam or sauté them until just tender. Beans are wonderful with just butter, or sautéed in olive oil with garlic and fresh parsley. They're also lovely in salads and in all sorts of vegetable medleys, soups, and pasta dishes. Bear in mind that green and yellow ("wax") bean pods keep their color when cooked, but those with red-streaked or purple pods do not. But raw beans of mixed colors do look beautiful together, arrayed around a dip.

Shelling fresh beans is a great job for children, grandparents, spouses, and guests who ask a cook, "What can I do to help?" How long shell beans will take to cook depends on the age of the bean, but it's usually less than half an hour. They are fine just simmered or steamed and then buttered, with salt and pepper, but we also like them cooked in a broth flavored with aromatic herbs and vegetables. A bit of bacon doesn't hurt either.

As for dried beans, opening a can of them is certainly a quick way to put food on the table but it can't compare with ones made from scratch. Yes, they take longer to cook, but it is one of those jobs that becomes simple once you get into the habit. We rinse them clean, then soak them in water overnight, although soaking is not essential. Common wisdom urges you to discard the soaking water, then rinse the beans again, to diminish their flatulent effect, but some flavor will be lost, so we'll leave that decision to you. To cook them, put them in a big pot that will hold more than double the volume of the beans, then cover them with plenty of water and bring to a boil. They can then be simmered either on top of the stove or in the oven. With the oven method there's less risk of the water boiling away quickly and causing the beans to burn.

One of the most important advantages of home-grown dried beans over store-bought ones is that you know the age of the bean. Cooking times are always somewhat unpredictable with bean seeds, and it is frustrating to prepare them for a meal and not have them done in time. Acidic water might be the culprit, and can be corrected by adding a pinch of baking soda to the pot as a last resort, but it makes the texture mushy. Another safeguard is to wait until after the beans have softened before adding other ingredients, especially acidic ones such as vinegar. But the most important factor is the age of the beans, because the older they are, the longer the cooking time, and the ones you grew yourself during the current year are always a safe bet.

THE SUNFLOWER FAMILY

- **ARTICHOKES**
- **SUNCHOKES**
- **LETTUCES**
- **CHICORIES**
- **TARRAGON**

YOU MIGHT JUST AS WELL CALL THIS the lettuce family or the daisy family or the artichoke family. All these are members in good standing of the Asteraceae (sometimes called the Compositae), one of the largest families in the plant kingdom. Often taprooted, with flowers that attract large numbers of beneficial insects, the Asteraceae are better represented in the flower garden, which they populate with zinnias, asters, daisies, marigolds, dahlias, and a host of other highly decorative species, their flowers all composed of ray flowers emanating from the center like the rays of the sun. Over in the veggie plot you might find the related chicory tribe, which includes endive, escarole, and radicchio. Let those go to seed and you'll see flowers like those of the common chicory that grows along the road, with its ray flowers a brilliant sky-blue. Or sunchokes (still called Jerusalem artichokes by some, as noted on page 192) with their sunflower-like blooms. Artichokes and cardoons, which are related to thistles, have nests of ray flowers in an extraordinary neon bluish-purple color. And lettuce? Few gardeners tolerate bolted lettuce long enough to let it bloom, but if they did they'd enjoy the floral display shown on page 112, a familiar sight to those who save their own seeds. Tarragon, the oddball of the group, is a member of the genus *Artemisia,* known for its dainty white flowers. But the French form of tarragon that gardeners grow is sterile, and will rarely bloom in your garden.

Artichokes

ARTICHOKES ARE NOT A COMMON SIGHT in gardens, but with today's varieties and sometimes a little tinkering, they are an easy and satisfying crop to grow.

An artichoke is the immature flower bud of a domesticated thistle. It looks a little scary, its armored leaves concealing and protecting the delicious flesh within. You pick it before these spiny leaves (actually leaflike bracts) can open outward and allow the beautiful neon-violet flower to develop. Often called globe artichoke, because of its rounded form, this bud has a number of edible parts. Its bottom is a flat, meaty disk, full of flavor. At the base of each leaf there is similar tissue, which becomes more plentiful and tender as you move toward the center. These tender central leaves, along with the bottom disk, constitute the artichoke heart. Sitting on top of the disk is the fuzzy, scratchy choke,

An artichoke is the immature flower bud of a domesticated thistle.

well named because of its inedibility, but in small artichokes it is sometimes nonexistent or soft enough to be eaten. The part most often neglected is the artichoke's stem, which discloses more of that yummy flesh when peeled.

GROW. Artichoke is a perennial crop, but not a very cold-hardy one. In some of the mild coastal parts of California (and similar parts of other countries such as France and Italy) plants survive from one year to the next. But where temperatures drop below 14 degrees, it's best grown as an annual. This is easy to do with modern varieties that are bred to mature the first year. But you can grow even the old varieties as annuals too. It just requires a bit of gardening trickery.

The plants would not normally produce those toothsome buds the first year. In areas where they would not survive the winter, you therefore have to create an artificial winter for them. This is called "vernalization," or "cold treatment." You do it by sowing the plants in pots indoors or in a greenhouse at least eight weeks before the last expected frost, then putting them in a spot where they'll experience cool temperatures (around 50 degrees) for about two weeks. (To have larger plants to set out, we actually start this process on February 15 and give them a six-week growing period in a greenhouse, followed by six weeks of chilly outdoor spring weather.) It's important to keep them above 25 degrees during the outdoor phase, either by using a cold frame, by covering them with a tarp on cold nights, or by whisking them back inside when needed. As soon as the danger of hard frost has passed, you can transplant them into the garden. They will respond as if a true winter had just occurred, and make buds in summer. Although this whole process is less crucial with the new varieties that grow more easily as annuals, we still give those a chilling period too, as insurance. And vernalization allows us to get any old-time variety to produce edible chokes the first year, including the pointed purple European varieties.

Since they will grow into large plants, artichokes need to be 2 feet apart in each row (even more, if you're growing them as perennials in a mild climate), in rows 42 inches apart, so this is usually not a crop for a small garden. But it is a beautiful one, with its dramatic, spiny gray-green foliage. Consider making a bed for it as a landscape feature—along a fence, say. These mighty plants, with their taproots, appreciate a deeply dug, rich soil, with lots of organic matter. The better the soil, the more buds you'll be able to harvest; we usually hope for about twelve per plant. A hay mulch will help to conserve moisture. We grow a variety called Imperial Star, which has been bred for spring vernalization.

HARVEST. The plants will start to bear in midsummer and will keep going well into fall. Pick the buds when they are still firm and tight, before they begin to open, with about 4 inches of stem. You'll have a bitter taste on your fingers after handling them, but don't worry about that. Cooking transforms the beast. We keep picking them as long into the fall as they are produced, but the stems eventually turn hard and fibrous. Sometimes it's best to cut them to the ground after their big flush of growth in summer, and let new foliage come up. Even

FACING PAGE (Top to bottom):
Butterhead lettuce.
Lolla Rossa lettuce.
Red romaine lettuce.

in Maine we get some late buds this way. On the other hand, if you leave the first growth alone you'll get a bed of spectacular flowers when the last buds bloom.

STORE. They are best if eaten fresh-picked, but can be refrigerated for a few days if necessary.

COOK. The simplest cooking method is steaming. We give them a minimal trimming first, pulling off the tough outermost ring or two of leaves with a downward motion. Then we peel the stem. To keep cut surfaces from darkening you may rub them with lemon, or place them in a bowl of water acidified with lemon or vinegar, but for a quick trim we often don't bother. How long you steam an artichoke depends on its size. Full-sized ones take 45 minutes, small ones 30 minutes or less. To test for doneness, tug at an outer leaf, and if it releases quickly, give it the tooth test.

There are few pleasures more delightful than pulling off the leaves of a just-picked, freshly steamed artichoke, dipping them in melted butter and scraping the flesh off them with your teeth. (We set a big bowl into the middle of the table to toss the leaves into.) The tender innermost ones can be lifted out as one unit by their tips, like a little crown, then dunked and eaten. Finally, after plucking or scraping out the choke, the bottom disk and stem are dunked too. If served cold or at room temperature, a vinaigrette or aioli is good for dipping. Artichokes make a fine appetizer, but we often make a whole supper of them when they first come into season.

For grilling or oven-roasting we prefer to use just the hearts and stems, so that

there is nothing for the diner to fish out and discard. Small artichokes, which grow lower on the plant after the large ones have formed above, can be eaten whole, with little or nothing to waste. One of the great luxuries of growing your own artichokes is having these little gems in abundance.

Sunchokes

YOU MAY HAVE HEARD of this vegetable by an older name, Jerusalem artichoke. Sunchoke, though less common, avoids the confusing reference to the artichoke, which this is not, and Jerusalem, with which it has no connection. It is, however, a type of native sunflower, with cheerful yellow flowers and tall majestic growth. Underground, the plants form clusters of little potato-like brown tubers, which grow more numerous as the plants multiply. That's the part we eat.

GROW. This is not a crop to grow among dainty salad greens and radishes. It is a plant of sidewalk-lifting power, and we would call it indomitable if we had not, once, lost it entirely to hungry, pawing deer. It's a great candidate for edible landscaping, grown as a grove, or as an untrimmed flowering hedge. When establishing a new planting in spring, set the tubers 1 to 2 feet apart, 4 inches deep. Water and mulch them while they are getting established, but after that they will mulch themselves, as the tops die back in fall, and will shade out most weeds.

HARVEST. Pry the current year's crop of tubers out of the soil with a digging fork in fall and on into winter. You can continue to dig them while the ground remains

Roasted whole, these sunchokes will be crisp on the outside and soft within.

unfrozen. In late winter or early spring, new growth will start to emerge from any that remain.

STORE. Unlike other root crops, these do not store well. You can keep them for a couple of weeks in the fridge but they will soon start to deteriorate. Better to dig them fresh for as long as you can.

COOK. If you grow sunchokes you'll have a lot of them to harvest in fall, and fortunately they are versatile in the kitchen. Our favorite way to treat them is to roast them in whole clusters, as in the recipe on page 402, in which they come out crisp on the outside and tender in the middle. They are also quick and delicious to steam, boil, or fry. Their flavor is unassertive, and while they do acquire a pleasant sweetness in cold weather they benefit from the addition of seasonings and the enrichment of butter, oil, or cream. We like them in a creamy soup with chicken broth and with leeks, which are also plentiful in fall and winter.

Sunchokes are very popular eaten raw in salads. They have a wonderful crunch, a bit like that of jicama roots or water chestnuts. Slice them thin for best effect.

Although sunchokes don't need to be peeled, a thorough scrubbing with a vegetable brush is essential, to remove any grit from all those nooks and crannies. A few other things to watch out for: Cooking them in reactive metal pans such as aluminum or iron will discolor them; and for a small number of people, they have a flatulent effect similar to that of beans. If this is your fate, alas, this may not be the tuber for you—unless you just think of it as a sunflower.

Lettuces

WHEN MOST PEOPLE THINK OF salad greens they think of lettuce. Indeed, if you have a head of lettuce you have a salad, just awaiting a dressing and perhaps an herb or two. Since lettuce tends to be very mild tasting, it's a good background green to which you add the flavors of dressings, seasonings, other vegetables and fruits, or more assertive greens such as arugula and watercress. But this is not to say that lettuce is dull. Because of its long-standing popularity, numerous kinds have been developed, with different shapes, colors, and textures, each with their own role to play in the kitchen. These are as beautiful combined in a bowl as they are in the garden.

Butterheads

Beautiful, roselike heads have outer leaves that lie relatively flat, and make a great base on which to set other ingredients in a composed salad (page 296). The inner leaves are more tightly folded and thereby become blanched to some degree. This makes a nice contrast of light and dark when both are tossed together. Though classically green, many butterheads are red at the tips, shading to pale green or chartreuse in the center—a gorgeous combination. Butterheads are the softest-textured lettuces, often called Boston lettuce. Bibb types, such as the popular buttercrunch lettuces, are a slightly crisper type. Soft lettuces are the quickest to wilt when used with warm dressings.

Leaf Lettuces

These lettuces form an open head that lets in the sun, so that the leaves are usually quite uniform in color, in shades of green or red. Varieties range from large to mini in size, and in texture from the super-frilly Lollo types to the flatter, lobed oakleafs. All are handy for the cook, because you can easily pluck individual leaves as needed for sandwiches or small salads, without cutting the whole head.

Romaines

These long, upright heads, also called cos after the Greek island of Kos, were grown in Ancient Egypt, as bas-reliefs show. According to food historian William Woys Weaver, the romaine shape was developed in ancient Syria for use "as an edible scoop or spoon when eating tabbouleh-like foods." An excellent use indeed. The small, crisp inner leaves make a fine cracker substitute for dips. Modern romaines are popular as crisp, sturdy, nutritious lettuces that stand up well to heavy dressings (Caesar salad dressing, with its egg yolk, garlic, anchovies, and parmesan cheese, is a classic example). Varieties include not only green and red but also wonderfully red-speckled ones such as Freckles or Flashy Trout Back. Some, such as Rouge d'Hiver, are good for cold weather. Others, such as the Israeli-bred Jericho, withstand summer's heat.

Crisp Heads

The most familiar crisp heads form a hard, pale green ball at the center of the head, and are epitomized by the old variety Iceberg. Once the dominant lettuce in America, thanks to its rugged shipping capability, Iceberg was nearly swept from the market by softer, greener, tastier lettuces, as appetites became more adventurous and eclectic. But a crisp head of lettuce has its use in a salad—think of it as a milder, gentler cabbage. And breeders

are developing greener varieties with more flavor, vitamins, and personality.

When using a crisp head, don't neglect the green outer leaves, where more of the nutrients lie. A class of crisp heads often called Batavian or summer crisp lettuces are especially useful in areas with hot summers. Often they're the only lettuces left standing as temperatures rise.

Baby Leaf Lettuces

These are not a particular type of lettuce, but a technique for growing and harvesting a wide range of them. Planted thickly and cut while only a few inches tall, they make a delicious, tender salad. Pick them frequently by cutting just above soil level with a sharp knife or scissors, and they will regrow for successive harvests—a wonderful way to use garden space. Washed thoroughly, spun or patted dry, and lightly dressed, they make a great instant salad, either by themselves or with other baby leaf crops.

GROW. Lettuce can be sown directly in the row, then thinned, but to make the most of garden space and keep it productive we prefer to sow lettuce in soil blocks (see page 230) and have three-week-old transplants ready to go in when a bed is empty. Most lettuces can be planted 10 to 12 inches apart in the row, with three rows to a 30-inch bed. Smaller ones such as Little Gem can be spaced even closer. The rake and marker teeth on page 232 can be used to make a perfect grid for setting out lettuce.

Lettuce needs a fertile soil, well enriched with compost. Grow it as a fall, winter, and spring crop in warm climates

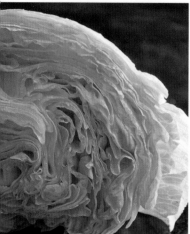

TOP: Crisp head lettuces, such as the Iceberg types, are firm and long-keeping.
BOTTOM: Five Star Greenhouse Lettuce Mix combines a number of varieties and is designed for harvest at the baby leaf stage.

These salad crops were sown in a cold frame for spring harvest.

and a spring, summer, and fall crop in cool ones. Certain lettuces are hardier than others in cold weather, especially the oak leaf types. And any lettuce is hardier when grown as baby leaf, rather than heads. Another trick is to sow them a week or two after your first fall frost date, and transplant them to a cold frame a few weeks later. They will overwinter as small heads and make the rest of their growth in springtime.

Like most greens, lettuces are succulents with a high moisture content so plenty of compost and attention to irrigation are called for. Mulching can help keep moisture in the soil, but we don't recommend that practice with the salad crops. Mulching will encourage slugs under most conditions (not pleasant when you find one in your salad), and all those stray bits of hay or straw have a bad habit of falling into the heart of your lettuces.

HARVEST. Any head lettuce can be picked either by plucking outer leaves or by picking the whole head. The best way to do that is by grasping the head from above and twisting it as if you were unscrewing a light bulb. The stem will snap off at soil level, leaving the taproot in the ground. Lettuces grown for baby leaf production are harvested by the cut-and-come-again method described above.

In the garden, you'll notice that as a lettuce head matures and grows past the edible stage, the center starts to rise as if it wants to become a little tree. This means that it is bolting, that is, sending up a stalk in order to bloom, and produce seeds. As the stalk grows, the leaves may become bitter—but not always, especially in cool weather. Take a nibble and see. You might get a bit more mileage out of

them yet. Even the stalks, when young and tender, can be edible. Taste them, and if they are sweet and mild, strip off the leaves, peel them, and steam them like asparagus. Then douse them with butter or vinaigrette while still warm.

STORE. The softer the lettuce, the less time it will keep. A loose head of oak leaf lettuce might last a week in the fridge in a plastic bag, or wrapped in a moist dish towel, but a crisp head will stay edible for weeks. All lettuces keep better with the head intact than they do as loose leaves. If you find you're not using up your lettuce fast enough, grow small succession plantings, smaller heads, or cut-and-come-again rows, rather than hoarding bags of it in the fridge.

Head lettuces will keep best after harvest if you wait until just before you need them to wash them. If you need just part of the head, break off what you need rather than storing the leaves loose. Tearing the leaves does less damage than cutting them, especially if the knife is dull, but in either case the severed edges will soon oxidize and turn brown. Drying lettuce and other greens with clean towels is the most gentle method, but a lettuce spinner is a great time-saver.

COOK. Some uses for the various types of lettuce are noted above, but have you ever

considered cooking lettuce? There are several popular methods, and whichever one you choose must take into account the textural difference between the lettuce's core and its more tender leaves. Long, slow braising in a flavored broth softens both and makes a tasty dish, although the leaves take on a slightly grayish hue. Cream of lettuce soup, made with just the green leaves and no core, is light and delicious, especially when enriched with egg yolk and cream. Make it in spring when there are beautiful fresh herbs to toss in as well. It can be pureed—or not. We also love a simple sauté in which the core is cut out, diced and cooked gently in olive oil or butter; the chopped leaves are added later, along with herbs. Another way to use up those extra lettuces!

Chicories

IN THEIR VARIOUS FORMS, chicories are widely popular in Europe, especially in winter, and over here they definitely have their place. Although they're less commonly grown than lettuce, many appreciate their firm texture. Some chicories can have a slightly bitter edge, although this is less evident when they are well grown, and they can be blanched to make them milder still. They lack lettuce's milky sap, and hence do not turn brown at the edges the way lettuce does when cut.

Endive

This member of the chicory group forms a robust, thick-ribbed head and tastes best in cool weather. Its most popular form is curly

THE MANY FACES OF THE CHICORY TRIBE:
TOP: Blanca Riccia endive.
CENTER: Natacha escarole.
BOTTOM: Indigo radicchio.

endive, also called frisée, and its varieties range from moderately curled to finely frizzled. This quality gives loft to salads, and helps the leaves to hold dressings well.

Escarole

With its huge heads of slightly wavy leaves, escarole makes a terrific salad. It's great in summer in our climate, but more important, it's the green we go to in late fall when the head lettuce is over for the season.

Radicchio

This too is a chicory, distinguished by dramatic red markings. There are a number of different types, identified with towns in Italy's Veneto region. The most striking ones are from Chioggia, firm round heads with brilliant carmine red leaves and white ribs, or the elongated ones from Treviso, with similar coloration. Castelfranco's lettuce-like heads are pale green speckled with red.

GROW. Curly endive is quite cold hardy, and even more so when grown as a baby-leaf crop. Some varieties such as Bianca Riccia have been bred just for this purpose. Since it regrows vigorously from repeated cuttings, it's a frequent component of our winter salads. With escarole and radicchio we stick to whole heads. Modern radicchio varieties such as Indigo, which do not need cold weather to form heads, have been developed for summer production.

In Europe, winter growers blanch heads of endive and escarole in the field by placing white plastic domes over their centers, pegged down with stiff wire. These are left on for a week, excluding the sun, and it's amusing to see fields with some rows wearing these little hats. The result is a head with a pale yellow-green center. The contrast between light and dark foliage is beautiful in the salad bowl, and the blanching makes the center sweet and mild. As a result, the salad as a whole becomes more mild tasting without totally sacrificing the nutrients and more pronounced flavor you get from the greener leaves. Some modern varieties of escarole are described as self-blanching, and are indeed quite pale in the middle, but we blanch a few anyway for dramatic effect, by inverting terra cotta pots over their centers for a week. (We tape up the hole in the bottom of the pot to make it dark under there.) Blanching can also be done by tying up the centers of the heads with twine or rubber bands, but there is some risk of rot with this method. Whichever way you do it, it's best to initiate blanching when the foliage hasn't been moistened by rain or irrigation.

We have also practiced a more extreme method of blanching in which entire endive heads of the witloof varieties are forced in total darkness. This produces the little pointed heads of Belgian endive (also called witloof chicory) that you see for sale in markets—very white, crisp, and sweet-tasting. Here's how you do it. Plant in early June and dig up the mature plants in October, roots and all. Then cut the foliage off about half an inch above the tops of the roots, being sure to keep the growing tips intact. Trim all the roots to a uniform nine inches or so, and stand them upright in two-gallon buckets, at least twelve roots to a bucket. (If need be, you can use sand to make them stand upright.) Place heavy-duty black plastic bags over the buckets so that not one speck of light can come in. Mature them for a few months in the root

cellar or some other dark, cold but frost-free place. After that they're ready to be sprouted. (Don't worry if they've already started to sprout a bit.) Bring a bucket into the warmth of the house, and fill it with water up to the roots' shoulders. Re-cover with a black plastic bag and place the bucket in a dark place. Elegant little firm, pointed heads four to six inches long, with unexcelled crispness and sweetness, will soon grow. If you do this with radicchio the tips of the heads will be a jaunty pink or red. Even heads that are not tightly folded will taste delicious. Harvest the heads by cutting them at the base, and bring up a new bucket every time an old one has been used up.

HARVEST. Chicories are harvested as whole heads. Though you might pick a few outer leaves of radicchio for a color accent, the inner ones have a more dramatic contrast between red and white, so often the outer foliage is discarded in favor of the tight, firm centers.

STORE. All these keep as much as a week in the fridge except for the curly endives, whose foliage is more fragile.

Hats On, Hats Off

Blanched heads of escarole and endive are a winter staple in France. The salads from which they are made are a blend of pleasantly bitter green leaves mixed with the sweet, pale hearts.

BLANCHING. White plastic hats, pegged to the ground with wire legs, cover the heads to exclude the light.

THE UNCOVERING. After a week, the hats are removed, revealing the heads' blanched hearts.

THE RESULT. The center of the head is a gorgeous pale yellow, its texture tender, its flavor mild.

COOK. We love all of these greens, especially in cold-weather salads. Little heads of Belgian endive are especially choice and give a salad a unique crispness. Their leaves also make perfect spoons for scooping up a dip.

Escarole keeps its body well in cooking, and is a good green to serve those who are put off by the strong flavors of spinach and some brassicas. Try it braised the Italian way with olive oil and garlic, or simply sautéed with butter.

As a salad ingredient, radicchio supplies a striking red accent. Its characteristic hint of bitterness, which lends some character, is said to reflect its virtues as an appetite stimulant and digestive aid. In Venice we often saw long Treviso leaves, blanched the way you would Belgian endive (see previous page), standing upright in a glass to nibble at the start of a meal. As a firm-textured green, radicchio holds up well with heavy dressings containing bacon or pancetta (unsmoked Italian bacon). It also responds well to cooking, though its red color is dulled in the process. Grilled or roasted with garlic and a little olive oil, radicchio is a good foil for rich meat dishes, or on an antipasto plate along with grilled or roasted half onions, eggplant, zucchini, and peppers.

Tarragon

THERE IS SOMETHING ELEGANT about tarragon, with its long, soft, slender leaves, its hint of anise flavor muted by a refined grassiness. But make sure you're growing the true French tarragon, not the large, abundant Russian type, whose flavor is pallid at best. The French type is propagated vegetatively (by division, or from cuttings) and does not breed true to seed, so don't bother with any tarragon seeds, or seed-grown plants. Where it is happy, tarragon is a perennial that grows abundantly, and the appearance of its first apple-green shoots in spring is as exciting as the first crocus.

GROW. Tarragon will sometimes be set back by winter cold—or even killed—in northern climates. Poor drainage, especially in winter, is also its enemy. Our tarragon, in a sheltered spot, grows luxuriantly, and the more we cut it back, the more healthy and bounteous it is.

HARVEST. Pick and use generously, to encourage regrowth. We never bother to bring it indoors in winter, since it will just go dormant for the season, so gather ye foliage while ye may.

STORE. Tarragon dries well, and we often use it that way. But drying, freezing, and even long cooking can sometimes darken the plant to near-black, so fresh use will always be the first choice. Poking some sprigs into bottles of white wine vinegar is also a good way to preserve its flavor for winter use in salads.

COOK. Tarragon marries so well with shallots, in dishes such as the French classic sauce Béarnaise, that I often pair the two in salad dressings, with egg dishes, and with chicken. A toasted open-faced sandwich featuring tarragon, shallots, and mayonnaise is a near-Béarnaise experience without the fuss. This is also an excellent herb for stuffing under the skin of a chicken before roasting. And

Tarragon is a must-grow herb for salads and sauces. Cutting and using it frequently keeps the plant bushy and productive.

it is a salad herb par excellence, with a flavor just assertive enough. Snipping it with scissors is less bruising to the tender leaves than chopping is. Often we'll just leave them whole. Sprigs keep easily in a glass of water, and make a simple enhancement for cauliflower, carrots, green beans, and numerous other vegetables.

SALAD GREENS FROM OTHER PLANT FAMILIES

- MÂCHE
- CLAYTONIA
- SALAD MIXES

ALL OVER THE WORLD there are greens that people pick for nourishment, many of them growing in the wild. And not all of them fall into the brassica family, or the sunflower family just described. Many are weeds in your own garden, such as dandelions and purslane. And among them are several that, because they have come late to the American table, tend to have a cachet as gourmet items. But these peasant greens, in some cases still foraged in the wild in their places of origin, have a longer-standing popularity in Europe. Even when domesticated, a number of them are little changed from their primitive form. Here are just a few unrelated gems that you should try if you have not already discovered their virtues.

Mâche

THIS SALAD GREEN IS BEST KNOWN by its French name, mâche, probably because its English one, corn salad, is too confusing. Before New World corn (maize) was brought to Europe, the word *corn* simply meant grain in general, and this little plant (*Valerianella locusta*) has long been a weed of European winter grain fields. Because of its extreme cold hardiness, it has brought many a forager through the long winter, bearing the gift of green flavors and vitamin C. A Swiss friend reminisces fondly about farm women bringing barrows of it into town, and customers rushing up gleefully for this early spring tonic.

A member of the valerian family, Valerianaceae, mâche makes tidy little rosettes of soft green leaves, that are harvested when about 3 to 4 inches across, and never get much bigger than that. It has a pleasantly chewy texture and a very mild taste.

GROW. It's hard to germinate mâche in summer's heat, and even in Maine we grow it as a three-season crop, direct-sowing through September and October to overwinter in a cold frame or unheated greenhouse. In climates where snow and ice do not cover the ground, you can grow it outdoors in wintertime. A light mulch of straw, autumn leaves, or evergreen boughs will protect the plants if needed. January sowings, for us, grow very slowly

Harvesting mâche.

The trick is to cut just above the root and just below the base of the head, so that it comes away intact.

but we can start picking in early spring. Soon after the ten-hour day returns, in February, any uneaten fall-planted mâche plants will start to go to seed, so we like to have a winter-sown crop of mâche coming along to take their place.

HARVEST. Mâche heads are picked whole by running a sharp knife under them right at soil level. The trick is to cut just above the root and just below the base of the head, so that it comes away intact. This is not a crop you cut for regrowth. As a result you might get less of a yield from it, but on the other hand it can be picked even while frozen, and there aren't many crops like that.

You will need to clean the heads thoroughly. Because they hug the ground they pick up a lot of soil and debris. Just toss them into a sink full of water, where they will form a floating raft. Swish them gently and the dirt will sink to the bottom.

Claytonia in bloom.

STORE. You can keep the little heads in a moist dish towel or a bag in the fridge for a brief time, but they are fragile and do not keep well. That's why you rarely find them for sale in a store.

COOK. We might wilt mâche a little with a warm dressing, but that's as close as we come to cooking it. The light, fluffy nature of the leaves give a wonderful loft to the salad bowl. It mixes fine with other greens but we like it best by itself, or with baked beets, as in the recipe on page 298. Another nice thing about the leaves is that they have a cupped shape that holds the dressing well. But they are very absorptive, so dress lightly, perhaps with a little lemon and oil, lest they turn soggy. If the heads are 4 inches across or more, we

might trim the head at the base so that it separates into individual leaves.

Claytonia

LIKE MÂCHE, CLAYTONIA (*Claytonia perfoliata,* also called *Montia perfoliata*) is relatively unchanged from its wild form. But unlike most foraged crops in the salad repertoire, it is a North American weed. Another name for it, miner's lettuce, recalls its place in the diet of California's gold prospectors working in rustic settings. It is a member of the Portulacaceae family and a distant relative of the summer weed purslane; in fact, in Europe it is called winter purslane.

As with mâche, claytonia's leaves are fleshy and succulent; when you wash them they pile up and float on the water. They are about the size of a quarter (considerably larger in the western species) and round, with a few little points in the margins. A long slender stem holds each leaf aloft like a parasol, then pierces its center at bloomtime with a tiny white or pinkish fragrant flower. The stem then elongates to produce a few more flowers.

GROW. For all its daintiness, claytonia is a vigorous plant that regrows when cut and self-sows with abandon—only a minor nuisance when you've come to love this crop. We direct-sow it for fall, winter, and spring harvest.

HARVEST. The plants are best picked before flowering, or at the single-flower stage, by grasping a bundle of stems and cutting them as if they were a little bouquet. We try to cut them so that there is only an inch or two of stem, because trailing stems in a salad are awkward to eat. If long stems are left on the plant, we trim those, leaving just an inch or two on the plant to encourage tidy regrowth.

STORE. Claytonia may be kept for a few days in the fridge but is best cut and eaten fresh.

COOK. While we have used claytonia alone for salads and garnishes, it is usually mixed with other salad leaves. The flavor is very mild and not very pronounced. Dress it lightly to keep it from absorbing too much oil. It becomes limp when cooked and is best eaten raw. It doesn't store or travel well, which is why it is an unfamiliar crop, rarely encountered in stores.

Salad Mixes

VARIOUSLY CALLED MESCLUN mixes, baby leaf mixes, or spring mixes in stores, these are popular for their variety of colors, flavors, and textures. Sometimes they are just assorted lettuces; other times they are made up of leaves from several different plant families, thus providing a more varied range of nutrients. The best ones are made from small, whole young leaves, not large ones torn up, and are far superior when locally grown and picked fresh, especially if they're your own.

GROW: Many companies offer seed mixes with a lot of variety in one packet, but it's also fun to compose your own by growing many leaf crops for cut-and-come-again use, and picking them at baby leaf size. Choose them by flavors you especially like, and by how they look in the bowl or on the plate. For instance, you might combine dark green baby spinach, tiny crimson leaves of Bull's Blood beet, and pale, frilly curly endive leaves, picked small. Arugula, Swiss chard, and all of the Asian greens described on pages 137 to 139 can be picked at baby leaf size for a salad mix.

We have grown and enjoyed some mixes that are already combined in the seed packet, but more often we sow the crops individually, since the ones we like do not always mature at the same rate. Most are sown in rows 2 inches apart, one inch apart in the row. Some exceptions are spinach, Swiss chard, and claytonia (see the chart on page 457).

HARVEST. Most baby leaf crops are cut when about 3 to 4 inches tall by grasping them with one hand and slicing along the row with a sharp knife. Some people use scissors. If the leaves have grown too long,

Most baby leaf crops are cut when about 3 to 4 inches tall.

cut just the desired length, then trim what is left in the ground to about an inch tall, for tidier regrowth.

STORE. Our salad mixes store up to ten days in plastic bags in the fridge—much longer than the ones you buy because home-grown ones start out fresh. If one ingredient starts to deteriorate first it's usually the soft lettuces.

COOK. All these salad mixes should be handled gently and dressed lightly. Sometimes you'll see collections of the firmer greens sold as braising greens, but braising implies a longer cooking process than suits these young, tender plants. If you cook them, give them a very brief sauté instead.

THE GRAIN FAMILY

* CORN

THE POACEAE, also called the Gramineae family, is populated by grasses. Agriculture was born from the domestication of these crops, which, in large part feed the world. The big three are wheat, rice, and corn (maize) but a number of others, such as oats, rye, barley, millet, sugar cane, and sorghum are of major economic importance. Grain crops, most of which are grown chiefly for their seeds, have jointed, hollow stems, but they vary widely in their growth habits and needs. Wheat, for example, is a cool-weather annual but corn is a warm-weather one.

Whether these can be grown in home gardens depends partly on how easy the seeds are to thresh without mechanized equipment, and space is often a consideration as well. Corn is the only one that home gardeners grow with any frequency, so we've included it here. But those with an interest in exploring grains further should take a look at millet, wheat, and the hulless varieties of oats and barley. Amaranth, though not a grass, is a protein-rich seed crop that is easy to grow and harvest.

Corn

WITH TODAY'S SWEETER CORN VARIETIES you no longer need to sprint from field to stove before the kernels turn starchy. To our taste, the "super-sweet" ones are too sugary, at the expense of corn flavor, so we favor either the old-time, open-pollinated ones with a normal amount of sugar, or the sweeter ones that are merely "sugar-enhanced." We also think that freshly harvested corn still tastes best, whether it loses its sweetness or not.

Try growing one of those beautiful Indian corns such as Mandan Bride. The multicolored ears can be used as fall decorations, and/or ground into cornmeal. You'll need a corn mill to grind it (see page 453), but a sturdy hand-crank model costs little more than a good bottle of olive oil.

GROW. Corn is a big, hungry plant that needs fertile soil. If you know where your corn will go in spring, spread compost lavishly on the bed the fall before. You will also need to keep it irrigated in dry weather.

The usual recommendation is to plant corn in blocks of four rows for proper pollination, but that requires a lot of garden space. You can make a small

Try growing one of those beautiful Indian corns. The multicolored ears are not only decorative but can also be ground for cornmeal.

planting more space-efficient by growing in hills (clusters) instead of rows. To do that sow four seeds in a clump every 18 inches down the center of the bed. Thin to the three best plants. The plants growing together in a clump will pollinate each other more effectively than they would in a line, and the extra space between the clumps satisfies the space requirements of each corn stalk. Although corn seedlings will grow fine in cool soil, the seeds will not germinate in it. So in a cold climate, you can get a jump on the season by growing corn from transplants, set out as soon as the first green shoots appear.

See pages 108 to 109 for advice on planting both sweet corn and corn for grinding in a way that allows you to save their seeds for next year.

HARVEST. When the silks have turned brown on the ears, start checking to see if the kernels have ripened. Squeeze the tip of an ear with your fingers to see if it is still pointed, or if it has acquired a more blunt shape. If you're in doubt, peel back the husk just enough to glimpse the kernels. Look for ones that have attained full size and exude a milky juice when pierced with your fingernail. To pick, pull the ear downward to strip it away from the stalk, holding the stalk firmly so that it isn't broken while you're yanking off an ear. There may be one or more ears still to ripen on it.

STORE. For fresh eating, cook right after picking. Any extra can be frozen if it is done promptly. Although it is possible to freeze cobs whole, the kernels may be mushy, and we find they are tastier (and take up less freezer space!) if the kernels are removed. First blanch the ears very briefly—only a minute or two—in boiling water, plunging them into ice water immediately afterward to stop the cooking. Then cut the kernels off the cob with a heavy, sharp knife. Stand the ear upright on a cutting board, or for a tidier job, use an angel food cake pan. Poke the pointed end of the ear into the pan's central core, slice downward, and let the kernels collect in the pan (see page 360).

Even ears that have passed the optimal point of tenderness can be used in dishes such as succotash (page 355), or frozen. We will often scrape over-mature corn to extract the tender, sweet centers, leaving the tougher jackets on the cob. The way to do this is to slice down the center of each row with the tip of a knife, then turn the knife around and use the back of it to scrape the pulp of the kernels with a firm downward motion. There are also old-fashioned corn-cutting tools that make the job a little easier (see page 453).

If you're growing field corn to be dried and made into cornmeal, you can let it

mature and dry itself right on the stalk, but if the weather is wet you can bring mature ears indoors, husk them, and let them continue the drying process in a warm place sheltered from the rain. It's important not to let them get moldy. The kernels are dry when pressing them hard with your fingernail does not dent them. Store them in a cool, dry place away from rodents. To remove them from the cob, pop them off with your fingers, or use one of the simple, old-time, hand-powered corn-shelling machines (page 453).

COOK. It's hard to beat the simple ritual of husking corn, boiling or steaming it for ten minutes, and slathering it with butter. Leftover ears, whether cooked or raw, are perpetually useful for corn-off-the-cob dishes such as succotash, salsa, or the Real Creamed Corn recipe on page 360. Toss kernels in a skillet with olive oil and other summer vegetables such as red peppers and zucchini, or into pancake batter. Put them in muffins and in shepherd's pie. Make the corn soufflé on page 332, which is easier than you might think.

Asparagus spears start to emerge in our garden in late spring, through a hay mulch.

THERE ARE OTHER PLANTS with food value in the family Asparagaceae, notably agave and yucca, but asparagus is the one most often seen in kitchen gardens. It is a perennial crop that will come up on its own for many years if it is well cared for.

Asparagus

ASPARAGUS ARRIVES during a hungry time of year. Spring has sprung, blossoms have bloomed, and trees are leafing out, but the root cellar is nearly empty and the garden is not yet bountiful. Warm-climate gardeners might still be harvesting overwintered spinach and kale. Provident gardeners might be picking early salads from under protective devices. And anyone who planted parsnips last summer has unearthed them by now. But for the most part, it's a time of waiting for newly sown crops to bear. For a week you've squinted at the asparagus bed to see if any little green tips have poked up, and then suddenly they have, just when you need them most.

GROW. It's very important to prepare a good bed for this permanent crop, so naturally any extra compost or rotted manure you can amend the soil with before planting the asparagus will be of long-lasting benefit. (See page 53 for the placement of the bed.) We have

always grown ours from seed and then transplanted them in, but it's less trouble for the average home gardener to start them from one-year-old roots that are available at garden centers every spring. You'll also be able to harvest them sooner.

Although many old garden books talk about the extensive digging and trenching involved in setting out asparagus transplants, we haven't found that to be necessary as long as the roots are spread out in a wide hole about 8 inches deep, and covered with 4 inches of soil; add more soil as the stems emerge and grow taller, until it is level with the rest of the bed. Just be sure to add enough limestone when preparing the soil to neutralize soil acidity and provide the asparagus with adequate calcium. We keep our asparagus bed heavily mulched between the rows with spoiled hay (see page 184), both to keep down weeds and to provide continuous nutrition from the slow decomposition of the hay. Don't neglect the asparagus in summer just because it is no longer feeding you. The bed must be kept weeded and be irrigated as often as the rest of the garden. In fact, more asparagus beds are lost to weeds—especially grasses—than any other factor.

In late fall, cut the tall, fernlike foliage down to the ground when it turns brown, and compost it along with the previous year's mulch. Then spread compost or manure around the plants and re-mulch them with hay, as above.

HARVEST. Asparagus will usually not be fully productive until it is three years old, depending on how fertile your soil is. At two years you can pick a few spears, but otherwise it's best to let the plants direct their energies into building up their mighty root systems. In the third year cut for two weeks, then for about six weeks in the years thereafter. We use a sharp little kitchen knife or a forked asparagus knife, severing the stem just at the surface—any deeper and there's a risk of injuring new shoots on their way up. Asparagus spears can be snapped so that they break just at the point where the stem becomes tender and succulent, but we do that *after* picking at soil level to leave a tidier, healthier bed.

STORE. The spears taste better when picked immediately before eating. So unless you're planning a dinner for ten and must save up large quantities, don't hoard them for long.

COOK. Home-picked bundles of asparagus rarely enter the house the way store-bought ones do—all the same thickness and all the same length—but that's fine. After washing them, it's a simple matter to pare down the stems of the thicker ones or slice their stems lengthwise so that they take the same time to cook as the thinner ones. It's important not to overcook asparagus, especially the tips, which will begin to fall apart. Although the tips are the most prized, the stems are delicious too, even though the thick ones might need peeling. We're happy to have them when spears are scarce and we're feeding large numbers.

The first time you eat asparagus in spring you want their fresh flavor unadorned, so they're best just simmered or steamed whole for five minutes or so until barely tender, then slicked with butter. If only a small handful appears

After its early summer harvest, asparagus stems are allowed to grow tall with lush, ferny foliage.

daily, chop them into an omelet, a stir-fry, or a sauce for pasta. Serve them steamed and coated with vinaigrette to top a salad. When they are producing abundantly, dress them with sauces, make cream of asparagus soup, quiche, and gratin, or invite friends to an asparagus pig-out party to celebrate.

THE MORNING GLORY FAMILY

• SWEET POTATOES

THIS FAMILY, the Convolvulaceae, is well known for noxious weeds such as bindweed, and the ornamental morning glory, itself invasive in some locales. It also includes the common sweet potato, grown for its tasty and nutritious underground tubers. Like its showy blue-flowered cousin, it is a vine, but one that is content to creep along the ground rather than twine around whatever is at hand in order to gain height.

Sweet Potatoes

NO RELATION TO the white-fleshed so-called "Irish" potato, the sweet potato is at least true to its name when it comes to sweetness. For many, its bright orange, carotene-rich flesh is a must at Thanksgiving dinner.

We can remember when it often lay beneath a carpet of marshmallows, an embellishment for which there is no need.

Not all sweet potato varieties are bright orange. Their interiors range from white to yellow to deep orange-red. The paler ones have a different texture as well: firmer, less moist, and less sweet. Often you'll see the orange type sold or served as yams, another misnomer. The true yam, a black-skinned tuber, is rare in this country and is unrelated.

Though you'd never confuse a sweet potato root with the fruit of a pumpkin or winter squash, I've seen diners mistake the flesh of one for the other on the plate, thanks to their similar appearance. Taste carefully though, and you'll find no touch of squash flavor. Sweet potatoes sing their own song.

This is a crop that needs plenty of space, although there are some relatively compact varieties. We've often taken advantage of its sprawling nature and let it cover a large area with its roving vines to prevent weeds from taking hold. It is well worth growing because it is one of the easiest and most satisfying vegetables to store for winter eating.

GROW. When growing sweet potatoes, the gardener's goal is to produce fat, rounded roots to eat through the winter. For that you need a balanced, moderately fertile, mineral-rich, slightly acid soil. Fertilizers too high in nitrogen will give you lots of lush foliage but skimpy tubers. Better to use plenty of mature compost.

Sweet potatoes also need about four months of nice warm weather. But even in our cool-summer garden we can grow them by warming the soil before planting with

Sprouting Sweet Potatoes

Sweet potato "slips" can be sprouted at home by setting a tuber in moist sand. The slips can then be pulled off and rooted in water (if more roots are needed) before being planted in the garden.

sheets of black IRT plastic (see page 174), and then planting through slits cut in the sheets. Plastic isn't pretty to look at, but the plants' vines cover it in short order. We've also had great luck growing sweet potatoes in summer in a plastic-covered greenhouse.

Unlike most garden vegetables, this one is not grown from seed but from "slips," which are simply the shoots that sprout from a tuber's eyes. These can be purchased by mail order (see page 452 for a source). They will arrive looking quite wilted and pitiful, but will soon revive. You'll want to wait to plant them until the danger of frost has passed, but they can be held for several weeks if needed by placing them root-end-down in a jar of water. Plant the long stems deeply, a foot apart, with the foliage sticking out above the ground. Then keep the plants irrigated throughout the season. In addition to good soil, rotating the crop and providing good drainage will help to avoid pests and diseases. You might need to experiment a bit to find the right variety for your garden. Beauregard has been the best one for us in Maine.

HARVEST. Dig up the roots carefully when the vines start to turn brown. It is okay to let the first frost kill the vines, but harvest the tubers right after it. You don't want to let them spend too much time in soil that is below 50 degrees. Spread them out in a warm, dry place to cure for about ten days; this matures the skin.

STORE. After curing, store them in a cool room in the house (*not* in a moist root cellar), discarding any with signs of rot.

COOK. Most harvests have a few long, thin tubers as well as the fat ones, less

versatile but worth saving if you don't have a large crop. We use these up first, peeling off the rather tough skin, then boiling and mashing them, or cutting them up for a Red Thai Curry (page 404). The fat ones are the ones to bake whole and unpeeled, served with a slit on top and pats of butter slipped in.

As with most vegetables, roasting intensifies their flavor. Bacon and onions make a good foil for their sweetness in the recipe on page 397. And if, for you, sweet potatoes at Thanksgiving dinner should taste like dessert, bake them peeled and mashed in a shallow casserole, sprinkled with brown sugar and pecans. The marshmallows will not be missed.

A successful sweet potato harvest.

THE BUCKWHEAT FAMILY

- **SORREL**
- **RHUBARB**

THE POLYGONACEAE INCLUDE some infamous weeds, such as Japanese knotweed, but several excellent food plants as well. Buckwheat itself, which yields the groats used in the Buckwheat Kasha recipe on page 352, has been useful to us as a weed-smothering cover crop and soil enricher that we till into the soil before the buckwheat has a chance to go to seed. (We'd prefer to harvest it first for cooking, but the seeds' inedible hulls can't be removed without special equipment.) Sorrel and rhubarb, on the other hand, are indispensable for those who are partial to them. One is a flavorful green, the other a perennial stem crop.

Red-veined sorrel is both beautiful and delicious in salads. Here it has been sown in soil blocks.

Sorrel

SORREL IS A MEMBER of the buckwheat family and a distant relative of the cloverlike weed oxalis, sometimes called wood sorrel. There are several cultivated types of the true sorrel, all of them excellent greens. The one generally called French sorrel (*Rumex scutatus*) has smaller leaves than common sorrel (*R. acetosa*), but in fact both are grown in France and are prized by cooks for their sharp lemon flavor. A wild form called sheep sorrel (*R. acetosella*) is a familiar weed in gardens, and is edible. There's a gorgeous red-veined sorrel that is very ornamental. And we also grow a patented sorrel variety called Profusion from the Canadian company Richters. It is sterile, and therefore does not go to seed; thus it is usable for more of the season—all year, with protection.

GROW. Sorrel is a hardy perennial that will come up year after year in spring, just when you need fresh greens on the table. We always have a few clumps of it in our herb garden, along with the perennial herbs, but it can also be grown in greater quantity in the vegetable garden, for cooking. We will usually transplant it to a greenhouse in September, where it will be surprisingly productive.

HARVEST. Pick leaves as needed. More will grow.

STORE. The soft, tender leaves are best used fresh.

COOK. Any sorrel will enliven a salad; just add as much or as little as you like, for just the right amount of lemony bite. We toss in small leaves whole. With larger ones we make a chiffonade by stacking them, then slicing them crosswise into thin ribbons.

Sorrel is also cooked, primarily in creamy soups, where it lends an extra bit of viscosity, making the addition of flour unnecessary. It also can be sautéed and used for a bed on which to set strongly flavored fish, which it complements well. Sorrel's only drawback in cooking is that it turns a dull khaki color when heated, but you can green it up somewhat by adding lots of parsley to the dish. The flavors go fine together.

Rhubarb

IN EARLY SPRING when not much is going on in the outdoor garden, rhubarb springs to life from thick underground tubers. The leaves are huge and handsome, the flowers that appear a little later on are towering plumes. Looks alone might earn a spot for it in the garden, but most people grow it for its succulent, usually red leaf stalks—the only parts of the plant that do not contain toxic levels of oxalic acid.

GROW. Rhubarb is a cool-weather plant that needs a winter chilling period and appreciates some shade and ample watering in hot summers. It may even go dormant in summer, only to reemerge in fall. Give it a place of its own where it can grow undisturbed from year to year, in a deeply dug, well-drained bed enriched with compost or well-rotted manure. It is usually planted from crowns (tubers with growth points on them called eyes), either purchased or obtained from a friend who is dividing a mighty clump in fall. When you plant, make sure the eyes are no more than one inch below the soil surface. Give each plant a 3-foot by 3-foot space. Rhubarb can also be grown from seed but it takes longer.

HARVEST. Wait a year or two after planting to harvest your first leaf stalks, so that the plant can build up some reserves, and always leave half of them on the plant. Leave the toxic flower stalks alone. Pick by giving the leaf stalks a twist followed by a tug, and keep picking until the weather warms, the plant blooms, and the stalks toughen.

STORE. The stems will keep fine in the fridge for a while, much the way celery does. Many people like to can or freeze them for use beyond their season.

COOK. Because rhubarb is mouth-puckeringly tart it is almost always used with lots of sugar or some other sweetener. Hence it's often treated like a fruit, even though it isn't one. Rhubarb stewed with honey is a tasty way to end a meal—topped with a big dairy dollop such as sour cream, ice cream, or mascarpone cheese. Other favorite dishes are rhubarb crisp, and the ubiquitous strawberry-rhubarb pie. That one is a bit of a mystery, since strawberry season just barely overlaps with rhubarb's prime. Our pet theory is that since the first red rhubarb was sometimes called strawberry rhubarb, for its color, the name morphed into a recipe.

SMALL FRUITS

- **STRAWBERRIES**
- **RASPBERRIES**
- **BLUEBERRIES**
- **GRAPES**

FOR THE MOST PART, the subject of sweet fruits lies outside the practice of vegetable-growing explored in this book, just as the plants themselves tend to be grown apart from them. As we noted in

Rhubarb is grown for its flavorful red leaf stalks. (The rest of the plant is toxic.) Pull them off with a twist and a sharp tug.

Rhubarb is a cool-weather plant that needs a winter chilling period and appreciates some shade and ample watering in hot summers.

Chapter 2, these are largely perennial crops whose position is fixed from one year to the next, and therefore do not take part in the crop rotations so central to good vegetable-garden hygiene. Two exceptions are melons, which are annuals (see page 174), and strawberries, which we grow as a two-year crop (see below). Both of these can be incorporated into the vegetable garden proper.

Many small fruits, including strawberries and bramble fruits such as raspberries, blackberries, and black raspberries, are members of the rose family (Rosaceae). The resemblance to roses is particularly strong in the brambles, with their prickly stems. It's not always possible to fit even fruits such as these into a small yard, but one way to do this is by planting them along a fence line or, in the case of grapes, as a shade-casting vine over an arbor. For us, they are an essential part of a homegrown diet. With all these small fruits it's important to shop for varieties that are advertised as suitable for your region (the resources listed on pages 454 to 455 will also guide you).

GROW. In general, all the small fruits appreciate a deeply dug organic soil. It is especially important to keep small fruits in permanent plantings weed-free, because once grass and other weeds are established in a permanent bed they can be hard to remove.

Strawberries

THESE CAN BE GROWN as an annual crop, but are often managed as a perpetual one, since the plants are so good at self-propagating. Thus you can make an initial purchase, then keep them going from year to year. Strawberries spread by sending out runners along the ground, which root and form new plants. If you assign them a bed and plant them in a neat row, they will soon fill that bed with plants until it becomes matted with foliage. We let this happen, but the following spring we dig up some of the healthiest, most vigorous runners and transplant them into a new bed, pinching any blossoms that appear, so that energy is put into establishing roots. This way we always have two beds going at once: one that's two years old and bearing heavily, and a second one of transplanted runners that are not yet ready to support fruit production.

You can also grow a crop of the so-called "everbearing" strawberries, which tend to bear light crops in both early and late summer, taking a break in the hottest weather. We set these out as young plants as early as possible, to get them well established. Then we pick off any blossoms that appear for the first two months. By

Although straw, as the crop's name suggests, is the traditional mulch for strawberries, pine needles work well too if you have them.

late summer their root systems have grown enough to produce fruit, which they'll do until frost. We also grow, and cherish, the tiny alpine strawberries, which are richly flavored, aromatic, and reliably perennial. While regular strawberries are usually grown from purchased plants, alpine strawberries are very easy to grow from seed. The plants do not send out runners, and they make a charming, compact edging. We find that all of our strawberries benefit from a mulch, for winter protection, moisture retention, weed control, and for keeping the fruits clean and free of rot. Straw, as the crop's name suggests, is the traditional material and is still the best one, although we have sometimes used pine needles (see photo at bottom left). For more about strawberries, see page 116.

Raspberries

WE GROW OUR RASPBERRIES on the old-fashioned "hill system" that we learned from a neighbor years ago, and have found it easier to manage than the systems using wire stretched along trellis supports. The first step in the hill system is to drive in a sturdy wooden stake every 6 feet in the row, and then plant one raspberry next to every stake. Each fall we prune out all but the eight most vigorous canes (as raspberry stems are called) closest to the stake, and tie them to it for support. Next year's fruit will be borne on those canes the following summer. We maintain the fertility with a permanent hay mulch, except in a circle around each stake where we spread compost or manure.

We use the hill system for our everbearing raspberries too, growing them in clusters tied to a central stake in their own separate row. Everbearers would normally bear an early and a late crop, but we manage them by having them produce a late crop only, borne on canes grown that same year. To do this we cut *all* the canes right to the ground every fall after they have finished bearing. We leave all the canes that grow up during the summer and harvest them in fall. The result is a very bountiful late-summer harvest that goes on until heavy frost.

Raspberries are typically purchased as one-year-old plants, and you should never have to buy new ones. But it's important to follow the pruning program described above so they don't get out of hand and become a prickly jungle. Their habit is to send out numerous runners in the surrounding soil, which need to be pulled out regularly, saving only the ones you need for bearing.

Blueberries

THE BLUEBERRY, a bush fruit, is a North American native and a member of the heath family (Ericaceae), which also includes heathers, rhododendrons, and azaleas. These all require acid soil in order to thrive, and the blueberry is no exception. That's an advantage at our place, since we have acid soil to begin with. We simply give the blueberry bushes their own bed, and refrain from liming it. Gardens with neutral soil can succeed with blueberries by digging in lots of peat moss, which is acidic. As the years go by, mulching with acidic materials such

Raspberries Grown on the Hill System

WINTER. We leave eight stems per plant and tie them to a stake.

SUMMER. The highly productive bushes can then be picked from all sides.

as autumn leaves and evergreen needles will help keep the pH down—and the weeds as well. Gardeners with alkaline soil (that is, a pH above 7.0) can add elemental sulfur pellets as a soil acidifier. But in our view the far-ranging roots will eventually encounter alkaline soil and alkaline water, and gardeners in alkaline areas would be better off with the other berry fruits that tolerate it better. Also, blueberries are a cool-climate crop. Gardeners in the southern states substitute another native species called rabbiteye blueberry.

The other concern with blueberries is that they need plenty of moisture, but at the same time good drainage. (In nature, highbush blueberries perch on hummocks in or near wetlands, well above the water level.) Whenever possible, we choose a site for them that is moist but not soggy. That leaf mulch will also help keep the soil from drying out.

Grapes

GRAPES DON'T REQUIRE PAMPERING and can grow in most soils as long as the drainage is good. But like any plants they will respond to good care. We grow them on an arbor, planted 8 feet apart. As part of our late-fall work, we top-dress them by spreading a layer of compost about an inch deep, 2 feet on either side of the vines. And we keep the bed cultivated and weed free during the growing season. Since they are growing on an overhead arbor, rather than one of the specialized wine-grape systems, we prune to keep them from becoming too rampant but still nicely covering the arbor and producing grapes. We do the work in late winter, when the branches are still bare, by cutting the new shoots from the previous year back to one bud and removing some altogether where the vines look crowded. We allow a canopy to form above, but pull off any small shoots that form along the vertical trunks of the vines. There are certainly more sophisticated ways to prune grapes, but this more casual system has worked well for us.

HARVEST. Judging by the behavior of very young children, the ability to spot a perfectly ripe berry is, if not inborn, then very quickly learned. When a berry tastes sweet and flavorful, you look for another one like it. Then another and another. We give the kids quart yogurt containers with two holes punched at the rim so you can tie on a string to drape around your neck. We use these ourselves when we pick for dessert, or to put on top of cereal.

Strawberries will ripen after picking if they are almost ripe, but picking ripe is always best. Look at the underside before picking to see if the fruit is red throughout. Raspberries are ripe when they're just the right shade of red, purple, or gold, depending on the variety. Blueberries grow in clusters and ripen gradually. Always look at the bottom of a blueberry before you pick it. If its underside is not dark blue, it is not ripe. Grapes are ripe when a grape picked from the tip of a bunch has brown seeds and tastes sweet. Pick grapes by the bunch. Bunches should be snipped off, not yanked, using heavy-duty scissors or grape shears.

Keeping up with the picking of small fruits is important, if for no other reason than that the birds will get there first if you don't. We've been known to protect strawberries with floating row covers and blueberries with black plastic netting made to deter birds. In wet weather it helps to pick raspberries regularly. Dampness promotes molds and other ills that can spread from overripe berries to ripening ones.

STORE. Strawberries, if perfect, will last a few days. Raspberries, black raspberries, and blackberries are the most fragile, and are best eaten right away, though they might last a few days if chilled. Gather and eat them while you can, or turn them into jams. Blueberries will often keep in good shape for a week in the fridge. Grapes can sit out on the table for that amount of time, or for several weeks chilled.

COOK. When berries are plentiful they are turned into pies, shortcakes, and cobblers, or used in simpler desserts such as fools (see page 446) and raitas (see page

Grapes ripening on our grape tunnel alongside the vegetable garden.

445). By growing varieties with different ripening times, we have a berry parade all summer long, ending with fall raspberries and a few everbearing strawberries. The tiny alpine strawberries make up for their small size by bearing continuously from early summer to frost. A dedicated picker will harvest a small bowl or two, but these are primarily berries for outdoor snacking. Children consider their harvest a treasure hunt and appreciate their ground-level habit. These gems are also perfect for scattering on a whipped-cream-topped cake or pie.

We are not frugal with our berries, preferring to consume as many as possible while they are bearing, then waiting for their time to come round again next year. But a large excess does sometimes result in jams and syrups.

We grow some grapes to be made into a very rustic wine, others for savoring out of hand, some seeded and some not. Heavy clusters of the tastiest ones are a sufficient ending to a meal, set right on the table under a candle or two, with a wedge of good room-temperature cheese. And each year our Worden grapes (a Concord type) are boiled down for hours to make a thick syrup, sweetened with honey. We put this up in half-pint jars to pour over ice cream when a quick dessert is needed, or to give a little extra flavor dimension and color to an apple pie.

We're not big on berries in savory dishes, but grapes are another story. Cut them in half, remove seeds as needed, and add to chicken salad and tuna salad, or sprinkle them over the top of a tossed salad, along with cheese. Serve them as a condiment with curry, with couscous, or whenever you're looking for a winning combination of sweetness, tartness, and crunch.

TREE FRUITS

- APPLES
- PLUMS
- PEACHES
- CHERRIES
- PEARS

WHAT'S NOT TO LIKE about food that grows on trees? There's something wonderful about the way a fruit or nut tree delivers its harvest to you year after year. And you don't need to have space for a whole orchard. As we discussed on page 58, appropriate trees can be introduced into the landscape even on a small property. Most fruit trees are grafted, and you can choose ones on dwarf or semi-dwarf rootstocks if space is limited.

We do, however, want to emphasize the importance of choosing trees wisely. An apple tree might be with you for more than a lifetime, and a nut tree for centuries. It can be disappointing to make a choice and then find out some years down the road that the tree will not survive in your area, or is not well adapted and hence prone to pest and disease problems. Most annual food crops can be made to do well in average garden conditions, and even when they don't, little time or space is sacrificed. But tree crops are very climate-specific. The possibilities vary greatly from state to state or even county to county. For example, we need a very short-season grape for our cool sliver along the Maine coast, and only one variety of peach, called Reliance, has worked consistently well for us. Southern and West Coast gardeners need to match their mild winter temperatures to the chilling

Apple trees are the mainstay for us.
Since they are such a long-term investment,
we spent two years improving our less-than-ideal
soil before planting the trees.

requirements of certain low-chill peaches and apples.

We urge you to look around and see which species and varieties have done the best for your neighbors. Other local resources such as universities and the Extension Service can also be of help, as can books with a more detailed treatment of fruit culture (page pages 454 to 455). As you narrow down your choices, make sure you get information on which varieties are self-fertile and which need another tree to pollinate them. In the latter case, the recommended companion trees will have bloom times that overlap enough for pollination to take place. You'll also want to grow fruits that please your taste buds and suit your purposes in the kitchen. Visiting a pick-your-own orchard in your area is a fun and useful way to educate your palate—and pick up some tips on choosing and growing local varieties.

As with small fruits, a great many tree fruits, such as apples, peaches, pears, plums, and cherries, are members of the rose family (Rosaceae) and have a number of requirements in common.

GROW. The ideal spot for most fruit trees is on a gentle south slope, except when a fruit's blossoms are at risk of being killed by early frosts and would be unable to set fruit. In that case a north-facing slope would foster a later, safer bloom time. If you have no such options, just pick a sunny, well-drained spot for your trees, and do your best to make a wise selection.

Apple trees are the mainstay for us. Since they are such a long-term investment, we spent two years improving our less-than-ideal soil before planting the trees. In most parts of the country you wouldn't have to do this, but it is nice to know that with a little extra effort, one can successfully grow tree fruits anywhere. Here is what we did. The first spring we brought in as much extra organic matter as we could round up, spread limestone and rock powders, tilled it all in, and planted buckwheat as the first of a series of green manures (that is, crops grown and tilled under to add fertility to the soil). Buckwheat is a wonderful pioneer green manure since it feeds well on less soluble nutrients and is tolerant of any remaining soil acidity. We followed the buckwheat by tilling under some composted animal manure we were able to find, and in late summer we sowed the area to a mixture of oats and field peas, which we left there for the winter. The second spring, with the soil on its way to being fertile, we sowed biennial sweet clover, a vigorous deep-rooted legume that grew all that summer and remained over the following winter. We tilled it under thoroughly before planting the apple trees. We did the same thing with our young peach orchard, and we'd recommend this program for most any area where fruit trees will be grown.

Peach trees are much more short-lived than apples but they generally bear at a younger age. Peaches also need to be thinned on the branch, with a distance the size of your fist between fruits. This leads to healthier fruits and less weight for the relatively fragile branches to bear. Apricots need long, warm summers and fairly mild winters. With cherries you can choose between the sweet cherries for fresh eating, best grown in moderate climates, and the sour ones that are more hardy and great for baking. With plums, the red ones are not as cold hardy as

Besides bearing wonderful fruit, a peach tree makes a graceful addition to even a small yard.

smaller purple ones. If you find a pear tree that is right for your area, it will be long lived if cared for well.

It might seem logical to splurge and purchase fairly mature trees if you are in a hurry to get fruit, but in the long run you're better off buying ones that are just one or two years old. They will get established better and are likely to be healthier and more fruitful. But it's important to protect these young treasures from predators. The black plastic netting sold to keep birds from eating berries is also useful for deer protection of young fruit trees. But as the trees get larger you may have to put up tall fences if you live in serious deer country. Various repellents are sometimes effective. The other major threats are meadow voles and rabbits, which can kill a young tree by nibbling the lower bark. We encircle the trees with 18-inch-tall cylinders of hardware cloth or aluminum screen material at planting time, burying them an inch or so in the ground. The screen is also useful against borers that drill into and enter the base of fruit trees and lay eggs there; the larvae that emerge tunnel in and injure or even kill the trees. After the tree is planted we mulch it with spoiled hay (see page 184), hay mixed with manure, or mowings from any thick mat of tall grasses we can cut locally, replenishing it each year in late fall, after the leaves have been shed.

An old-timer once remarked that the best time to prune apple trees is when your knife is sharp—in other words, when you have the time to do it. Dormant pruning in late winter is traditional, but we also prune our apple trees then because that is convenient for us. Like many home-garden orchardists we don't follow any specific system. When the trees were young we selected sturdy branches arranged around the trunk. Since then, we've tried to use common sense and pay attention to the basic principles. That means we thin out branches to let the sun in to ripen the fruit. There's an old New England saying that one wants to keep the center of the tree open enough to throw a cat through it; so we cut out any inward-pointing branches. We prune any rubbing or crossing branches and all suckers and water sprouts (those shoots that grow straight up, with few leaves and no fruit). We also take out any broken or dead branches. This advice can be applied to most other fruit trees as well. However, peach trees are not pruned in very cold weather, and certain upright plum and cherry varieties are better trained to have a central leader rather than an open center. Pear trees, which can grow quite tall, are best pruned for lower growth. Pruning, as well as thinning of the fruit, will also help keep pests and diseases at bay.

The pests and diseases that can sometimes plague fruit trees can be frustrating for home gardeners. Most prefer not to spray poisons on what they are going to eat, and would not have the time or expertise for a spray program anyway, even with safe products such as horticultural oils or benign dusts like Surround, which is made from a powdered clay called kaolin. Hanging red sticky ball traps two weeks after petal fall can lessen damage by attracting and killing pest insects such as the apple maggot fly, before they can do their work. Gathering up fallen leaves from trees with scab diseases can be helpful. Breaking apart

An old-timer once remarked that the best time to prune apple trees is when your knife is sharp—in other words, when you have the time to do it.

the tent caterpillar nests in the crotches of cherry trees and stomping on the larvae is not a pleasant job but it is an effective one. And turning out your chickens to gobble up insects such as plum curculio is always a good idea (their manure is a plus!). But to us the most logical course is to choose appropriate, resistant varieties, keep the trees happy with yearly applications of hay mulch and well-rotted manure, and maintain a biologically diverse environment. Avoiding poison sprays can encourage the presence of birds and other creatures that feed on insect pests. And growing nectar-rich flowers such as clovers, mints, asters, and coneflowers will attract both insect pollinators and beneficial insect predators. Professional organic apple growers sometimes plant strips of these between their rows of trees, and you can buy seed mixes specially formulated for this purpose. The home gardener's flower garden can have the same healthy influence.

These Reliance peaches are hardy enough even for our northern farm.

HARVEST. Picking would seem to be the simplest task but there is an art to it. Low-hanging fruit, naturally, comes first. After that your options are shaking the tree, with its risk of bruising the fruits when they fall, climbing the tree, which has its upper limits and risks bruising you if *you* fall, and using an apple-picking tool—a little basket on the end of a long pole. Nudge the fruit a bit and if it is ripe it will usually fall in.

So when is a fruit ripe? With apples, bright color is not always an indicator, but dark-colored seeds are, so cut open a few fruits to see if the tree is ready. Peaches lose all but the slightest green color when ripe and feel a little soft and yielding. Apricots and red plums should be picked plump and ripe; but pears, cherries, peaches, and purple plums will ripen off the tree if picked a little early.

How you pick is important too. Try to be gentle with fruits, especially those that bruise easily, and also be gentle with the twigs on which they grow. You don't want to injure the spurs on which new ones will be borne next year. Use two hands and release the fruit with a careful twisting motion.

STORE. The storage life of fruits ranges from that of the delicate fig, with its brief moment of honey-dripping perfection, to the almighty apple, crisp in its all-winter basket or bin. In between are fruits like pears and peaches, which go oh-so-quickly from ripe to rotten. Even among apples, some are borne in late summer and need to be eaten fairly quickly, and others, like the russets, come in late but last for months and months. Storage conditions must be cool and moderately moist. A root cellar works fine for apples, but since the ethylene gas they give off can turn root crops like carrots bitter and cause them to sprout prematurely, it's best to find a separate spot.

There's also the option of preserving fruits by drying, freezing, and canning. Apricots and apples are particularly tasty dried, and there's nothing like a good stash of cherry jam, plum chutney, and applesauce for winter eating. And while we're visiting the rose family, how about the bright red or orange fruits of the rose itself, called hips? Small and seedy they may be, and not as versatile in cooking, but you can make a beautiful jelly out of them. Or fill jars with them, pour boiling water and honey over them, and can them for an old-fashioned drink called shrub, extremely rich in vitamin C and named for the thorny plant on which they grow.

COOK. The fruits that we harvest are there to be eaten out of hand, unadorned. But often we'll turn them into puddings, tarts, pies, and cakes. Each fruit's season is a festival in its honor, especially if, as is the case with peaches, that season is a short one. For weeks there's peaches and cream, peach shortcake, peach cobbler, and peach custard. We also love peaches in salads, such as the one for Chicken Salad with Spiced Peaches on page 309. The same thing happens with a gift of a neighbor's pears or cherries.

Although apple season is almost year-round, that fruit has its sub-seasons as well. Our old orchard, which Eliot planted over forty years ago, contains only varieties that have settled into the climate and soldier on from one year to the next. We enjoy the first pies of the season with the Summer Rambos, which appear in August. Then come the big, juicy Spigolds, and the IdaReds, whose red-pigmented skin tints applesauce pink. The beautiful little Golden Russets are sweet, crisp, and khaki colored—our best keepers, lasting all winter long in a spare fridge along with other good keepers such as the Macouns. We also press gallons of delicious sweet cider with a mix of whichever apples are most plentiful. What we don't drink right away we can in gallon jars to have on hand until the supply is gone.

Apples vary in their degree of sweetness and tartness, their juiciness, their firmness, and some are best suited to specific purposes. An apple's age adjusts the equation as well. But I find it is always possible to add or subtract sugar, to vary the amount of liquid—or thickeners—and the length of cooking time, so that any apple you use in a recipe will do fine. They needn't be perfect, either. I have no problem cutting out the odd blemish. Stored apples, however, do need to start off in good shape, and be checked frequently so that the proverbial rotten one doesn't spoil the rest.

Apart from winter desserts, we count on apples for use in salads (page 300), soups (page 270), and even sandwiches (page 266). And there's no better snack than an apple, with a piece of well-aged Cheddar cheese. ☼

> Each fruit's season is a festival in its honor, especially if, as is the case with peaches, that season is a short one.

CHAPTER

5

Making It Easy

WHEN ADAM AND EVE WERE THROWN OUT OF EDEN they were told: "By the sweat of your brow you will eat your food." In other words, the Garden of Eden was paradise, but now you've been expelled and have to work for your supper. It's true enough that gardening is work, but it should be pleasant work. It should not be drudgery. Since the two of us are engaged in vegetable growing as a business, we've spent a lot of time figuring out how to enjoy our daily work. And you can too, in your own home garden.

PLANNING AHEAD

FIRST ON OUR MAKING-IT-EASIER LIST is thinking ahead, which starts with lists and reminders of what to get and when to get it. Seeds need to be on hand when you need them, as do bags of limestone and other garden soil amendments. It's also important to have a garden map. We have a very simple blank map layout of our home garden's growing areas, so that we can fill in what we're planting and when we're planting it each year, just as we do on our farm. We want to know what will be growing where, and whether we've forgotten anything. We make extra blank copies so we can redo the plan if we want to make changes in the future or just want to visualize what future changes might look like, and we save all these maps, marked with the actual results of each year's garden, so we can learn from our experiences. The plan at left is an example.

We also use our map to plan succession cropping (see page 50). We mark on each section an estimate of the date when the present crop will be harvested and the remaining plants can be pulled. At that point the area will be available for replanting. For example, our usual date for planting fall peas in the home garden is between July 15 and August 1, so they will mature in the cool fall but before hard frosts. A glance at the dates written on the garden map tells us which beds should be available on that date (crops without dates are there until frost). A quick thought about crop rotation lets us decide whether the area is appropriate for peas. Then all we have to do is plant on the desired date.

Garden Plan 2013

Corn	
Corn	
Corn 8/25	Peas 7/15
Corn 8/15	
Cucumbers Climbing Zucchini	Beefsteak Tomatoes
	Plum Tomatoes
Artichokes	Cherry Tomatoes
	Onions 8/5
Early Broccoli 8/1	Leeks • Garlic
Kale • Collards • Chard	Beets 8/1
	Carrots 8/1
Potatoes	Bush Beans 9/1
Peppers & Eggplants	Spinach • Lettuce Asian Greens
Celery • Celery Root Fennel	

ORGANIZING YOUR TOOLS

ANOTHER THING that makes our work easier is organization. Let's say you have the seeds on the day you wish to plant, but no hoe to make the furrow with. Of course you can always use a stick or whatever else is at hand, but the right tool makes for pleasant work. You can find that tool more easily when you need it if there is some sort of garden shed with hooks, a tool wall in the garage where your tools can be hung, or even just a garbage can in the garage that stores tools, working end up.

A relaxing winter gardening activity is to go to the tool shed with a can of boiled linseed oil and a rag and coat the wooden handles ahead of the garden season, so they're pleasant to hold and don't dry out and get brittle. If there are rough spots on the wood, smooth them with sandpaper before applying the linseed oil. Use a file to make sure the metal edges are sharp, not just on the hoes but on the shovels and spades also. A 10-inch metal file from the hardware store (commonly called a "mill bastard") is best for the job. We humans are a tool-using species and we develop affection for the simple tools we garden with, so it's satisfying to maintain them in A-1 condition. Sources for tools can be found on pages 453.

DO YOU NEED POWER TOOLS?

ON THE WHOLE, motorized tools are not necessary for the home food garden. A tiller is obviously useful if you want to turn your lawn or some other vegetated area into a garden. But you don't have to own one. You can always rent one or hire somebody who has one. Do you need a tiller once a garden is established? The answer depends on how well you maintain the garden, both when it's in production and at the end of the season. In many gardens a tiller is used to erase all the messy weeds and plant waste left over from last year, so as to be able to start over

again with a clean slate. The tiller will do an excellent job of that, but if you maintain the garden by keeping up on weeding, removing old plants to the compost heap, and replanting harvested areas to new crops, you won't have any mess that needs erasing. When you want to incorporate more rock powders or compost, you can do the job very efficiently by working the soil shallowly with back and forth strokes using a tine cultivator. If you have loosened the soil first with a fork, that work will be quite easy.

USING A BROADFORK

YOU MIGHT HAVE HEARD of the laborious practice called double-digging, an energetic turning over and deep mixing of the soil, from the surface down to the subsoil layer. This task does create a loose and deep soil. But since we want our work to be pleasant, we use a simpler and more effective method to achieve just that. The tool that will do the job is called the broadfork (see the how-to on page 224). The broadfork is not used to turn over the earth, merely to lift and loosen it from underneath to relieve any soil compaction. If you ever dig down into a deep fertile soil, you'll see the beautiful structure of crumbs, worm tunnels, and root channels created by the plants and all the soil creatures. This ideal structure forms naturally when the soil is fed compost and left to its own devices. That is the well-aerated structure that plant roots have evolved to exult in. We see no sense in destroying the structure by turning the soil over and rearranging it—we're only interested in letting air into it. That's because the garden vegetables

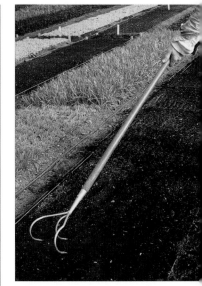

Using a three-tine cultivator to mix amendments into the soil.

It's important to keep essential tools organized and within easy reach. We erected this freestanding "tool wall" at the hub of our farm.

we're growing are almost all annuals, and so our garden soil does not have the much more extensive root system and natural aeration that would be established by perennial plants in a natural setting. Our work with the broadfork makes up for that lack. Another advantage to broadforking is that it does not bring up weed seeds from down below.

The broadfork has two handles. The crossbar between them is ideally as wide as the bed. Ten-inch-long teeth, made for penetrating the soil, extend below the cross bar. In use, you hold both handles upright and press the teeth into the soil by stepping on the crossbar.

Then the handles are pulled back toward you just enough to lift and loosen the soil before returning the handles to the upright position and raising the tool out of the soil. It is then moved back 6 inches or so, inserted into the soil again, and the process is repeated. The idea is to prevent any soil compaction from forming in the top 10 inches, by lifting and loosening the soil to allow more aeration but without destroying the soil structure. The broadfork is designed to do just that, and with the force of gravity doing most of the work, it's a delightful tool to use. In a new garden you may not be able to insert the teeth

Using a Broadfork

DRIVE IT IN. Gravity helps you to sink the tines into the soil without much effort.

PULL TOWARD YOU. Pulling the handles toward you lifts the soil and aerates it without turning it over.

REPEAT. With the handles upright again, raise the tool out of the soil, move it toward you 6 inches, and drive it in again. Repeat until the whole bed is aerated.

to their full length, but over time your efforts will pay off and a deeper soil will result. We have seen broadfork designs with longer teeth (up to a ridiculous 18 inches), but that's unnecessary. Soil compaction forms between 6 and 8 inches down, and any extra depth of tine makes for unnecessary work.

In a small garden you can achieve similar results by inserting a garden fork into the soil and pulling back similarly on the handle. In either case, just rake the surface smooth after you've finished aerating, and you're ready to plant. Remember, you're not doing this to the whole garden all at once, but rather on a bed-by-bed basis as you progressively sow spring crops and replant summer ones. ☼

SPREADING OUT THE WORK

ALTHOUGH GARDEN WORK often seems to pile up at certain times, there are ways to spread it out more evenly throughout the year. Yes, spring and early summer are busier than late fall and winter, but try this: After the final harvest of each garden bed in the fall, consult your garden plan and do as much of the preparation for next year's first crop in that space as seems appropriate. In our garden that's when we spread an inch or so of compost and mix it in shallowly. If your soil test calls for more lime, phosphate rock, or greensand, fall is the best time to add it. If a bed won't be used for the earliest crops, you might also spread a layer of spoiled hay or straw over it. That will protect the soil

from erosion and also provide some extra plant food next summer from the slow decomposition of the covering layer over the winter. That's just the kind of thing that happens in the natural world. Next spring you'll rake off any un-decomposed residue and add it to the compost heap. The great benefit of doing a lot of the preparation work in fall is that you have the time to do it without being rushed. In spring the season advances so quickly that it's easy to get behind, especially in a wet spring when you must wait for the soil to be workable. When you're ready to get seeds into the ground, it's so much better if the garden is ready for you. ☼

Pelleted seeds are easy to see, and easy to sow with the desired spacing.

SOWING SEEDS

BESIDES SPREADING OUT THE WORK over the year, you can also find ways to do less of it. One excellent way is through efficient sowing and transplanting. Let's start with the first. Seed catalogs that sell to commercial growers as well as home

gardeners offer seeds that have been made easier to sow by pelleting, sizing, or decorticating them. The pelleting process encases odd-shaped seeds like carrot and lettuce in enough clay coating to make them into small round balls. Seed-sizing is used to ensure that each lot of seeds is within a narrow range of diameter since seeds of the same crop can vary in size depending on where they are in the seed pod. Both pelleting and seed-sizing make using the seeds in a precision seeder much more efficient. Similarly, decorticating removes the rough edges on irregularly shaped seeds like beets and chard, also making them easier to sow with a precision seeder. Although these selected and prepared seeds are more expensive, we think the extra expense is worth it in greater efficiency at planting time.

If you sow by hand, the ease of picking up pelleted seeds one by one with your fingers will allow you to accurately sow crops like carrots and lettuce at the ideal spacing, so that you need fewer seeds and avoid the long, tedious job of thinning rows that were too closely sown. If you choose to use a small home-gardener-size precision seeder (see pages 452 to 453 for sources), any one of the seed treatment options will help in assuring evenly spaced seeds. Precision seeders offer a range of hole or cup sizes to pick up and deliver seeds. The more closely your seed size fits that hole or cup, the better things work and the fewer seeds are wasted. This is a tool best suited to an experienced gardener with a large vegetable plot. ☼

If you do a lot of direct-sowing, a precision seeder saves time and gives you perfectly straight, accurately spaced rows. Seeds are poured into small hoppers and fall into holes in the axle, which turns by means of the rotation of the wheels as you pull it along. The tool comes with interchangeable axles, each designed to sow seeds of a specific size.

STARTING SEEDLINGS

SOWING SEEDS IN CONTAINERS rather than directly into the garden, then setting out the crops as transplants, has long been a popular garden technique. For the crops for which this is appropriate, transplants allow you to place seedlings at the ideal spacing for best growth right off the bat, rather than thinning them to that spacing later on. Some vegetables, such as tomatoes, peppers, and eggplants, need to be started ahead of outdoor planting time in order to get them to mature a decent crop, especially in cool climates. Others, such as broccoli, kale, and lettuce, will simply feed you sooner if you can give them a head start. Some seeds, those of cucumbers for instance, germinate poorly in cool soil, and will give a more assured crop if they begin their life in a warm and sheltered spot. Other crops, although they germinate well, are especially pest susceptible when young. For this reason cabbage, cauliflower, and broccoli often succeed better if set out as three-week-old seedlings.

Transplants that you started, or purchased at the local garden center, and then set out on the first suitable spring day, give a great sense of accomplishment. What was previously bare ground is suddenly a green symbol of the summer to come. Whether you transplant the seedlings into tidy rows or varied artistic patterns, there's something about their young green vigor that you'll never tire of.

STARTING SEEDLINGS OUTDOORS

ONE OF THE SIMPLEST WAYS to start a wide range of vigorous seedlings with very little effort is to sow seeds directly into a cold frame. (See pages 87 to 89 for more about cold frames.) The extra daytime warmth and nighttime cold protection offered by the cold frame makes it an easy place to start seeds ahead. It isn't a greenhouse, but with a bit of ingenuity you can use it like one. Gardeners for the past 400 years have done very well getting early crops off to a healthy start with nothing but a cold frame. We have used ours to start all of the following: beets, broccoli, cabbage, chard, fennel, kale, lettuce, leeks, and onions. And the way we do it allows us to dispense entirely with the usual pots and flats. We just spread potting soil 2 inches deep in a section of the cold frame and sow seeds directly into it (see page 228).

If you're starting a number of crops, it helps to edge each separate area with thin strips of wood as if it were a flat. We make narrow straight furrows in which to sow the seeds with the sharp corner edge of a board. Once the seedlings are up, we prick them out, lifting them very gently, and transplant them to wider spacing on a grid in another section of the frame. Depending on the eventual size of the seedlings, they can be spaced at 2 by 2 inches or 3 by 3. You then let them grow to the size you wish, cut the soil into cubes with a knife like a tray of brownies, and transplant each well-rooted seedling with its own cube of soil into the garden. To avoid the expense of potting soil, you can make an effective substitute by mixing equal parts of fine compost, sifted garden soil, and peat moss. Just remember that weeds will grow along with your seedlings in that mix, which won't happen with purchased potting soil if it has been properly made.

Instead of starting your transplants under cold frames, you could do it equally well under quick hoops, which we described on pages 90 to 91. Setting them up takes less work or money than building or buying cold frames, so if you're starting a lot of seedlings they may make more sense.

Some gardeners who are used to direct-sowing all or most of their plants into the spot where they are to grow, then thinning them, may wish to continue to do so. Others may want to stick to the traditional indoor methods described below for the warm-weather crops. But we offer the cold frame/quick hoop method for several reasons: First, it's hard to find a window with adequate sun. Light doesn't come from enough directions, and

Choose a warm sunny spot, sheltered from the wind, to set up your seedlings.

Starting Seedlings in a Cold Frame

MAKE A FURROW. Spread potting soil in the cold frame, 2 inches deep. Then press the corner edge of a stick or board into the potting soil to make straight, narrow furrows.

SOW THE SEEDS. Make a crease in the seed packet and tap the packet with your finger to make the seeds come out one by one. When the seedlings germinate, thin them to the desired spacing as needed.

PRICK THEM OUT. Lift the seedlings gently, one by one, and transplant them to another part of the cold frame at a wider spacing.

LET THEM GROW. Leave the young plants in the cold frame, protected from severe weather, until they are of proper transplanting size.

CUT CUBES OF SOIL. When ready to transplant, take a knife and cut a cube of soil around the seedling, then carefully lift it out.

TRANSPLANT. Plant the seedlings in your garden bed, using the grid-marking system shown on page 232.

seedlings are likely to be leggy. Second, the cold frame/quick hoop method is simple and goes with the flow. It takes advantage of the tolerance many crops have for cool weather. Third, it's more secure. If you forget to water a flat you can lose the seedlings very quickly, but if their roots are in the ground there's much more leeway. And fourth, both are handy devices you might already have in order to extend the growing season; you're simply adding another use for them. You just need to be sure to vent them on sunny days, or always keep them open a crack to avoid cooking the plants inside.

Another solution, if you have a warm, sunny spot sheltered from wind in springtime, is to set up a table there—it could even be planks or a sheet of plywood on sawhorses—and start moving your cool-weather transplants out there as soon as you dare (see page 227). Keep some floating row cover material handy (page 90) for covering them at night. You won't have the advantage of inground growing, but it will ease your space crunch indoors.

STARTING SEEDLINGS INDOORS

WHEN STARTING SEEDS of tomatoes, peppers, eggplants, or cucumbers, you'll probably need more warmth than outdoor systems provide, and you should start them indoors. One ideally warm place for germinating is on top of the refrigerator. The compressor on the back gives off heat that rises toward the top. Just be sure to pay attention and move the flats to a sunny window just as soon as the seeds germinate. The ideal sunny window is a bay window, in which the seedlings receive light from the sides as well as the front, but use the best window you have. Light is key to growing stocky, healthy transplants. If you have no sunny windows you can use fluorescent plant lights. We've used them, but find them to be a fussy and expensive substitute for sunlight. Unless you're growing varieties that garden centers do not sell as starts, it sometimes makes more sense to purchase your tomato, pepper, and eggplant seedlings there. (For advice on shopping for seedlings see page 175).

People often have their favorite seed-starting devices, and there are a lot of them on the market. But it's also possible to keep life very simple and create your own. A seed tray can be made by turning an empty half-gallon milk container on its side, cutting it in half lengthwise, and punching a few holes in the bottom of each half for drainage (see page 231). Fill it with the seed-starting mix described on page 227, sow your seeds, keep them watered gently with a fine spray, and wait for little green shoots. We ignore the standard advice about "waiting for the first true leaves to appear," and move the tiny seedlings up to a larger container as soon as possible. The British horticulturist William J. C. Lawrence, writing in *Science and the Glasshouse* in 1948, demonstrated that the sooner you move a new seedling to a bigger container the better. That container could be a plastic tray, but if you prefer to avoid plastic you can make wooden flats. For another option see "Starting Seedlings in Soil Blocks" on page 230.

After these plants have been in the flats for two or three weeks, move them up to four- or five-inch pots (measured

Light is key to growing stocky, healthy transplants.

Starting Seedlings in Soil Blocks

SOIL BLOCKERS. These handy tools, which come in several sizes, compress moist potting soil into cubic blocks by means of a plunger. There is then no need for plastic cell trays or peat pots. (See pages 452 to 453 for sources.)

INSERTS. A nipple inside the blocker makes an indentation into which you can drop a seed. You can buy inserts for the two-inch blocker that replace the nipple and make a ¾-inch-cube-shaped hole in the soil block instead.

THE MINI-BLOCKER. This blocker makes ¾-inch cubes exactly the size of the holes you've made with the inserts.

SMALL FLATS OF MINI-BLOCKS. By sowing into these tiny cubes, you can produce a large number of seedlings—from which to select the best—without using a lot of space or potting soil. We use a very fine potting soil mix sifted through a ¼-inch screen for mini-block cubes.

MOVING THEM UP. As soon as the seeds have germinated, you can move them up to the larger blocks. Simply drop the mini-block into the mini-block-sized hole.

READY TO PLANT. As the roots of these tomato seedlings grow, they fill the block, which does not fall apart and is easy to handle. There is less transplant shock with soil blocks than with any other method.

horizontally at the top). This is the size pot often used to sell perennial flowers at nurseries, so if you or a friend shop for these they can be saved for potting up seedlings. If you have timed your sowing right, you can move the plants into the cooler conditions of a cold frame or quick hoop to give them more light. This will keep them from becoming leggy, and it will also harden them off and get them ready for life in the real world at a time when outdoor conditions are *almost* warm enough. You want plants like tomatoes to be robust, stocky, and well on their way when they're six to eight weeks old and the soil and air are warm enough to plant them.

We suggest that you'll do better by starting your warm-weather seedlings later than most books recommend, and putting younger plants into the garden. In our experience five- to six-week-old transplants of these crops are old enough. Your transplants will not have been made leggy and stressed by inadequate light and they will produce better. Although your first harvest may be slightly delayed, a younger more vigorous plant will give you a far larger total harvest by the end of the season. ✹

Starting Seedlings in Milk Cartons

An economical way to start warm-weather crops indoors is to sow them in cut-down milk cartons. Make a seedling tray by cutting the carton in half lengthwise. You can then move the seedlings along to larger containers, which could be milk containers as well. Here, a tomato seedling is growing to planting size in its own milk carton "pot."

PLANTING FOR WEED CONTROL

THE BEST WAY to make garden work easier is efficient weed control. That overcomes what we've always considered the biggest constraint to successful home gardening—the sense of hopelessness many gardeners feel in the face of heavy weed pressure. Not only are weeds competing with the vegetables for garden nutrients and moisture, but they're making you feel bad. They give the garden a look of untidiness and neglect. It's not a pleasant place to hang out. And once weeds have gained the upper hand, the task of getting rid of them seems almost impossible. The key is to not let weeds get ahead of you. And there are tools and techniques designed to help you achieve that goal. Let's start with our favorite weeding tool, because our planting system is designed to accommodate its use.

USING A HOE

WORKING ON HANDS AND KNEES to pull weeds can be hard on the body, especially on the back. It's much more comfortable to work in an upright position, cultivating with a hoe. The seeding and spacing suggestions described below will help to make that cultivating easier. But even better, if the ideal hoe is selected for the job, this can be truly enjoyable work. In our experience that means a hoe designed for skimming (shallow cultivating) rather than chopping. That difference depends on the angle of the blade to the handle.

Marking Rows for Transplants

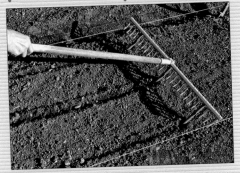

MARK THE ROWS. Use the same bed-forming rake shown on page 42, along with the red plastic marker tooth extensions that can be purchased with it. (See page 453 for a source.) Placing the markers on the teeth of the rake gives you parallel rows the desired distance apart. (See page 457 for a chart of plant spacing.)

MAKE A GRID. Reset the markers for the desired plant spacing within the rows. Draw the rake across the bed to make the grid.

PUT IN YOUR TRANSPLANTS. Use the intersections of the grid lines as your guide.

The chopping hoe, the standard model that hangs on racks in every hardware store, has a 90-degree angle between the handle and the blade. By contrast, the skimming hoe design, better known as the collinear hoe, has a 70-degree angle between the blade and the handle. The collinear hoe also has a lighter, narrower blade.

In order to use a chopping hoe you have to hold it with your thumbs pointing down the handle. That causes you to work in a bent-over position, resulting in a sore back. A collinear hoe is used standing upright with the thumbs pointing up the handle, the same way you'd hold a broom or a leaf rake. It's a comfortable position, rather like standing in the ballroom dancing stance, with your back straight and your arms held naturally. The angle of this hoe makes it perfect for shaving off small weeds at the surface of the soil. Here's a case where tool design is in harmony with best practices. For even smaller spaces between plants, a similar tool called a wire weeder can be used—an ultra-narrow version of the collinear hoe that removes weeds between closely spaced plants with surgical precision.

The ideal time to control weeds is when they are tiny, right after they first appear. Small, newly germinated weeds have no staying power. Shave them off at the surface and they're history. Furthermore, when you cultivate the soil by shaving shallowly, as the collinear hoe is designed to do, you don't disturb the soil deeply enough to injure your plants' roots or bring up new weed seeds from below. If you wait too long before going after the weeds, you create more work for yourself. Large weeds do have staying power and are harder to cut off. You have to cut deeper in order to un-root them. Very often they just get dragged around and then they'll re-root in even slightly moist conditions. Get them when they're small and it's no contest. And this is peaceful, meditative work—the kind of thing you might actually want to do in the cool of a summer's evening.

There are times, even in the best of gardens, when weeds get ahead of you and you might feel like reaching for that chopping hoe. But the alternative we prefer for stubborn weeds is the stirrup hoe, named after its shape. It has the force to cut larger weeds off just below the soil surface, even in compacted soil.

Evenly spaced seedlings are easier to keep weed free.

A deluxe model, called the wheel hoe, is a lifesaver for those with large vegetable gardens. Rolling along by means of a wheel mounted in front of the stirrup blade, it makes quick work of weeds in well-trodden paths.

When is the best time to weed, in wet weather or dry? Certainly weeds pull out more easily when the soil is moist, but on the other hand a weed already stressed from dry weather, cut off and lying on the ground, will perish quickly in the hot sun, and not re-root. We try to do all our cultivating when the sun shines.

And what about mulch? For several crops a mulch makes good sense: for peas with their fragile root systems, easily harmed by hoeing; for strawberries, whose fruits mold easily when they rest on the soil; for potatoes, to prevent moisture stress. (See page 237 for more on mulching to conserve moisture.) If you're trying to keep annual weeds from germinating, a mulch of hay, grass clippings, or pine needles can be effective. But if the roots of perennial weeds such as dandelions, ferns, wild blackberries, and grass lurk beneath the soil surface, a mulch will only make your job harder if it fails to keep such weeds from coming up through it. You'll have to pull the mulch aside to remove them, and soil will likely scatter on top of the mulch when you do. So the moral of the story is: Remove all perennial weeds before you plant crops, then cultivate or mulch to keep annual ones from sprouting.

THE ROLE OF PLANT SPACING

PRECISION SEEDING and precision transplanting also help in weed control. A three-week-old seedling placed in newly prepared soil has a three-week head start on weeds, since the weed seeds haven't germinated yet. But your cultivating dance will be even more effective at controlling weeds if you've taken the extra time to sow the seeds and/or set out the transplants in

A wire weeder is like a surgical tool for removing weeds. Scuffle it in the soil between plants even when they are closely spaced.

The stirrup hoe at left cuts off weeds below the soil surface. It has a swinging motion that gives it the power to dispatch weeds that are well rooted in, and can even be used in the compressed soil of garden paths. The collinear hoe at right is best used to cultivate the loose soil of garden beds, when the weeds are still small.

Scallions in soil blocks, sown in clumps of multiples.

straight rows. The best way to do that is to stretch a string, usually called a garden line, either down the row you're planting or along the edge of the bed, to guide your seeder if you're using one. In both cases the line is tied to a stake at either end and pulled taut. To sow a straight line of seeds you make a shallow furrow with a board or the corner of a hoe blade along the garden line, and drop in the seeds. Evenly spaced seedlings are easier to keep weed free because you can use a hoe effectively both between rows and between seedlings.

For setting out transplants in straight rows with even spacing, we enlist the help of our 30-inch-wide garden rake, the same one shown on page 42 for bed-forming, but with marker teeth extensions. We slip these extensions over the rake's teeth at the appropriate spacings for each crop, to line out a grid pattern on our 30-inch-wide beds. First we run the rake lengthwise down the bed, using the garden line along the edge of the bed as a guide for the edge of the rake. If we are planting at three rows to the bed, as with the multiplant system below, we place three marker teeth on the rake, one in the center and one

10 inches to either side. Then we reset the marker teeth at the desired in-row spacing and run the rake across the bed. Then we set out transplants at every place where the marks on the soil intersect. (See the how-to on page 232.)

MULTIPLE-PLANT SEEDING

GROWING PLANTS in clumps rather than in rows is another seeding technique that makes weed control easier. When crops like onions, beets, or scallions are sown in rows, the in-row weeding can be tedious. Instead of direct-sowing in the garden, we start these crops ahead in the cold frame or in soil blocks. But the difference here is that we sow more than one seed in each of the 3- by 3-inch grid locations that we spoke of above. With onions, for example, we sow four seeds together. With beets we sow two (beet "seeds" are actually pods containing more than one seed), and with scallions we sow twelve. The aim, given average germination, is to end up with three to four onions, four beets, or ten scallions in each clump. When the seedlings are ready to be set out (The chart on page 457 indicates time from sowing to setting out), we transplant all these crops at three rows to a 30-inch bed. The rows are 10 inches apart, and the clumps are set out 12 inches apart in the row.

If you direct-sow onions or beets they are usually thinned to 3 or 4 inches apart in the row, and scallions ideally to one inch apart. Transplanting our clumps of seedlings at the 10- by 12-inch spacing gives each plant an equivalent amount of total space and, yes, they all grow normally in the clump. But the advantage for eventual weed control is that you now have no in-row weeding to contend with. You can use the collinear hoe to cultivate just as effectively within the row as between the rows.

By harvesttime there are four onions or four beets growing in a cluster at each site. They can be harvested individually, as you need them, or all at once. We harvest the scallions by pulling the whole clump. It looks just like the bunch of scallions you're used to buying, and fits nicely in the crisper drawer.

Multiplant growing also allows you to control the size of crops that might otherwise grow larger than you can deal with at a meal. For example, if you use this technique with broccoli, cabbage, or cauliflower (at three to four plants per clump), and set out the clumps 2 feet apart each way, you will get smaller heads but more of them, and in less space. Many gardeners with small households prefer a 4-inch-diameter head of broccoli rather than one at 6 inches or more. ☼

IRRIGATION

IT IS NATURAL TO HOPE that rainfall will always provide all the water your garden needs. In some years and in some parts of the world that may be true. But how do you determine when it's necessary to supplement rainfall? First off, when it rains, ask yourself, Did it rain enough? In New England there is a traditional old-timer's question after a rain: Did the moisture meet? In other words, was the rain sufficient to wet the dry surface far enough down to meet up with the moist soil underneath, with no dry layer in between, and thus add to the soil's moisture storage? If the moisture didn't meet, especially during dry spells, you'll have to add some yourself.

HOSES

WHEN THE GARDEN IS SMALL, the simplest irrigation practice is to use a hose with a spray nozzle. However, when you water you want to moisten more than just the surface. So think of your time with the hose as a meditation moment in your day and take long enough to do it thoroughly. One inch of rainfall per week during the growing season is a generally accepted target, whether it is supplied by actual rainfall or by irrigation. It's easy to calculate how long to water your garden with a hose by timing how long it takes your hose to fill a 5-gallon bucket (1,155 cubic inches). That amount of water will cover 8 square feet of garden to a depth of 1 inch. Say you have an 80-square-foot garden (8 feet by 10 feet). You can provide an inch of water to your garden by doing irrigation meditation for the time it takes to fill that bucket multiplied by ten. Of course, you want to make your meditation slightly active by moving the hose in an even pattern so as to apply the same amount of water to all parts of the area. Another tip: In order to water evenly you need to start spraying the area just outside the edge of your plot, then move the spray pattern

> Think of your time with the hose as a meditation moment in your day.

at a constant speed across the plot, and finish up just outside the edge on the other side. That way the plants at the edge of the garden get the same amount of water as do those at the center.

IRRIGATION SYSTEMS

EIGHTY SQUARE FEET is about as large an area as most people would want to water by hand, so the next step for a larger garden is to set up some sort of sprinkler system. On our commercial farm we use an irrigation system we put together ourselves. It is so simple and flexible that we also use it in our home garden.

The key component is a commercial sprinkler head called the Wobbler. Its advantage over other types of sprinkler heads is that it has only one moving part and delivers water in larger drops rather than fine spray. The larger drops are less affected by wind and will give surprisingly good coverage even on windy days so that no water is wasted. It also operates at standard water pressure. We mount our Wobblers on commercially available stands (see below), but you can make your own uprights out of whatever length you want of the ½-inch threaded pipe that is easily available at box stores. The other

Watering with a Wobbler

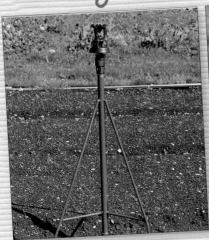

WOBBLER ON A STAND. This device sprays water around the garden with a rotary motion powered by the water itself. A series of stands can be connected with each other by attaching hoses, to cover a large area.

THE WOBBLER HEAD. The head is purchased separately and screwed on.

THE WOBBLER IN ACTION. What makes this device so useful is the size of the droplets. They are large and heavy enough to resist being blown around, so you can irrigate on windy days without wasting water.

end of the pipe is screwed into a stable base. That way you can have sprinklers that operate at different heights. We use two heights in our garden. In one the Wobbler is attached to a 6-foot stand for irrigating the tall crops in the trellised section of the garden, and the other is 30 inches tall for irrigating the lower-growing crops. A source of Wobbler heads and stands is given on page 453.

Both of us draw most of our gardening experience from the eastern states rather than the dry West, so we've had minimal experience with the drip irrigation systems that are so popular there. If you wish to use drip irrigation, take a look at pages 453 and 454 in the Resources sectio. We've used drip systems in our greenhouses and found them quite complicated and bothersome compared with the overhead sprinklers we now use almost exclusively, as described on page 239. We also recommend good quality soaker hoses (page 453), which we use outdoors from time to time, especially in permanent plantings. In addition, we've both had gardens with no access to running water at all, and offer the following options for dealing with such situations.

OTHER SOLUTIONS

WHERE NO WATER IS AVAILABLE except from rain, two very valuable solutions are found in organic matter and mulching. The soil organic matter we celebrated in Chapter 1 has another important virtue beyond providing the ideal habitat for your plant's roots and for all the soil creatures that provide plants with nourishment. Organic matter holds water in the soil. To look at this comparatively, let's say a cubic foot of sandy soil holds one unit of water. The water-holding ability of a silt soil is somewhat better than that, two units; and that of a clay soil is double that, four units. From the point of view of resisting drought, the clay soil is better than the sandy soil because it holds four times as much water. Since we have sandy soil, those figures are of particular concern for us. But there is something better yet. A cubic foot of soil organic matter holds sixteen units of water.

Thus, the more organic matter you're able to add to your soil, the more drought resistant that soil becomes. The unwatered gardens we have had—once we filled the soil with plenty of compost— were only noticeably affected by dry summers, on average, one year in ten. That was the delightful extra benefit of raising the percentage of soil organic matter. But you can do even better. The organic wastes that you add to the compost heap to rot down into that priceless crumbly black stuff can start their rotting as mulch on *top* of the soil, between the rows of plants in your garden. It may not look tidy, but it will be effective.

Hay and/or straw are the mulching materials most commonly used for vegetable gardens, and very satisfactory they are. (Bark mulches are more appropriate for ornamental plantings.) But hay and straw are not the only options. Any type of organic matter, any type of leaf or stem or vine that might be added to the compost heap, can serve duty first as moisture-conserving garden mulch. Think of the natural world, where everything that grows falls back to the surface of the earth when it is spent. That's nature's mulching system, and it helps hold water

Organic matter holds water in the soil.

The largest and most efficient French watering cans hold about three gallons. If you fill them up they weigh around 25 pounds each.

in the soil for the growing plants to use. How much water does mulching save? The figure most often given is that a 4-inch-thick mulch is worth the equivalent of an additional 4 inches of rain during the growing season. And since the residues of the mulch itself add organic matter to the soil as they decompose in situ, these practices complement each other. So if you're gardening with no access to water, your "irrigation" system will be based on collecting all the organic matter you can find, mulching your garden with it, and then, at the end of the season, composting it and eventually incorporating the compost into your garden soil. If you can't bring in extra water, plan on preserving as much as possible of what you do have.

Another garden reality is one where you have access to water, such as a dug well or a rain barrel, but no pump or hoses to get it to the garden. We've been in that situation too, as have many gardeners over the centuries. The result of their ingenuity is shown in the design of watering cans. The best one was developed by the Parisian market gardeners of the 19th century and is still known today as a French watering can. The handle on this can runs in a curved shape from just above the spout at the front of the can over the opening at the top and down to the back end near the bottom. While you're holding the can with one hand, that shape allows you to slowly adjust where your fingers rest on the handle to progressively tip the can. In this way, French gardeners could walk between two beds, a can in each hand, watering the soil of the two beds simultaneously. As they walked they moved their fingers back along the handle, to tip the can and dispense water.

When you have to carry water by hand you quickly start to think about how to use it most effectively. Newly sown rows of not-yet-germinated seeds (especially the slow-to-germinate crops like carrots, parsley, and onions) are the first and best use since it is important for good germination to keep the seeds moist. Quick-growing succulent leafy greens such as lettuce or spinach are the next most needy plants. With further thought you soon realize that if you do your irrigation toward the end of the day, the soil will remain moist all night and up to about 10 o'clock the next morning. If you do it at midday, when the hot sun will quickly evaporate the moisture you just applied, it won't be as effective. So our recommendation is to do the job in the late afternoon. If you are moistening rows of seedlings, keep doing it every day until the seeds germinate. Once germination occurs and the seedling roots go down into the earth, you can stop the daily watering because the young plants then have access to more moisture than they did as seeds at the surface of the soil.

If you're growing seedlings in a cold frame or hoop tunnel seedbed (see pages 87 to 91), it will take less water to get them up to size in that confined area. When you're ready to set them out in the garden, water the seedlings thoroughly before you transplant. A seedling in a well-watered cube of earth has the best chance of getting established, even if it's transplanted into dry soil.

The largest and most efficient French watering cans hold about three gallons. If you fill them up they weigh around 25 pounds each. When we were carrying a lot of water in those earlier gardens, we helped support the weight of the two cans with an old-fashioned yoke across our shoulders. Our yoke was a piece of wood, long enough to extend across the shoulders, wide enough to sit comfortably on the shoulders, and with a section carved out to fit around the neck. A short piece of rope, the length of one's arm, hung from each end. A hook attached to the bottom of each rope helped hold the handles and took the weight of the two cans off the arms by supporting it on the shoulders. The yoke is a wonderful piece of old-time technology. Yokes for carrying water are not commonly available for purchase these days, but in this case a little imagination can help come up with a solution. When searching for an odd item like this, the question we always ask is where else in today's world would something like it be used? In this case we realized that canoeists use a yoke on their shoulders when portaging, and we quickly found one in a canoe supply catalog. We added the short lengths of rope ourselves.

WATERING IN GREENHOUSES

ONCE YOU'RE GROWING PLANTS in the protection of a greenhouse, you can make use of the newer irrigation technology designed for watering greenhouses (see page 453). These systems consist of very small, lightweight nozzles that hang down every 3 feet from a plastic water pipe attached below the central connector that runs along the roof of the greenhouse (see photo at right). With such a system you can hook a hose to one end of the pipe and the nozzles will water the whole greenhouse from above. Since the nozzles have very small

An overhead sprinkler system used in a small movable greenhouse.

apertures that are easily clogged, these systems use a filter for the water to pass through before entering the delivery pipe. Different-colored nozzles are offered to provide varying widths of spray coverage. You'll want the nozzle that delivers a 12-foot-wide coverage for the modular greenhouse described on pages 93 to 95.

These specialist greenhouse systems water very evenly and when we've tested ours by placing collecting cups in various places around the greenhouse, we found the same level of water in all the cups. Because of the extra heat and accelerated growth of the plants in a summer greenhouse, the soil seems to dry out faster, especially when the doors are open for venting. Slight lapses in providing water that would seem unimportant in an open garden are magnified in the greenhouse. A simple, dependable irrigating system will make the greenhouse growing experience that much more enjoyable.

The winter greenhouse is a different situation entirely. In winter the sun is low in the sky and there is very little evaporation from the soil. In addition, plant growth slows down and considerable moisture is available from the soil because the water table is higher in winter. Therefore we've found very little need to irrigate during the low-sun months of winter. The extent of the low-sun months varies with your latitude and its effect on the length of day. When day length drops to ten hours or less, the whole system is in a slow-production hibernation, still producing food but needing almost no care. For us on the 44th parallel of latitude, the low months extend from November 5 to February 5. For the rest of the country, see the map and chart on page 456. Don't, however, let the vacation from irrigating make you complacent. Once the days get longer and the sun gets stronger, you need to start paying attention to irrigation again. ☼

THE VERTICAL GARDEN

GROWING VERTICALLY can double, triple, and even quadruple the produce from a given area of soil. Crops trained vertically maximize access to the sun (more photosynthesis), stay cleaner (no soil spatter), are easier to harvest (no bending over), and can provide shade or wind protection for other crops at their base, which grow in the space they would have taken up if not trellised. A surprising number of crops are suitable for vertical growing techniques. We support them all with the same trellis support.

AN ALL-PURPOSE TRELLIS

THE SIMPLEST TRELLIS support has two parts: upright posts and a crossbar on the top. The crossbar eliminates the sagging and post-bending of systems that use a wire as the top support. We used to make these trellis supports out of wood by using 2-by-2s for both the uprights and the crossbar. However, wood rots in contact with the soil after a few years, and it took some effort to drive the uprights into the soil. We now use galvanized metal electrical conduit (EMT) for both the uprights and the crossbar—the same type of material used to build the modular greenhouse and quick hoops in Chapter 3.

The uprights should be one diameter larger than the crossbar to allow a hairpin-shaped piece of flexible wire to fit in and secure the bar on top (see photo on page 242).

EMT is sold in standard 10-foot-lengths. To create a 4-foot-tall pea trellis we cut each 10-foot-long 3/4-inch diameter conduit into two 5-foot lengths and set them upright every 5 feet along the row. We drive them 12-inches into the soil with a hammer or mallet. A 10-foot length of 1/2-inch conduit serves as the crossbar. A lightweight plastic mesh with 6-inch-square holes, sold in garden catalogs, is hung from the crossbar for the peas to climb on. The hanging is achieved by weaving the crossbar in and out through the upper edge of the mesh.

When you drive pipe with a hammer, the force of the blows can deform the end of the pipe. You can prevent that by inserting a 6-inch-long bolt, with a diameter just smaller than that of the pipe, into the top of the pipe, and hammering on that. For 3/4-inch EMT a 5/8-inch bolt is ideal. Be sure to wear eye protection when hammering on metal.

For taller crops that need more support, we use one-inch conduit for the uprights and 3/4-inch for the crossbar. For a 6 1/2-foot-tall trellis we cut the posts 8 feet long and try to drive the uprights 18 inches into the soil. That makes a sturdy support to contend with both the weight of a bumper tomato or cucumber crop, and the wind pressure on a taller structure. The medium on which the plants climb depends

Our trellis system supports tomatoes in the home garden.

on the crop. As described below, peas climb on a plastic mesh and the other crops climb on strong twine tied to the trellis support at the top and to a short stake driven into the ground at the bottom. We could use the pea mesh for tomatoes, cucumbers, or climbing beans but the work of getting the vines and stems out of it at the end of the season is daunting. The biodegradable twine makes cleanup so much easier because everything can be thrown into the compost heap—vines, twine, and all—and it will decompose. The tomatoes and cucumbers are pruned to train them to a single stem (see the illustration on page 244). and are encouraged to twist around the twine for support as they grow upward. The beans climb the string by twining around it without any help from us. You can also use plastic clips sold for this purpose (see the photo on page 169 and sources on page 454).

This same simple trellis construction can be put to other uses in the garden. In fall, either floating row cover or sheets of plastic can be draped over the crossbar to create a low A-frame greenhouse for

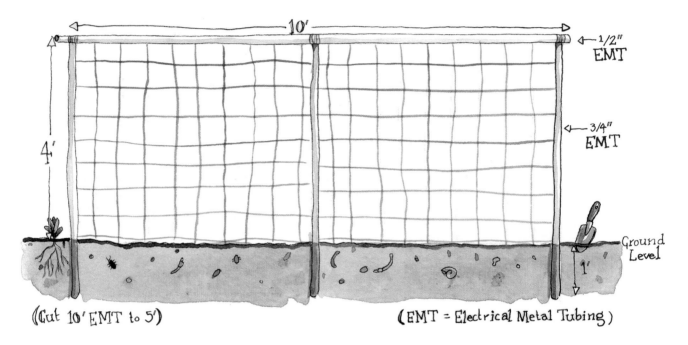

10'

1/2" EMT

3/4" EMT

4'

Ground Level

1'

(Cut 10' EMT to 5')

(EMT = Electrical Metal Tubing)

Pieces of bent wire secure the crossbar on top of the trellis to the uprights that support it.

season extension. The same structure can be erected over your strawberry beds to make a bird-netting tent to foil feathered berry-eaters. In that case you might wish to attach the bottom edge on one side to a board so the netting can be easily folded back for harvest.

Instead of removing the trellises at the end of the season and storing their parts, you may wish to erect them permanently in a section of the garden reserved for trellised crops. You could then rotate those crops between the trellised beds. You can see how this might work with the sample rotation for tall crops on page 46. When any of the non-trellised tall crops like sweet corn are included in such a rotation, you just skip the crossbar. The uprights alone are not inconvenient and cast no shade.

CROPS THAT CLIMB
Peas

PEAS HAVE TENDRILS that will cling to a vertical support. Traditionally, gardeners have grown them on "pea brush," that is, brush cuttings, usually birch, stuck into the ground at intervals along the row. We've also used structures of fanlike spruce branches tied together. But we now find it less work to hang a plastic trellis mesh (with 6-inch by 6-inch holes) from our trellis support and grow the peas up both sides of it. Sow in two rows, 6 inches apart, one on each side of the trellis (see page 188). In order to support a heavier crop, it helps to run a line of twine horizontally along the outside of the pea vines for every foot tall they grow. That prevents the vines from being pulled off the trellis by careless harvesters—especially eager children who love eating fresh raw peas. We use the trellis even for the peas that can be grown without support, since we think they grow better vertically and are much easier to pick.

Pole Beans

POLE BEANS ARE natural climbers. Plant three or four seeds around the stake, and as the vines grow upward, they will circle around and hold on to the string tied to the stake. Place each clump of vines 2 feet apart. Make sure the twine you use is untreated and biodegradable so that it can be composted at season's end.

Cucumbers

ALTHOUGH most cucumbers can be grown on the ground, the epicurean European types do better and produce longer, straighter fruit when grown vertically. They are not natural climbers like beans and peas, even though they do have clinging tendrils. However, with a little pruning and training you can get them to grow vertically, giving you cleaner fruit and avoiding soil-borne diseases. Install the twine as for beans. As the main stem of the cucumber grows, twist it gently around the string for support. Prune off all suckers and fruit for the first 30 inches (see illustration at left).

TALL TRELLIS FOR TOMATOES, CUCUMBERS, AND BEANS

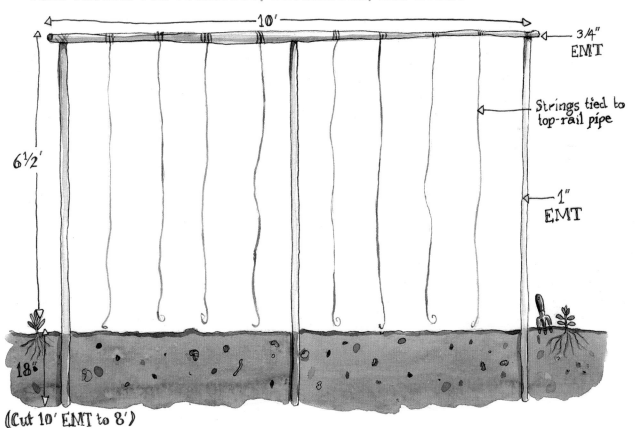

10'

3/4" EMT

Strings tied to top-rail pipe

6½'

1" EMT

18"

(Cut 10' EMT to 8')

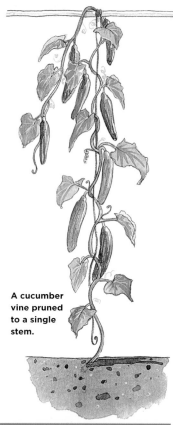

A cucumber vine pruned to a single stem.

tiny cucumber

sucker

In order to prune a cucumber vine to a single stem, you must pinch out the suckers that grow in the fork between the leaf stems and the main stem. Do this carefully so as not to injure the tiny cucumber that emerges from this fork as well.

Then just prune off suckers as the vine continues its vertical growth. When the vine reaches the top support bar, encourage it to grow over the bar and trail back down to the ground. It will continue producing fruit the whole way.

Tomatoes

LIKE MOST GARDENERS we grow determinate tomatoes without staking them because they grow to a certain point, stop growing, and then produce fruit. But with the indeterminate varieties (the ones that keep growing and fruiting as long as the season lasts), we like to grow them vertically on a trellis support. We use the same system as for the cucumbers, shown at left, and plant the tomatoes 24 inches apart. We prune out all the suckers (the new growth at the base of each leaf branch) in order to have a single stem that we twist around the string as it grows vertically. Not only do we appreciate the clean fruit and ease of harvesting, but also find the sight of that green wall splashed with red fruits to be a gorgeous expression of home garden bounty. (For growing in tomato cages, see page 176.) ☀

FENCING

WHEREAS the trellis is a fence for vegetable support, it's a good idea to have a second fence for what we might call garden support: protecting the garden from wild creatures. Depending on where you live in North America, the list of invaders can include rabbits, groundhogs, woodchucks, skunks, porcupines, raccoons, wild turkeys, deer, and moose. Gardeners in South America worry about llamas, alpacas, and vicunas; gardeners in Australia need to exclude kangaroos; while gardeners in Africa have the unenviable challenge of holding elephants at bay. In every one of these cases there are many ingenious methods that have evolved over the years to keep the animals from eating everything.

We've used a number of local techniques ourselves in times of need, such as smelly repellents like dried blood for deer, a radio tuned to an all-night talk show to keep the raccoons out of the sweet corn, or a box trap baited with a cut-up apple covered with salt to capture the porcupines that delight in destroying our raspberry plantings. Although these solutions are often effective for temporary relief, none of them offer the permanent security of a good fence. The same tall fence that keeps out deer can also deter smaller creatures if the bottom of the fence is tight to the ground and has a small mesh. A single strand of electric fence wire attached to the outside of that fence at the appropriate height (between 6 and 12 inches) will ensure that the more agile invaders don't climb over. For those creatures that invade by digging, you can bury a 2-foot-wide section of wire mesh a couple of inches deep horizontally around the perimeter of the fence. When animals dig in the soil at the bottom of the fence, they quickly encounter the wire mesh.

DEERPROOFING THE YARD

ONE OF GARDENERS' MOST COMMON COMPLAINTS is the presence of vegetable-munching, shrub-nibbling, flower-destroying deer. Here's how we solved the problem in our former home, which had a half-acre front yard. A variety of different fencing materials kept them out: a stockade fence hidden behind plantings, decorative lattice fencing that supported both food-bearing and ornamental vines, and a black plastic mesh fencing material strung from tree to tree in a wooded corner. The lattice fences were attached to the house, with two gates for entry.

A black mesh fence is invisible when strung from tree to tree.

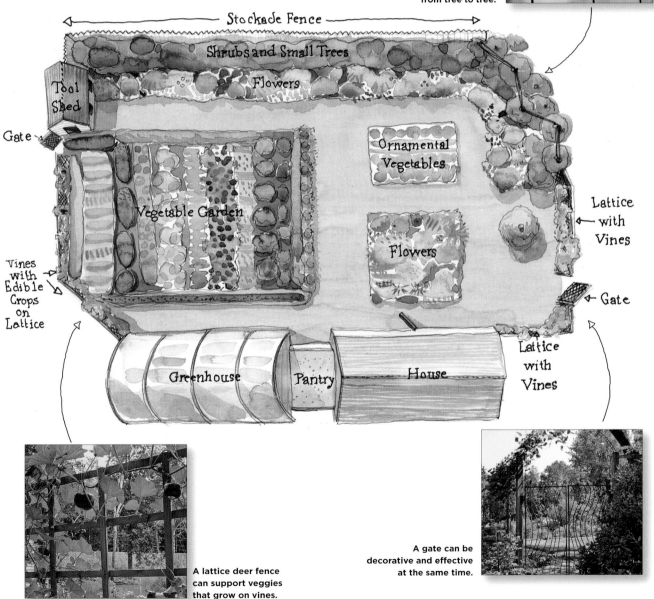

Stockade Fence

Shrubs and Small Trees

Flowers

Tool Shed

Gate

Vines with Edible Crops on Lattice

Vegetable Garden

Ornamental Vegetables

Flowers

Lattice with Vines

Gate

Lattice with Vines

Greenhouse

Pantry

House

A lattice deer fence can support veggies that grow on vines.

A gate can be decorative and effective at the same time.

> Fencing doesn't have to be expensive or make your garden look like a prison compound.

We would love to offer simpler solutions that are less expensive than a fence, but in the long run it makes the best sense. This is one of those cases in our garden experience where dealing with the whole problem right up front is the only surefire solution. But it doesn't have to be expensive or make your garden look like a prison compound. We once fenced a whole half-acre yard with a combination of a black plastic mesh and a 7-foot-tall homemade lightweight trellis made of wood. The plastic mesh was a commercial product, sold to be used as deer fence, which we strung through the trees along two sides of the property. Its black color disappeared visually among the green leaves and even in winter there were enough twigs or evergreen boughs to still render it invisible. The wooden trellis, which attached to both ends of the house, took care of visible areas with no trees to hide the mesh. Between the fence posts we used 1-by-2 spruce boards for both uprights and crosspieces to make a diaphanous structure of square holes, 16 inches on each side, that the deer regarded as a fence and we regarded as a trellis on which we could train vines. A 2-foot-tall strip of chicken wire mesh along the bottom kept out small creatures such as rabbits, and attractive gates welcomed in human visitors. That fence kept the deer out, kept our ducks in, and secured the fruits and vegetables for our use. ☀

THE $100 TOMATO?

THERE IS AN EASY WAY TO CALCULATE the value of your garden produce without weighing and recording each item you harvest. Let's take lettuce as an example. A space 9 inches by 10 inches is adequate for a head of lettuce. That means you can grow one and a half lettuces on every square foot. The 80-square-foot garden we used as an illustration back in the irrigation section could easily grow over 100 lettuces. The cost of a head of lettuce in the store multiplied times 100 is the dollar value of just growing lettuce in that small garden. However, two further factors need to be considered. First, that's a lot of lettuce to have maturing at once. Except for selling it or giving lettuce to all the neighbors, it would be hard to dispose of. So it would make sense if some of the garden were planted with lettuce and some with other crops like carrots or snap peas or potatoes. Closely planted carrots can produce three bunches or so on that square foot and are a very good value. Snap peas could yield a quarter of a pound, and a good early potato harvest might make a pound per square foot. Their dollar value for space used will be less. But in all these cases there is room for a second crop on that square foot before the end of the season, which can easily double your production.

The best return-for-effort crops are the ones we started with in Chapter 3—the leafy greens. Since kale and chard, for example, keep producing new leaves all season long and are so versatile in cooking, they more than pay for their garden space.

Harvest bounty to inspire the cook.

Fresh herbs also, which are enormously expensive sold in small bunches enclosed in plastic clamshells at the market, repay their keep many times over and can be used profligately in countless dishes. A study done at the University of Saskatchewan found that the following additional crops always covered their expenses: carrots, cauliflower, tomatoes, lettuce, eggplants, peppers, spinach, blackberries, and raspberries. Sweet corn and green cabbages on the other hand either need a lot of space to grow (corn) or are sold inexpensively in the market (cabbages) and will, therefore, bring in the least dollar value for their square footage. This is where the choice of what to grow depends on your passion for that particular crop and your appreciation for its eating pleasure when harvested right before it's prepared. Sweet corn makes up for its low return per square foot by being so much more tender and flavorful when it is just out of the garden, whereas with cabbage, that is less noticeable. But then cabbage, as a succulent leafy crop that can be easily stored for winter use, has virtues for year-round eating that neither fresh corn nor leafy greens can offer. ☼

THE NEXT GENERATION

THE REAL DOLLAR VALUE of the garden in our estimation is based not only on the superior quality of whatever vegetables you decide to grow, and your peace of mind in having access to food that exceptional, but also on its value to your children's future. It is comforting that you no longer have to ask, "Where has this lettuce been and what have they done to it?" It is equally comforting that you no longer have to force vegetables on your family because, as we have seen with our children and grandchildren, food that

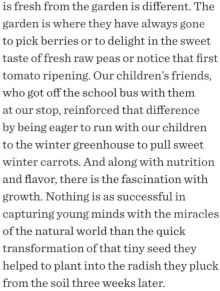

is fresh from the garden is different. The garden is where they have always gone to pick berries or to delight in the sweet taste of fresh raw peas or notice that first tomato ripening. Our children's friends, who got off the school bus with them at our stop, reinforced that difference by being eager to run with our children to the winter greenhouse to pull sweet winter carrots. And along with nutrition and flavor, there is the fascination with growth. Nothing is as successful in capturing young minds with the miracles of the natural world than the quick transformation of that tiny seed they helped to plant into the radish they pluck from the soil three weeks later.

If we expect today's young people to find solutions to ensure the future of their world (which they will have to do), they need to be introduced to the garden. What could be better than the direct knowledge that compost—the world's best fertilizer, which is made for free in your backyard from plant and animal waste products— is a model for other simple solutions to the problems that will be faced by future generations? We believe that if what we are doing in our garden is in any way complicated it is probably wrong, and we modify our practices accordingly. The biologically based garden is not just a subject. It is also a skilled teacher.

Modern education has been far too often co-opted by the spectacular and the industrial while ignoring the fundamental and the biological. Schools spend millions to familiarize students with Internet systems in the ether above their heads,

while little is spent to introduce them to the vital systems in the earth beneath their feet. Our schools impress students with the spectacle of millions of stars in the heavens but neglect to awe them with the miracle of millions of living organisms in a single teaspoon of fertile soil.

Students are introduced to the chemical table of elements but are left unaware of the susceptibility of the creatures in that teaspoon to the daily chemical residues of our industrial production. How can we hope to train our children to care for the planet, when they are unfamiliar with the irreplaceable role of the skin of that planet in the miracle of their life? Our educators are doing a reasonable job at explaining the intricacies of 21st-century human society to students in lab and classroom, but they are neglecting to make them aware of the web of life in field and forest. If we wish to teach reverence for the earth, we need to get our children into the garden. ☀

PART TWO

The Kitchen

COOKING FROM THE GARDEN is not like cooking from the store. If you're a shopper-cook, most often you'll start with a recipe and a list of ingredients, go out and buy them, then make your dish. A gardener-cook does it backwards: The garden provides a list of ingredients, inspires the recipe, and collaborates on the menu. It's more interactive. It's more fun.

A supermarket looks pretty much the same every day of the year, but not so a garden. If the market is a dictionary of ingredients, the garden on a given day is the front-page news. Not every standard item is there. But if you have grown some storage crops and extended the growing season using the tricks in this book, your kitchen can speak with a pretty wide vocabulary most of the time. And the food is only a few steps away. Once you're set up, apart from your labor and a few minor gardening expenses, it's also free. If you've grown it with care, in a good organic soil, it's better than anything you can buy—and it's open twenty-four/seven. You can eat food that is fresh-this-minute, and you soon learn what a difference that makes. It's like tasting a potato, or spinach, for the first time.

Another discovery, which kind of creeps up on you, is the power of seasonality. Yes, the market has perfect-looking food, all of it available year-round so that you can make any recipe you want, any day. But the story behind that array is not very appetizing. Fruits and vegetables often come from halfway around the world, where our winter is their summer or our spring their fall. Ethylene gas

has given the tomatoes a strange sort of ripeness, with no taste.

If you decide to pass up this modern entitlement, you'll find that eating with the seasons is not a limitation but a gift. You'll look forward to a food's seasonal appearance with excitement. Not only is it better-tasting because it is fresh and naturally ripened in its prime, it is more satisfying to eat, your appetite for it sharpened by anticipation. You begin to see the year as a series of little festivals in which perfect asparagus arrives, followed by perfect peas, perfect tomatoes, perfect winter carrots, and all the other winter roots and greens whose flavor and sweetness are improved by cold air and soil. You associate their life stages with certain activities and celebrations. Your social life may even change as power lunches are replaced by picnics, or as formal dinners give way to spontaneous feasts. Last-minute invitations start with "Come help us eat up all these strawberries" or "The corn is ready."

Speaking for ourselves, we have never once felt constrained by our seasonal diet, and we sometimes marvel at how dull the perpetual global diet can seem, day by day, and how disappointing it tastes. We've found it especially hard to eat while traveling, faced with dishes like "Seasonal Berries" (in December) or "Seasonal Salad" (topped with cucumbers and tomatoes in January), for which so much fuel has been burned with such a bland result.

My own garden-to-table experience has made me not only a more satisfied diner but also a better cook. I've become more creative, better at improvising, more knowledgeable and confident about ingredients. An interesting development at our farm has been the number of professional cooks who have come to work with us, and what they've gained from the experience. You really have to see a vegetable or fruit through its life cycle to fully appreciate its complexity. By the time you harvest a crop, you have an understanding of how it developed its flavor, texture, and color. You discover that some vegetables taste better young, some when fully mature, and some either way. And their treatment in the kitchen may change according to their age—for example, cooking times vary greatly with both age and freshness. You learn about size. Is a particular "baby" vegetable small because it's been picked young, because it was bred to be small, or because it grew poorly? If you grew it yourself, you know the answer to questions like that and will be a more discerning shopper when a purchase is necessary. Some edibles have just a brief moment when they arrive at perfection. You learn how they taste before, during, and after that moment.

When you get to know a vegetable, you know all its parts, not just the ones that are trimmed and groomed for sale. We use the phrase "nose to tail vegetables," cribbed from chef Fergus Henderson's approach to meat in his book *The Whole Beast: Nose to Tail Eating*. When you expand your view of which parts of a plant can be eaten, it's like having a bigger garden. You may already know that turnips and beets have edible greens, but let's hear it for the refreshing but little-used foliage of celery, and the wonderful tuber-like globe you get from celeriac—the same plant as celery, but bred for an enlarged stem base. Explore radish leaves and pods, fennel bulbs and fronds, pea tendrils, and the stems of lettuce and garlic. You'll find few of those at a typical market.

There's a dance that edible garden plants do when they're hanging out together, coming into season at the same time. They fall into cliques. A time-honored dish like ratatouille wasn't invented by a recipe writer—it developed from the simultaneous summertime fruition of eggplants, tomatoes, peppers, and squash. The key players in succotash—lima beans and corn—grew literally entwined in Native American gardens, and still do, the corn stalks supporting the beans, until both are reunited in the pot. The mâche and baked beets in the salad on page 298 are a

Even when I'm busy with a dozen things, there's always a way to produce a good meal.

traditional pairing in France: perfect in winter, impossible in August.

This is not to say that such combinations should always follow tradition; in fact, the heart of garden cookery is serendipity. Every day in the garden, cellar, or cold frame, there are meals waiting to be created or modified based on what's there and what looks best. Sometimes a new dish is sparked by an ingredient's absence—a great tomato-less lasagna, perhaps—or from an excess. It was a wheelbarrow full of extra cucumbers that got me to try them sautéed.

Like anyone, I have my own style of cooking and eating, and it supports a goal that Eliot and I share: to combine healthy eating with maximum pleasure. I try to approach cooking vegetables and fruits in a way that retains the most nutrients. I don't boil them and then throw away the water. I'll steam them, or I'll sauté them, often in such a way that their cooking liquid has evaporated at the point when they're tender. We like our greens cooked only briefly, but we have never understood the fad of rock-hard firmer vegetables, like broccoli and green beans, cooked too briefly to develop their flavors. We prefer them with just a bit of crunch—not mushy, and not underdone. We rinse or scrub vegetables well, but peel them only when the skin is unpleasantly tough.

Another trend that has passed us by is the pervasive fear of fat. Depriving ourselves of cream, butter, or bacon would only backfire and prompt us to gorge on them. What works better for us is portion control (stopping when we're no longer hungry) and a good dose of exercise, much of it gained by growing food. The one thing we're a bit strict about is our avoidance of processed foods, which tend to be oversalted and full of additives and empty calories. We try to avoid refined foods, especially refined carbohydrates, that have been stripped of nutrition. Recent research emphasizes, over and over, that they do us more harm than good.

I like to serve food with visual appeal, and when the fruits and vegetables are beautiful, the picture is not hard to paint. I might give some thought to which plate or bowl I use to display a dish, and to the food's arrangement on the plate, but ultimately, great-looking food is not about decoration, it's about its inherent quality. The ability to recognize the ripeness and healthiness of edible plants is part of our DNA, a fact that is confirmed every time we watch our grandchildren grazing among our berries, cherry tomatoes, and peas. As scientists tell us, the phytonutrients that give fruits and vegetables their bright colors are signaling us to partake. And if our instincts haven't given us the power to recognize the green of a healthy kale or spinach leaf, a bit of time spent in the garden will. In the kitchen we observe how those colors behave: oil-soluble ones such as the carotene in carrots or the lycopene in tomatoes do not leach out in cooking, but the anthocyanins in many foods such as red cabbage, or the betalains in beets, require an approach to cooking that conserves them.

If cooking from your backyard plot is improvisational, why have recipes at all? I find I don't use them often, and even when I do, I don't follow them to the letter. Every time I make a favorite thing it's a little bit different, and I try to keep a kitchen diary for jotting down concoctions we've especially liked. But recipes do give any cook a starting point. When the garden becomes your produce aisle, you'll find that certain themes and patterns emerge in the things you cook. For me they're a collection of versatile concepts, such as stir-fries, quiches, stews, omelets, soups, composed salads, and such, that I can adapt according to what's on hand each day.

One premise of this book is that knowing just a few basic ways to cook with vegetables can multiply your repertoire, since the selection will vary from month to month. I've proposed seasonal variations for many dishes, and my hope is that you'll come up with some of your own. It's also perfectly okay to go out and buy an ingredient to complete a recipe. We are not purists here, and although most of the produce we eat is homegrown, we've been known to purchase this or that, to see if we like it enough to grow it, or to get us through what the old-timers called the "hungry gap," when stored crops are running out in late winter and the spring ones have not yet gathered steam. We also allow ourselves to be a little extravagant when we do purchase ingredients, and we look for good quality. We figure we've earned that chunk of Parmigiano-Reggiano cheese or that pinch of saffron (bought more economically in quantity) because so much of what we eat is free from the garden.

This section sets out some of the pathways that have helped me integrate the garden into the whole breadth of my cooking life. Its goal is to expand the role of garden produce from that of the side dish to something that infiltrates the whole menu. As a result, it is not organized by individual crops. If you have a glut of a specific vegetable, the index will help locate a variety of ways to put it on the table.

People often complain that modern life leaves them too busy to garden and too busy to cook. I understand what they mean. Someday, I tell myself, I will find the time to bake my own bread, roast my own coffee, and make all my own cheese, yogurt, pasta, and jam. I doubt that's ever going to happen. But most of us have some choice as to how we spend the hours in our day. For me, what my family and I put into our bodies is important enough that I'm willing to make food from scratch. There's a Sicilian proverb that translates: "What you don't pay at the table you pay to the doctor." To me, that applies not just to money but also to time. Even when I'm busy with a dozen things, there's always a way to produce a good meal. And the time we spend at table, often with family and friends, is unrushed, with plenty of relaxed conversation. It's part of what we call our "feast philosophy." Eating good food that we have grown is one of our greatest pleasures, a luxury of time to which anyone can aspire. ❀

OPEN-FACED SANDWICHES WITH TOMATOES AND PESTO | PAGE 265

Appetizers and Sandwiches

THE GARDEN, FOR ELIOT AND ME, is a year-round snack bar. Look for us out there in the rows, popping cherry tomatoes into our mouths for a little energy boost during the day, munching a podful of green peas or a just-ripe ear of raw corn. When children and grandchildren visit us, they do the same.

An appetizer, like a snack, should sharpen the appetite but not spoil it for regular meals, and here again, the garden provides. As people start circling the kitchen, their hunger piqued by cooking smells, I quickly put out a bowl of small, freshly dug carrots, which are available almost year-round. Each season has similar treats to offer. In spring and fall there might be a plate of elegant red-tipped French Breakfast radishes with a little salt to dip them in. When sugar snap peas are in season, these are the snack of choice. In summer a bright blue bowl filled with a variety of cherry tomatoes might appear, or strips of red and yellow sweet peppers, or cucumber slices fanned out on a plate with coarse salt, freshly ground black pepper, and fresh dill. Even winter storage vegetables, such as Japanese white turnips or kohlrabi, provide crisp raw snacks when thinly sliced. My favorite is the exquisitely sweet Chioggia beet, with its red-and-white bull's-eye pattern, sliced paper-thin and laid out on a green plate at holiday time.

Crudité platters are easy to assemble from whatever the garden is serving up. If you like yours with a dip, that can be vegetable-based as well. Fixings for quick sandwiches, too, are always close at hand, a blessing for a busy gardener-cook.

I love cheese platters as much as the next person, but I'm more apt to bring them out with dessert. Whether for the family or for a guest, nothing starts a meal off better than a special garden treat that says, "This was grown here. It's just been picked. And today it's at its prime. Welcome."

ROaSTeD PePPeR anD TOmaTO DIP

MAKES ABOUT 2½ CUPS

3 tablespoons olive oil

6 medium-size plum tomatoes, cut in half lengthwise (about 2½ cups)

2 large red, yellow, or orange bell peppers, stemmed, seeded, and cut lengthwise into wide strips

2 medium-size onions, peeled and cut in half crosswise

Cloves from ½ head garlic (about 8 cloves), separated but not peeled

1 teaspoon dried thyme

½ cup sour cream

Salt and freshly ground black pepper, to taste

Sure, summer is hot, but firing up the oven to roast the vegetables for this dip will give them so much extra flavor that it's worth it. At the same time, you'll make a considerable dent in your late-summer tomato-and-pepper glut. Grill the rest of the meal outdoors, or bring out a bowl of potato salad from the fridge, made the night before.

I like to set the dip in the center of a platter and surround it with raw vegetables in many colors: yellow bell peppers, orange carrots, young purple string beans, small tender side shoots of broccoli, or whatever crudités the garden offers.

Roasting tomatoes brings out the most delicious flavors.

1. Preheat the oven to 350°F.

2. Oil a rimmed baking sheet with some of the olive oil. Place the tomatoes, peppers, and onions on the sheet, sprinkle them with the remaining oil, and using your hands, rub the oil all over them. Press down hard on the pepper strips, with their cut sides down, to flatten them. Then arrange the tomatoes and peppers with their cut sides up, and the onions with their cut sides down, on the baking sheet. Scatter the garlic cloves around the vegetables and roast for 30 minutes.

3. Take the baking sheet out of the oven. Remove the garlic cloves and set them aside. Sprinkle the thyme over the other vegetables and return the baking sheet to the oven. Roast for about 20 minutes.

4. Turn the baking sheet around and flip the onions so they are cut side up. Roast until the vegetables have reduced in size and are caramelized but not burned, about 30 minutes.

5. If there are some blackened flecks on the vegetables, cut these out. Combine the tomatoes, bell peppers, and onions in a food processor, blender, or food mill. Squeeze or scrape the garlic pulp out from its papery skin and add the pulp to the food processor. Add the sour cream, and blend until smooth. (If you are using a food mill, wait to stir in the sour cream after pureeing.) Stir in salt and black pepper to taste.

6. Serve the dip warm or at room temperature.

"EDIBOWL" PEPPERS

Here's a fun way to serve this dip, if you have grown some miniature bell peppers or found them at the farmers' market. They are single-serving size, perfect for an hors d'oeuvre, and because bells are not pointed on the bottom, they will sit flat on a platter. Cut off their tops, clean out their ribs and seeds, and spoon a few tablespoons of the dip into each one. Then add a bouquet of colorful raw vegetables cut into sticks, along with a sprig of purple basil and a nasturtium flower. Our friend Marada Cook created this technique for her "Edibowl" booth at Maine's Common Ground Fair, in the interest of zero-waste packaging. After strolling fairgoers finished dipping their carrot and celery sticks, they could eat the container as well.

PARSNIP AND FETA DIP

MAKES ABOUT 1½ CUPS

1 large parsnip, trimmed
  but not peeled, cut into
  1-inch chunks
  (2 packed cups)

3 large cloves garlic,
  unpeeled

2 tablespoons olive oil

5 ounces feta cheese,
  crumbled (about ¾ cup)

¼ cup heavy (whipping)
  cream

Freshly ground black
  pepper

This vegetable dip surprises people because the normally strong, sweet flavor of parsnip roots is balanced by the tanginess of feta cheese. You can make the dip as soon as your parsnips mature in the fall, and then throughout the winter if the ground is soft enough to dig. Since our soil freezes solid for many months, we are especially grateful for this dish when early spring rolls around.

For dipping, crackers or chips are fine, but try the high-fiber option of spreading this on a thin slice of raw beet, or on the crisp end of a Belgian endive leaf. It also makes for a good bruschetta, spread on a toasted slice of Italian bread.

1. Preheat the oven to 350°F.

2. Place the parsnip chunks and the garlic cloves on a rimmed baking sheet. Sprinkle with the olive oil and toss, coating them thoroughly. Bake for 20 minutes.

3. Take the baking sheet out of the oven, and using tongs, flip the parsnip chunks over. Return the baking sheet to the oven and bake for another 10 minutes. The parsnips should be very soft and golden brown but not charred, and the garlic soft inside.

4. Squeeze or scrape the garlic pulp from its papery skin, and place the garlic pulp in a food processor, blender, or food mill. Add the feta, cream, and pepper to taste.

5. When the parsnips are done, add them to the processor and blend until smooth.

6. Serve the dip right away, or cover and refrigerate it (it will keep for several days); then reheat it in a small saucepan over low heat. The warmth enhances the flavor, but the dip is also fine at room temperature.

Bagna Cauda

SERVES ABOUT 20 AT A MEAL WITH LOTS OF OTHER FOOD, 8 TO 10 AS THE SOLE APPETIZER

This pungent dipping sauce, accompanied by raw fall or winter vegetables and pieces of crusty bread, is the one to make when friends gather on a cold evening. A specialty of the Piedmont region of Italy, it is pronounced *bahn-ya-COW-da* and translates as "warm bath." As an appetizer, it is very filling, and you could make a meal of it if you were so inclined. Essentially it is garlic and anchovies, dissolved in hot butter and cream or in olive oil. Eliot and I like a creamy bagna cauda because of the way it thickens up and clings to whatever morsels you plunge into it. When dipping a vegetable, hold a slice of bread beneath it to catch the drips. When the bread is soaked, eat it and start a new one.

The garlic flavor is very pronounced, the anchovy less so, despite the amount added, and I have yet to see it offend the anchovy-averse.

2 cups heavy (whipping) cream

4 large cloves garlic, peeled and pressed

1 cup (2 sticks) butter

2 ounces canned anchovy fillets

4 to 6 carrots, scrubbed but not peeled, cut into sticks

3 ribs celery, cut into sticks

6 to 8 baby white turnips, peeled (if needed) and sliced

1 small daikon radish, unpeeled, cut into sticks; or 8 to 10 whole small red radishes

1 or 2 heads Belgian endive, separated into individual leaves

1 or 2 heads fennel, trimmed, cored, and sliced lengthwise

1 loaf crusty Italian bread, or 1 baguette, sliced ½ inch thick

1. Combine the cream and the garlic in a saucepan, and bring to a simmer over medium heat. Reduce the heat to low and cook, stirring frequently, until very thick, 30 to 40 minutes.

2. Combine the butter and the anchovies in another saucepan (I toss in some oil from the anchovy can or jar as well), and cook over low heat, stirring frequently, until the butter has melted and the anchovies have thoroughly dissolved, about 5 minutes.

3. When the cream has thickened, gradually add the anchovy butter to it,

When dipping a vegetable, hold a slice of bread beneath it to catch the drips.

whisking or using an immersion blender. There is no need to strain the finished bagna cauda.

4. Serve hot or warm, in a bowl or crock. Set the bowl in the center of a large platter, and surround it with the carrots, celery, turnips, radish, endive, and fennel. Put the bread slices in a basket and place it within easy reach.

TRY THIS TOO . . .

Other cold-weather vegetables might include scallions, broccoli, and cauliflower. Try dipping other firm salad leaves, such as romaine or escarole.

If there are still some summer vegetables in the garden, use thin spears of zucchini, cucumber, and red or yellow bell peppers.

STUFFED SQUASH BLOSSOM FRITTERS

SERVES 4 LUXURIOUSLY, 6 TO 8 AS A SMALLER APPETIZER

SEXING A BLOSSOM

Squash blossoms are truly a gardener's reward. Pick early in the day, while they are still wide-open golden trumpets. You can stuff them after they have closed, but it's hard to do without tearing them.

The male blossoms are the best because they come with a stem "handle." They're also less needed in the garden— you don't need many to pollinate the female flowers that grow on the same plants. That said, you can make perfectly good stuffed squash blossoms with the females; the little round swelling at the base, which would eventually form the fruit, is edible.

We discovered this wonderful appetizer on a trip to Rome years ago, and since then we have seen numerous variations cropping up on American menus.

It is very important to eat these fritters right away, before they lose their crispness. I fry them in small batches, and as I'm setting them out on a platter, diners congregate and gobble them up as soon as they're cool enough to touch. It's a great start to a meal.

Even with the thin batter, the flowers pick up a good bit of the oil, so these are filling morsels. I would not serve them before a heavy meat-and-potatoes meal. They go best with a table full of summer salads and a light seafood soup.

8 ounces medium-soft, slightly tangy cheese, such as raclette (my favorite), Fontina, or Monterey Jack

16 squash blossoms, preferably males with 3-inch stems (see "Sexing a Blossom," page 262), picked while open, laid out on a baking sheet, and refrigerated (uncovered) immediately

16 large fresh sage leaves

½ cup plus 2 tablespoons whole wheat flour

¼ teaspoon salt

Freshly ground black pepper, to taste

About 1 cup olive oil

Flaky salt for serving (optional)

1. Cut the cheese into sixteen 1-inch-long logs, about ½-inch thick.

2. Gently part the petals of a blossom to gain access to the column of fused stamens at its center (or the pistil if it's a female). Trying not to tear the petals, carefully cut out this column with small scissors or flower snips. Insert 1 cheese log and 1 sage leaf into the base of the blossom, where the column was. Fold the petals back in, surrounding the cheese and sage. Repeat with the remaining blossoms, cheese, and sage. Set aside.

3. Combine the flour, the ¼ teaspoon salt, and pepper in a shallow bowl. Add ¾ cup water, and whisk together to produce a thin batter. (You'll find that whole wheat flour turns less gummy as a breading than white flour does, and picks up less oil. If the batter thickens too much before you are done, add a little water to thin it out.)

4. Have a warmed platter handy, lined with several thicknesses of paper towels.

5. Pour enough olive oil into a 9- or 10-inch skillet to be ¼-inch deep, and heat it over medium heat until it is fragrant but not smoking.

6. One at a time, holding them by their stems, swirl 3 or 4 blossoms in the batter until they are well coated and the twisting motion has pushed the petal

tips into a point (this helps to seal in the cheese). Place the blossoms in the skillet, separating them so that they are not touching. Fry them on each side, turning them with a spatula, until they are crisp and golden but not browned, 2 to 3 minutes per side. Make sure the oil is hot enough to do this quickly, before the cheese can ooze out.

7. Remove the squash blossom fritters from the skillet, place them on the platter, add a bit more salt (sprinkle with flaky salt, if desired) and pepper if needed, and serve immediately. (If they sit around too long, they still taste good but will lose their crispness.) Meanwhile, repeat the process with the remaining blossoms until they are all done (and eaten!).

TRY THIS TOO . . .

The blossoms we sampled so long ago in Rome were stuffed with good Italian mozzarella and one anchovy apiece. I have experimented with numerous kinds of cheeses, including goat cheese and Cheddar, and all but the hardest ones are meltingly delicious. I've found a sage leaf is a more popular addition than an anchovy, but sometimes I make half of them with the latter. A bit of hot pepper is also tasty; or use a hot Pepper Jack cheese.

OPEN-FACED SANDWICHES

Sandwiches, pockets, and wraps are all fine when we're on the go, but when we're at home Eliot and I prefer a lower-carb version with the focus on the filling. An open-faced sandwich employs a slice of bread the way a pizza employs a crust: to support and display a savory and eye-pleasing array of ingredients, which can be hot or cold, raw or cooked. Eating it may require a knife and fork. This form of sandwich is popular in the Scandinavian countries and in France, where it is called a *tartine*.

The three examples here all start with a generous layer of whole-egg mayonnaise, which helps to hold the toppings in place. Thanks to its egg content, the mayonnaise puffs and bubbles lusciously when broiled.

TOMATO AND PESTO TOPPING

MAKES 4 SANDWICHES

HERE'S A GREAT WAY to turn tomatoes and basil into a quick but satisfying lunch.

1. Preheat the broiler (to "high" if yours has settings).

2. Place the bread slices in a single layer on a baking sheet, and broil on one side until a bit crisp but not browned, 2 to 3 minutes. Remove the baking sheet but leave the broiler on.

3. Turn the bread slices over, and spread the mayonnaise over the untoasted side. Arrange the arugula, then the tomatoes, and then the onion on top of each slice.

4. Drizzle the pesto over the onions. Season with black pepper, and then scatter the Cheddar on top.

5. Broil until the edges of the bread just start to brown, 2 to 3 minutes. The tomatoes will have given up a bit of their juices, and the cheese should be well melted and bubbly. Serve immediately.

TOMATO AND PESTO TOPPING

4 slices whole-grain bread

½ cup whole-egg mayonnaise (see page 323 for a homemade version)

1 small handful fresh arugula leaves, coarsely chopped

2 large tomatoes, thinly sliced

1 small onion (any kind), peeled and sliced into thin rounds

2 tablespoons pesto (see page 320 for a homemade version)

Freshly ground black pepper

1 cup coarsely grated sharp Cheddar cheese

ONION AND PARMESAN
TOPPING

4 slices whole-grain bread

⅔ cup whole-egg
    mayonnaise
    (see page 323 for a
    homemade version)

1 tablespoon minced fresh
    tarragon leaves, or
    2 teaspoons dried

Freshly ground black
    pepper, to taste

1 small onion (any kind),
    peeled and sliced into
    thin rounds

½ cup freshly grated
    Parmesan cheese,
    preferably Parmigiano-
    Reggiano

APPLE AND BRIE
TOPPING

4 slices whole-grain bread

½ cup whole-egg
    mayonnaise
    (see page 323 for a
    homemade version)

2 tablespoons finely
    chopped fresh sage
    leaves, or 1 tablespoon
    dried

1 small onion, peeled
    and finely chopped
    (about ¼ cup)

2 large apples (any kind),
    peeled, quartered,
    cored, and finely sliced

12 ounces Brie cheese,
    rind removed (unless
    you love the rind)

ONION AND PARMESAN TOPPING

MAKES 4 SANDWICHES

THERE IS SOMETHING ABOUT the combination of onion, Parmesan, tarragon, and mayonnaise that is infinitely satisfying. Cut into small rounds or squares, these little toasts make quick canapés, but we like them best whole, for a winter supper.

1. Preheat the broiler (to "high" if yours has settings).

2. Place the bread slices in a single layer on a baking sheet, and broil on one side until a bit crisp but not browned, 2 to 3 minutes. Remove the baking sheet but leave the broiler on.

3. Turn the bread slices over, and spread the mayonnaise over the untoasted side. Sprinkle with the tarragon and pepper. Distribute the onion among the bread slices, pulling the rings apart. Then sprinkle the cheese over the onions.

4. Broil until the edges of the bread just start to brown, the mayonnaise starts to puff up, and the cheese bubbles, 2 to 3 minutes. Serve immediately.

TRY THIS TOO . . .

✦ Substitute sliced scallion for the onion.

✦ Add chopped fresh spinach, arugula, sorrel, or watercress, arranging it on top of the mayonnaise before you add the onion.

APPLE AND BRIE TOPPING

MAKES 4 SANDWICHES

APPLE AND CHEESE IS a time-honored combination. For this dish we love Brie because of the way it melts quickly over the apples, leaving them somewhat crisp.

1. Preheat the broiler (to "high" if yours has settings).

2. Place the bread slices in a single layer on a baking sheet, and broil on one side until a bit crisp but not browned, 2 to 3 minutes. Remove the baking sheet but leave the broiler on.

3. Turn the bread slices over, and spread with mayonnaise over the untoasted side. Sprinkle with the sage and onion, and then distribute the apple slices over the top. Finally, add the Brie (because it will stick to your fingers, it is easiest to use two knives—one to cut it into pieces and the other to scrape the pieces onto the sandwiches).

4. Broil until all the edges of the bread just start to brown, the ingredients are hot, and the cheese is well melted, 3 to 4 minutes. Serve immediately.

CaRROT anD RaISIn SanDWICHES

MAKES 4 SANDWICHES

My mother made this sandwich for me when I was a kid, and I loved it. She used an old-fashioned meat grinder to mash and mix the carrots and raisins. The grinder creates the best texture, but a food processor does a decent job too. This is a good sandwich to take to school or work. For a more substantial meal, serve it with a salad or a light, nonstarchy soup such as Farmer's Tomato Bisque (page 277).

10 small, tender carrots, scrubbed but not peeled, cut into 1-inch sections (2 cups)

1 cup raisins

½ cup mayonnaise, homemade (see page 323) or a good brand

Salt and freshly ground black pepper

8 slices whole-grain bread (slices not too thick, hard, or dense), crusts removed

8 leaves soft lettuce, such as a Boston or Bibb type

1. *If using a meat grinder,* grind the carrots and raisins together into a bowl; then mix in the mayonnaise. *If using a food processor or blender,* pulse the carrots and raisins together until they are thoroughly combined but have not turned to a paste. This will take less than a minute. Add the mayonnaise and pulse for a few seconds more. *If you have neither of these implements,* grate the carrots on the medium-fine holes of a box grater and finely chop the raisins with a sharp heavy knife. Combine in a bowl and stir in the mayonnaise.

2. Stir in salt and pepper to taste.

3. To make a sandwich, spread one fourth of the mixture over a slice of bread. Top it with 2 lettuce leaves, and then top the lettuce with a second slice of bread. Repeat three more times to create 4 sandwiches.

This is a good sandwich to take to school or work.

Soups

A SOUP CAN BE CHUNKY OR SMOOTH, heavy or light, thick or thin. It can be a simple introduction to a meal or, as is common in our household, the meal itself, followed by salad and a bowl of fruit.

The busy pace of modern life, much of it lived outside the home, has taken its toll on soup making, and most households have made their peace with a shelf full of soup in cans. This chapter may be taken as a small effort to banish them. The vegetables in those soups seem dead, the broth usually oversalted, chemical-tasting, and metallic.

Some long-simmered soups require your presence for several hours and are best as weekend fare. But even these allow stretches of time when only a cook's awareness is required, not his or her hand or eye. Many words are written and rows weeded while soups bubble on our stove. Some soups, on the other hand, are made quickly. Many on the following pages can be made in less than an hour.

CHICKEN SOUP WITH APPLES

SERVES 5 TO 6

12 tablespoons (1½ sticks)
 butter

2 large onions, peeled and
 coarsely chopped

3 cups chicken stock
 (see page 289)

2 cups dry white wine or
 dry vermouth

2 large ribs celery,
 coarsely chopped

2 cloves garlic, peeled
 and pressed or finely
 minced

4 to 8 apples, peeled,
 cored, and coarsely
 chopped (about 4 cups)

8 ounces mushrooms,
 sliced (2½ cups)

1 pound cooked chicken
 (or turkey) meat,
 cut into 1-inch pieces

6 tablespoons whole
 wheat flour

2 teaspoons ground
 cardamom

1½ cups heavy (whipping)
 cream

½ cup coarsely chopped
 fresh flat-leaf parsley
 leaves

Salt and freshly ground
 black pepper

This is a good cold-weather soup, but it can be prepared any time you have apples on hand. It requires both cooked chicken (or turkey) meat and stock, so I often make the soup the day after I have roasted a bird (see Roast Chicken with Potatoes and Sage, page 421), as there is always plenty of meat left to pick off the carcass, as well as the makings of stock. A good full-flavored stock is important to this soup. I also think it's important to include some dark meat, to contribute more flavor.

There is a lot of browning of individual items here, and the reward is a great depth of flavor. Excess butter can be skimmed off toward the end if desired.

1. Melt 3 tablespoons of the butter in a large skillet over medium-low heat. Add the onions and sauté, stirring frequently, until they are golden brown, 10 minutes.

2. Meanwhile, combine the stock and the wine in a large soup pot, stockpot, or Dutch oven, and bring to a simmer.

3. Remove the onions from the skillet with a slotted spoon, leaving as much of the butter behind as possible, and add them to the soup pot. Add the celery and garlic to the soup pot, and simmer over very low heat.

4. Meanwhile, add 3 tablespoons butter to the butter remaining in the skillet, and set it over medium-low heat. When it has melted, add the apples and simmer, stirring occasionally, until they are tender and medium brown, 10 to 15 minutes. Then use a slotted spoon to transfer the apples to the soup pot.

5. Melt 1 more tablespoon of the butter in the skillet and add the mushrooms. Sauté, stirring occasionally, until they have browned, 5 minutes. Add them to the soup pot.

6. Add the chicken pieces to the soup pot.

7. Melt the remaining 5 tablespoons butter in the skillet over low heat. Add the flour and cardamom and cook, stirring vigorously with a spatula or a flat whisk, for 3 minutes. Add 1 cup of hot water and stir vigorously to make a thick roux, mashing any lumps with the spatula or whisk.

8. Add the roux to the soup and stir vigorously with a large spoon to mix it in thoroughly. Simmer for 2 minutes.

9. Add the cream and parsley. Simmer for 2 minutes.

10. Season the soup with salt and pepper to taste, and serve hot.

TRY THIS TOO . . .

✦ This soup will work with any type of poultry, including duck. (If you've begun with a whole duck or a duck carcass, use some of its plentiful fat for browning the mushrooms and vegetables.)

✦ When I must suddenly feed more people than expected, I stretch this soup by adding cooked rice, which I often have on hand in the refrigerator or freezer, or by adding some potatoes that have been chopped into small cubes and quickly simmered in water for 15 minutes. If the soup needs enrichment after these additions, more stock can be added as well. Additional flour is not needed, since either the rice or the potatoes will thicken the soup slightly.

Beef Borscht

2 ounces slab bacon, cut into ¼-inch cubes (¼ cup), or 2 regular bacon strips, chopped

2 tablespoons butter

2 tablespoons sunflower oil

3 pounds stewing beef, cut into 1-inch pieces

Salt and freshly ground black pepper

3 cups dry red wine

3 cups homemade beef stock (see page 291) or water if you don't have homemade stock

2 bay leaves

1 small bundle fresh thyme sprigs, tied together with twine, or 1 teaspoon dried thyme leaves

2 large beets, trimmed, peeled, and shredded in a food processor or on a box grater (about 5 cups)

4 medium-size carrots, scrubbed but not peeled, cut into ¼-inch-thick rounds

2 large onions, peeled and coarsely chopped

¼ cup dry vermouth or additional red wine (optional)

INGREDIENTS CONTINUED ▶

A traditional borscht is a robust peasant soup, or sometimes a stew. Originally a Ukrainian dish, it has its variants in other parts of the former Soviet Union and far beyond. Some are cold, some are smooth, some are chunky. Ingredients and methods may vary, but beets are essential to its character. My version is a one-pot meal I often make when feeding a large crowd of hungry farmworkers on a cold day. The bright color alone is a good warm-up. Even if I am serving only four people, I often make the full amount because this borscht is just as good, if not better, the next day—so a repeat performance is welcome.

1. Sauté the bacon in a large skillet over medium heat, stirring, until it has browned uniformly, 3 to 5 minutes. Using a slotted spoon, remove the bacon to a plate and set it aside, leaving the fat in the skillet.

2. Add the butter and sunflower oil to the fat in the skillet, and heat over medium-high heat until the butter's foam subsides, about 2 minutes.

3. Meanwhile, pat the pieces of beef dry with a paper towel.

4. Season the beef cubes with a dash of salt and black pepper, add them to the skillet (in batches so as not to crowd the pan and cause the meat to steam), and brown them on both sides, 3 to 4 minutes per batch. As each batch is done, transfer it to a plate.

5. Remove the skillet from the heat. Place all the meat in a large heavy pot or Dutch oven, leaving the fat in the skillet. Add the wine, stock, bay leaves, thyme, and beets to the meat. Stir, bring to a simmer, and cook, partially covered, for 1½ hours.

6. While the beef is simmering, return the skillet to medium heat. Add the carrots and onions and cook until browned, 5 minutes. Then set the vegetables aside in a bowl.

7. Deglaze the skillet by adding the vermouth or wine and simmering it over medium heat, scraping the bottom of the skillet with a spatula to loosen the delicious brown bits. Add this liquid to the simmering mixture.

8. Place the potatoes in a medium-size saucepan, add water to cover, and bring to a simmer. Cook until tender, 10 to 15 minutes. Remove the pan from the heat but leave the potatoes in the pan.

9. When the meat has been simmering for 1½ hours, fish out the bay leaves and the thyme bundle. Drain the potatoes and add them to the pot along with the carrots and onions and the chopped cabbage. Simmer until the cabbage is tender, 20 minutes. This dish should have the consistency of a soup, so if too much liquid has boiled away, add water. Thanks to the beets, all the vegetables will be colored varying shades of red. It will smell irresistible, and flavors will have blended together. Taste; add salt if needed, and season with a grinding of black pepper to taste.

10. Ladle the borscht into individual bowls, and top each one with a dollop of sour cream and a scattering of scallion tops.

TRY THIS TOO . . .

For a lighter version, substitute yogurt for the sour cream—although sour cream will taste better.

◄ INGREDIENTS CONTINUED FROM PREVIOUS PAGE

3 large potatoes (any kind), scrubbed but not peeled, cut into 1-inch cubes

½ small red cabbage, cored and coarsely chopped

2 cups sour cream

1 bunch scallions (green parts only), cut into medium-fine pieces

BLACK BEAN SOUP

SERVES 6 TO 8

Black beans color their cooking liquid, making any soup seem richer and more substantial, an effect that is possible when you cook them as mature dried beans, not at the fresh shell bean stage. I've found that by cooking black beans an extra half hour after other ingredients have been added, the liquid thickens wonderfully without exploding the beans and making them mushy.

This is a summer or early fall soup, made with fresh peppers and tomatoes. (In winter you could substitute ones that you have canned, frozen, or dried.) I often prepare it when I am feeding a crowd, and even if we are few at the table I like to make the full amount because it is so nice to find it in the fridge the next day. We like to eat it with dark sourdough bread and a green salad.

I always allow extra time to cook dried beans—up to 3 hours—because the cooking time can be unpredictable.

3 cups dried black beans, such as black turtle beans

2 bay leaves

1 cinnamon stick (3 inches long), or ½ teaspoon ground cinnamon

8 ounces slab bacon or thick-cut breakfast bacon, cut into small cubes (1 cup)

2 medium-large onions, peeled and chopped

2 to 3 yellow or red bell peppers, stemmed, seeded, and chopped

2 jalapeño peppers, or to taste, seeded and finely chopped (see Note)

2 cloves garlic, peeled and pressed or finely minced

2½ cups coarsely chopped peeled fresh tomatoes, preferably plum type

Salt and freshly ground black pepper

1 to 2 cups sour cream or yogurt

Tabasco sauce, for serving

1. The night before, rinse the beans, place them in a large pot, and add 6 cups water. Let them soak at room temperature overnight.

2. When you are ready to prepare the soup, preheat the oven to 350°F.

3. Drain the beans in a colander and rinse them under cold running water. Drain again. Place the beans in a Dutch oven (or if it is ovenproof, rinse out the pot they soaked in and return the beans to that pot). Add the bay leaves, cinnamon stick, and enough cold water to cover by 2 inches. Bring to a simmer over medium heat.

4. Transfer the pot to the oven and bake, uncovered, until the beans are just tender, usually about 1½ hours. (This could also be done on top of the stove, but there is less danger of the beans sticking to the bottom of the pot if they are cooked in the oven.) Remove the pot from the oven.

5. Sauté the bacon, stirring it frequently, in a large skillet over medium heat until just crisp, about 7 minutes. Remove the

bacon with a slotted spoon to a plate and set it aside, reserving the fat in the skillet.

6. Add the onions, bell peppers, and jalapeños to the fat in the skillet, cover, and sweat over low heat until they are softened and lightly browned, about 10 minutes.

7. Stir the cooked vegetables and the garlic into the beans. Remove the bay leaves and cinnamon stick. Simmer the soup, uncovered, over low heat for 20 minutes.

8. Add the tomatoes and the bacon, and simmer for another 10 minutes to blend the flavors. Season with salt and pepper to taste.

9. Serve hot in individual bowls with a dollop of sour cream on top of each one, or pass the sour cream at the table. Pass the Tabasco for those who like extra heat.

NOTE: After chopping hot peppers, thoroughly wash your hands, the knife, and the cutting board to avoid painful irritation of your fingers and anything they might touch.

SOUPE au PISTOU

SERVES 4 TO 6 AS A MAIN COURSE

Make this main-course soup in summer when the garden yields bunches of basil, the herb upon which it depends for its flavor. Summer is also the time when shell beans abound. For more about them, see page 186.

There are many versions of this soup—some with noodles, some with potatoes, some with both. This recipe uses neither—just some light summer vegetables, beans, hearty kielbasa, and, of course, pesto.

2 cups fresh shell beans

2 kielbasa sausages, or
  1 U-shaped kielbasa
  (about 12 ounces total)

2 tablespoons olive oil

2 medium-size onions,
  peeled and coarsely
  chopped

1 rib celery, coarsely
  chopped

1 medium-size zucchini,
  cut into thick rounds

1 large handful green
  beans (about 6 ounces),
  cut into 1-inch pieces

3 cups chopped peeled
  fresh tomatoes

Salt and freshly ground
  black pepper

1 cup Pesto Sauce
  (page 320),
  made without nuts

1. Place the shell beans in a large soup pot, add water to cover by 1 inch, and bring to a boil. Reduce the heat to a simmer and cook until tender, 15 to 30 minutes.

2. While the beans are cooking, cut the kielbasa into ¼-inch-thick rounds. Heat the olive oil in a large skillet over medium heat until fragrant, 1 to 2 minutes. Add half of the kielbasa rounds and sauté, flipping them with tongs or a spatula, until they are browned on both sides but not burned, 10 to 15 minutes. Using a slotted spoon, transfer the kielbasa to a bowl. Repeat with the remaining rounds. Leave the oil and drippings in the skillet.

3. Place the onions in the skillet and sauté over medium heat until tender and translucent, about 10 minutes. Add the onions to the bowl of kielbasa, leaving the drippings in the skillet.

4. Add ½ cup of water to the skillet and deglaze it over medium heat, scraping the bottom with a spatula to loosen the tasty brown bits. Add this to the cooked shell beans.

Pistou is French for the sauce we know as pesto, named for the mortar and pestle it's traditionally made with.

5. Stir the kielbasa and onions, the celery, zucchini, and the green beans into the shell beans. Add water to cover, and bring the mixture to a boil. Reduce the heat to a simmer and cook, uncovered, until all the vegetables are just tender, 20 to 25 minutes.

6. Add the tomatoes and cook for a minute or two just to heat them through. Add a little water if needed to keep things soupy, simmering briefly to reheat. Season with salt and pepper to taste.

7. Serve very hot (so the cheese in the pesto will melt when it is added). Either pass the pesto in a small bowl, or put a dollop of it (about 2 tablespoonfuls) in the center of each individual bowl of the soup.

TRY THIS TOO . . .

✦ You can omit the kielbasa for a meatless version, or substitute other meats such as bratwurst, ham hocks, lamb shanks, or leftovers from a roast chicken.

✦ To use dried beans instead of fresh shell beans, substitute 1 cup dried beans such as navy beans or cannellini, and instead of step 1, do the following: Soak the beans overnight in water to cover. Drain, rinse, and pick out any bad beans or stones. Preheat the oven to 350°F. In a large soup pot or Dutch oven, combine the dried beans and water to cover by 1 inch, and bring to a boil over high heat. Cover the pot, set it in the oven, and cook until the beans are tender, usually 1 to 2 hours. Drain. Then proceed with the recipe starting at step 2.

FARMER'S TOMATO BISQUE

SERVES 4 TO 6

I make this rustic, chunky soup a lot when tomatoes are abundant in the garden. Although plum tomatoes yield a thicker puree, it's fine to use an equivalent volume of other kinds. The addition of medium-dry sherry, to my mind, is the magic touch. An inexpensive brand will do fine, as long as it has a tawny color and a bit of sweetness.

This would make a good lunch dish served with a composed salad topped with fruit, or with a platter of open-faced sandwiches.

1. Chop half of the tomatoes into large pieces, and set them aside. Puree the remaining tomatoes in a food processor, blender, or food mill. Pour the puree into a large saucepan, and set it aside.

2. Cook the sausage in a large skillet over medium heat, breaking it into crumbles with a spatula, until no pink color remains, about 4 minutes. Using a slotted spoon, remove the sausage and add it to the pureed tomatoes. Leave the fat in the skillet.

3. Melt the butter in the skillet over medium-low heat. When the foam subsides, add the onions and garlic, and sauté, stirring frequently, until the onions have softened, about 10 minutes.

4. Add the sherry to the skillet and boil gently, stirring constantly with a spatula to scrape up the brown bits, until the alcohol has evaporated, about 2 minutes.

5. Add the onions, with all their liquid, to the sausage-tomato mixture, and heat over medium heat until warmed through, about 5 minutes.

6. Shortly before serving, stir the reserved chopped tomatoes into the soup and cook until they are heated through but have not started to disintegrate. Add the cream very gradually, stirring to incorporate it, and heat to just below a simmer to avoid curdling. Season the soup with salt and pepper to taste, stir, and serve immediately in a deep serving bowl or in individual soup bowls.

TRY THIS TOO . . .

This soup is a brick color, accented by

---

2 pounds (about 30 small, 20 medium, or 10 large) fresh plum tomatoes, peeled

1 pound country-style (bulk) pork sausage

2 tablespoons butter

2 medium-size onions, peeled and chopped

1 large clove garlic, peeled and pressed or finely chopped

1 cup medium-dry sherry

1½ cups heavy (whipping) cream

Salt and freshly ground black pepper

red spots of fresh tomato. If you prefer a brighter red, prepare an extra ½ cup of chopped peeled tomatoes, at room temperature or slightly warmed, mix them with 1 tablespoon finely chopped fresh basil, and scatter this garnish on top of the finished soup.

For a meatless version, omit the sausage and serve grilled cheese sandwiches with the soup.

FISH SOUP WITH TOMATOES AND FENNEL

SERVES 4 TO 6

4 tablespoons extra-virgin olive oil

2 small to medium-size onions, peeled and finely chopped (about 1½ cups)

1 fennel bulb, finely chopped (about 1 cup)

2 teaspoons fresh thyme leaves, or 1 teaspoon dried thyme leaves

½ teaspoon saffron threads

1½ cups dry white wine

½ teaspoon Tabasco sauce

Salt and freshly ground black pepper

1 pound fillet of haddock or other white fish

2 cups heavy (whipping) cream

2 large fresh tomatoes, peeled and finely chopped

Served with bread, cheese, and fruit, this soup could be a lunch or supper in itself. In smaller portions it could be the first course for a summer dinner featuring grilled steak or ribs.

1. Heat the olive oil in a medium-size saucepan over low heat. Add the onions and fennel, and sauté until they are soft and translucent, about 10 minutes.

2. Add the thyme, saffron, wine, Tabasco, ¼ teaspoon salt, black pepper to taste, and 1½ cups water. Simmer for 10 minutes.

3. Cut the haddock into ½-inch cubes and add them to the mixture. Simmer, stirring, until the fish is just cooked through, about 2 minutes.

4. Stir in the cream and bring the soup to a simmer, but do not let it boil. Taste, and add salt if needed.

5. Add the tomatoes gradually and stir until they have just warmed through. Serve immediately.

SPICY SHRIMP SOUP

SERVES 4 AS A LIGHT MEAL, 6 AS A FIRST COURSE

¼ cup peanut oil or
   sunflower oil

2 medium-size carrots,
   scrubbed but not
   peeled, finely chopped
   (1 cup)

2 medium-size leeks
   (white part only),
   cleaned (see page 142)
   and chopped into
   medium-fine pieces
   (1 cup)

1 large red bell pepper,
   stemmed, seeded, and
   finely chopped (1 cup)

2 fresh jalapeño peppers,
   stemmed, seeded, and
   very finely chopped (½
   cup), see Note, page 274

1 bunch scallions
   (white and green parts),
   chopped (1 cup)

1 medium-size cucumber,
   peeled, seeded, and
   finely chopped (1 cup)

2 teaspoons grated fresh
   ginger

3 cups vegetable stock
   (see page 292)

1 cup semi-sweet Riesling,
   Gewürztraminer, or
   other semi-sweet white
   wine

Juice of 2 limes
   (no more than
   2 tablespoons)

Salt

1 pound small shrimp
   (about 4 cups), peeled
   and deveined

1 cup chopped fresh basil
   leaves

The accent is on the veggies in this soup, made with vegetable stock rather than fish stock and with the shrimp added just at the end. Omit the shrimp and you still have a savory bowl. None of the ingredients are cooked very long, so there is plenty of crunch, bolstered by the deep flavor base of the long-simmered stock.

This is a light summer dish, and a good thing to make after a period of overindulgence in rich food. It might also be the first course to precede a heavier main one.

1. Heat the oil in a large saucepan over medium heat. Add the carrots and leeks, reduce the heat to medium-low, and sauté, stirring, for 4 minutes.

2. Add the bell pepper, jalapeño peppers, scallions, cucumber, and ginger. Sauté, stirring, for another 4 minutes.

3. Add the vegetable stock, wine, lime juice, and a dash of salt. Bring the mixture to a simmer, and then let it simmer for 2 minutes.

4. Add the shrimp and cook, stirring with a wooden spoon, until they are firm and no longer translucent, 3 to 5 minutes, depending on their size.

5. Remove the pan from the heat and taste for seasoning. Add a bit of salt if needed. Stir in the basil, and serve immediately.

This summer soup is more chopping than cooking, and doesn't heat up the kitchen.

CREAMY FALL VEGETABLE SOUP

SERVES 4 AS A MAIN COURSE, 6 AS A FIRST COURSE

Despite its name, there isn't a lot of cream in this soup. The creamy richness comes mostly from the flavor of the vegetables, the background of beef stock, and the smoothness of the puree. Butternut squash predominates but doesn't overwhelm. I like to make this when the squash has matured and cured but there are still some late tomatoes in the garden, along with fresh celery.

We make a meal of it for lunch or supper, along with a salad. It also makes a good first course if the main course is a fairly light one.

1. Preheat the oven to 350°F.

2. Cut the squash into large chunks and scrape out the seeds, but do not peel it.

3. Sprinkle the sunflower oil on a baking sheet and place the squash chunks on it, smearing all their cut surfaces with the oil. Bake, turning the pieces once or twice, until they are very tender when pierced with a fork, 30 to 40 minutes. Set aside to cool slightly.

4. Melt the butter in a large heavy-bottomed saucepan, soup pot, or Dutch oven over low heat. Add the leeks and sauté, being very careful not to burn them, until just tender, 2 to 3 minutes.

5. Add the celery, turnip, garlic, bay leaf, cayenne, a dash of salt, and black pepper to taste. Cover, and sweat the vegetables, stirring them now and then, for 10 minutes. Continue to watch the leeks carefully.

6. Add the tomatoes and beef stock, and simmer, covered, for another 5 minutes. Remove the bay leaf.

7. Peel the cooled cooked squash and add it to the saucepan. Stir briefly. Then puree the mixture, in batches, in a blender or food mill, pouring each batch of puree into a large bowl. (If using a blender, be careful not to fill it too full, lest it erupt at the top and burn you.) When all the soup has been pureed, return it to the saucepan. (An immersion blender, placed directly in the pan, works too—but only a heavy-duty version. The fibers of the leeks will get caught up in the blade of a standard immersion blender.)

1 small butternut squash (1 pound or less) or part of a larger one

1 tablespoon sunflower oil

2 tablespoons butter

2 large leeks (white and pale green parts only), cleaned (see page 142) and chopped into 1-inch pieces

1 large rib celery, coarsely chopped

1 small turnip, coarsely chopped

2 cloves garlic, peeled and chopped

1 large bay leaf

Dash of cayenne pepper

Salt and freshly ground black pepper

12 small plum tomatoes, peeled and chopped (1½ cups)

2 cups beef stock, preferably homemade (see page 291)

1½ cups cooked brown rice

¾ cup heavy (whipping) cream

2 tablespoons minced fresh flat-leaf parsley leaves

8. Add the rice to the puree and cook, stirring, over low to medium heat to heat it through, 3 to 4 minutes.

9. Add the cream and heat to just below a simmer. Taste for salt and pepper and add more if needed. Sprinkle with the parsley, and serve hot.

TRY THIS TOO . . .

✦ If it's winter, I use plum tomatoes that I have frozen, and I replace the celery rib with celery root. If there are no leeks, substitute 2 medium-size onions.

✦ Chicken stock can be substituted for the beef. For a meatless version, substitute water.

CREamy ASPARAGUS anD SCALLIOn SOUP

SERVES 4 TO 6

4 cups poultry stock, preferably homemade (see page 289)

16 medium-size asparagus spears, trimmed and cut into 1-inch pieces

6 tablespoons (¾ stick) butter

16 medium-size scallions (white and green parts), cut into 1-inch pieces

4 tablespoons all-purpose flour

1½ cups heavy (whipping) cream

4 tablespoons coarsely chopped fresh tarragon leaves, or 2 tablespoons dried

Freshly ground black pepper

Salt

When the asparagus spears first come up, there may not be much else on hand to combine them with. But scallions are a good possibility, either as an early-planted crop in the garden or cold frame, or as green onions from an early onion row (see page 66). If you grow tarragon, you are sure to have plenty of that to add, well before asparagus season is over.

This soup is light enough to serve as a starter, or to accompany sandwiches and a salad at lunchtime.

1. Bring the stock to a simmer in a large saucepan over medium-high heat. Add the asparagus and simmer until just tender, about 5 minutes. Remove the asparagus with a slotted spoon and set it aside in a bowl. Leave the stock in the pan and set it aside.

2. Melt 2 tablespoons of the butter in a large skillet over medium heat. Add the scallions and sauté, stirring frequently, until soft and golden, about 5 minutes. Add the scallions to the asparagus.

3. Melt the remaining 4 tablespoons butter in the skillet over medium-low heat. Add the flour and stir vigorously with a whisk or a spatula to form a roux. Cook, stirring constantly, until the flour loses its raw taste but does not brown, about 2 minutes.

4. Pour about half of the still-warm stock into the skillet and whisk or stir vigorously until the mixture is thickened and smooth. Pour this into the remaining stock in the saucepan, stirring to incorporate.

5. Add the asparagus and scallions, and stir to combine.

6. Stir in the cream, 3 tablespoons of the fresh tarragon (or all of the dried tarragon) and black pepper to taste. Heat the soup to a low simmer; then remove the pan from the heat.

7. Taste, and add salt as needed. Serve hot, sprinkled with the remaining 1 tablespoon fresh tarragon.

VARIATION:

For a more elegant version, puree the soup at the end, and add a dollop of crème fraîche to each serving, topped with the tarragon.

Leek and Potato Soup

SERVES 4 AS A MAIN COURSE, 6 AS A STARTER

Here's a hearty soup for fall and winter days. Serve it as a main course or as a warm-up for skiers, woodcutters, and snow-shovelers. You can use brown-skinned potatoes, which often keep better through the winter, but the red ones look nice with the pale yellow-green of the leeks. For a meatless version, substitute butter for the bacon and add 1 teaspoon of curry powder.

4 ounces slab bacon, cut into small cubes (about ½ cup), or 4 regular bacon strips, chopped

6 medium-size leeks (white and pale green parts), cleaned (see page 142) and chopped (about 4 cups)

4 medium-size red potatoes (about 2 pounds total), scrubbed but not peeled, cut into ½-inch cubes

1 bay leaf

1 teaspoon fresh thyme leaves, or ½ teaspoon dried

Small pinch of nutmeg, preferably freshly grated

Salt and freshly ground black pepper

1 cup heavy (whipping) cream

2 tablespoons finely chopped fresh flat-leaf parsley leaves

1. Sauté the bacon, stirring, in a large heavy-bottomed saucepan, soup pot, or Dutch oven over medium heat until it has browned uniformly, 5 to 7 minutes. Using a slotted spoon, transfer the bacon to a plate. Drain off a little of the bacon fat in the pan if you like, but leave enough to cook the leeks in.

2. Add the leeks to the pan and sauté them over low heat, stirring frequently to make sure they do not burn, until wilted, 5 to 10 minutes.

3. Add the potatoes, 4 cups of water, and the bay leaf, thyme, nutmeg, a dash of salt, and black pepper to taste. Bring to a boil. Then reduce the heat to medium-low and simmer until the potatoes and leeks are both very tender, 15 to 20 minutes. Remove the bay leaf.

4. Puree the mixture, in batches if necessary, in a food processor or blender. (If using a blender, be careful not to fill it too full, lest it erupt at the top and burn you. A potato masher will also do the trick, but the texture will not be as smooth.)

5. Return the soup to the pan, add the bacon, and simmer, stirring often, until the bacon flavor permeates the soup, 5 minutes.

6. Just before serving, stir in the cream and heat the soup to just below a simmer. Taste, and add salt and pepper if needed. Serve in individual bowls, sprinkled with the parsley.

RED GAZPACHO

SERVES 4 TO 8

A spicy gazpacho is the soup to make when the summer fruiting vegetables are in abundance. It's light, healthy, quick, and since the vegetables are all raw, it doesn't heat up the kitchen. Tomatoes, peppers, and cucumbers are traditional. But as any child with a paint box can tell you, red and green make brown. This effect is much less evident if the ingredients remain coarse enough to be distinguishable, but if it is pureed, the soup is more appetizing when either green or red predominates. Here is the red version. It depends heavily on the quality of the vegetables, so if you haven't grown them yourself, try to fill in with some from a good local farmers' market.

For a simple lunch or supper, serve this in soup bowls with a platter of egg salad sandwiches in the center of the table, or with a shrimp or crabmeat salad. For a more dressed-up dinner, serve it as a first course in little bowls, or as an hors d'oeuvre in short glasses on a tray, with small spoons alongside.

3 cups coarsely chopped
   red tomatoes

2 cups coarsely chopped
   red bell peppers

2 cups coarsely chopped
   peeled cucumbers

1 small onion, peeled and
   chopped

Juice of ½ lemon

2 tablespoons honey

1 teaspoon Tabasco sauce,
   or 2 teaspoons chopped
   fresh hot chile pepper
   (more if you like your
   food with extra heat)

1 tablespoon balsamic
   vinegar

1 teaspoon salt, or to taste

Coarsely ground black
   pepper, to taste

2 tablespoons olive oil

¼ cup whole-milk yogurt

1 tablespoon finely
   chopped fresh cilantro

1. Combine half of the tomatoes, peppers, cucumbers, onion, lemon juice, honey, Tabasco, vinegar, salt, and pepper in a food processor or blender. Process to form a coarse puree. Transfer the puree to a large bowl, and repeat with the remaining half of the ingredients. Taste for seasoning.

2. Gently stir the olive oil into the soup.

3. Refrigerate the soup until it is thoroughly chilled, about 2 hours.

4. Serve the chilled gazpacho in individual bowls, topping each one with a dollop of the yogurt and a sprinkling of cilantro. Serve cold.

GREEN GAZPACHO

SERVES 4 AS A MAIN COURSE, 6 TO 8 AS AN APPETIZER

This gazpacho is a chlorophyll explosion, refreshing and pungent. It's ideal for the early part of summer, when you crave a cold vegetable soup but neither the tomatoes nor the peppers have ripened to red. Serve it with a platter of sandwiches, or pass it in cups, with spoons, while meat or fish is cooking on the grill.

Instead of using a food processor, you can puree the soup in a blender, although you might have to do this in three batches instead of two. Alternatively, finely chop all the ingredients by hand with a large sharp knife or a mezzaluna.

1. Combine the bell pepper, jalapeño pepper, cucumber, celery, and scallions in a large bowl, and stir together briefly. Spoon half of the mixture into a food processor and add 1 cup cold water. Pour the remainder into a smaller bowl and set it aside. Pulse the food processor until the mixture is just pureed, about 30 seconds, and return it to the large bowl.

2. Put the reserved vegetable mixture in the food processor, and add the parsley, cilantro, agave syrup, lime juice, lemon juice, a dash of salt, black pepper to taste, and 1 cup cold water. Pulse until just pureed, about 30 seconds.

3. Combine both vegetable mixtures in the large bowl, add the olive oil, and stir to mix thoroughly. Taste, and add more salt as needed (this soup tastes best with enough salt to accent the flavors). Refrigerate if not serving right away.

4. Just before serving, pour the gazpacho into individual bowls or glasses. Top each serving with 1 to 2 tablespoons sour cream and a pinch of the chives.

TRY THIS TOO . . .

If you are growing any green tomato varieties, such as Green Zebra or Green Grape, these may be added once they're fully ripe. A few tomatillos, either raw or cooked, would add another flavor dimension and an even sharper tartness.

- 1 medium to large green bell pepper, stemmed, seeded, and cut into small chunks (1½ cups)
- 1 green jalapeño pepper (or more if desired), stemmed, seeded, and chopped
- 1 medium-size cucumber, peeled, seeded, and coarsely chopped (¾ cup)
- 2 medium-size ribs celery, coarsely chopped (⅔ cup)
- 6 scallions (white and green parts), coarsely chopped (1 cup)
- 1 cup (packed) fresh flat-leaf parsley leaves
- ¼ cup (packed) fresh cilantro leaves, or to taste
- 1 tablespoon agave syrup, or 4 teaspoons raw sugar
- 2 tablespoons fresh lime juice
- 2 tablespoons fresh lemon juice
- Salt and freshly ground black pepper
- ¼ cup extra-virgin olive oil
- ½ cup sour cream
- 1 tablespoon very finely snipped fresh chives

STOCKS

Many recipes, including some in this book, call for stock, a simmered-down essence of meat or fish flavored with vegetables. Bones are included in meat and fish stocks for their nutritious gelatin. There are also stocks made from vegetables alone. The word *broth* is sometimes used instead; both terms usually indicate a strained liquid.

Stocks give a huge flavor boost to soups, stews, grain dishes, and vegetable dishes, and they can also be used as a simple warming soup, great to have on hand when someone isn't feeling well. Most restaurants prepare their own stocks and always have them available, but making stock is not always part of a typical home cook's routine. What with chopping, browning, simmering, and straining, stock-making is often considered too much trouble.

The alternatives are to use water, which will make the result less flavorful, or to use a canned stock or broth or one compressed into a powder or paste. While some of these products are definitely better than others, I've never found any that made an adequate substitute because all have a processed taste. So I got into the habit of making stocks a long time ago. Since it's something I always keep in mind, I take advantage of opportunities: a harvest of extra or imperfect vegetables, a carcass from poultry I've roasted, or the least tender cuts from an animal, or part of an animal I've bought in bulk. Backs, wings, and giblets are a good beginning for a poultry stock.

The process is not burdensome, because most of the time the stock is just simmering along while you do something else. You need to be at home to keep an eye on it, but that's all. You can even omit the browning step if you're rushed.

I freeze stock in straight-sided pint jars that fit neatly in the door racks of my freezer (straight sides are necessary for freezing to prevent jar breakage).

If I lacked the space to do this, I would simply reduce the stocks further to concentrate them, and then freeze them in smaller containers. They can even be reduced to a pastelike glaze, then frozen as cubes in an ice cube tray for later dilution. However it's done, these stores are money in the bank. I use them up gradually, replacing them whenever it's convenient. The more I make, the more I use them, and the more they enhance my cooking.

Fish stocks are made quickly, like the one described in the halibut recipe on page 428. A fish "rack," which includes the head, tail, bones, and some of the flesh, is worth its weight in gold if you have a fisherman friend, or a market that can order a rack for you. Fish stocks don't keep as well as other stocks, and if I freeze them at all, I use them in the next month or two.

CHICKEN STOCK

MAKES 4 TO 5 QUARTS

I use this stock more than any other, so I make sure I have plenty in the freezer to have on hand whenever I need it. It tends to be lighter in color than beef or vegetable stocks, and lends a subtle background of meatiness to vegetable dishes, such as the Baked Leeks on page 392. And it is essential in many soups, whether to boost the flavor, to act as the broth, or to make the soup go further. Sometimes I'll make it very quickly while I have chicken bones to work with, without the addition of vegetables—whose flavor can be more easily added later—because just a simple broth is useful too. But the more earthy and herbal a stock is, the richer the final soup will be.

1 chicken (4 pounds)

½ teaspoon salt

2 medium-size carrots, scrubbed but not peeled, coarsely chopped

1 rib celery, coarsely chopped

1 medium to large onion, peeled and coarsely chopped

3 cloves garlic, peeled and smashed

2 sprigs fresh parsley

Several sprigs fresh thyme, or 1 teaspoon dried

1 bay leaf

6 whole black peppercorns

1. Cut the chicken into pieces, separating the drumsticks from the thighs, severing the wings, and splitting the breast down the middle, then cutting in half crosswise to make 4 pieces. Cut the back in half. (One easy way to make all these cuts is to hold the blade of a meat cleaver on the spot where the cut should be, then strike a blow on the back edge of the cleaver with a rubber mallet. Poultry shears are also useful for splitting the breastbone.)

2. Place the chicken pieces in a stockpot, and add 4 quarts of cold water and the salt. Bring just to a boil over high heat, 20 to 30 minutes. Then reduce the heat to a very low simmer, with just a few bubbles rising. During this time a gray foam will float to the surface. As it collects, skim it off with a skimmer or a slotted spoon, and discard it. (It is easiest to skim the stock before any vegetables or herbs have been added.) Simmer for 15 minutes.

3. Start to remove the chicken pieces, beginning with the breasts, which take the least time to cook. Place the breast pieces on a cutting board or a plate and

THE MAKINGS OF A CHICKEN STOCK

There are other ways to assemble the materials for a chicken stock, the most important of which are the gelatin-rich bones, and it pays to be on the lookout for opportunities to collect them. Save the carcass from a roast chicken, along with the drippings. When you're making fried chicken, buy a whole chicken, rather than the standard pack of parts, in order to have some carcass left over. Ask a local poultry farm or butcher to save you necks, backs, and giblets (exclude the livers, which are good for pâté or chopped liver but are too strongly flavored for stock). Collect all these, both raw and cooked, in the freezer and save them to make a big batch of stock.

Everything in this recipe applies equally to turkey, either from purchased parts and giblets or from the bonanza that Thanksgiving presents. Since the bird is much larger, you'll need to increase the amounts of water, vegetables, and seasonings proportionally.

cut off the meat, reserving the skin and bones in a bowl. Next, do this with the wings and the back. Do the thighs and drumsticks last. While you are skinning and deboning the meat, continue to skim off the foam. The meat can be reserved for another purpose, such as chicken salad, chicken curry, or soup.

4. Return the skin and bones to the pot and add the carrots, celery, onion, garlic, parsley, thyme, bay leaf, and peppercorns. Simmer, uncovered, for 3 hours, or until the desired strength has been reached.

5. Place a strainer over a large bowl, and strain the stock through it, pressing the vegetables to extract as much liquid as possible. I find it helps to remove most of the bones from the strainer first with tongs, then press the vegetables. (For a clear stock, strain out the vegetables but do not press them. If it is still cloudy, re-strain it through a strainer lined with several layers of cheesecloth.)

6. Skim off the fat with a large spoon, by using a fat separator, or by chilling the stock so that the fat solidifies on top for easy removal. Either discard or preserve the fat for another use. (Sometimes, when freezing poultry stock, I'll deliberately leave a half inch or so of fat in the top of the jar, then use it for frying onions or other aromatics in order to add even more chicken flavor to a recipe where the stock is being used.) For freezing information, see page 288.

Making a stock is not burdensome, because most of the time it is just simmering along while you do something else.

BEEF STOCK

MAKES 3 TO 4 QUARTS

It's a great feeling to have homemade beef stock on hand to make a soup more substantial, whip up some gravy, or flavor a rice dish. Even in stews and braises that make their own juices, adding stock instead of water doubles the flavor, especially if you start the stock by roasting both the bones and the vegetables. As with any stock, the corps of basic "soup pot" vegetables plays a big part.

1. Position a rack in the preheat to 450°F.

2. Smear a large shallow roasting pan with the olive oil, place it in the middle of the oven, and heat it for 2 minutes.

3. Remove the pan from the oven, and add the soup bones. Using tongs or a long fork, rub the bones in the oil to coat them. Sprinkle the salt over the bones, and space them in the pan so that they are not touching. Set the pan in the middle third of the oven and roast the bones, flipping them over once, until they are evenly browned but not burned, about 30 minutes. (This could also be done in a large skillet on top of the stove, but it's easiest, and involves less cleanup, to do the bones in the oven while you're chopping the vegetables.)

4. When the bones are done, place them in a large stockpot, leaving the oil and fat in the roasting pan.

5. Put the onions, carrots, and celery in the pan and stir to coat them with fat. Return the pan to the oven and cook, stirring the vegetables from time to time, until they are browned, 15 to 20 minutes. Remove the pan quickly if there is any danger of burning.

6. While the vegetables are cooking, fill the stockpot with 5 quarts of cold water, or enough to cover the bones, and set it over high heat. Add the garlic, bay leaves, peppercorns, tomatoes, thyme, rosemary, oregano, and parsley.

7. When they have finished browning, add the vegetables to the stockpot. When the liquid begins to boil (this will take about 30 minutes), lower the heat to a slow simmer and cook, uncovered, for 4 to 5 hours. (If the bones have a lot of meat on them, it's okay to steal a bit of it partway through, and enjoy it for lunch with the horseradish cream on

2 tablespoons olive oil

5 to 6 pounds meaty beef soup bones, such as the shank (lower leg) and the oxtail

1 teaspoon salt

2 large onions, coarsely chopped

4 large carrots, scrubbed but not peeled, coarsely chopped

4 ribs celery, coarsely chopped

3 large cloves garlic, peeled and chopped

4 bay leaves

1 teaspoon whole black peppercorns

6 plum tomatoes

4 sprigs fresh thyme, or 1 teaspoon dried thyme

1 sprig fresh rosemary, or 1 teaspoon dried rosemary

1 sprig fresh oregano, or 1 teaspoon dried oregano

4 large sprigs fresh parsley

Adding
stock to
stews and
braises
doubles the
flavor.

page 427.) At the end, the liquid level will have dropped by a few inches and the meat will be falling off the bones. Keep an eye on the liquid to make sure it doesn't get to a rolling boil and reduce too fast, since a slow simmer extracts more flavor.

8. Taste the stock to see if it has reached the desired strength, and reduce it some more if it seems weak. Add a small pinch of salt if needed, but don't over-salt the stock in case you need to reduce it further when you use it in a recipe.

9. Remove just the bones and discard them. Strain the liquid through a large strainer into a container, pressing on the solids with the back of a large spoon to extract as much liquid as possible.

10. Use as desired, or freeze (see page 288).

TRY THIS TOO . . .

The stock can be reduced still further to produce a meat glaze, a thick paste used for lending a concentrated beef flavor to a dish without adding liquid. The glaze can be frozen and used by spoonfuls as needed. If you plan to do this, reduce the total amount of salt to a pinch.

VEGETABLE STOCK

MAKES 4 TO 7 CUPS, DEPENDING ON THE DESIRED CONCENTRATION

A vegetable stock is excellent for enriching soups, especially meatless ones. It also gives great flavor to risotto and other rice dishes, and to couscous and other grains. Add vegetable stock to curries, stews, bean dishes, potato dishes, creamy sauces, and anything that could use a little beefing up—without the beef. You can also enjoy the stock plain, as a light meal or as a soothing tonic for someone who is ailing. Freeze or can some to have on hand for such occasions.

The vegetables that work best are the old standbys that serve cooks so well as a flavor base—onions, celery, carrots, garlic—plus, of course, some herbs. I like to add fennel as well, if it's in the garden. Chopping or shredding the vegetables creates more surface area, which helps them yield up their essence. It also makes them easier to strain.

1. Combine all the vegetables and seasonings in a stockpot, add 12 cups cold water, and bring to a simmer over medium-high heat.

2. Reduce the heat to low and simmer, uncovered, for 2 hours.

3. Place a large strainer over a large bowl or saucepan, and strain the mixture through it, pressing on the vegetables with the back of a large spoon to extract as much liquid as possible. (Do this lightly, or not at all, if a recipe calls for a very clear stock.) Discard the solids.

4. Taste the stock. If it seems too weak and you'd prefer a richer, more flavorful stock, return it to medium heat and simmer to reduce it until the right strength has been reached.

5. Use right away, or store, covered, in the refrigerator for up to 4 days. For freezing information, see page 288.

TRY THIS TOO . . .

Other vegetables can be used for stock when they are in season: bell peppers, pea pods, potatoes, zucchini, tomatoes. Parsnips too, but just a bit, as they are strong and sweet and you don't want the stock to overwhelm whatever dish you're making. Brassicas such as cabbage are generally too strong as well, although I've tossed in a mild young kohlrabi or a few baby turnips with good results.

5 medium-size ribs celery, finely chopped

3 medium-size onions, peeled and finely chopped

6 to 8 medium-size carrots, scrubbed but not peeled, finely chopped or shredded

1 cup chopped parsley stems

1 small fennel bulb, or a few fennel stems, finely chopped (optional)

3 medium-size cloves garlic, peeled and finely chopped

2 bay leaves

Several fresh thyme sprigs, or ½ teaspoon dried thyme leaves

4 whole cloves

¼ teaspoon salt

¼ teaspoon whole black peppercorns

Try using fresh herbs when you can.

CHAPTER 8

Salads and Dressings

THE STANDARD "GARDEN SALAD" on restaurant menus is a little time-travel trick in which lettuce is topped with summer vegetables such as tomatoes, peppers, and cucumbers . . . 365 days of the year. A real-life garden salad, on the other hand, changes with the garden itself, and is more interesting. Why eat the same salad every day when you can enjoy 365 different ones? Greens can be grown year-round if you choose ones that are right for each season, and most salads begin with a partnership between raw greens and oil, spiked with the acidity of vinegar or citrus. *Fresh*—or better yet, *fresh-picked-right-now*—is the key to salad-making. But beyond that, anything goes. A salad can come

before the main course, after it, next to it, or it can be the main course itself.

Our salads fall into two groups: tossed salads and composed ones.

TOSSED SALADS. Tossing greens in a bowl is certainly the best way to coat them with a dressing. When you add other ingredients, you want ones that will stick to the greens with the help of the dressing. For this, it works best if they are either light, as with as herbs, or flat-surfaced, as with shaved carrots, thinly sliced cucumbers, or grated cheese. Heavier additions such as grapes, hard-cooked eggs, tomatoes, or any cubed item such as cheese, apples, or croutons, will tend to fall to the bottom of the bowl during tossing. With these, use a wide, shallow bowl and scatter the heavies over the top. You might need to toss the top items separately with dressing.

Edible flowers stick just fine to greens, but they should always be sprinkled on top and not tossed. Nothing takes the bloom off a rose petal like gumming it up with oil. For more on using flowers, see page 166.

Fresh herbs give a bowl of salad something to sing about. I like to use them boldly, especially if the greens have been chosen more for their color and crunch than for assertive flavor. Mixtures are fine, but I often like to feature a single herb such as basil, tarragon, or dill, matching the other ingredients to it. And herbs do not always have to be minced. Whole leaves or sprigs give a salad a rustic, just-gathered quality. Look also for plants with strong flavors that can function like herbs—the pale inner leaves of a celery head, for instance, or tangy sorrel.

COMPOSED SALADS. When the heavier components of a salad become numerous or worthy of a special focus, it is time to think outside the bowl and make a composed salad. This is simply one that is carefully arranged on a flat dish or platter, rather than tossed. I love making these. With very little effort it is possible to come up with something so beautiful and enticing, just by arranging a few elements that taste great together and complement one another visually. It can be done with individual servings or with one large platter from which diners may help themselves.

So often, when Eliot and I come indoors at the end of a day in the garden, I'll put out two dinner plates, spread out some greens, and then start adding whatever is at hand. It might be vegetables I've picked from the garden on the way in: some raw ones such as tomatoes, fennel, sugar snap peas, and carrots, or some that I'll cook lightly, such as asparagus, broccoli, or cauliflower. Often I'll have some baked beets in the fridge, ready to be sliced for a salad. Sometimes the focus is fruit, with a few generous slices of cheese. The salad might accompany pasta or a meat dish if we are very hungry, but just as often the protein goes right onto the salad: a bit of leftover cold steak, ham, or chicken, say, or a couple of poached eggs. Shrimp, lobster, crabmeat, and scallops are perfect choices when they are in season.

Sometimes I'll toss the greens with the dressing first, saving some of the dressing for drizzling over the additions. Other times I'll just wait and drizzle everything at once, then sprinkle on some herbs. But in any case, it always ends up being exactly what we need: hearty enough to fill us up, but light enough to ensure a good night's sleep.

LeTTuce WiTH Pan-RoasTed PeaRs

SERVES 4

This simple salad is fine with raw pears, but pan-roasting the pears in butter adds luxurious flavor. It goes well with any hearty fall soup.

1. Rinse and dry the lettuce leaves, and tear them into large pieces. Distribute the lettuce over four salad plates or a single platter. Sprinkle the scallions and the blue cheese over the lettuce.

2. Melt the butter in 2 tablespoons of the oil in a medium-large skillet over medium heat until the butter's foam subsides, 2 minutes.

3. Add the pear quarters and sauté them on both flat sides until golden brown, about 20 minutes in all. Remove the skillet from the heat.

4. Place the roasted pear quarters on top of the lettuce, leaving the oil in the skillet.

5. Just before serving, add the remaining 2 tablespoons oil and the lemon juice to the oil in the skillet. Simmer over medium heat, stirring with a spatula, for no more than a minute, scraping the bottom of the skillet to incorporate any brown bits. Pour this evenly over the salad. (Parts of the greens may wilt just slightly.) Add salt and pepper to taste, and serve immediately.

NOTE: Blue cheese doesn't have to be imported to be good. There are many fine domestic brands, such as Point Reyes Farmstead and Great Hill Blue.

1 small or ½ large head red-tipped lettuce

4 scallions (white and green parts), chopped

4 ounces firm, mild blue cheese, chopped or crumbled (¾ cup; see Note)

2 tablespoons butter

4 tablespoons walnut oil or sunflower oil

4 medium-size ripe but slightly firm pears, peeled, cored, and quartered lengthwise

2 tablespoons fresh lemon juice (½ regular lemon or 1 Meyer lemon)

Coarse sea salt and freshly ground black pepper

I think composed salads such as this one are the most fun to make.

MÂCHE, LETTUCE, AND BEET SALAD

SERVES 4 TO 6

2 medium-size beets

6 tablespoons extra-virgin olive oil

2 tablespoons balsamic vinegar

1 tablespoon maple syrup

Coarse sea salt and freshly ground black pepper

1 small butterhead lettuce

2 handfuls (about 2 ounces) mâche

This is one of our favorite hearty wintertime salads. It makes a fine light supper dish, accompanied by a loaf of bread with butter or cheese, but it could also be paired at lunch with soup, sandwiches, or pasta. The contrast between the pale lettuce heart, the deeper green of the mâche, and the crimson beets makes it handsome to look at, too.

Baked beets are singularly delicious, so you may want to cook more than this recipe calls for and set some aside. I find that the extra-long baking time pays off abundantly in flavor and texture—the beets become very soft, full-flavored, and caramelized. A bit of maple syrup in the dressing adds to their natural sweetness.

1. Position a rack in the center of the oven and preheat the oven to 350°F.

2. Trim the beets so that just a bit of stem remains. You can leave the tails (the thin roots) on. Scrub the beets and let them dry. Do not peel them.

3. Wrap the beets individually in aluminum foil and place them in a small casserole or ovenproof pot. Cover, and bake for 3 hours (4 hours if you are using large beets, 2 for small ones).

4. While the beets are baking, make the dressing: Combine the oil, vinegar, and maple syrup in a small screw-top jar. Set it aside.

5. Remove the beets from the casserole and unwrap the foil. Set them aside to cool for about 5 minutes. Then trim off the stems and tails, and peel off the skin.

6. Cut the beets in half lengthwise; then slice them crosswise and place them in a bowl. While they are still warm, vigorously shake the dressing in the jar to mix it well, and immediately pour half of it over the beets. Season the beets with salt and pepper to taste, and stir gently to coat them with the dressing.

7. Rinse and dry the lettuce leaves, discarding any outer leaves that are at all tough and less than perfect, so that what you have is mostly the pale yellow-green

heart. Gently tear the leaves into smaller pieces and place them in a bowl.

8. Rinse the mâche thoroughly and pat it dry. If your mâche plants are 3 inches across or less, leave the heads whole. If larger, pinch off the root ends to separate the heads into individual leaves. Add the mâche to the lettuce.

9. Shake the rest of the dressing in the jar, and add it to the greens. Season with salt and pepper to taste. Toss gently, and then spread the greens out over a platter or shallow dish. Distribute the beets over the center of the greens, and serve immediately.

TRY THIS TOO . . .

In place of the mâche and lettuce, you might substitute baby spinach and the pale hearts of chicory or endive.

COLD-WEATHER SALAD WITH APPLES AND CHEESE

SERVES 4, OR 2 HUNGRY EATERS

1 tablespoon sherry vinegar

3 tablespoons extra-virgin olive oil

1 clove garlic, pressed

1 tablespoon butter

1 to 2 slices hearty bread, such as a sourdough rye, crusts removed, cut into ½-inch cubes (1½ cups)

1 teaspoon fresh thyme leaves, or ½ teaspoon dried thyme leaves

INGREDIENTS CONTINUED ▶

Here's a fortifying salad for a cold evening when there are baby greens in the greenhouse or cold frame and apples in storage. It covers enough food groups to be a complete meal. For easy assembly, have all the ingredients at the ready.

1. Prepare the dressing: Combine the vinegar, olive oil, and garlic in a small glass. Whisk, and set aside to steep.

2. Melt the butter in a medium-size skillet over medium heat. Add the bread cubes and the thyme, and sauté, stirring constantly to coat the bread with butter, until the cubes are crisp on all sides, about 3 minutes. Remove the croutons from the skillet and set them aside.

3. Fry the bacon in the same skillet over medium heat, stirring, until the pieces

are uniformly crisp, about 6 minutes. Using a slotted spoon, transfer the bacon to paper towels to drain. Discard the fat or save it for another purpose.

4. Rinse and dry the romaine, and combine it with the arugula and endive in a medium-large salad bowl. Toss the greens together with your hands. Whisk the dressing again.

5. Add the dressing, season with salt and pepper to taste, and toss gently with your hands or with salad servers to coat the greens completely. Add the cheese and toss again.

6. Sprinkle the croutons, then the apples and bacon, and then the scallions over the salad, and serve.

◀ *INGREDIENTS CONTINUED FROM PREVIOUS PAGE*

4 ounces slab bacon, cut into ⅜-inch cubes, or 4 strips regular bacon, cut into ½-inch pieces

4 cups baby romaine lettuce leaves; or 1 small head romaine, cut crosswise into 1-inch pieces (4 cups)

2 cups baby arugula

1 head Belgian endive, cut crosswise into 1-inch pieces

Coarse sea salt and freshly ground black pepper

⅔ cup shredded sharp Cheddar cheese

2 medium-size apples, unpeeled, cored and cut into ½-inch cubes

2 scallions (green and white parts), chopped

Baby leaf lettuces—
more winter hardy than full heads—
are just head lettuces picked as
single leaves when 3 inches tall.

SALAD WITH FENNEL AND ORANGES

SERVES 4 AS A SIDE DISH

- 1 head soft-leaf lettuce, such as Boston
- 1 medium-size fennel bulb, trimmed and scrubbed
- 2 oranges
- ¼ small red onion, very thinly sliced
- 3 tablespoons extra-virgin olive oil
- 1 tablespoon sherry vinegar
- Coarse sea salt and freshly ground black pepper
- 1 ounce Parmesan cheese, preferably Parmigiano-Reggiano, coarsely shredded with a box grater or in a food processor (¼ cup)

This salad is good with lunch, dinner, or even as a light supper in itself, along with crusty bread.

1. Rinse and dry the lettuce leaves. Arrange them on a platter or on individual salad plates.

2. Quarter the fennel bulb lengthwise, and then cut out the core from each quarter with a large sharp knife. Break the overlapping pieces apart, and nesting them two at a time, slice them crosswise on the fine blade of a mandoline or on a box grater. Distribute the fennel over the lettuce.

3. Cut off the ends of the oranges and stand them on a cutting board. Using a sharp knife, peel them from end to end, removing both peel and bitter pith. Slice the oranges crosswise into rounds and distribute them over the lettuce and fennel.

4. Separate the onion slices and scatter them over the salad.

5. Combine the oil and vinegar in a small glass jar, and whisk or shake to blend thoroughly. Pour the dressing over the salad.

6. Sprinkle the salad with salt and pepper to taste, and finally with the Parmesan cheese. Serve immediately.

1 fruit + 2 vegetables + a dressing + a little cheese = a perfect little light meal.

Shredding Fennel

This inexpensive mandoline, available at Asian food stores, is perfect for slicing vegetables thinly.

MÂCHE SALAD WITH BLOOD ORANGES

SERVES 4

We love the combination of mild mâche with strong-flavored blood oranges in winter, when both are in season. Alas, we can't grow oranges in Maine without supplemental heat, but this salad is worth the indulgence of an imported fruit. Our unheated winter greenhouse has lush beds of mâche all winter long, and the red streaks in a blood orange are beautiful against the background of dark green. The creamy chervil dressing balances the tartness of the oranges.

Serve this salad as a refresher after a hearty soup, stew, roast, or casserole.

4 large handfuls (about 5 ounces) mâche

4 blood oranges

⅔ cup Creamy Chervil Dressing (page 319)

Coarse salt and freshly ground black pepper

1. Rinse the mâche thoroughly, and pat it dry. If your mâche plants are 3 inches across or less, leave the heads whole. If larger, pinch off the root ends to separate the heads into individual leaves.

2. Spread the mâche out on individual medium to large plates, or on a single round platter.

3. Cut off the ends of the oranges and stand them on a cutting board. Using a sharp knife, peel them from end to end, removing both peel and bitter pith. Cut the oranges into the thinnest rounds possible without letting them fall apart (5 or 6 slices per orange). Arrange them in a loose cluster in the center of the individual plates or platter.

4. Drizzle the dressing over the oranges and the greens.

5. Sprinkle salt and pepper to taste over all, and serve immediately.

TRY THIS TOO . . .

Any other type of orange will work as a substitute if blood oranges are not available. The pinkish-fleshed Cara Cara navels are good in salads like this one because they're firm and easy to slice.

"THINNINGS" SALAD WITH ASPARAGUS

SERVES 4

24 asparagus spears
(use just the top
6 inches)

4 tablespoons
Basic Vinaigrette
(page 315)

Coarse sea salt,
to taste

Freshly ground black
pepper, to taste

4 handfuls small thinnings,
such as lettuce, Swiss
chard, beet greens,
spinach, radish leaves,
fennel tops, pea shoots,
and brassicas such as
kale (5 to 6 ounces total)

¼ cup mixed chopped
fresh herbs, such as
chives, tarragon, dill,
cilantro, chervil, anise
hyssop, and parsley

Asparagus comes up so early in the spring that it has few companions in the garden. But you can often assemble a delightful salad by thinning rows of greens that have been thickly sown. Combine these with steamed asparagus and you have a treat that only a garden can give you. Pull the greens while they are no more than 2 or 3 inches tall. If they are small enough, many can be eaten without snipping off the roots, but be sure to wash them thoroughly to get rid of the soil: Submerge them in a sink full of water and swish them around, repeating if needed. Dry them on towels or in a lettuce spinner.

The young shoots of chives and tarragon are up by the time asparagus emerges, soon joined by volunteer annual herbs such as dill and chervil. Any of these would make a fine addition.

This salad is reason enough to invite people over to celebrate the first delicate tastes of the season. It goes with just about anything.

1. Using a vegetable peeler or a small sharp knife, peel the ends of any asparagus spears that are thicker than ¼ inch in diameter. Pare down the ends of any extra-thick ones so that they will all cook uniformly.

2. Bring water to a simmer in the bottom of a vegetable steamer. Add the asparagus to the steamer basket, cover, and steam until just tender (easily pierced with the tip of a knife but not limp), 3 to 5 minutes. Drain well and pat dry.

3. Pour 1 tablespoon of the vinaigrette onto a small plate, and roll the asparagus in it. Sprinkle with a dash of salt and pepper to taste.

4. Place the salad thinnings in a bowl, add the rest of the dressing, and season with salt and pepper to taste. Toss.

5. Distribute the greens over individual plates or on a single platter. Arrange the asparagus spears over the greens, in either a tidy row or a casual jumble, and sprinkle the herbs over them. Serve immediately.

TRY THIS TOO . . .

To make this more of a meal, add 1 or 2 hard-cooked eggs, sliced or quartered, to each plate. Prepare a vinaigrette using nothing but lemon juice and olive oil, and sprinkle 1 teaspoon of capers over each plate.

Celery Heart Salad

SERVES 4 AS A SIDE DISH

A celery heart is just a head of celery with the outermost ribs removed. When you buy packaged celery hearts in the store, the tops are often chopped off so that very few leaves remain, so if you have not grown your own, look for a whole celery with some foliage included. In this recipe, use the cleanest, tenderest ribs, and reserve some of the best tender leaves, ranging from yellow to pale green in color. Although the celery could stand alone, I like to add a bit of lettuce for a more harmonious texture overall, and lots of parsley.

The addition of eggs adds protein to the meal, which might consist of this salad and a bowl of tomato bisque or a pasta dish. For a light supper for two, we cut the recipe in half but eat two eggs apiece.

2 celery hearts, very thinly
sliced (3 cups)

4 large eggs

4 large leaves red-tipped
lettuce, rinsed and dried

About ½ cup coarsely
chopped celery leaves

⅓ cup coarsely chopped
fresh flat-leaf parsley
leaves

½ cup Anchovy Dressing
(page 318)

1. Place the celery heart slices in a bowl of cold water and chill in the refrigerator for at least 30 minutes (this will make them very crisp).

2. Bring a saucepan of water (enough to cover the eggs) to a gentle simmer. Add the eggs and cook for exactly 5 minutes.

3. While the eggs are cooking, rinse the lettuce leaves and pat them dry with a dish towel or dry them in a salad spinner. Tear the lettuce into pieces and distribute them over individual plates or a platter.

4. Drain the celery and spread it on a kitchen towel. Pat it dry, and then scatter it over the lettuce. Sprinkle the celery leaves and the parsley over the celery.

5. Drain the eggs and let them cool slightly—until they are still warm but not too hot to handle.

6. Peel the eggs carefully, beginning at the large end. Since they are not fully hard-cooked, this will seem like peeling little water-filled balloons, but they are stronger than you might think. Set the peeled eggs aside for a moment.

7. Drizzle the dressing over the salad. (If there seems to be too much dressing, reserve some for another time.)

8. Holding an egg over one of the salads, or over the platter, slice it lengthwise and lay the two halves, with their cut sides up, on the greens. With some eggs the yolk might run a bit; with others it will stay moist and deep gold in color, but firm. Either is okay. Repeat with the remaining eggs.

9. Serve right away, while the eggs are still slightly warm.

Tomato Salad with Balsamic Dressing

SERVES 4 AS INDIVIDUAL SALADS, 6 FROM A PLATTER

When tomatoes are at the height of their season, there is no side dish that is simpler, more welcome, and easier to make than a platter of them, sliced—especially beautiful in a mixture of colors. Here, arugula adds a peppery note and onions offer a little bite of their own. The maple syrup in the dressing is a counterpoint to the tomatoes' acidity. Serve this with a nonsweet dish such as pasta, a vegetable gratin, or a quiche.

1 large handful (4 ounces) fresh arugula, rinsed and dried

6 large ripe tomatoes, or the equivalent, sliced ¼-inch thick

½ small red onion, very thinly sliced

Coarse sea salt

Freshly ground black pepper

3 tablespoons extra-virgin olive oil

1 tablespoon balsamic vinegar

1 tablespoon maple syrup

2 tablespoons coarsely chopped fresh basil leaves

1. Remove any long stems from the arugula. If the leaves are more than 6 inches long, cut them in half. Distribute them over a platter.

2. Spread the tomato slices over the arugula, overlapping them in a random pattern.

3. Separate the rings of the onion slices and distribute them over the tomatoes. Sprinkle with salt and grindings of black pepper.

4. Combine the oil, vinegar, and maple syrup in a small jar with a lid. Screw the lid on tightly and shake thoroughly to mix; then pour the dressing over the salad.

5. Sprinkle the basil over all, and serve.

TRY THIS TOO . . .

You can substitute lettuce or other greens for the arugula. Flat leaves will make a tidy salad, crinkly ones a more rustic, three-dimensional one.

This is also delicious with just tomatoes and the dressing alone. If you are multiplying the recipe for a large crowd, make one layer of arugula and then alternate the layers of tomatoes, onions, dressing, salt and pepper, and basil.

CHICKEN SALAD WITH SPICED PEACHES

SERVES 4

Peaches ripen just after the peak of summer's heat, when the arugula is starting to sweeten up and thrive. Bring the two together in a chicken salad and you have a refreshing midday meal. This is a good way to use the meat left over from making chicken stock, or from day two of a roasted bird. You'll need to poach the peaches well ahead of time in order to give them time to soak.

For extra-hungry diners, set out a loaf of robust bread and a wedge of good slicing cheese, such as Manchego or Idiazabal.

1. Peel the peaches with a small sharp knife. Cut them in half, and carefully remove the pits, keeping the halves intact. Set them, cut side down, in a skillet or shallow saucepan that is just big enough to hold them all in one layer.

2. Combine the cider, cumin, and cloves in a small measuring cup or bowl, and pour the mixture over the peaches. The liquid should just cover the fruit. Bring the liquid to a simmer over low heat, and cook until the peaches are tender, about 10 minutes.

3. Using a slotted spoon, gently transfer the peaches to a flat-bottomed plate or dish, still cut side down, leaving the liquid in the skillet.

4. Bring the liquid to a boil over high heat, and boil until it is thick, syrupy, and reduced to about 2 tablespoons, about 5 minutes.

5. Pour the syrup over the peach halves. Refrigerate them, covered, for about 2 hours.

6. When you are ready to serve the salad, combine the chicken, celery, scallions, mayonnaise, and black pepper to taste in a medium-size bowl. Stir to mix thoroughly, and then add salt to taste.

7. Toss the arugula with the vinaigrette in a large bowl.

8. Divide the greens among four medium to large plates, scattering them in the center of each plate. Place a mound of

---

4 ripe peaches

2 cups apple cider or apple juice

½ teaspoon ground cumin

4 whole cloves

2 cups chopped cooked chicken (chopped medium fine)

2 medium-size ribs celery, chopped medium fine

3 medium-size scallions (white and green parts), chopped

½ cup Basic Mayonnaise (page 323) or mayonnaise with green herbs (page 325)

Freshly ground black pepper

Salt

4 handfuls (about 8 ounces) arugula or other soft greens, such as Boston lettuce

2 tablespoons Shallot Vinaigrette (page 316)

the chicken salad, slightly off-center, on top of each serving of greens. Set two peach halves next to each mound of chicken salad. Serve right away so that the greens do not wilt.

TRY THIS TOO . . .

The spiced peaches can be used on their own in other ways. For example, garnish a platter of sliced roast pork with them, allowing at least one peach half per person.

After peach season is over, add halved fresh grapes to the chicken salad and stir to combine.

You can also use the chicken salad in sandwiches, increasing the amount of mayonnaise slightly if desired.

Trellised peas in bloom.

Salad with New Potatoes, Smoked Salmon, and Peas

SERVES 4 TO 6 AS A SIDE DISH

The best time to make this salad is when the potato plants have just started to bloom, signaling that new potatoes have formed underground. If this coincides with a crop of fresh garden peas, better yet. The flavors of fresh new potatoes, peas, and tarragon will carry the day, but smoked salmon is a tasty addition that can turn the salad into a light meal for two people. Served as an appetizer or a side dish, the salad would complement Meat Loaf with Vegetables (page 413).

1½ pounds small new potatoes, scrubbed but not peeled, cut into ½-inch-thick slices

1 cup shelled garden peas (from about 12 ounces pods)

3 tablespoons extra-virgin olive oil

1 tablespoon white wine vinegar

Pinch of dry mustard

Coarse sea salt, to taste

1 tablespoon chopped fresh tarragon or dill leaves, or 1 teaspoon dried

1 small onion, peeled and finely chopped

2 ounces smoked salmon, cut into small pieces (optional)

1. Bring water to a boil in a medium-size saucepan. Add the potatoes, reduce the heat to a simmer, and cook until they are soft when pricked with a knife, about 15 minutes. (Be careful not to overcook them, or they will become mashed potatoes when stirred.)

2. While the potatoes are cooking, bring water to a simmer in the bottom of a vegetable steamer. Add the peas to the steamer basket, cover, and steam until they are just tender, about 5 minutes. Drain.

3. Prepare the dressing: Combine the olive oil, vinegar, mustard, salt, and the dried tarragon, if using, in a small glass or jar. Set aside.

4. Drain the potatoes and combine them with the peas in a large bowl. Toss, and then stir in the onion, the salmon if using, and the fresh tarragon or dill if using. Serve at room temperature.

Peruvian Potatoes

SERVES 4 TO 6

4 small yellow-fleshed potatoes such as Yukon Gold (about 1 pound total), scrubbed but not peeled, cut in half or in 2-inch chunks

2 large eggs, at room temperature

¼ cup heavy (whipping) cream

1 teaspoon mildly hot pepper flakes, such as Aleppo (or a hotter type if desired)

1 teaspoon ground turmeric (for color; optional)

6 ounces mild, slightly tangy cheese such as queso fresco or Monterey Jack, cut into ½-inch cubes

Salt

½ head butterhead lettuce

1 small onion, peeled and thinly sliced

10 strongly flavored black olives, such as Alfonso or Kalamata, pitted

2 tablespoons finely minced fresh pepper, either a red, yellow, or orange bell type or a mildly hot type such as ancho

E ven in Peru there are many ways to make *papa a la huancaina,* a traditional dish named for the city of Huancayo, high in the Andes. I make a somewhat Americanized version. It is very colorful to look at, and can be enjoyed at room temperature. Make it mild or spicy, according to your taste. Because it requires some artful arrangement, this is a not for a picnic far afield, but it is still good to eat outdoors, matched with barbecued chicken.

1. Bring a large saucepan of salted water to a boil. Add the potatoes, reduce the heat, and simmer, uncovered, until they are fork-tender but still hold their shape well, about 15 minutes. Remove the potatoes with a slotted spoon, keeping the water at a simmer, and set them aside in a bowl.

2. Drop the eggs into the simmering water and cook for 10 minutes. Remove them with a large spoon and hold them under cold running water for a minute until they are cool enough to handle. Then peel the eggs and cut them lengthwise into quarters. The yolks should be slightly soft and well colored. Carefully set the egg quarters on a plate, keeping them yolk side up.

3. Bring water to a simmer in the bottom of a double boiler. Combine the cream,

pepper flakes, and turmeric in the top of the double boiler, and heat the mixture until you see steam rising. Then gradually drop in the cheese cubes and stir them as they melt, 10 to 15 minutes. (This can also be done in a saucepan directly on the burner, but keep the heat very low and stir constantly with a wooden spoon.) Taste, and add a dash of salt unless the cheese is very salty.

4. Rinse and dry the lettuce leaves, and arrange them around the edge of a platter or on individual salad plates.

5. Cut the potatoes into ½-inch-thick slices and arrange them in the center of the platter or plates. Pour the cheese sauce over them. Distribute the onion slices, egg quarters, and olives around the edge, on top of the lettuce. Sprinkle the minced fresh pepper over everything, and serve.

RICE SALAD WITH SUMMER VEGETABLES

SERVES 4 AS A LIGHT MAIN COURSE, 6 AS A SIDE DISH

2 cups cooked brown rice, lukewarm

3 tablespoons extra-virgin olive oil

2 tablespoons fresh lemon juice (½ lemon)

½ red bell pepper, chopped into medium-fine pieces (about ½ cup)

1 cucumber (6 to 7 inches long), peeled, seeded, and chopped into medium-fine pieces (about ½ cup)

2 scallions (white and green parts), chopped into medium-fine pieces (about ¼ cup)

⅓ cup chopped walnuts

1 tablespoon finely chopped fresh basil leaves

Salt and freshly ground black pepper

The veggies in this dish make it bright and colorful, but they go beyond decoration, making up more than a third of its volume. The result is a healthy starch-and-vegetable meal in one dish. Adding the dressing while the rice is slightly warm will help the rice to absorb it.

1. Place the rice in a medium-size bowl. Whisk the olive oil and lemon juice together in a cup or small bowl, and add this to the rice. Stir gently but thoroughly.

2. Add the bell pepper, cucumber, scallions, walnuts, basil, and salt and pepper to taste to the rice. Stir gently to mix, and then add more salt and pepper if needed.

3. Serve at room temperature. (If you make the salad ahead, take it out of the fridge about 30 minutes before serving. It is best made with freshly cooked rice, so the rice does not have a chance to harden.)

TRY THIS TOO . . .

✦ An early summer version might feature scallions and just-picked raw peas.

✦ In fall or winter you might use baby white turnips, chopped medium fine, and very finely chopped carrots.

✦ To make a more pungent version, add capers and chopped olives.

✦ To turn this into a heartier main course, add sautéed baby shrimp, small pieces of cooked chicken, or grilled fresh tuna.

Basic Vinaigrette

MAKES ABOUT ⅔ CUP

1. Combine the vinegar, oil, and any other ingredients you are using in a small glass or bowl.

2. Whisk vigorously. If the dressing separates, whisk it again. Another method is to place the ingredients in jar, such as a used mustard jar, close it tight, and shake vigorously. A shaken emulsion will hold for hours, and just a quick shake or two refreshes it. Using mustard, which is an excellent emulsifier, also helps.

NOTE: I sometimes add fresh herbs to a salad, but I add *dried* herbs to a vinaigrette. Fresh herbs soaking in a jar of vinaigrette would become soggy and unappetizing, but dried herbs actually need that rehydration.

2 tablespoons good-quality vinegar (sherry, balsamic, red wine, white wine, champagne . . .)

½ cup good-quality extra-virgin olive oil

½ teaspoon Dijon-style mustard (optional)

1 teaspoon mixed dried herbs such as thyme, oregano, and tarragon (optional)

1 clove garlic, pulverized in a garlic press or mashed to a paste with the tip of a knife (optional)

Vinaigrettes

The concept of a basic vinaigrette may seem simple: You mix oil and vinegar until they form an emulsion, pour it over a salad, then toss. But when it comes to the proportions, people are passionate in their preferences. My mouth puckers so much from vinaigrettes in France (some mixed half and half) that I can barely form the vowels I'd need to protest—tricky under the best of circumstances. Even in my own family, the three-to-ones battle the four-to-ones, and the two-to-ones are forbidden to make dressing at all.

When a recipe has only two major ingredients, they had better be good ones. A dressing made of all-purpose vegetable oil, mixed with plain red or white wine vinegar, will not taste as good as one made with a fruity extra-virgin olive oil and a flavorful sherry or balsamic vinegar, of which only a scant amount might suffice. Sometimes the use determines the choice: for instance, I tend to use balsamic vinegar for tomatoes.

Then there are the add-ons. I've suggested a few, but I invite you to come up with others that please you. (My favorite addition, pulped shallots, deserves its own recipe—see page 316.) I've omitted salt, pepper, and fresh herbs in the dressing because I always add these directly to the salad (see Note above).

And finally, vinaigrette isn't just for tossed salad. Use it on finely chopped raw vegetables, and on cooked vegetables such as asparagus, beets, and summer squash, served warm, cold, or room temperature. Substitute it for mayonnaise in dishes like chicken salad and potato salad.

SHALLOT VINAIGRETTE

MAKES ABOUT ½ CUP

1 medium-size shallot, peeled and coarsely chopped

½ teaspoon coarse sea salt

Freshly ground black pepper, to taste

2 tablespoon white wine vinegar

½ cup extra-virgin olive oil

French gray shallots taste the way real shallots should (see page 145).

I've found that the best way to add a delicately oniony flavor to a simple vinaigrette is to add some crushed shallot. A jar of this dressing, with a mini whisk protruding, often sits on my kitchen counter, ready to dress a quick salad from the garden. I like it best when made with a pale vinegar that doesn't color the shallot pulp. And since the flavor of the olive oil will stand out, I use my best bottle.

1. Place the shallot pieces, in batches, in a garlic press and press them over a glass or an empty jar, discarding what remains in the press at the end. You will collect about 1 teaspoon of shallot pulp.

2. Add the salt and pepper to taste to the shallot pulp. Then add the vinegar and olive oil.

3. Whisk or shake thoroughly before using. The dressing will keep for several days on the counter, or for a week in the refrigerator.

Shallots used to be expensive items imported from France. Now they're a common American crop that any gardener can grow.

SPICY DRESSING

MAKES ABOUT ½ CUP, ENOUGH FOR AT LEAST 4 SALAD SERVINGS OR TO BRUSH ON 8 PORK CHOPS

I use this dressing with a salad of robust greens such as romaine lettuce, radicchio, shredded cabbage, curly endive, Belgian endive, or escarole—alone or in combination. It's also good brushed on pork chops before grilling them.

1 large clove garlic

½ teaspoon ground cumin

1 teaspoon Aleppo pepper flakes, or ¼ teaspoon hot pepper flakes

1 teaspoon mild paprika, preferably smoked

1 tablespoon plus 1 teaspoon fresh lemon juice

6 tablespoons extra-virgin olive oil

Pinch of salt

Freshly ground black pepper, to taste

1. Place the garlic in a garlic press and press it over a glass or an empty jar, discarding what remains in the press at the end.

2. Add all the remaining ingredients to the garlic pulp.

3. Whisk or shake thoroughly to combine before using. The dressing can be kept for about a week in the refrigerator.

ANCHOVY DRESSING

MAKES ABOUT ½ CUP

4 bottled or canned
   anchovy fillets,
   preferably packed in oil
   (see Note)

2 tablespoons sherry
   vinegar

½ cup olive oil

¼ teaspoon salt

Freshly ground black
   pepper

Too many anchovies can overwhelm a dish with their intense fishiness, and even anchovy-lovers are usually happy with just a few lightning bolts of anchovy sparking up a pizza or a Caesar salad. On the other hand, the thorough incorporation of just a small amount of anchovy flavor is a magic trick verging on alchemy. Because it is high in glutamates, it conveys an earthy richness and resonance— *umami,* to use the Japanese word—that enhances other flavors without being identifiable.

My mother used to sneak a wee squirt of commercial anchovy paste into a number of things and it seemed to improve them all. This dressing, for which I use a few of the tiny fish fillets, is especially good on salads of firm-textured greens such as escarole, endive, and radicchio. The bold anchovy flavor works nicely with the slightly bitter flavor of these winter chicories.

1. Place the anchovies on a cutting board, and mash them with the tip of a large knife until they form a paste. Scrape the paste into a small jar or glass. Add the vinegar, oil, salt, and pepper to taste.

2. Shake or whisk thoroughly just before using.

NOTE: I prefer to use the anchovies that come in a glass jar because they can easily be stored in the refrigerator after opening. If you are using anchovies packed in a tin, remove any that are left over, along with their oil, and place them in a glass container, adding oil to cover if needed; then refrigerate. Anchovies cured in salt, although less readily available, are preferred by some cooks, but they require rinsing and tend to be a little bony.

CREAMY CHERVIL DRESSING

MAKES ABOUT ⅔ CUP

We like the rich mellowness of this dressing and use it often on salads that combine greens with fresh fruit. Chervil is a wonderfully delicate herb with a bit of anise flavor, not quite as strong as tarragon. It thrives best in cool weather and will grow in winter, even in cold climates, with some protection. In summer, when chervil tends to bolt quickly, I use tarragon in this dressing instead and enjoy it just as much.

1. Combine the mayonnaise, sour cream, and chervil in a small bowl, and use a small whisk or a fork to blend.

2. Whisk in the lemon juice, and then the cream. The dressing will be quite thick. If a thinner one is desired, whisk in the milk. Add salt to taste.

3. Refrigerate if not using immediately; it will keep for about 4 days.

2 tablespoons mayonnaise, preferably homemade (see page 323)

2 tablespoons sour cream

2 tablespoons very finely minced fresh chervil leaves, or 4 teaspoons very finely minced fresh tarragon leaves (if neither is available, use 2 teaspoons dried tarragon)

1 teaspoon fresh lemon juice

¼ cup heavy (whipping) cream

1 tablespoon whole milk (optional)

Salt

Chervil is a wonderful herb to have in your garden all year long.

Pesto Sauce

MAKES ABOUT ¾ CUP

Pesto is one of the great joys of the summer garden, and fresh basil, its primary ingredient, is easy to grow. Pick only perfect leaves, with no darkened patches, just before you are ready to make the sauce. Large-leaf green Italian varieties such as Genovese are the most authentic for pesto, but the smaller-leaf lemon basil is wonderful too.

Pesto was traditionally made by hand with a mortar and pestle, and the pestle is what gives it its name. Although the hand method takes more time, and some arm muscle, there is less oxidation of the leaves than when you make pesto in a food processor or blender—and hence more flavor. (Use a good heavy mortar and pestle with a large capacity. A Japanese suribachi, which has fine grooves in the ceramic that speed up the process, works well too.) You can also make a rustic but entirely satisfying version by very finely chopping the nuts, garlic, and basil by hand with a large sharp knife or a mezzaluna, and then grating the cheese.

Realistically, though, most cooks are grateful for the ease and speed that a modern food processor or blender offers when making pesto, and the result will not disappoint you. This recipe—whether made by hand or in a processor—makes more than enough sauce to stir into pasta for four people. I like to have some left over in the fridge to add to a salad dressing, season a quiche or savory custard (having made the pesto without nuts), or spoon over grilled chicken breasts and fish. Pine-nut-less pesto is also the essential ingredient in Soupe au Pistou (page 275).

USING A FOOD PROCESSOR OR BLENDER:

1. Toast the pine nuts in a small dry skillet over low heat, stirring constantly, until they are fragrant and golden but not brown, 3 to 5 minutes. Watch them carefully because they will burn very quickly if they get too hot.

2. Combine the pine nuts and garlic cloves in a food processor. Cut the cheese into small chunks and add them, along with a good grinding of pepper. Process until the ingredients are pulverized, 1 to 2 minutes.

3. With the machine running, pour in the oil in a steady stream, processing to form a paste. Add the basil and pulse briefly, stopping as soon as the leaves are pulverized.

4. If you are not using the pesto right away, place it in a small container and cover it with a thin film of olive oil to prevent darkening. Cover the container and refrigerate.

2 tablespoons pine nuts

2 cloves garlic, peeled and minced

1½-inch cube of Parmesan cheese, preferably Parmigiano-Reggiano

Freshly ground black pepper

¼ cup extra-virgin olive oil

1 cup (packed) fresh basil leaves (all stems removed)

Italian basil and pink-flowered cinnamon basil are a handsome pair in the garden.

2 tablespoons pine nuts

2 cloves garlic, peeled and minced

Freshly ground black pepper

1 cup (packed) fresh basil leaves (all stems removed)

1½-inch cube of Parmesan cheese, preferably Parmigiano-Reggiano

¼ cup extra-virgin olive oil

USING A MORTAR AND PESTLE

(Note that the ingredients are added in a different order than is listed on the previous page.)

1. Toast the pine nuts in a small dry skillet over low heat, stirring constantly, until they are fragrant and golden but not brown, 3 to 5 minutes. Watch them carefully because they will burn very quickly if they get too hot.

2. Combine the pine nuts, garlic, and a good grinding of pepper in the mortar and pound with the pestle for about 30 seconds.

3. Coarsely chop the basil leaves, and add them to the mortar. Pound with a twisting motion until you have a well-mixed paste, about 7 minutes.

4. Finely grate the cheese with a cheese grater and add it to the mortar. Add the olive oil and stir with the pestle until thoroughly mixed.

TO FREEZE:

Pesto is best when made fresh for immediate use, but it is so delicious and useful that it is tempting to freeze some, especially if you have an abundant supply of basil. Spoon it into clean half-pint canning jars and store them in the freezer. The pesto will stay just soft enough to allow you to chip away the desired amount without thawing it first. Another method is to freeze it flat in stacked pint or quart freezer bags, then break off pieces as needed. Still another is to freeze it in ice cube trays, then place the pesto cubes in plastic freezer bags. For freezing, I make pesto with just olive oil and basil, adding any other ingredients—including the cheese and pine nuts—at the time of use. This makes it more versatile in cooking.

TRY THIS TOO . . .

✦ Pesto can be made with other pungent herbs, such as parsley and chives, or in combination with them.

✦ You can also substitute other nuts, such as walnuts, hazelnuts, or pecans.

Lemon Pesto Dressing

MAKES 1 SCANT CUP

This is a lighter, less intense version of traditional pesto, more liquid than pastelike. I use it to dress tossed salads, sometimes adding finely grated Parmesan cheese while tossing. It's also good for basting meat or fish.

½ cup (firmly packed) fresh basil leaves

1 small clove garlic

2 tablespoons fresh lemon juice

½ teaspoon salt

Freshly ground black pepper

½ cup olive oil

1. Place the basil, garlic, lemon juice, salt, and pepper to taste in a blender or food processor.

2. Turn the processor on and gradually pour in the olive oil. Process just long enough to make a coarse puree, about 20 seconds. (Too much blending will over-oxidize the basil.)

3. This dressing will keep, covered, in the refrigerator for several days.

TRY THIS TOO . . .

Using lemon basil, with the lemony flavor right in the leaf, is another good way to make the dressing. If it's not lemony enough for you, add lemon juice to taste.

Basic Mayonnaise

MAKES ABOUT 1⅓ CUPS

Long ago I performed the cookery initiation rite of making mayonnaise by hand, but as soon as my mother taught me how to make it in the blender, I never looked back. It is much faster, much less laborious, and nearly foolproof. As a result, I make homemade

1 large egg

Juice of 1 lemon
  (about ¼ cup)

¼ teaspoon salt

Small pinch of cayenne
  pepper (optional)

¼ teaspoon dry mustard
  (optional)

¼ cup extra-virgin olive oil

¾ cup sunflower oil,
  grapeseed oil, or other
  neutral oil

mayonnaise far more often than I would if I still did the old dribble-and-whisk.

Blender mayonnaise is best made with a whole egg rather than just the yolk. This affects the texture of the result, which is looser and more easily poured than the yolk-only hand-whisked version. I find it more versatile this way: It works equally well as dressing, spread, dip, or sauce. I like it with some olive oil, but if that predominates, the taste is a little harsh, so I use only a little and combine it with a milder-flavored oil.

1. Combine the egg, lemon juice, salt, cayenne (if using), mustard (if using), and olive oil in the jar of a blender.

2. Blend for a few seconds. Then, with the blender running on low speed, very slowly dribble in a few tablespoons of the sunflower oil. Raise the speed to high and continue, adding the remaining sunflower oil. Partway through, you'll notice that the sound of the blender has deepened a bit and the mayonnaise has begun to thicken.

If the mayonnaise thickens too much and stops blending, pulsing a few times will usually get it going. Otherwise, just pour it into a bowl, using a narrow rubber scraper or long-handled spoon, and whisk in the last bit of oil by hand.

If the mayonnaise doesn't thicken at all, pour it into a spouted measuring cup or pitcher. Clean and dry the blender jar, put 1 egg yolk into the jar, and then, while blending slowly, pour the mixture back in, adding just a few

drops at a time, then a very thin trickle, until it emulsifies.

3. Cover and refrigerate immediately. The mayonnaise will keep, chilled, for up to a week.

TRY THIS TOO . . .

Mayonnaise can be made with either vinegar or lemon juice; there are vinegar people and lemon people, and I'm one of the latter. Either way, this is a great basic sauce to which other flavorings may be added. I prefer to blend or whisk most of these additions in at the end, adding a little and then tasting to see if more is needed. Often I'll make the full recipe plain, then make additions to smaller amounts on subsequent days—for specific uses or simply for variety's sake. Here are some favorite additions, any of which would be great on a composed salad (page 296), in a dip for raw vegetables, or as a topping on cold meat

or fish. The amounts (which you may vary to taste) are for the whole recipe; adjust smaller amounts.

✦ ¼ to ½ cup minced fresh herbs, such as tarragon, chervil, parsley, cilantro, and chives, either singly or as a mix. Add after blending. Dill mayonnaise, by itself or with chives, is especially good on salmon, or in a cucumber and watercress salad or sandwich.

✦ 1 to 3 cloves garlic, combined with a little salt and pressed into a paste with the tip of a knife. Mix after blending. This turns it into a version of aioli, beloved in the South of France and named for the French word for garlic. (For a less harsh taste, roast the unpeeled garlic, then squeeze it out of its skins.) You can also add a pinch of sweet or hot paprika.

✦ 1 canned anchovy fillet for a subtle depth of flavor, more if you want a pronounced anchovy taste. This can be added to the blender at the end and whirled briefly to mix.

✦ A pinch of saffron threads soaked in the lemon juice for 20 minutes before blending. Add garlic as well to make saffron aïoli, great on crab cakes.

✦ Ground cumin or curry powder, to taste. This is excellent for chicken salad.

✦ 1 to 2 tablespoons Pesto Sauce (page 320), or to taste—great in a BLT.

✦ 1 tablespoon prepared horseradish, or to taste—good on a roast beef or meatloaf sandwich.

✦ 1 tablespoon Dijon-style mustard, 1 tablespoon capers, 1 tablespoon minced fresh parsley, and 1 tablespoon finely chopped pickles (optional). Spoon over fried fish or use in a celery root salad.

OPEN-FACED OMELET WITH SUMMER VEGETABLES | PAGE 328

CHAPTER 9

Egg Dishes

IN OUR HOUSE, eggs are not just for breakfast time. We often combine them with vegetables for a complete protein-rich meal. If you are not lucky enough to have eggs from your own chickens or ducks, it is worth seeking out fresh organic pasture-raised ones from a local source. Fresh eggs from birds that have foraged on greens and bugs have bright orange yolks that stand up in the pan like rising suns, not pale yellow disks, flat with age. Here are some of our favorite ways to cook with them. You'll find more egg dishes in the Desserts chapter.

OPEN-FACED OMELET WITH SUMMER VEGETABLES

SERVES 2

3 large eggs

¼ cup heavy (whipping) cream

2 tablespoons butter

½ yellow bell pepper, stemmed, seeded, and finely chopped

3 scallions (white and green parts), chopped

8 cherry or grape tomatoes, cut in half

1 tablespoon coarsely chopped fresh cilantro or basil leaves

Freshly ground black pepper

Tabasco sauce, for serving

Coarse sea salt, for serving

This is the supper dish we fix when we want something quick and light. It's also great as a breakfast or brunch dish when family or friends are visiting. Because the omelet is not folded, it is foolproof and you avoid the risk of overcooking the bottom while you're waiting for the inside to set. The brevity of the cooking keeps the eggs very tender. The trick is to start them in a skillet on top of the stove, add whatever ingredients inspire you, then run them under a hot broiler just long enough to finish cooking the eggs.

Our omelets use the vegetables that are in season. This is a summer one, made for two people. Double the recipe and it will serve four, but the omelet will be thicker. Increasing the skillet size makes it hard to cut wedges, so it's best to keep making small ones until everybody has been fed. They're that quick.

1. Preheat the broiler (to "high" if yours has settings). If it is adjustable, position the rack 4 to 6 inches from the heat.

2. Whisk the eggs and cream together in a medium-size bowl until the mixture is uniform in color but not frothy, about 30 seconds.

3. Melt the butter in a 9- or 10-inch ovenproof skillet, preferably cast iron,

over medium heat. Pour in the egg mixture and let it set for 1 to 2 minutes to put a skin on the bottom; then remove the skillet from the heat.

4. Sprinkle the bell pepper, scallions, tomatoes, and cilantro over the eggs. Sprinkle with black pepper to taste.

5. Put the skillet under the broiler and watch as the eggs cook. After 2 minutes, carefully shake or tilt the skillet a bit to test for runniness, or insert a knife to see if it comes out clean. (Do this carefully to avoid burning yourself.) If the eggs are still runny, put the skillet back in the oven and test the omelet once every minute. Remove the skillet as soon as the eggs are done to avoid overcooking.

6. Slice the omelet into 4 wedges and serve immediately, right from the skillet. Pass the Tabasco sauce and salt at the table.

TRY THIS TOO . . .

In winter, we use snips of our potted rosemary, greens such as spinach or tatsoi, and maybe a few thinly sliced radishes for crunch. In spring we're ready for asparagus, then peas, scallions, and young green garlic tops, often with a bit of smoked salmon. Some ingredients, such as corn, eggplant, mushrooms, and crumbled sausage, must be cooked first, but most are sprinkled on as is. Cheeses of all sorts can play a role. It's a bit like making a pizza, only easier.

SAVORY CUSTARDS WITH GARLIC AND TARRAGON

SERVES 4

A salad with a flavorful custard as the centerpiece draws you irresistibly. This one can be made any time you have fresh tarragon and garlic in the garden. I find that steaming the custards in a covered skillet on top of the stove, rather than baking them, gives them a smoother texture. Unmolding them on the plates works best if you use little Pyrex cups with sloping, rather than vertical, sides. Although the recipe is designed for one custard for each plate, I make four for the two of us, since it is so hard to eat just one. Also, extras can be refrigerated for the next day. They are fine to eat cold, but we like them best warmed or brought to room temperature. Because of

4 medium-size cloves garlic, unpeeled

1 tablespoon butter, at room temperature

2 large eggs

1 cup heavy (whipping) cream

3 ounces (⅓ cup) creamy goat cheese

Pinch of nutmeg, preferably freshly grated

2 tablespoons finely chopped fresh tarragon leaves

Salt and freshly ground black pepper

4 small handfuls fresh arugula (about 3 loosely filled cups)

¼ cup extra-virgin olive oil

1 tablespoon tarragon vinegar or white wine vinegar

its richness, I'd serve this salad with a light soup such as gazpacho, or with a simple piece of grilled fish.

1. Preheat the oven to 350°F.

2. Place the garlic cloves in a small ovenproof pan or dish, and roast in the oven until tender, 20 to 30 minutes. Set the garlic aside to cool slightly.

3. Smear the bottom and sides of four custard cups with the butter. Place the cups in a skillet that is deep enough so that the custards can puff up a bit when a lid is placed over the cups. Add water to the skillet to reach halfway up the sides of the cups. Then remove the cups and set them aside.

4. Combine the eggs, cream, goat cheese, nutmeg, tarragon, a dash of salt, and pepper to taste in a medium-size bowl. Squeeze the garlic pulp out of its papery skins and add the pulp to the bowl. Whisk until thoroughly mixed (an immersion blender also works well for this). Then pour the mixture into the prepared custard cups.

5. Bring the water in the skillet to a simmer over high heat; then reduce the heat to very low. Carefully lower the filled custard cups into the water and place a lid over the skillet so they will steam. The custards will begin to puff up after about 5 minutes. The tarragon will float to the surface and the nutmeg and pepper will sink to the bottom. This is fine.

6. Cook until the custards are firm and a knife inserted into the center of one comes out clean, about 15 minutes. Remove the skillet from the heat. If you like, leave the cups in the skillet, uncovered, to keep the custards warm while you prepare the salad.

7. Place the arugula in a large bowl. Whisk the oil and vinegar together in a small bowl or cup, and pour over the arugula. Season with salt and pepper to taste, and toss. Arrange the arugula on four small to medium-size plates, leaving a bare spot in the center of each.

8. Run a knife around the inside of the custard cups to loosen the custards, and then invert one over each plate, letting the custard drop into the center of the salad (if necessary, letting the cup drop gently right onto the plate will help to jostle the custard). Serve immediately.

TRY THIS TOO . . .

Savory custards can be made with other herbs, such as parsley, chervil, or basil, and with a variety of pureed vegetables, such as spinach, tender young Swiss chard, or carrots. These are all delicious, although not always as smooth-textured as the version here.

Vary the surrounding greens according to the season and according to what you happen to have in the garden. If it is too hot for any greens to fare well, make a ring of sliced small tomatoes or of green beans tossed in a vinaigrette.

CUSTARD-STUFFED BAKED TOMATOES

SERVES 6 AS A SIDE DISH, 3 AS THE MAIN ATTRACTION

There is more than one way to stuff a tomato, but this is our favorite. The simplicity of the custard filling—just cream and egg—makes it very smooth and tender. We like these for brunch, perhaps on a plate with grilled sausage, steamed kale, and warm crusty bread. A platter of these tomatoes, sitting on lettuce leaves, looks great at a lunch buffet table, but they are not finger food. Eat them sitting down, with knife and fork in hand.

6 medium-size tomatoes

2 large eggs

1 cup heavy (whipping) cream

Dash of salt

Freshly ground black pepper, to taste

1 tablespoon olive oil

2 teaspoons finely minced fresh chervil or other soft fresh herbs such as tarragon, parsley, or basil

1. Preheat the oven to 350°F.

2. Hollow out each tomato from the stem end, leaving a generous opening at the top. You'll need a small, sharp knife to cut along the ribs, and a small spoon to scoop out all the pulp, leaving as much of the wall as possible. A serrated grapefruit spoon works beautifully for this. Turn the tomatoes upside down to let the juice drain away.

3. To make the filling, combine the eggs, cream, salt, and pepper in a medium-size bowl, and beat lightly with an eggbeater or whisk. The mixture should be uniform but not foamy.

4. Smear the olive oil over the bottom of a small baking dish that is just large enough to hold the tomatoes upright. Set them in the dish and, using a spouted

A few large grape leaves, snipped from the vines above the terrace, are a nice contrast and keep the tomatoes from sliding around.

pitcher or measuring cup, pour the filling into the cavities so it reaches to within ¼ to ½ inch from the top.

5. Bake until the filling is set and no longer jiggles when you gently shake

the dish, or until a knife inserted in the center of the custard comes out clean, about 45 minutes.

6. Sprinkle with the chervil and serve warm.

CORN SOUFFLÉ

SERVES 4

4 ears fresh corn

4 large eggs, separated

1 cup whole milk

4 tablespoons (½ stick) butter

3 tablespoons all-purpose flour

¼ teaspoon salt

½ teaspoon fresh thyme leaves, or ¼ teaspoon dried

Dash of cayenne pepper

½ cup finely grated Parmesan cheese

Small pinch of cream of tartar

A vegetable soufflé is not difficult to make, especially if your ingredients—in particular the eggs—are farm-fresh. While this version rises dependably for me, do not be disheartened if yours does not ascend to tall, fluffy heights. The combination of sweet corn, eggs, and cheese is luscious, and you can always call it a spoonbread or pudding. Serve it at lunch with BLTs made with homegrown tomatoes.

1. Preheat the oven to 400°F.

2. Fill a large saucepan half full of water and bring it to a boil. Drop in the corn and cook it over medium heat until very tender, about 10 minutes. Drain.

3. Holding an ear of corn, pointed end up, on a cutting board, draw a sharp knife down the center of each row of kernels, cutting through the kernels. Then scrape out the pulp by applying strong downward pressure with the back of a

large, heavy knife. You'll end up with very soft, milky corn. Measure out ¾ cup and set it aside, discarding the rest.

4. In a large bowl, whisk the egg yolks until they are well blended and thickened. Set aside.

5. Warm the milk in a small saucepan (do not let it boil).

6. Melt 3 tablespoons of the butter in a medium-size saucepan over low heat. Add the flour and cook, stirring constantly with a spatula or whisk, for 2 minutes. Add the warm milk and stir rapidly until a thick paste forms, 1 to 2 minutes.

7. Gradually stir the paste into the beaten egg yolks, mixing thoroughly. Stir in the reserved corn and the salt, thyme, and cayenne. Set aside to cool to lukewarm.

8. With your fingers, smear the remaining 1 tablespoon butter over the sides and bottom of a 2-quart soufflé dish. Coat the sides with the grated cheese, reserving any that is left over. (The cheese will help the soufflé to climb the sides as it cooks.)

9. Using a large whisk or an eggbeater, beat the egg whites in a large bowl until foamy, about 30 seconds. Add the cream of tartar, and continue to beat the whites until they form stiff peaks that hold their shape. Use a spoon or a scooped rubber spatula to fold the whites gently into the cooled corn mixture, using as few strokes as possible to incorporate them.

10. Pour the mixture into the prepared soufflé dish and sprinkle the remaining cheese over the top. Reduce the oven temperature to 350° and bake until the top rises into a uniform dome and a knife inserted in the center comes out clean, 30 to 40 minutes. Serve hot, right away.

TRY THIS TOO . . .

This could be made with other cooked vegetables, such as 1 cup finely crumbled cooked cauliflower or 1 cup pureed cooked spinach.

ASPARAGUS GOLDENROD

ASPARAGUS GOLDENROD

SERVES 4

My mother used to make a beautiful dish called Eggs Goldenrod, named for the grated egg yolk sprinkled on top like goldenrod pollen. Eliot and I like to add a vegetable, especially asparagus when it is in season. I also sharpen the sauce with Gruyère, Cheddar, or whatever tasty cheese I have on hand. This makes a fine brunch or supper dish, with a salad alongside and fresh fruit for dessert.

4 large eggs

1½ cups heavy (whipping) cream

4 ounces Gruyère cheese, shredded (1 cup)

40 medium-size fresh asparagus spears

4 large or 8 small slices whole-grain bread, crusts removed

2 tablespoons butter, at room temperature, for the toast (optional)

Freshly ground black pepper, to taste

1. Hard-cook the eggs: Place them in a small saucepan and add water to cover. Bring the water just to a simmer over high heat; then immediately lower the heat and cook at a bare simmer for 10 minutes. Remove the pan from the heat, drain off the water, and fill the pan with cold water to cool the eggs. Let them sit in the cold water for about 5 minutes.

2. Peel the cooled eggs and then carefully remove the yolks, keeping them as intact as possible. They should be firm enough to grate. Set the whites aside.

3. To form the "pollen," grate the yolks fine, using a box grater held over a dish. The yolks will break apart while you are doing this, so hold the grater horizontally and rub the yolks on it (watch your fingers). Tilt the grater to empty the yolk onto the dish, scraping the grater with a small knife to get all the yolk out.

4. Coarsely chop the egg whites, and set them aside.

5. Pour the cream into a medium-size skillet and bring it to a slow simmer over medium heat. Simmer, stirring constantly, until it has thickened slightly, 1 to 2 minutes. Then gradually add the cheese, stirring until it has melted and the mixture is smooth. Stir in the egg whites. Keep the sauce warm over very low heat.

6. Trim the asparagus spears to about 5 inches in length. Bring water to a simmer in the bottom of a vegetable steamer. Add the asparagus to the steamer basket, cover, and steam until just tender, 2 to 5 minutes.

7. While the asparagus is cooking, toast the bread and divide the slices among four plates. If you like, butter the toast— buttering softens it nicely but is optional.

8. Distribute the asparagus spears over the pieces of toast, and then cover with the creamy sauce. Top with the grated egg yolk and some grindings of black pepper, and serve immediately.

TRY THIS TOO . . .

Other vegetables can be substituted for the asparagus, according to the season. Broccoli, cauliflower, green beans, leeks, and garlic scapes are all tasty in this dish.

SPINACH QUICHE WITH BUCKWHEAT CRUST

SERVES 4 AS A HEARTY MEAL, 6 TO 8 IN COMBINATION WITH OTHER DISHES

3 large eggs

1½ cups heavy (whipping) cream

¼ teaspoon nutmeg, preferably freshly grated

½ teaspoon fresh thyme leaves, or ¼ teaspoon dried

Freshly ground black pepper, to taste

2 tablespoons butter, at room temperature

¾ cup buckwheat groats, also called kasha (see page 352)

6 ounces fresh spinach, chopped (about 4 cups)

6 ounces sharp Cheddar cheese, coarsely grated (1½ cups)

I used to consider quiche a time-consuming dish, reserved for special occasions because of the need to prepare a pastry crust. The crust in this recipe takes about one minute to make! A healthy layer of raw buckwheat groats cooks along with the filling, which contains enough moisture to make the groats soften and swell while they retain a pleasant crunch. Pop the quiche in the oven and while it is cooking you have time to make a salad and a fruit dish for dessert.

I make quiche fillings with a ratio of 1 egg to ½ cup of cream. The flavor and texture when the filling is made with cream are so much better than with milk, cottage cheese, or other substitutes that a few extra calories are worth it, especially since the lighter crust more than compensates. To make a larger quiche, you can move up to a 10-inch pie plate and use 4 eggs, adjusting other ingredients proportionately. To serve two people, use a 7-inch dish and 2 eggs.

These quiches are a quick solution when I foresee a motley crowd swarming in for lunch. I might make two or three different ones, with one, like this, a vegetarian option.

1. Preheat the oven to 350°F.

2. Combine the eggs, cream, nutmeg, thyme, and pepper in a bowl, and set the bowl aside. It is best, but not essential, that the mixture reach room temperature.

3. Using your fingers, smear 1 tablespoon of the butter over the bottom and sides of a 9-inch pie plate or round baking dish—preferably ovenproof glass or ceramic, not metal. Pour the buckwheat groats into the pie plate, and turn it while holding it at a tilt to coat the sides and bottom with the groats. Then hold the pie plate flat and shake it to distribute the remaining loose groats over the bottom.

4. Melt the remaining 1 tablespoon butter in a medium-size skillet over medium-low heat. Add the spinach and sauté, stirring, until it has wilted, about 5 minutes.

5. Gently distribute the spinach over the bottom of the pie plate without disturbing the buckwheat. Sprinkle half of the grated cheese over the spinach.

6. Beat the egg mixture thoroughly with a whisk or eggbeater until it is uniform but not foamy. Carefully pour the mixture into the pie plate, and top it with the rest of the cheese.

7. Bake until the center is firm and the top is rounded and golden brown, 45 to 50 minutes. The quiche is done when a knife inserted into the center comes out clean. Let the cooked quiche sit for 5 minutes or so. It will sink slightly as it cools.

8. Cut the quiche into wedges and serve while it is still warm.

TRY THIS TOO . . .

Over the years I have varied this recipe in endless ways (the Garden Pea Quiche on page 338 is one example). Selecting whatever vegetables are in season is a good way to begin, but I don't recommend watery ones such as zucchini and tomatoes that will dilute the filling. Broccoli, Swiss chard, and leeks are good choices, and a bit of ham or cooked bacon is a welcome addition. In winter, when tiny Maine shrimp are in season, we might add a small handful of those, sautéed briefly in butter.

This dish is just right for lunch or brunch.

Garden Pea Quiche with Buckwheat Crust

SERVES 4 AS A HEARTY MEAL, 6 TO 8 IN COMBINATION WITH OTHER DISHES

3 large eggs

1½ cups heavy (whipping) cream

1 teaspoon snipped fresh dill leaves, or ½ teaspoon dried

Freshly ground black pepper, to taste

2 tablespoons butter

¾ cup buckwheat groats, also called kasha (see page 352)

⅔ cup shelled fresh garden peas

⅔ cup coarsely chopped scallions (white and green parts)

6 ounces feta cheese, crumbled (1½ cups)

Like the spinach quiche on page 336, this one has a crust of buckwheat groats that takes almost no time to make and cooks along with the filling. This tangy version is perfect for early summer or fall when there are fresh peas in the garden. It's just right for a lunch or brunch dish.

1. Preheat the oven to 350°F.

2. Combine the eggs, cream, dill, and pepper in a bowl, and set the bowl aside. It is best, but not essential, that the mixture reach room temperature.

3. Using your fingers, smear 1 tablespoon of the butter over the bottom and sides of a 9-inch pie plate or round baking dish—preferably ovenproof glass or ceramic, not metal. Pour the buckwheat groats into the pie plate, and turn it while holding it at a tilt to coat the sides and bottom with the groats. Then hold the pie plate flat and shake it to distribute the remaining loose groats over the bottom.

4. Melt the remaining 1 tablespoon butter in a small skillet over medium heat. Add the peas and scallions, and sauté for 5 minutes.

5. Gently distribute the pea mixture over the bottom of the pie plate without disturbing the buckwheat. Sprinkle half the feta cheese over the peas.

6. Beat the egg mixture thoroughly with a whisk or eggbeater until it is uniform but not foamy. Carefully pour the mixture into the pie plate, and top it with the rest of the cheese.

7. Bake until the center is firm and the top is rounded and golden brown, 45 to 50 minutes. The quiche is done when a knife inserted into the center comes out clean. Let the quiche sit for 5 minutes or so. It will sink slightly as it cools.

8. Cut the quiche into wedges and serve while it is still warm.

BROCCOLI BREAD PUDDING

SERVES 6 TO 8 AS A SIDE DISH

Savory bread puddings are great for brunch or as a side dish at a buffet. They might eliminate the need for serving potatoes or rice. This pudding goes well alongside ham, chicken, or grilled sausages.

1. Preheat the oven to 350°F.

2. Spread the bread chunks out on two large baking sheets and bake until they are crisp and dry but not browned, 15 to 20 minutes.

3. While the bread is crisping, sauté the bacon in a medium-size skillet over medium-high heat until crisp and lightly browned, 3 to 4 minutes. Set aside. Using a slotted spoon, transfer the bacon to paper towels to drain. Discard the fat or save it for another purpose.

4. Bring water to a simmer in the bottom of a vegetable steamer. Add the broccoli florets to the steamer basket, cover, and steam until they are just tender, 4 minutes. Remove the basket from the steamer and run cold water over the broccoli to stop the cooking. Set it aside to drain.

5. Using an eggbeater, a whisk, or an electric mixer, beat the eggs in a large bowl. Add the cream, milk, nutmeg, salt, and pepper, and beat well. The mixture should be thoroughly combined but not frothy.

6. Mix the two cheeses together in a bowl.

7. Butter a medium-size baking dish (9 by 13 inches is ideal) or a shallow casserole. Spread half of the crisped bread pieces in the bottom, followed by half of the broccoli, half of the bacon, half of the scallions, and half of the cheese mixture. Pour half of the egg mixture over all. Then add the remaining bread, broccoli, bacon, scallions, and egg mixture, in that order. Press the bread down with the back of a spoon to help it absorb the liquid. Then sprinkle with the remaining cheese mixture.

8. Bake until the pudding is lightly browned on top and no longer runs into the corners of the pan when tilted, about 45 minutes. Let it rest for about 10 minutes, and then serve warm.

TRY THIS TOO . . .

Seasonal substitutes might begin with asparagus in spring, then move on to summer squash, corn, leeks, or Swiss chard.

- 1 large loaf fairly dense, medium-firm bread such as multigrain sourdough, or an eggy bread such as challah or brioche, crust removed, bread torn into irregular 1-inch pieces (you'll need 10 lightly packed cups)
- 4 ounces slab bacon, cut into ¼-inch cubes (½ cup)
- 1 large head broccoli, cut into florets with 1-inch heads and short stems (4 cups)
- 3 large eggs
- 3 cups heavy (whipping) cream
- 2 cups whole milk
- ¼ teaspoon nutmeg, preferably freshly grated
- ¼ teaspoon salt
- Freshly ground black pepper, to taste
- 1¼ cups shredded sharp Cheddar cheese
- 1¼ cups shredded Gruyère cheese
- 2 tablespoons butter
- 1 cup chopped scallions (green part only)

MEDITERRANEAN SUMMER PASTA | PAGE 346

Pasta, Grains, and Legumes

IF YOUR PANTRY IS STOCKED with a few types of whole grains, pastas, and beans, you can always turn the garden's yield into a complete meal. They offer a great background canvas on which to display the colorful and flavorful produce of your garden.

The combination of grains, grain-based pastas, or protein-rich beans with vegetables has traditionally been the food that people have turned to when meat is too expensive or scarce—but as some of these recipes show, these dishes can be made even heartier when a little meat protein is added. More of them can be found in other of these chapters as well—such as Soups, on page 268.

ORZO PASTA WITH SHRIMP, PEAS, AND CHEESE

SERVES 4

1 cup (about 6 ounces) orzo (rice-shaped pasta)

⅓ cup extra-virgin olive oil

12 ounces small shrimp, fresh or frozen, peeled and deveined

1 medium-size onion, peeled, halved lengthwise, and then sliced into very thin half-rounds

1 medium-size rib celery, white base trimmed off, rib chopped (⅔ cup)

½ red bell pepper, chopped (1 cup), or ½ cup crumbled dried red bell pepper (see page 179) if peppers are not in season

1 teaspoon minced fresh rosemary or thyme leaves, or ½ teaspoon dried thyme

1½ cups green peas, fresh or frozen (thawed if frozen)

½ cup heavy (whipping) cream

4 ounces feta cheese, crumbled (about ⅓ cup)

⅓ cup (about 2 ounces) grated Parmesan cheese, preferably Parmigiano-Reggiano

Freshly ground black pepper

Salt (optional)

Tiny pink, sweet wild-caught Maine shrimp are the jewels of winter for us. At other times we buy them frozen, in order to have them on hand. The peas of early summer are, likewise, a fleeting pleasure, so we freeze them as well. As a result, the two often end up together, despite being at odds with our eat-with-the-seasons philosophy. On a busy evening, it's possible to have this one-dish meal on the table in half an hour. The flavor of feta is essential—don't substitute another cheese.

1. Fill a large saucepan or a pasta pot with 4 quarts salted water, and bring it to a boil over high heat. Add the orzo, lower the heat slightly, and cook at a rolling boil, stirring from time to time, until tender, about 10 minutes.

2. While the pasta is cooking, pour all the olive oil into a very small saucepan or skillet and heat it over high heat. Add a small batch of the shrimp and sauté until no longer translucent, 1½ to 2 minutes if fresh, 2 to 2½ minutes if frozen. Remove them with a slotted spoon and set them aside in a small bowl. Repeat with the remaining shrimp. Reserve the oil.

3. Drain the orzo in a colander and rinse it under hot running water. Leave it in the colander, set over the empty saucepan. Stir it occasionally with a fork to keep it from clumping.

4. Pour the reserved oil into a large skillet and set it over medium heat. Add the onion, celery, and bell pepper, and sauté, stirring with a spatula, for 5 minutes. Then add the rosemary, peas, cream, feta, and Parmesan. Reduce the heat to low and simmer, stirring constantly, until the peas are just tender and the feta has softened, 3 to 5 minutes.

5. Add the reserved orzo and shrimp. Stir for a minute or two to heat them

thoroughly. Then season to taste with black pepper. Taste for salt and add some if needed (the cheeses are quite salty). Serve immediately.

Don't forget the feta— the flavor is essential.

TRY THIS TOO . . .

✦ Depending on availability, you can substitute other forms of sustainably harvested shellfish, such as bay scallops, in this dish.

✦ For a vegetarian version, substitute strongly flavored black olives, such as Kalamatas, sautéed mushrooms, or both.

SPAGHETTI WITH SUMMER VEGETABLES

SERVES 6

- 2 cups heavy (whipping) cream
- 1 cup grated Parmesan cheese, preferably Parmigiano-Reggiano
- Freshly ground black pepper
- 1 pound spaghetti
- 3 tablespoons olive oil
- 2 medium-size onions, peeled and chopped into 1-inch pieces
- 2 red bell peppers, stemmed, seeded, and sliced into strips
- 3 medium-size carrots, scrubbed but not peeled, sliced on the diagonal into ½-inch-thick rounds
- Salt, to taste
- Kernels from 4 ears fresh corn

INGREDIENTS CONTINUED ▶

This one-dish vegetarian meal makes the most of the garden's summer abundance. Since it contains too many vegetables to sauté all at once in one pan, the trick is to steam the ones that are most likely to fall apart from overcooking. Since the sautéing, steaming, and pasta-cooking all happen together, the sauce is made first, then set aside for a quick reheat at the end. All will go smoothly if you have the vegetables cleaned and cut up ahead of time, ready to go. Before you start cooking, read the recipe through so you can see how the steps overlap.

1. Bring a large pot of salted water to a rolling boil on a back burner.

2. While the pot of water is heating, pour the cream into a large shallow saucepan and simmer it over low heat, stirring, until it has reduced by a third, about 5 minutes. Then gradually add the grated Parmesan, stirring constantly to keep the mixture smooth. Add a generous grinding of black pepper and set the pan aside.

3. Add the spaghetti to the boiling water and cook according to the package directions or until just al dente (9 to 12 minutes), stirring it occasionally to separate the strands. Then drain the pasta, return it to the pot, and toss it with 1 tablespoon of the olive oil. Cover the pot and set it aside.

4. As soon as the pasta goes into the pot, heat the remaining 2 tablespoons olive oil in your largest skillet over medium heat until it is fragrant, about 30 seconds. Add the onions, bell peppers, and carrots, season lightly with salt, and sauté over medium-low heat for 5 minutes. Then add the corn and cook until the vegetables are just tender but not browned, another 5 minutes.

5. As soon as the onions, peppers, and carrots have started to cook, bring water to a simmer in the bottom of a vegetable steamer. Place the zucchini and broccoli in the steamer basket, cover, and cook until they are just tender, about 10 minutes. As soon as they are done, pour the water out of the pot and return the vegetables to it. Cover, salt lightly, and set aside.

6. When all the vegetables are done, combine them in whichever is larger, the skillet or the vegetable steamer pot. Stir very gently to mix.

7. Reheat the sauce, stirring, over low heat for a minute or two to reheat it. Using tongs or a pasta server, divide the pasta among six plates or shallow bowls. Spoon the vegetables over the pasta, and the sauce over the vegetables. Garnish with the parsley and marjoram, and serve immediately.

TRY THIS TOO . . .

✦ Don't feel limited to the vegetables listed here. You could also use green beans, fennel, scallions, peas, and cauliflower—especially the golden-colored kind. In fact any vegetable that is at its prime could be included, with the exception of tomatoes, which are watery and would dilute the sauce. The more colors you include, the more festive it will look.

✦ Any type of pasta can be used. With spaghetti and other long strands, it is best to serve individual portions on plates or bowls to make sure the vegetables are evenly distributed. To serve buffet- or family-style—with the pasta, vegetables, and sauce combined before serving—use a shorter shape such as penne, macaroni, or fusilli, which is easier to mix and spoon onto plates.

◀ *INGREDIENTS CONTINUED FROM PREVIOUS PAGE*

2 zucchini, each about 8 inches long, cut into ½-inch-thick rounds

½ head broccoli, cut into small florets

2 tablespoons minced fresh flat-leaf parsley

1 tablespoon minced fresh marjoram or tarragon leaves

All will go smoothly and quickly if you have the vegetables cleaned and cut up ahead of time.

MeDITeRRanean summer Pasta

SERVES 2 TO 4 SERVINGS AS A MAIN COURSE, 4 TO 6 AS A SIDE DISH

¼ cup pine nuts

8 ounces narrow egg noodles, such as tagliolini

4 tablespoons extra-virgin olive oil

¼ cup Pesto Sauce (page 320; see Note below)

Juice of 1 lemon (about ¼ cup)

12 large, strongly flavored olives, such as Kalamatas, pitted and coarsely chopped

8 scallions (white and green parts), coarsely chopped

2 tablespoons capers, drained

30 dime-size or 15 quarter-size cherry tomatoes, left whole

¼ cup coarsely chopped fresh flat-leaf parsley

This pasta dish is colorful to look at and quick to make on a warm day. Serve it by itself for a light lunch or supper—or as a major side dish at a cookout with chops or burgers. Having a jar of homemade pesto in the fridge makes for a handy shortcut.

1. Have all the ingredients laid out and ready. Bring a large pot of salted water to a boil for the pasta.

2. While the water is heating, toast the pine nuts in a small dry skillet over very low heat, stirring them constantly, until they turn a pale tan color and give off their rich aroma, 3 to 5 minutes. Watch them carefully because they will burn very quickly if they get too hot. Set the nuts aside.

3. Add the pasta to the boiling water and cook, following the directions on the package, until just tender. (Bite one with your front teeth to check.) Drain, and return the pasta to the pot.

4. Stir 2 tablespoons of the olive oil into the pasta. Then add the pesto, lemon juice, reserved pine nuts, olives, scallions, and capers. Stir briefly and cover the pot to keep warm.

5. Heat the remaining 2 tablespoons olive oil in a large skillet over medium heat until fragrant, about 1 minute. Then add the tomatoes and sauté, stirring constantly, until they brown slightly and soften but do not disintegrate, 5 to 6 minutes. If a few of them burst, it's okay. Remove the skillet from the heat.

6. Place the pot containing the pasta over low heat and stir for 2 minutes to warm it further. Add the parsley and stir to combine.

7. Serve in a single large shallow bowl or in individual bowls, sprinkling the tomatoes over the top.

NOTE: Instead of making Pesto Sauce, you could just add ½ cup chopped fresh basil leaves and 2 pressed cloves of garlic along with the other ingredients in Step 4, and then pass grated Parmesan cheese at the table.

SOBA NOODLES WITH VEGETABLES AND TAHINI SAUCE

SERVES 4

When friends arrive unexpectedly at lunchtime, this Asian noodle dish is the perfect solution; in fact, it is such a good backup that we make a point of keeping the pantry ingredients on hand. It stands alone as a healthy meal, and the zesty sauce makes the most of whatever vegetables are in the garden or root cellar. We especially like this made with the fall vegetables suggested here.

1. Have all the vegetables cut up and at hand. Place the tahini, warm or at least at room temperature, in a medium-size bowl or 1-quart Pyrex measuring cup.

2. Heat the sesame oil in a large skillet over medium heat until fragrant, about 1 minute. Then add the carrots, onions, garlic, and ginger. Sauté, stirring occasionally, until the vegetables are slightly browned and the carrots are just tender but still have a bit of crunch when pierced with a knife, 15 to 20 minutes.

3. While the vegetables are cooking, bring a large pot of salted water to a boil. Add the noodles and cook according to the package directions, stirring occasionally, until tender, usually 8 to 10 minutes.

4. While the noodles are cooking, ladle out 1 cup of the boiling water and add it to the tahini. Whisk or stir vigorously to make a thick sauce. Add the lemon juice, which will thicken it a bit more. Then add the tamari, which will thin the sauce slightly. Set the sauce aside.

5. Bring water to a simmer in the bottom of a vegetable steamer. Add the broccoli to the steamer basket, cover, and steam until just tender, about 4 minutes.

6. When the carrot mixture is done, remove the skillet from the heat and set it aside, covered.

7. Drain the noodles and place them in one large shallow bowl or divide them among four individual bowls.

- 1 cup organic tahini (see Notes on next page)
- 2 tablespoons toasted sesame oil or peanut oil
- 6 to 8 medium-size carrots, scrubbed but not peeled, cut on the diagonal into ½-inch-thick rounds (about 2 cups)
- 3 medium-size onions, peeled and coarsely chopped (about 4 cups)
- 2 cloves garlic, peeled and minced
- 1 teaspoon minced peeled fresh ginger, or ¼ teaspoon ground dried ginger
- 12 ounces buckwheat soba noodles (see Notes on next page)
- Juice of 1 lemon
- ½ cup tamari (Japanese soy sauce)
- 1 pound broccoli, cut into small florets (about 8 cups)

8. Add the broccoli to the other vegetables in the skillet, and stir gently to mix. Distribute the vegetables over the noodles. Pour the sauce over the noodles and vegetables, or, if you wish, pass it separately. Serve immediately.

NOTES:

✦ Tahini, a Middle Eastern paste made of ground sesame seeds, is available at natural food stores and often in more mainstream stores as well. It can be found raw or roasted. Both are fine for this dish, but we usually buy the raw since it is more often available in bulk. Bulk tahini or opened jars should be stored in the refrigerator.

✦ Buckwheat soba noodles and Japanese tamari are also widely available, but can be purchased in bulk, and of better quality, at natural food stores.

TRY THIS TOO . . .

Leeks, kale, and fennel would also work well in a fall or winter version. For summer, try red bell peppers, zucchini, eggplant, and green beans.

COUSCOUS WITH PINE NUTS AND RAISINS

SERVES 6 AS A SIDE DISH

½ cup raisins

¼ cup Marsala or another sweet fortified wine, such as port or cream sherry

½ cup pine nuts

8 tablespoons (1 stick) butter

1½ cups couscous, preferably whole wheat

Generous pinch of saffron threads (optional)

Dash of salt

The modern forms of couscous, whether the typical small-grain variety or the larger Israeli-style couscous, are a great help to the cook because they can be prepared much more quickly than longer-cooking grain dishes such as rice. We make this dressed-up version for vegetarian guests, with sautéed vegetables on the side, when the main course contains meat. Couscous pairs beautifully with stews and curries and is especially good with lamb.

1. Combine the raisins and Marsala in a small saucepan, and bring to a boil over medium heat. Lower the heat to a simmer and cook until the raisins have absorbed most of the wine, about 10 minutes. Set aside.

2. Toast the pine nuts in a small dry

skillet over very low heat, stirring constantly to keep them from burning, until they are light brown, 3 to 5 minutes. Watch them carefully because they will burn very quickly if they get too hot. Set aside.

3. Melt the butter in a small saucepan over low heat, and cook until it turns a golden brown, being careful not to let it burn, about 5 minutes. Set aside.

4. Put the couscous in a medium-size saucepan, add 3 cups of water, cover, and bring slowly to a simmer over medium-low heat. Stir in the reserved raisins, pine nuts, butter, the saffron if using, and the salt. Cover and cook over very low heat until the couscous has absorbed almost all the water but has not begun to stick to the pan, about 5 minutes.

5. Remove the pan from the heat, and stir the couscous briefly and gently so that any ingredients that have floated to the top are well distributed. Let the couscous sit, covered, for a few minutes to absorb the last bit of liquid.

6. Serve the couscous as soon as possible in a medium-size bowl, fluffing it with a fork as needed to break up any clumps.

Toasting pine nuts brings out their flavor. Watch them carefully.

FRIED RICE WITH PORK AND VEGETABLES

SERVES 2 TO 4 AS A MAIN COURSE, 4 TO 6 AS A SIDE DISH

4 large fresh Swiss chard leaves, preferably yellow- or gold-stemmed

1 pound boneless pork

2 tablespoons toasted sesame oil

2 tablespoons peanut oil

4 medium-size carrots, scrubbed but not peeled, sliced into ¼-inch-thick rounds

2 cloves garlic, peeled and finely chopped

1 tablespoon finely chopped fresh ginger, or 1 teaspoon ground dried ginger

6 golf-ball-size white Japanese turnips, unpeeled, cut in half; see Notes)

2 tablespoons fermented black soybeans (optional; see Note)

4 cups cooked brown rice (from 1½ cups uncooked), cooled to room temperature

6 scallions (green and white parts), cut into 1-inch pieces

Soy sauce, for serving

Tabasco or your favorite hot pepper sauce, for serving

M aking fried rice is a great way to use whatever vegetables you have at hand, whether in the garden or from storage. It can be meatless or, as here, it can include a small amount of meat for extra protein and flavor. The pork can be an inexpensive cut such as shoulder chops or country-style ribs. With or without meat, this can be a meal in itself.

This particular recipe uses fall vegetables. Yellow-stemmed chard makes a colorful addition after the bright colors of summer vegetables are gone. Small Japanese turnips are so sweet and tender in the fall that they need almost no cooking, and their crunch is a wonderful substitute for water chestnuts in any Asian dish.

Both the pork and the rice can be left over from another meal—in fact I will often make extra rice one day, knowing that it might form the basis for fried rice the next.

1. Cut along the sides of the center ribs of the chard leaves to separate them from the green part of the leaves. Slice the ribs and the stems diagonally into 1-inch pieces. Cut the greens into roughly 2-inch squares.

2. Cut the meat into ½-inch cubes, and blot them with a paper towel to dry the surfaces.

3. Heat the sesame and peanut oils together in a large skillet over medium-high heat. When the oil is hot, add half of the meat. Sauté, stirring or flipping the pieces with tongs so they brown uniformly, about 5 minutes. Using a slotted spoon, transfer the meat to a bowl. Repeat with the remaining meat. Leave the oil in the skillet.

4. Put the chard ribs and stems in the

skillet, and add the carrots, garlic, and ginger. Cook over medium heat, stirring frequently, until the carrots have started to soften, 5 minutes.

5. Add the turnips and soybeans, and cook for 2 minutes.

6. Add the rice, scallions, chard greens, and the reserved pork. Cook, stirring constantly and scraping the bottom of the pan with a spatula to keep the rice from sticking, until the rice is heated through and the greens are slightly wilted, about 5 minutes.

7. Serve right away, passing the soy sauce and Tabasco at the table.

NOTES:

✦ Regular turnips do not make a good substitute for the tender white Asian kind. If you don't have these, use radishes or broccoli stems instead.

✦ Fermented black soybeans are small and soft, with a pungent, salty flavor

like that of soy sauce. Adding just a few will give a dish a unique zing. They can be found in Asian groceries or ordered online, and will last at least a year in the refrigerator.

TRY THIS TOO . . .

✦ Other cool-weather vegetables might include radishes of all kinds, especially the red-skinned ones for color. Substitute kale or bok choi (pac choi) for the Swiss chard. Try broccoli, with its crisp stems sliced. In summer, use snow peas or sugar snaps, red bell peppers, summer squash, and green beans—all lightly cooked.

✦ Although pork is our favorite meat for fried rice, I also use beef or lamb. Sometimes I'll start by frying small cubes of slab bacon, in which case I'd pour off some of the bacon grease and add just the toasted sesame oil, omitting the peanut oil. Fried rice is also delicious made with shellfish—especially shrimp, lobster, or scallops.

Japanese turnips—small in size—add a crisp spark of flavor.

Yellow-stemmed chard makes a colorful addition after the bright colors of summer vegetables are gone.

BUCKWHEAT KASHA

SERVES 4 TO 6 AS A SIDE DISH

1 large egg

1 cup buckwheat groats

½ teaspoon salt

Freshly ground black
  pepper

Butter, to taste

Buckwheat is not a grain, if you define *grain* as the one-seeded fruits of cereal grasses, such as wheat, barley, and corn, but it is used like one. The fruit seed of a round-leaved plant related to sorrel and rhubarb, buckwheat is delicious, full of fiber and nutrients, and gluten-free. It also cooks much faster than most cereal grains, including rice, which makes it a great instant side dish. Buckwheat seeds with the hulls removed are called *groats.* These are often sold as *kasha,* but since that word can sometimes refer to a variety of grain porridges, *buckwheat kasha* is a more explicit term. You can buy both raw and toasted buckwheat groats; I've found the latter to be more readily available, more flavorful, and slightly easier to cook.

Buckwheat kasha goes well alongside almost any meat or vegetable—try it with the Zucchini and Onions on page 371. We love it just topped with lots of butter, salt, and pepper.

Buckwheat expands quite a bit in cooking. Coating the individual grains with beaten egg helps to keep them separate so they don't become mushy. If you double the amount of buckwheat in this recipe, one egg will still suffice.

1. Beat the egg in a small bowl. Add the buckwheat and stir to coat the grains with the egg.

2. Place the buckwheat in a medium-size saucepan and cook over medium heat, stirring constantly to break up the clumps, until all the grains are separate, about 5 minutes.

3. Add 2 cups hot water and stir briefly and vigorously to mix, scraping any egg crust off the bottom of the pan with a spatula. Add the salt. Cover the pan, turn the heat to very low, and simmer very gently until most of the water has been absorbed, about 20 minutes.

4. Taste to see if all the groats have softened. If they are still a bit hard, add 1/2 cup water, cover, and simmer some more. It's important to watch carefully, lest the water boil away and the grains stick to the bottom of the pan. Toward the end, you may take the pan off the heat and let it sit, covered, until the last bit of water has been absorbed.

5. Season to taste with salt, black pepper, and butter. Serve hot.

TRY THIS TOO . . .

✦ You can also make brown butter to drizzle over the buckwheat, as in the Potato and Celery Root Mash on page 396.

✦ Make a pilaf with buckwheat kasha by combining it with lightly sautéed vegetables, substituting chicken, beef, or vegetable stock for the water, and baking it in a 350°F oven until all the liquid has been absorbed, 10 to 15 minutes.

SHELL BEANS WITH TOMATOES AND SAGE

SERVES 4 TO 6 AS A SIDE DISH

Long-cooking baked beans might be perfect for a cold day, but in summer you want something quicker, something that won't heat up the kitchen. Tender young shell beans are the answer (for more on shell beans, see page 186). If they have just swelled in their pods and the plum tomatoes have ripened, you have a winning combination.

4 cups fresh shell beans (from about 3 pounds unshelled)

4 cloves garlic, peeled and pressed or very finely chopped

8 ounces fresh plum tomatoes, peeled (see page 178) and coarsely chopped

1/4 cup olive oil

12 large fresh sage leaves, finely chopped

Dash of salt

Freshly ground black pepper

1. Place the beans and the garlic in a saucepan, add just enough water to cover, and bring to a boil over medium-high heat. Then lower the heat to a simmer and cook until just tender, 10 to 30 minutes depending on the age, size, and type of

beans. If the mixture becomes too dry before the beans are cooked, add a little water. You can drain them if they are still soupy when they are done, but I try to use just enough water so that it has cooked away by the time the beans are tender.

2. Remove the pan from the heat and while the beans are still warm, gently stir in the tomatoes, olive oil, sage, salt, and pepper to taste. Serve warm or as a room-temperature salad.

TRY THIS TOO . . .

We often make this dish in wintertime with dried beans and frozen plum tomatoes. In this case, the beans will take much longer to cook (see page 189).

SHELL BEANS WITH TOMATOES AND SAGE

SUMMER SUCCOTASH

SERVES 3 TO 4 AS A MAIN COURSE, 6 AS A SIDE DISH

Succotash, a Native American staple combining beans and corn, has become a modern classic. The typical version uses lima beans, but any shell bean—such as white kidney beans, Vermont cranberry beans, or flageolets—will do.

This dish could stand alone as a meal, but it would be even better if accompanied by a salad—with tomatoes, perhaps, in summer, or with winter greens later on. It could also be a side dish to accompany a meat platter, such as fried chicken.

2 cups fresh shell beans (from about 1½ pounds unshelled)

Kernels from 4 ears fresh corn (2 cups)

2 ounces slab bacon or salt pork, finely diced (¼ cup)

2 tablespoons finely chopped fresh flat-leaf parsley

1 tablespoon sunflower oil

1 medium-size onion, peeled and finely chopped

¼ teaspoon salt

Freshly ground black pepper

1. Place the beans in a saucepan, add just enough water to cover, and bring to a simmer. Cook, adding a little water if needed, until tender, 10 to 20 minutes, depending on the age, size, and type of bean.

2. Add the corn and cook until it is tender, 5 minutes. If the mixture is soupy, drain off the excess liquid or simmer the mixture for a few minutes more (the goal is to use just enough water so that it has cooked away by the time both vegetables are tender). Set the pan aside.

3. Heat a small skillet over medium heat, add the bacon, and sauté, stirring, until it is slightly crisp, 5 minutes. Remove the bacon with a slotted spoon and add it to the corn and beans, leaving the fat in the skillet.

4. Stir the parsley into the corn and beans.

5. Add the sunflower oil and onion to the skillet, and sauté over medium-low heat until the onion is tender but not browned, about 10 minutes. Add the onion to the corn and bean mixture, season with the salt and pepper to taste, and serve hot.

TRY THIS TOO . . .

In wintertime it is fine to substitute dried or frozen beans and corn for fresh. Dried corn will take longer to cook (see page 189 for cooking dried beans).

11

Summer Vegetables

THE FIRST CROP OF SUMMER ACTUALLY BEGINS IN SPRING.
The closed buds of asparagus tips are delicious until they sprout branches, like ferny shrubs. After that, summer's harvest basket holds a luscious collection of what we typically call vegetables but are actually fruits, brought to ripeness by the sun. Tomatoes, cucumbers, peppers, beans—these are all, properly speaking, the fruiting bodies of plants. Their purpose is to protect and nurture the seeds within them until it is time for those seeds to disperse. No wonder they are full of succulent, nutritious flesh. Most are tropical in origin, so we pamper them like babies in hopes of making the most of their season. We gorge on them, celebrate them, raw or cooked, and flavor them with the herbs that are

also abundant in summertime. Since they ripen when it's often too hot to enjoy spending time in the kitchen, preparations tend to be simple. This is fine, because the produce itself carries the day.

In a few cases, the stem is what we eat. Celery, which tolerates only light frosts, is a food of summer, much appreciated for its crispness. Bulb fennel is an enlarged stem base, also appreciated for its crunch. It deteriorates in very cold weather. Artichokes arrive in summer and carry on into the fall—or winter in warm climates—their prickly buds daring you to find their exquisite hearts.

Summer vegetables, because they are plant parts experiencing rapid, time-sensitive growth, are soon past their prime, so their harvesting requires the cook's vigilant eye.

Our summer garden

OVEN-ROASTED ARTICHOKE HEARTS WITH LEMON AND ROSEMARY

SERVES 4 AS A SIDE DISH

This is our favorite way to eat the small artichoke heads that form on the plants' lower side branches. When you harvest them, leave several inches of the stem attached, because the stem is delicious too. Trimming them takes some time, but after that this dish cooks itself without much ado. We like these strongly flavored morsels as a side dish with a steak, or on top of firm salad greens such as romaine lettuce, endive, or radicchio.

1. Preheat the oven to 375°F.

2. Combine the olive oil, vermouth, lemon juice, and garlic in your largest nonreactive roasting pan or baking dish.

3. Trim each artichoke by slicing off the top third of the head, then pulling off the green leaves, leaving only those that are pale chartreuse in color. With a small, sharp nonreactive knife, trim off any green stubs left behind. Peel the stems and slice off their bottom surfaces. If the artichokes are large enough to have chokes, remove them (see pages 190 to 191). As each head is done, cut it in half, but leave any very tiny ones whole. Roll the trimmed artichokes in the mixture in the roasting pan, and then leave them in it, cut side down.

4. Scatter the rosemary, olives, and capers over the artichokes. Season with a dash of salt and a generous grinding of black pepper. Cover the pan tightly with a lid or with aluminum foil, and bake until the artichoke hearts are tender and all the liquid has been absorbed, 45 to 50 minutes. The cut sides should be golden brown.

5. Sprinkle with the parsley, and stir briefly. Serve hot or warm in a dish or shallow bowl, or at room temperature in a salad.

½ cup extra-virgin olive oil

⅔ cup dry vermouth or dry white wine

Juice of 2 Meyer lemons or 1 regular lemon (¼ cup)

2 cloves garlic, peeled and pressed or minced

20 baby artichokes (no more than 3 inches wide, 2 to 3 pounds total), or 10 small-to-average-size ones

4 teaspoons fresh rosemary leaves

8 large strongly flavored black olives, such as Kalamatas, pitted and coarsely chopped (optional)

2 tablespoons capers, drained

Salt and freshly ground black pepper

1 tablespoon coarsely chopped fresh flat-leaf parsley leaves

REAL CREAMED CORN

SERVES 4 AS A SIDE DISH

4 large ears fresh corn

½ cup heavy (whipping) cream

Dash of salt

2 teaspoons snipped fresh chives

2 teaspoons snipped fresh dill leaves

Freshly ground black pepper

Creamed corn is a dish sorely in need of rehabilitation. Replace that gooey, sugar-added canned glop with kernels cut off the cob, and simmered in a little cream that reduces and thickens as the kernels cook. Both the corn and the cream are naturally sweet.

1. Remove the kernels from each corn cob by standing the ear upright and carefully slicing down the sides with a large, heavy sharp knife.

2. Place the kernels in a medium-size skillet or saucepan, add the cream and salt, and bring to a boil over medium-high heat. Then reduce the heat and simmer until the kernels are tender and the cream is thick, 11 to 12 minutes.

3. Stir in the chives, dill, and pepper to taste. Serve hot or warm.

TRY THIS TOO . . .

You can also take this dish a step further and let the corn make its own cream: Holding each ear of corn vertically as described, use the tip of a small sharp knife to slice down the center of each row of kernels. Then use the back of a large knife to scrape down the rows, pressing heavily. This pops out the kernels' milky innards, leaving the less digestible kernel walls behind. The result is a sweet puddle of instant creamed corn, plain and simple. You can also buy a corn-cutting tool that performs this act by puncturing the kernels with metal teeth, then squeezing them out. Since the yield of scraped kernels is about half that of cut ones, you'll need 8 ears to get 4 servings. The amounts of the other ingredients remain the same, but because the inner kernels

Getting the Kernels off the Cob

CUTTING. An angel food cake pan catches the kernels tidily.

SCRAPING. An old-fashioned corn cutter releases the kernels' milky centers.

are very tender, they will take about half the time to cook.

Cutting or scraping the kernels off the cob is also the most space-saving way to freeze corn. After blanching the cobs for a minute or two in boiling water, remove the kernels and freeze them in bags of two or four portions each. Flatten the bags after filling them and stack them inside a plastic box.

CUCUMBER RAITA

SERVES 4 GENEROUSLY AS A SIDE DISH, 6 TO 8 AS A CONDIMENT

A *raita* is an Indian yogurt dish, usually served alongside curries and other spicy dishes. Most raitas are savory ones involving vegetables, but there are also sweet raitas, of which the grape version on page 445 is an example. I use the general concept as a model and make up my own versions. You should, too. Although some raitas include hot pepper seasoning, I prefer to use them as a cooling agent to complement hotter fare. This particular one is a good way to use cucumbers during the great summer glut, when you are picking them every day. I use fresh, young slicing cucumbers for this dish—some have such tender skins that they do not need peeling.

⅔ cup whole-milk yogurt

⅓ cup sour cream

½ teaspoon ground cumin

2 tablespoons finely minced fresh mint leaves

Salt and freshly ground black pepper

3 medium-size cucumbers (about 1½ pounds), peeled and coarsely grated (2 cups)

1 tablespoon finely grated onion

3 small red radishes, very thinly sliced

1. Combine the yogurt, sour cream, cumin, mint, a dash of salt, and a generous grinding of pepper in a medium-size bowl and mix until thoroughly combined.

2. Add the cucumbers and onion, and stir gently to mix. (Rougher treatment can break up the cucumbers, releasing their juice and making the sauce runny.) Refrigerate, covered, if not serving right away.

3. Just before serving, sprinkle the radish slices over the top. Served chilled or at room temperature.

SAUTÉED CUCUMBERS

SERVES 4 AS A SIDE DISH, 6 TO 8 AS A SAUCE OR GARNISH

2 tablespoons butter

4 small slicing cucumbers (1 pound), peeled and very thinly sliced (about 3 cups)

1 large sweet onion, preferably a Vidalia type or a Walla Walla, peeled, quartered, and very thinly sliced

½ cup heavy (whipping) cream

2 tablespoons finely chopped fresh dill leaves

Salt and freshly ground black pepper

The first time I cooked cucumbers, I was surprised to see how well they held their shape and their crunch. Sautéing them is simple and quick. I like this as a side dish with any meat, or as a garnish for seafood, especially a rich and strong-flavored type such as swordfish, bluefish, or salmon. You can either spoon it on top of the fish as a sauce or serve it alongside. If you are growing watercress, tuck a few sprigs under the fish just before serving.

1. Heat the butter in a large skillet over low heat until the foam subsides, about 3 minutes. Add the cucumbers and onion and sauté, stirring frequently, until the cucumbers are tender and translucent but retain some crispness, 8 to 10 minutes.

2. Add the cream, dill, a dash of salt, and black pepper to taste. Raise the heat to high and boil rapidly, stirring constantly, to thicken the sauce, 1 to 2 minutes. Serve hot or warm.

When you have a lot of fresh vegetables to play with, you're bound to experiment with them. Who knew that cucumbers could be cooked? Try them next in a creamy soup.

CRANBERRY-PEPPER RELISH

SERVES 4 TO 6 AS A SIDE DISH, 6 TO 8 AS A GARNISH

Cooked bell peppers and onions taste pretty sweet on their own, but we especially love them with the added tart-sweet flavor of dried cranberries. The ones we buy are sweetened with apple juice, but unsweetened ones are fine too if you add a bit of honey (1 tablespoon, or to taste). The combination is tasty alongside roasted or grilled meats, or with buckwheat kasha (page 352).

¼ cup olive oil

4 medium-size ripe bell peppers, either red or yellow (not green), stemmed, seeded, and cut lengthwise into eighths

2 medium-size onions, peeled and cut into thick rounds

Dash of salt

¼ cup dried sweetened cranberries

1. Heat the olive oil in a large skillet over medium heat until fragrant, 1 to 2 minutes. Add the peppers, onions, and salt. Reduce the heat to medium-low, cover the skillet, and cook, stirring the mixture from time to time, until the vegetables have started to caramelize, 10 to 15 minutes. Do not let them burn.

2. Add the cranberries and cook, uncovered, over low heat, stirring as needed, until they have softened, 5 to 10 minutes. Serve warm or at room temperature.

CRANBERRY-PEPPER RELISH

LamB-STuFFeD eGGPLanT

SERVES 4 AS A MAIN COURSE, 6 TO 8 AS A SIDE DISH

4 small eggplants
  (4 to 5 inches long)

Boiling water

4 tablespoons olive oil

8 ounces lamb, ground or
  very finely chopped

1 medium-size onion,
  peeled and finely
  chopped

4 small plum tomatoes,
  peeled, seeded, and
  chopped

1 clove garlic, peeled and
  pressed or minced

¼ cup pine nuts

1 teaspoon minced fresh
  oregano leaves, or
  ½ teaspoon dried

1 tablespoon minced fresh
  flat-leaf parsley leaves

Freshly ground black
  pepper

Salt

¾ cup grated Parmesan
  cheese, preferably
  Parmigiano-Reggiano

Stuffed eggplant is a wonderfully versatile dish. Depending on the size of the eggplant and the nature of the stuffing, it can be a main course, a side dish, or a plated appetizer (a bit too messy for finger food). Although you can stuff an eggplant of any size, small ones are the easiest to eat because they can be served as individual portions. These would go well with potato salad or a green salad, and maybe some crusty bread served with hummus and a plate of cheeses.

1. Preheat the oven to 375°F.

2. Cut the eggplants in half lengthwise, and run the tip of a sharp knife around the perimeter, ¼ inch in from the skin, making the cut as deep as you can without piercing the skin. Score the inner flesh in a checkerboard of ½-inch squares. (This will make the flesh easier to remove later.)

3. Pour boiling water into a baking dish to a depth of ¼ inch. Place the eggplants, cut side down, in the baking dish. Bake until they are tender when pricked with a skewer, about 15 minutes.

4. While the eggplants are baking, heat 2 tablespoons of the olive oil in a medium-size skillet over medium heat until fragrant, about 1 minute. Add the lamb and sauté, stirring with a spatula,

until browned, about 5 minutes. Using a slotted spoon, transfer the lamb to a medium-size bowl.

5. Add 1 tablespoon of the olive oil to the skillet, and then add the chopped onion. Sauté, stirring with a spatula, until translucent, 5 minutes. Add the onion and oil to the lamb.

6. Remove the eggplants from the baking dish and set them aside until they are cool enough to handle. (Leave the oven on.) Then scrape out the pulp with a small, sharp spoon, taking care not to tear the skin. It will sometimes pull out in a single piece. Chop it up and add it to the lamb and onions. Add the tomatoes, garlic, pine nuts, oregano, parsley, and a generous amount of black pepper, and stir to combine. Season with salt to taste.

7. Spoon the lamb mixture into the eggplant shells and sprinkle the tops with the Parmesan. Smear a rimmed baking sheet with the remaining 1 tablespoon olive oil, and place the stuffed eggplants on the baking sheet. Bake until the cheese has melted and the stuffing is hot, about 15 minutes. (You can run them under the broiler at the end to melt the cheese further, if desired.) Serve hot, warm, or at room temperature.

TRY THIS TOO . . .

It's fun to experiment with other fillings for this dish. We make a very tasty meatless version with a stuffing of cooked rice, feta cheese, toasted pine nuts, raisins, and minced fresh mint or basil, mixed with the eggplant pulp.

ROASTED FENNEL WITH APRICOTS

SERVES 6 TO 8 AS A SIDE DISH

The combination of fennel and fruit is a good accompaniment to meat, especially rich, fatty cuts such as pork shoulder or bratwurst. This dish might be a good way to introduce someone to fennel for the first time. I often make it for a large crowd, and while it takes quite a while to cook, it requires little attention and the house smells wonderful while it's in the oven.

1. Preheat the oven to 350°F.

2. Combine the fennel, onions, garlic, olive oil, sherry, salt, and pepper in a large roasting pan or casserole, and toss to coat everything with the oil. Cover tightly with the lid or with aluminum foil, and roast for 1½ hours, stirring the vegetables occasionally.

3. Stir in the apricots and roast until the vegetables are very tender and the apricots have cooked but have not yet begun to disintegrate, 30 minutes. Serve hot.

8 medium-size fennel bulbs (or the equivalent), trimmed and quartered lengthwise

4 medium-size onions, peeled and quartered

2 cloves garlic, peeled and finely chopped

3 tablespoons olive oil

¼ cup medium-dry sherry

½ teaspoon salt

Freshly ground black pepper, to taste

½ cup (loosely packed) dried apricots, cut in half

Anellini beans. The name means "little rings" in Italian.

HERBY, CREAMY GREEN BEANS

SERVES 4

You can buy a garlic-and-herb-flavored soft cheese and stir it into hot cooked green beans for a luxurious treat. But fresh-from-the-garden herbs taste much better.

This dish would go well with the meat loaf on page 413 and a platter of sliced vine-ripened tomatoes.

1. Make a paste of the garlic by mincing it and then mashing it on a cutting board with the side of a knife. (Or simply squeeze the pulp out of the skins of roasted cloves onto the cutting board.) Add the salt, and smear the paste a few times with the tip of the knife until smooth. Set aside.

2. Bring water to a simmer in the bottom of a vegetable steamer. Place the green beans in the steamer basket, cover, and steam until just tender, 6 to 8 minutes.

3. While the beans are cooking, combine the cream, thyme, tarragon, rosemary, reserved garlic paste, and cream cheese in a medium-size saucepan over medium-low heat. Cook, whisking or stirring constantly, until the cream cheese has melted and the sauce is very smooth, about 2 minutes.

4. When the beans are done, add them to the sauce and stir well over low heat until they are thoroughly coated, 2 to 3 minutes. Serve immediately, hot or warm, so that the sauce does not stiffen.

1 clove garlic, peeled, or 2 cloves garlic, unpeeled, roasted

Small pinch of salt

12 ounces fresh green beans, ends trimmed, cut in half

½ cup heavy (whipping) cream

½ teaspoon fresh thyme leaves, or ¼ teaspoon dried

½ teaspoon minced fresh tarragon leaves, or ¼ teaspoon dried

½ teaspoon minced fresh rosemary leaves (do not use dried)

2 ounces cream cheese, cut into pieces (¼ cup)

Buttered beans get monotonous in summer when the vines are bearing heavily. Try this decadent version.

SUMMER TART WITH ROASTED TOMATOES

SERVES 4 AS A MAIN DISH, 6 AS A SIDE DISH OR APPETIZER

- 4 tablespoons extra-virgin olive oil, plus more if needed
- 18 medium-size plum tomatoes (about 2 pounds)
- Coarse sea salt and freshly ground black pepper, to taste
- 1 tablespoon mixed dried herbs, such as parsley, thyme, rosemary, chervil, sage, and dill
- 3 medium-size onions (about 1 pound), peeled, quartered, and very thinly sliced
- 1 Butter Pastry Crust (page 434) in a 9-inch tart pan with removable bottom, partially baked

A favorite dish of ours, this tart takes several hours to make but is worth it for a lunch with special guests or as the opening salvo of a dinner celebration. Both the tomatoes and the onions sweeten while they cook.

1. Preheat the oven to 350°F.

2. Drizzle 3 tablespoons of the olive oil over the bottom of a rimmed baking sheet.

3. Cut the tomatoes in half lengthwise. Rub the cut sides of the tomatoes in the oil in the baking sheet, and then arrange them, cut side up, on the baking sheet. If the tomatoes look dry, drizzle a little more oil over them. Sprinkle salt, pepper, and the dried herbs over the tomatoes.

4. Roast for 1 hour, turning the pan around halfway through cooking to

Roasting Tomatoes

CUT IN HALF. Place cut-side-up on an oiled baking sheet.

SPRINKLE ON DRIED HERBS. Add these at the end if you're using fresh ones.

ROAST. The tomatoes are done when they're slightly browned but not charred.

ensure that they cook evenly. The tomatoes are done when they look smaller and somewhat drier. The cut sides will have browned a bit, but not charred, and the uncut sides will feel soft and pillowy. Take out the baking sheet but leave the oven on. Set the tomatoes aside.

5. Slick a medium-large skillet with the remaining 1 tablespoon olive oil, and warm it over medium heat until fragrant, 1 to 2 minutes. Add the onions, reduce the heat to very low, and partially cover the skillet to speed the cooking but still allow moisture to escape. Cook, stirring from time to time and making sure the onions do not stick to the skillet or burn, until they are tan and caramelized, with a jamlike consistency, and are reduced to about 1 cup, 45 minutes to 1 hour.

6. Spread the onions over the bottom of the partially baked tart shell. Then arrange the tomatoes, cut side down, in a single layer of rings, starting at the outside. Overlap them enough so that all of them fit.

7. Place the filled tart on a baking sheet (to make it easier to handle and to catch any drips). Bake until the crust is set and golden brown and all the ingredients are heated through, 15 to 20 minutes.

8. Release the tart from the pan by pressing up on the bottom from below, letting the fluted rim drop. Then gently slide the tart off the metal bottom and onto a flat plate, using a spatula to loosen it.

9. Serve hot, warm, or at room temperature, but not cold. It can be made ahead and reheated for 30 minutes at 200°F.

TRY THIS TOO . . .

Omit the dried mixed herbs and sprinkle 1 tablespoon finely minced fresh basil over the tart just before serving.

zucchini and onions

SERVES 4 AS A SIDE DISH

Too many zucchini? Pick them while they are small and tender, and make this simple dish often. Serve it with meat or fish.

1. Bring water to a simmer in the bottom of a vegetable steamer. Place the zucchini and onions in the steamer basket, cover, and steam until tender but still slightly firm, about 8 minutes. Stir gently to drain, and place in a warmed shallow serving bowl.

2. Melt the butter in a small saucepan or skillet over low heat. Let it cook until it turns a golden brown, but do not let it blacken, about 5 minutes. Remove the pan from the heat. Add the parsley and marjoram to the butter, and let it sit for a minute or two for the flavors to infuse.

3. Drizzle the butter over the vegetables, add the salt and pepper to taste, and then stir briefly and very gently to blend. (Rough stirring will cause the zucchini to give up its juices.) Serve immediately.

4 small zucchini (no more than 6 inches long), sliced into ⅛-inch-thick rounds (about 4 cups)

2 medium-size onions, peeled, quartered, and thinly sliced (2 cups)

2 tablespoons butter

1 tablespoon finely chopped fresh flat-leaf parsley leaves

2 teaspoons finely chopped fresh marjoram, tarragon, or dill leaves

Dash of salt

Freshly ground black pepper

Steam some carrot rounds along with the zucchini and onions, and your dish will look like the Italian flag.

BEET GREENS AND SCALLIONS | PAGE 375

Cooking Greens

MOST OF THE LEAFY GREENS WE COOK are closely related to one another and are members of the genus *Brassica,* a group described in more detail on page 126. They're sometimes referred to as "the cabbage family," although cabbage is just the beginning. There's broccoli, kale, collards, Brussels sprouts, turnip greens, mustards, and a host of Asian greens—as well as cauliflower, which is neither leafy nor green but has the familial flavor. These plants have long been recognized as nutritious. For centuries mothers have said, "Eat your greens—they're good for you." And they were right.

Greens that are not brassicas include the familiar Swiss chard, beet greens, and spinach, which are all closely related to one another, and another constellation of closely related plants called the chicories, which include endive, escarole, and radicchio. Sorrel and watercress are also popular players, though less commonly grown. Worldwide, the list of greens that people cook runs into the hundreds, each with its own virtues.

Beet greens.

These greens tend to have assertive flavors—some more than others. The brassicas range from the mildness of a Savoy cabbage to the sharp bite of a mustard. The chicory group tends toward bitterness and is tricky to tame both in garden and in kitchen, so they are sometimes blanched—that is, covered while growing to exclude light, thereby making them mild and sweet. Some people love their greens strong and bitter, many do not, and it's the grower's job to steer a middle path by fertilizing intelligently, irrigating as needed, and observing other cultural practices. Greens should not be bland and tasteless, either.

With a few exceptions, such as Malabar spinach, an edible vine, greens taste best when grown and harvested in cool weather. The cold sweetens them and smoothes out their rough edges. When they are at their best, they are delicious, and many can be eaten raw as well, especially when the leaves are young and tender.

Often people who think they don't like greens have only eaten ones that were overcooked, over-mature, or poorly grown. When they discover what greens taste like fresh from the garden in their proper season, it is a revelation.

The job of the cook is not to boil the dickens out of greens until their flavors and nutrients are gone, nor to mask their flavors, but to treat them delicately and pair them with ingredients that complement them. (The sweetness of onions and raisins, the emollience of butter and bacon, spring to mind.) Quick cooking methods such as sautéing, steaming, stir-frying, and simmering in a little flavored broth offer the best route to success.

BEET GREENS AND SCALLIONS

SERVES 4 AS A SIDE DISH

This dish is good when made with beet greens of any size, whether small bunches from a thinned row or the tops of mature beets that you will be storing in the cellar. Teaming them up with scallions, bacon, and maple syrup has won over many a greens-hater. They are especially tasty when served alongside a hearty piece of meat, but if it's pork, omit the bacon. Keep in mind that beet stems bleed just the way the roots do, and will color pale foods such as fish.

- 2 ounces slab bacon or salt pork, cut into ¼-inch cubes (¼ cup)
- 1 pound beet greens, leaves sliced into ribbons and stems cut into 2-inch pieces
- 1 bunch scallions (about 6 ounces), both white and green parts cut into 2-inch pieces
- 1½ tablespoons maple syrup
- Salt and freshly ground black pepper

1. Sauté the bacon in a large skillet over medium heat, stirring, until the pieces crisp uniformly and cook to a tan color, about 7 minutes. Remove the bacon pieces to a plate with a slotted spoon and set them aside, leaving the bacon fat in the skillet.

2. Add the beet greens, beet stems, and scallions to the skillet, cover, and cook over low heat, stirring from time to time, until the beet stems are tender and the scallions have turned slightly golden, 15 to 25 minutes, depending on the size and age of the greens.

3. Remove the skillet from the heat and stir in the maple syrup and the reserved bacon. Season with salt (if needed—the bacon might be salty enough) and pepper to taste. Serve immediately.

Any strong-flavored brassica— such as kale, collards, broccoli raab, or mustard greens—would be enhanced by this treatment.

STIR-FRY WITH ASIAN GREENS

SERVES 4 AS A SIDE DISH

2 tablespoons toasted sesame oil or peanut oil

1 clove garlic, peeled and minced

1 piece (1 inch long) fresh ginger, peeled and cut into thin matchsticks

8 ounces snow peas (about 2 cups), strings removed if any

8 scallions, white parts and green tops chopped separately into 1-inch pieces

2 to 3 heads (about 8 ounces) baby bok choy (pac choi), white bottoms and green tops chopped separately into 1-inch pieces

6 medium-size red radishes, thinly sliced

1 tablespoon soy sauce

A stir-fry is one of those wonderfully quick dishes you can make any time of the year, using whatever seasonal vegetables are at hand. Although the technique is Chinese in origin, you don't have to use Asian vegetables or seasonings, although they are awfully good. You don't need a wok either, or chopsticks. A large skillet and a spatula will do.

When you stir-fry, you cook the ingredients briefly in a small amount of oil over fairly high heat, keeping them in constant motion. In one style of stir-frying you then add liquid and thicken it into a sauce, but I favor the simpler, lighter method that highlights the textures, flavors, and colors of the vegetables.

Have all the vegetables washed, trimmed, chopped, and ready to go so that you can add them quickly as you cook. The trick is to add them in a sequence that gives each one just the right amount of cooking time. Firm ones go in first, followed by the softer ones. The most fragile are added at the end and are barely warmed so that they wilt a bit but do not shrivel up altogether. Those that are best eaten raw, such as radishes, can also be tossed in at the end.

This is a good dish to make while a casserole or roast is finishing up in the oven.

1. Heat the sesame oil in a large skillet over medium heat until fragrant, 1 to 2 minutes. Add the garlic and ginger and cook for 1 minute, stirring constantly, to flavor the oil.

2. Immediately add the snow peas, scallion whites, and bok choy bottoms. Stir-fry until the vegetables are tender but still have some crunch, about 3 minutes.

4. Add the bok choy tops, stir-fry for 30 seconds, and then remove the skillet from the heat.

5. Add the radishes and soy sauce, and stir to combine. Serve immediately.

TRY THIS TOO . . .

✦ Other vegetables that are excellent for stir-frying include green beans, carrots (whole baby ones or sliced larger ones), whole or sliced baby turnips, sliced bell peppers, tatsoi, coarsely chopped Swiss chard, broccoli florets, and cauliflower florets.

✦ Meat, seafood, and mushrooms can be included, but these are best browned separately and then added in at the end.

3. Add the scallion greens and stir-fry for 1 minute.

ROASTED BRUSSELS SPROUTS AND SHALLOTS

SERVES 4 AS A SIDE DISH, 6 TO 8 AS A GARNISH

In fall and early winter, when Brussels sprouts sweeten on their stalks, they make tasty side dishes for cold-weather meals. Try this one with pork chops, or with a sliced London broil, and the Potato and Celery Root Mash with Brown Butter (page 396). This would also make a nice garnish to encircle a hearty roast, popped into the still-hot oven after the roast has been removed and is resting prior to carving.

Both Brussels sprouts and shallots vary a great deal in size. Try to pair small with small or large with large so that the cooking times come out about the same.

1. Place a rimmed baking sheet in the oven and preheat the oven to 400°F.

2. Toss all the ingredients together in a bowl, distributing the oil evenly.

3. Spread the sprouts and shallots out on the preheated baking sheet, and roast for 15 minutes.

4. Turn the sprouts and shallots over with a pair of tongs, and continue to roast until both vegetables are very tender and browned but not blackened, another 15 minutes. Serve hot or warm.

TRY THIS TOO . . .

✦ Try substituting mini-cabbages for the sprouts. These might be ones that have been cut back to regrow (see page 72).

✦ Homegrown Brussels sprouts are rarely bitter, especially if picked in cold weather, and the sweetness of the shallots should amply compensate in case they are. If the flavor is still too strong for you, stir in a tablespoon of honey and/or balsamic vinegar at the end.

20 large Brussels sprouts or 30 to 40 smaller ones, trimmed

1 pound shallots (roughly equal in volume to that of the sprouts), peeled, root ends trimmed, and cut in half if needed to approximate the size of the sprouts

¼ cup olive oil

Salt and freshly ground black pepper, to taste

CABBAGE WITH CARAWAY BUTTER

SERVES 4 TO 6 AS A SIDE DISH

Cabbage and caraway seeds naturally go together. I like this dish best when it is made with green cabbage and paired with something dark-colored on the plate, such as a steak. For a paler meat such as chicken, you might use red cabbage instead. If you use a Savoy cabbage, which has a finer texture, shorten the cooking time by 5 minutes.

1 small head green cabbage, core removed, chopped into bite-size pieces

4 tablespoons (½ stick) butter

2 teaspoons caraway seeds

Salt and freshly ground black pepper

1. Bring water to a simmer in the bottom of a vegetable steamer. Add the cabbage to the steamer basket, cover, and steam until it is tender, about 15 minutes.

2. Melt the butter in a small saucepan or skillet over medium heat, and add the caraway seeds. Cook until both the butter and the seeds are golden brown but not blackened, 2 minutes.

3. In a large bowl, toss the cabbage with the caraway butter and salt and pepper to taste. Serve hot or warm.

TUSCAN KALE WITH RAISINS

SERVES 4 TO 6 AS A SIDE DISH

¼ cup raisins

½ cup Marsala wine or medium or cream sherry (not dry sherry)

¼ cup pine nuts or slivered almonds

¼ cup olive oil

1 clove garlic, peeled and finely chopped

8 ounces young Tuscan kale leaves, stemmed and chopped (about 8 cups)

Salt and freshly ground black pepper

There's a classic Catalan dish that combines the silky texture of spinach with wine-soaked raisins and toasted nuts. This version uses young Tuscan kale instead. Kale requires more cooking than spinach does, but with the tender Tuscan type, a fairly brief steaming does the trick. For best results, use the smaller leaves toward the center of the plant. We love this alongside salmon and baked potatoes.

1. Combine the raisins and the wine in a small saucepan and simmer over low heat until most of the liquid has evaporated, about 5 minutes. Set aside.

2. Toast the pine nuts in a small dry skillet over very low heat, stirring constantly, until they are fragrant and pale tan but not browned, 3 to 5 minutes. Watch them carefully because pine nuts burn very quickly. Remove the nuts from the skillet and set them aside.

3. Pour the olive oil into the skillet, add the garlic, and stir over low heat until the garlic has cooked slightly without browning, 2 minutes. Set aside.

4. Bring water to a simmer in the bottom of a vegetable steamer. Add the kale to the steamer basket, cover, and steam until it is tender, about 5 minutes.

5. Combine the kale, reserved raisins and pine nuts, and the garlic olive oil in a warmed bowl, and mix. Season with salt and pepper to taste, and serve hot or warm.

CREAMED SPINACH

SERVES 4 AS A SIDE DISH

There are various ways to make spinach creamy—the traditional steakhouse method is to boil it, drain it, and add a gooey, floury cream sauce. I prefer to cook it in cream and then puree it, so that none of its juices are lost. This concentrates the flavor so that it tastes as if you are eating essence of spinach. Pureed spinach seems luxurious by itself, even with nothing added, but a little cream, onion, and nutmeg is very satisfying. This is a versatile side dish, good with most anything.

1 tablespoon butter

1 medium-size onion, peeled and finely chopped (about ½ cup)

1½ pounds fresh spinach, any large tough stems removed

¾ cup heavy (whipping) cream

Pinch of nutmeg, preferably freshly grated

Salt and freshly ground black pepper, to taste

1. In your largest saucepan or pot, melt the butter over medium-low heat. Add the onion and cook, stirring, until it is soft and translucent, about 5 minutes.

2. Add the spinach, cream, nutmeg, and salt and pepper. Cook, stirring frequently, until the spinach is wilted and tender, 5 to 10 minutes. (It may help to cover the pan for the first 2 minutes or so, to reduce the volume more quickly. If only some of it fits in the pan, keep adding the rest as it cooks down.)

3. Transfer the mixture to a food processor or blender, in two batches if necessary, and puree. Taste, and add more salt if needed. Serve hot. (If the spinach is not to be eaten right away, you can return it to the pan for reheating over low heat.)

SWISS CHARD WITH ONIONS

SERVES 4 GENEROUSLY AS A SIDE DISH

1 large bunch Swiss chard (about 12 ounces)

2 tablespoons olive oil

2 medium-size onions, peeled and fairly finely chopped

2 tablespoons fresh oregano leaves, or 2 teaspoons dried

Salt and freshly ground black pepper, to taste

I often make this with one of the gaudy chard collections such as Bright Lights or Rainbow—each bunch includes stems in a variety of colors that extend on up into the leaves as central ribs. Although some of the pigments fade with cooking, you can still tell they are there. The colors might even coax kids into trying this delightful non-bitter cooking green. It's also fine to use the basic white-ribbed chard, or ones in single colors such as red or gold.

The trick here is to give the thick ribs more cooking time than the green leaves.

1. Cut the chard ribs from the leaves by folding the leaves in half lengthwise and running a sharp knife down the ribs' edges.

2. Slice the ribs on the diagonal into 1-inch pieces. Chop the chard leaves into pieces about 1 inch square.

3. Pour the oil into a large skillet and warm it over medium heat until fragrant, about 30 seconds. Add the chard ribs and the onions, and reduce the heat to low. Cover the skillet and sweat the vegetables, stirring them once or twice, until the stems start to soften, about 4 minutes.

4. Add the chard leaves, oregano, and salt and pepper. Sauté, uncovered, over medium-low heat, stirring frequently, until all the ingredients are tender, about 6 minutes. Serve immediately.

The multicolored chards are as handsome as a row of zinnias.

TURNIP GREENS AND SAUSAGE

SERVES 4

Here's a great way to introduce some healthy greens at the breakfast table, and it takes almost no time at all. Serve the sausage and the greens together on a warm platter, or divide them among individual plates. You might add scrambled eggs on the side, or place a poached egg over each serving of greens. We like it with country-style (bulk) sausage, but it would taste just as good with links.

- 1 pound country-style pork sausage meat
- 1 tablespoon olive oil or sunflower oil
- 8 ounces fresh turnip greens, any long stems removed, leaves coarsely chopped
- Salt and freshly ground black pepper

1. Form the sausage meat into 4 round, flattened patties.

2. Heat the oil in a large skillet over medium-low heat, and cook the sausage patties until they are browned on both sides and no longer pink in the center, about 10 minutes. Transfer the patties to a warmed platter, leaving any fat and drippings in the skillet. Keep the sausage patties warm.

3. Add the turnip greens to the skillet, reduce the heat to low, and cover. Sweat the greens until they have given up some of their moisture, dissolving the flavorful sausage drippings, about 3 minutes. Then uncover the skillet and cook, stirring, for another 2 minutes. Season with salt and pepper to taste, and serve immediately, alongside the sausage.

TRY THIS TOO . . .

✦ Turnip greens have a slightly bitter flavor, which is not unpleasant and is tempered here by the sausage. A squeeze or two of lemon juice, and/or a tablespoon of honey, will mellow them out even more.

✦ Try substituting other strong-flavored greens, such as mustard or broccoli raab.

The greens are as good as the turnip.

Earthy Vegetables

ROOTS, TUBERS, AND ENLARGED STEM BASES are all organs that certain plants use for food storage. As such, they are tasty and nutritious without having to be fresh. Over the years, humans have selected the best specimens of these plants for food, breeding varieties that emphasize richer stores of flesh, better flavor, and even seductive colors. Thus are we blessed with the baking potato, the carrot, the onion, the beet. (For beet recipes, see pages 272 and 298.)

Cooks count on these earthy treasures in times when meat is scarce, or on winter days when greens may be hard to find. No wonder they are the building blocks for soups and stews around the world. And lucky is the gardener who has enough space to grow and store them for winter fare, as well as the curiosity to try less familiar ones such as celery root (celeriac) and sunchokes. Though not a root, winter squash—a champion winter keeper—and cauliflower belong here too.

A collection of stored roots, treasure trove though it is, does not look appealing at first glance. Cached in crates or tubs in the moist dark, these grimy lumps require the cook's strong scrubbing arm and creative touch. But the superior flavor of homegrown root crops is a big reward. Here are a few starring roles they might play in your kitchen—look for more of them throughout the other recipes in this book.

CARROTS WITH HONEY AND ROSEMARY

SERVES 4 AS A SIDE DISH

8 medium-size carrots, scrubbed but not peeled, sliced diagonally into ½-inch-thick rounds (about 2 cups)

2 tablespoons butter

1 tablespoon honey or maple syrup

1 teaspoon minced fresh rosemary leaves

Dash of salt

Freshly ground black pepper

The sweetness in this carrot dish makes it a good complement to salty, rich meats, especially pork and lamb, and the bright color lights up a plate. Its ingredients are often at hand: carrots in the ground, in the root cellar, or in the fridge, and a pot of rosemary outside the kitchen door or near a sunny window.

1. Bring water to a simmer in the bottom of a vegetable steamer. Add the carrots to the steamer basket, cover, and steam until they are easily pierced with a knife, 8 to 10 minutes. Remove from the steamer.

2. Melt the butter in a medium-size skillet over medium heat. Add the honey and rosemary and cook, stirring constantly, until the mixture cooks down to a thickened sauce, about 2 minutes.

3. Add the carrots to the skillet, and stir to reheat them and distribute the sauce. If the steam coming off the carrots makes the sauce runny, keep cooking and stirring until it thickens a bit more and coats the carrots thoroughly.

4. Add the salt and pepper to taste at the very end, and serve immediately.

TRY THIS TOO . . .

If you don't have fresh rosemary, substitute 2 teaspoons finely chopped fresh flat-leaf parsley, adding it at the end.

CARROT AND PARSNIP PUREE

SERVES 4 TO 6

Combining equal amounts of carrot and parsnip results in a puree that has an appetizing pale orange color. The carrots tame the strong parsnip flavor and make it less sweet. This puree is hearty enough to replace a starch dish alongside greens and meat or fish.

1. Pour 4 cups of water into a medium-large saucepan and bring it to a rolling boil.

2. Add the parsnips and carrots, and return to a boil. Then reduce the heat and simmer, uncovered, until the vegetables are fork-tender, 15 to 18 minutes. Drain.

3. Pour the cream into the saucepan, and add ½ cup water (omit the water if you are using half-and-half). Add the nutmeg, thyme, a dash of salt, and pepper to taste. Simmer for about 1 minute to warm the cream.

4. Transfer the vegetables, along with the cream, to a food processor or blender and puree until smooth (or use an immersion blender directly in the pan). Return the puree to the saucepan and reheat, stirring, for 2 minutes. (If you prefer a chunkier, more rustic mash, skip the pureeing and instead mash the vegetables with a hand masher right in the saucepan.) Taste for salt, and add more if needed.

5. Spoon the puree into a warmed shallow bowl and dot it with the butter while it is still hot. Serve immediately.

TRY THIS TOO . . .

For a lighter version, substitute half-and-half for the heavy cream.

- 1 large parsnip (about 1 pound), peeled and cut into thick rounds or coarse chunks
- 5 to 6 medium-size carrots (about 1 pound), scrubbed but not peeled, cut into thick rounds
- ½ cup heavy (whipping) cream
- ¼ teaspoon nutmeg, preferably freshly grated
- 1 teaspoon fresh thyme leaves, or ½ teaspoon dried
- Salt and freshly ground black pepper
- 2 tablespoons butter

Earthy root vegetables perk up when spices are added, such as nutmeg, ginger, and cardamom.

ROASTED CAULIFLOWER GREMOLATA

SERVES 4 TO 6 AS A SIDE DISH

1 to 2 large heads cauliflower, leaves and stems removed but not the core (see Note)

8 tablespoons olive oil

2 tablespoons fresh lemon juice

1 clove garlic, peeled and pressed or finely minced

1 tablespoon capers, drained

Dash of salt

Freshly ground black pepper

2 tablespoons finely chopped fresh flat-leaf parsley leaves

This is a good side dish with just about anything. Sharp flavors and attractive overlapping slices help jazz up a vegetable that might otherwise seem too ordinary for a party. *Gremolata* is the Italian word for a topping made of parsley, garlic, lemon, capers, and olive oil. Add a few minced anchovies as well if you're a fan.

1. Preheat the oven to 400°F.

2. Using a large knife or a cleaver, cut the cauliflower vertically into ½-inch-thick slices.

3. Smear the bottom of a large baking pan with 2 tablespoons of the olive oil. Spread the cauliflower slices in the pan, overlapping them only if necessary. Sprinkle 2 more tablespoons of the oil over them. Roast the cauliflower until the slices have begun to brown on the bottom, 20 to 25 minutes.

4. Flip the cauliflower slices over with a spatula and roast until the other sides have browned slightly, 15 to 18 minutes.

5. Arrange the roasted cauliflower slices in one or two overlapping rows on a warmed platter.

6. In a small glass or cup, combine the remaining 4 tablespoons olive oil with the lemon juice and the garlic. Whisk to combine thoroughly, and then drizzle this over the cauliflower. Sprinkle the capers, salt, pepper to taste, and finally the parsley over the cauliflower. Serve warm or at room temperature, but not cold.

NOTE: Cauliflower heads vary as to size, and as to the size of the solid inner core. Some heads might yield 4 large intact slices, others no more than 2. If presenting perfect slices isn't important to you, go ahead and include all the smaller pieces in the baking pan; otherwise reserve the smaller crumbly bits for another dish, such as Cauliflower with Pine Nuts and Brown Butter (facing page).

TRY THIS TOO . . .

Lemon zest is often used in a gremolata and could be substituted for the lemon juice. Orange zest would also be delicious.

CauLIFLOWER WITH PINe NUTS AnD BROWN BUTTeR

SERVES 4 AS A SIDE DISH

Wonderful as cauliflower is, with its mild cabbage-y flavor, it sometimes needs a little perking up. We love to serve the golden variety described on page 133, but even the usual white kind gets a boost from brown butter and toasted pine nuts. This is good with salmon, with a green salad alongside.

5 tablespoons pine nuts

4 tablespoons (½ stick) butter

1 large head cauliflower, cored and cut into small florets (about 4 cups)

Salt and freshly ground black pepper

2 tablespoons minced fresh flat-leaf parsley leaves

1. Toast the pine nuts in a small dry skillet over very low heat, stirring constantly, until they turn a pale tan color and give off their rich aroma, 3 to 5 minutes. Watch them carefully because pine nuts burn very quickly if they get too hot. Set them aside.

2. To make the brown butter, use a small skillet or saucepan that is not aluminum and does not have a dark bottom, so you can track the changes in the color of the butter. Melt the butter in the skillet over low to medium heat. It will foam and bubble, and the trick is to keep the heat low enough so that it does not overflow the skillet and does not burn while it continues to brown. The milky particles will darken and sink to the bottom, but should not blacken. The butter will turn a golden brown color, with a wonderful rich flavor. Set the brown butter aside in the warm skillet.

3. Bring water to a simmer in the bottom of a vegetable steamer. Add the cauliflower to the steamer basket, cover, and steam until it is just tender when pierced with a knife, about 5 minutes.

4. Place the cauliflower in a warmed bowl and drizzle the brown butter over it. Scatter the toasted pine nuts on top, and season with salt and pepper to taste. Sprinkle with the parsley and serve immediately.

Fresh-picked cauliflower and zucchini.

CELERY ROOT CUTLETS

SERVES 4 AS A SIDE DISH

2 large celery roots
(each at least 1 pound)

¼ cup whole wheat flour

2 large eggs, well beaten

1 cup fine dry bread
crumbs (see Note)

6 tablespoons (¾ stick)
butter

Salt and freshly ground
black pepper

2 tablespoons finely
chopped fresh flat-leaf
parsley leaves

1 lemon, cut into 8 wedges

Although they are filling enough to stand as a main course, we find these butter-fried disks are excellent with a plate of fat sausages and a winter salad. We like the contrast between the crunchy exterior and the tender flesh inside, which has a subtle, artichoke-like flavor.

1. Fill a medium-large saucepan halfway with water and bring it to a boil.

2. While the water is heating, trim, peel, and scrub the celery roots. Before they have a chance to brown, slice them into ½-inch-thick rounds and drop the rounds into the boiling water. (If they must sit a while before cooking, float them in a bowl of cold water to which you have added 1 tablespoon distilled white vinegar.)

3. Reduce the heat to medium-low and simmer the celery root until it

is just tender when pricked gently with the tip of a small knife, 8 to 10 minutes.

4. While the celery root is cooking, prepare three shallow bowls: one containing the flour, one with the eggs, and one with the bread crumbs.

5. Drain the celery root, and while the rounds are still warm, dip each one in the flour to coat both sides, then in the egg, and then in the crumbs. Set them aside in a single layer on a large plate or sheet of wax paper.

6. Melt the butter in a large skillet over medium heat. When the foam subsides, use a spatula to gently place the breaded rounds in the skillet. (Do this in two batches if needed. I sometimes use two cast-iron skillets.) Sauté them on both sides until golden brown, 5 to 7 minutes per side. As you remove each round, set it on a warmed platter.

Try these Celery Root Cutlets as an appetizer with a garlicky mayonnaise.

7. Season the celery root cutlets with salt and pepper to taste, and sprinkle with the parsley. Then garnish with the lemon wedges, to squeeze at the table.

NOTE: To make dry bread crumbs, toast bread slices on both sides, cut off the crusts, and whir the toast in a blender until fine-textured.

TRY THIS TOO . . .

These disks are also tasty as an appetizer, served with the garlicky mayonnaise on page 325. Either pass the dressing in a sauceboat or spoon it next to 2 disks on each small plate.

KOHLRABI AND PARSLEY PUREE

SERVES 4 AS A SIDE DISH

Kohlrabi, delicious to nibble on as a crudité, has a mild flavor in this recipe. The parsley adds color as well as flavor. We think it's a pleasant change from mashed potatoes as a side dish with meat or fish.

1. Bring water to a simmer in the bottom of a vegetable steamer. Add the kohlrabi and the garlic cloves to the steamer basket, and steam until both are very tender, 30 minutes. Remove from the steamer.

2. Place the garlic cloves on a cutting board, sprinkle with a dash of salt, and using the tip of a knife, mash and smear them together to form a paste.

3. Combine the steamed kohlrabi, garlic paste, cream, parsley, nutmeg, and salt and pepper to taste in a medium-size saucepan. Simmer, stirring, over low heat to heat the cream and cook the parsley, 3 minutes.

4. Transfer the mixture to a food processor or food mill, and puree it. Return it to the saucepan and stir over low heat until it is thoroughly reheated. Swirl in the butter, add pepper to taste, and serve.

4 medium-size kohlrabi (about 2 pounds total), trimmed, peeled, and cut into ½-inch-thick slices

2 large cloves garlic, peeled and left whole

Salt

½ cup heavy (whipping) cream

1 cup (packed) fresh flat-leaf parsley leaves

Pinch of nutmeg, preferably freshly grated

Freshly ground black pepper

3 tablespoons butter, at room temperature

Baked Leeks

SERVES 4 AS A SIDE DISH, 6 AS A GARNISH

4 cups (packed) coarsely chopped cleaned leeks (white part only; see Note)

¼ teaspoon fennel seeds, or a dash fennel pollen (optional)

½ teaspoon fresh thyme leaves, or ¼ teaspoon dried

Freshly ground black pepper, to taste

¼ cup chicken stock (see page 289)

2 tablespoons butter

Salt, to taste

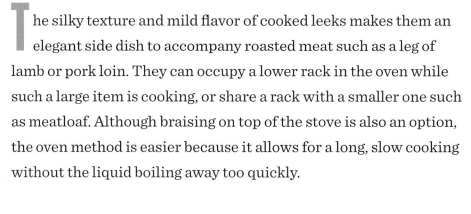

The silky texture and mild flavor of cooked leeks makes them an elegant side dish to accompany roasted meat such as a leg of lamb or pork loin. They can occupy a lower rack in the oven while such a large item is cooking, or share a rack with a smaller one such as meatloaf. Although braising on top of the stove is also an option, the oven method is easier because it allows for a long, slow cooking without the liquid boiling away too quickly.

1. Preheat the oven to 350°F. (If the oven is at a higher temperature to accommodate another dish, that is fine, but pay close attention to the leeks as they cook and be prepared to add a small amount of water to prevent them from scorching.)

2. Combine the leeks, fennel seeds if using, thyme, and pepper in a medium bowl, and toss. Transfer the leeks to a shallow baking dish. (Or toss the mixture in the dish itself if there is room.) Pour the chicken stock over the leeks, dot them with the butter, and sprinkle with a dash of salt.

3. Bake, uncovered, stirring the leeks from time to time so the tops don't dry out, until they are very soft, silky, and tender when pierced with a knife, 45 to 50 minutes. The leeks cook in a tiny amount of stock, so most of the liquid will have cooked away, leaving juices with a syrupy consistency. If not, cook a bit longer to reduce the liquid.

4. Taste for salt: If the chicken stock has been made with salt, you might not need any more. Serve hot or warm.

NOTE: Leeks vary greatly in size, not only in thickness but also in the length of the white shank. You will probably need about 6 medium-size leeks here. To clean leeks, slice them in half lengthwise and then hold them under cold running water, spreading the layers open to rinse away any soil.

CREAMED LEEKS ON TOAST

SERVES 4, OR 2 HUNGRY DINERS

This is one of our favorite light suppers—but it's equally appropriate at breakfast, lunch, or brunch. It involves a simple sauce of cream thickened with lemon and seasoned with nutmeg and thyme. Serve it with a bowl of apples.

1. Place the leeks in a medium-size skillet, add 1 cup of water and the salt, and bring to a simmer over high heat. Then reduce the heat to low and simmer, uncovered, until tender, about 12 minutes.

2. While the leeks are cooking, remove any hard crusts from the bread and lightly toast the slices. Set each slice on a warmed plate in a warm spot.

3. Using a slotted spoon, transfer the leeks to a strainer that you are holding over the skillet. Press on the leeks to extract some of the liquid, letting the liquid return to the skillet. Set the leeks aside in a bowl.

4. Raise the heat under the skillet and boil the liquid, stirring it frequently, until it has reduced to about 2 tablespoons, 10 to 12 minutes.

5. Remove the skillet from the heat and stir in the cream, nutmeg, and thyme.

Then return it to medium heat and cook at a low boil, stirring continuously, until the cream thickens, 5 minutes.

6. Reduce the heat slightly, drizzle in the lemon juice, and cook, stirring, until the sauce has reduced to the consistency of a medium-thick gravy, about 2 minutes.

7. Return the leeks to the skillet and stir them into the sauce. Reheat, stirring, for 1 to 2 minutes. Spoon the leeks and sauce over the pieces of toast. Grind black pepper to taste over them, sprinkle with the parsley, and serve immediately.

TRY THIS TOO . . .

We change the vegetable in this dish according to the season. In spring it might be asparagus, in early summer snow peas, then broccoli or cauliflower. Leeks are the mainstay for the winter months. A firm vegetable is preferable to a cooked leafy green, which would thin out the sauce.

2 medium-size leeks (white and pale green parts only), cleaned (see Note, facing page) and cut crosswise into 1-inch pieces

Dash of salt

4 slices hearty bread with a loose, open texture, cut about ½ inch thick

1 cup heavy (whipping) cream

Dash of nutmeg, preferably freshly grated

1 teaspoon fresh thyme leaves, or ½ teaspoon dried

Juice of ½ lemon (about 2 tablespoons)

Freshly ground black pepper

1 tablespoon finely chopped fresh flat-leaf parsley leaves

SKILLET POTATOES WITH ROSEMARY

SERVES 2 TO 4 AS A SIDE DISH

2 large baking potatoes, scrubbed but not peeled

4 tablespoons (½ stick) butter

1 teaspoon finely chopped fresh rosemary leaves

Coarse sea salt and freshly ground black pepper

This is one of our favorite dishes for a weekend breakfast. Covering the potatoes tightly while they cook allows them to absorb the flavor of the butter and to retain enough moisture to soften while the bottom becomes caramelized and crisp. Great with poached eggs on cinnamon-raisin toast.

1. Slice the potatoes into ⅛-inch-thick rounds.

2. Melt 2 tablespoons of the butter in a medium-size skillet, preferably one with a tight-fitting lid, over medium-low heat.

3. Remove the skillet from the heat, and starting at the center, arrange half of the potato slices in overlapping circles to form a rosette. Sprinkle with ½ teaspoon of the rosemary, and season lightly with salt and pepper.

4. Make a second rosette on top of the first with the remaining potato slices. Sprinkle lightly with salt and pepper. Add the remaining rosemary, and dot with the remaining 2 tablespoons butter.

5. Cover the skillet and cook very slowly, on a wide burner if possible, over low heat until the potatoes are soft when poked with a knife, 20 to 30 minutes. Watch carefully: You want the bottom to turn golden brown and smell buttery but not burn.

6. Remove the skillet from the heat and loosen the potatoes at the edges with a spatula. If you're feeling adventurous, try flipping your creation: Invert a large plate over the skillet, and using pot holders or oven mitts to hold them together tightly, flip them over so the potatoes land in the plate with their browned side up. On the other hand, if you're just plain hungry and ready to eat, simply cut the potatoes into wedges, right in the skillet, and then flip them brown-side-up as you serve them. Still elegant, still delicious.

TRY THIS TOO . . .

This is also good with fresh sage or thyme substituted for the rosemary. And if you like, you can add a finely chopped clove of garlic between the two layers.

POTATO AND KALE CASSEROLE

SERVES 4 AS A MAIN DISH, 6 AS A SIDE DISH

Although similar to scalloped potatoes, this casserole has enough vegetables in it to be a complete meal. We like it on fall or winter evenings, along with a bowl of raw sweet, crisp winter carrots.

1. Preheat the oven to 400°F.

2. Spread half of the potatoes over the bottom of a 9 by 13-inch baking dish, overlapping them. Grind pepper over them generously. Distribute half of the feta over the potatoes. Slowly pour ¾ cup of the cream over the top. Sprinkle with half of the scallions, half of the parsley, and half of the kale.

3. Repeat the layers: the rest of the potatoes, a grinding of pepper, and the rest of the feta, cream, scallions, parsley, and kale.

4. Sprinkle the Parmesan cheese uniformly over the top.

5. Cover the baking dish loosely with aluminum foil or parchment paper (so steam can escape), and bake for 30 minutes.

6. Remove the foil and bake until the Parmesan is lightly browned and most of the cream has been absorbed and does not run into a corner when the dish is tilted, 5 to 10 minutes. Let the dish cool for 5 minutes before serving.

TRY THIS TOO . . .

This is also good made with sharp Cheddar and/or Gruyère.

---

8 small potatoes (any type), unpeeled, sliced into thin rounds (about 4 cups)

Freshly ground black pepper

5 ounces feta cheese, chopped or crumbled

1½ cups heavy (whipping) cream

10 scallions (white and green parts), chopped (about ⅔ cup)

12 sprigs flat-leaf parsley (leaves and upper stems), coarsely chopped (about ½ packed cup)

8 small to medium-size Tuscan kale leaves, ribs removed, leaves coarsely chopped (about 1¼ loosely packed cups)

3 ounces Parmesan cheese, preferably Parmigiano-Reggiano, finely grated (⅓ cup)

POTATO and CeLeRY ROOT MaSH WITH BROWN BUTTER

SERVES 4 TO 6 AS A SIDE DISH

1 large celery root
(1 pound)

4 medium-size baking
potatoes

5 tablespoons butter

1 medium-size onion,
peeled and finely
chopped

1¼ cups heavy (whipping)
cream

1 large bay leaf,
preferably fresh

1 teaspoon fresh thyme
leaves, or ½ teaspoon
dried

Salt and freshly ground
black pepper

1 tablespoon chopped
fresh flat-leaf parsley
leaves

Potatoes and celery root are a natural match. They are combined at proportions of about two to one in this recipe, but use equal amounts if you want an even more pronounced celery flavor. For a hearty winter meal, serve this mash with some cool-weather greens (in a salad or cooked) and a few fat sausages.

1. Fill a medium-large saucepan halfway with water, and bring it to a boil over high heat.

2. While the water is heating, trim and peel the celery root, removing all brown parts and cutting off whatever remains of the leafy top. Scrub it clean, and then cut it into 1-inch chunks.

3. Scrub the potatoes but do not peel them. (The puree would be more elegant, but less nutritious, without the potato skins.) Cut them into 1-inch chunks.

4. Add the celery root and potatoes to the boiling water and return it to a boil. Then reduce the heat to a brisk simmer and cook, partially covered, until both vegetables feel soft when pricked with a fork, 15 to 20 minutes. Drain and set aside.

5. Rinse and dry the pan, and then put it back over low heat. Add 2 tablespoons of the butter, and when it has melted, add the chopped onion. Cook, stirring, until the onion is soft and translucent, about 10 minutes.

6. Add the cream, bay leaf, and thyme. Simmer very slowly so the herbs will steep in the cream and flavor it, about 5 minutes. Then remove and discard the bay leaf.

7. Add the potatoes and celery root to the cream mixture and stir for several minutes to combine and reheat. Mash with a hand potato masher or an immersion blender right in the pan. (Resist the urge to use a ricer, which works for potatoes but turns celery root into a grainy mess.) Add salt to taste, and then set the pan aside, covered.

8. Place the remaining 3 tablespoons butter in a small non-aluminum pan that does not have a dark bottom (so that you can track the changes in color), and melt it over medium-low heat. It will bubble and foam, so watch it and turn the heat down if it seems about to boil over. The milky particles will darken and sink to the bottom, but should not blacken. The butter will turn a slightly brown color, with a wonderful rich flavor.

9. Spoon the mashed mixture into a warmed shallow bowl, making a shallow pattern of swirls or ridges on top. Pour the brown butter over the top, so that it collects in the hollows. Grind black pepper to taste over the top, sprinkle with the parsley, and serve hot.

Celery root is the enlarged stem base of a certain type of celery.

ROASTED SWEET POTATOES WITH ONIONS AND BACON

SERVES 4 TO 6 AS A SIDE DISH

In fall or winter, this hearty roasted fare might accompany a main course you are preparing on the stovetop, such as lamb chops. If the oven is occupied by a large cut of beef, just add these ingredients to the same pan. They would also go well with venison.

4 ounces slab bacon, cut into small cubes (½ cup)

4 medium-size sweet potatoes (about 2 pounds total), peeled and cut into 1½-inch chunks

4 medium-size onions, peeled and quartered

2 tablespoons olive oil

2 cloves garlic, peeled and finely chopped

10 large fresh sage leaves, coarsely chopped

1 tablespoon coarsely chopped fresh flat-leaf parsley leaves

Salt and freshly ground black pepper

1. Preheat the oven to 350°F.

2. While the oven is heating, sauté the bacon cubes in a small skillet over medium-low heat until they render some of their fat, about 2 minutes. Using a slotted spoon, transfer the bacon to a plate and set it aside.

3. Pour the bacon fat into a roasting pan or baking dish that is large enough to easily hold the sweet potatoes and onions in one layer. Add the sweet potatoes, onions, and oil, and stir thoroughly to coat the vegetables with the oil. Roast for 40 minutes, stirring the vegetables occasionally.

4. Add the bacon, garlic, and sage, and roast for another 30 to 40 minutes, continuing to stir occasionally.

5. Add the parsley, season with salt and pepper to taste, mix thoroughly, and serve.

BAKED SPAGHETTI SQUASH WITH CHEESE

SERVES 4, OR 6 AS A SIDE DISH

In my view, spaghetti squash is an underused and often misunderstood vegetable. It's quite a wonderful thing: The tendency toward stringiness, characteristic of some hard-fleshed squash, has somehow been turned into an asset. The result is an interior that, when cooked, breaks into delicious spaghetti-like strands.

But I think the analogy with spaghetti can be taken too far. This might look like vermicelli, but it is distinctively vegetal—tender, with a bit of a crunch, and just slightly sweet. To me it does not call out for an aggressive red sauce, and the idea of pawning it off on your child as pasta insults his or her intelligence. I'm usually satisfied with just butter (lots of it) and salt and pepper, but the treatment here is a special-occasion departure with, I admit, a little Northern Italian influence. Serving it directly from the squash skins makes a fun and unusual presentation, but if you prefer, you can scoop the flesh out of the skin and serve it in a warmed shallow bowl or baking dish.

A spaghetti squash is ripe for use when it has turned slightly golden in color.

1. Preheat the oven to 350°F.

2. Place the squash on a cutting board, and with a large heavy knife or a cleaver, cut it cleanly in half lengthwise. Remove just the seeds by scraping them out with a spoon, leaving all the stringy flesh in place.

3. Sprinkle the olive oil over the bottom of a rimmed baking sheet. Place both squash halves on the baking sheet, cut side down, and slide them around to coat their cut surfaces with the oil. Bake until tender, 45 to 50 minutes—but start testing for tenderness after 30 minutes by flipping the squash over and poking it with the tip of a knife or a skewer, to see if it has softened inside. Some spaghetti squash cook faster than others, and if left in the oven too long they can turn watery.

4. Remove the baking sheet from the oven but leave the oven on. Set the squash halves cut side up on the baking sheet, and loosen the flesh by running a large spoon very gently just inside the skins, trying not to tear them. Then pry up and fluff the flesh lightly with a fork to separate it into strands, leaving the strands in the squash shells.

1 ripe spaghetti squash (2 to 2½ pounds)

2 tablespoons olive oil

4 tablespoons (½ stick) unsalted butter

2 cloves garlic, peeled and pressed

4 teaspoons very finely minced fresh sage leaves

Coarse sea salt, to taste

Freshly ground black pepper, to taste

⅔ cup finely grated Parmesan cheese, preferably Parmigiano-Reggiano

5. Melt the butter in a small saucepan over medium-low heat. Add the garlic and cook until it has browned slightly, 1 to 2 minutes.

6. Pour the butter and garlic over both squash halves. Then add the sage, salt, and pepper. Stir gently to mix. Sprinkle the cheese over the top of both halves, and return the baking sheet to the oven. Bake until the cheese has melted, 5 minutes.

7. Using two large spoons, or a spoon and a spatula, gently lift the squash onto a platter. Serve hot or warm, scooping the strands out of the skins.

BUTTERNUT SQUASH ROUNDS

SERVES 4

The long, straight necks of butternut squash are perfect for slicing into uniform rounds, shaped like hockey pucks. (The globe-shaped end of the squash can be used also, but since it has a hollow cavity, the slices will look more like a ring-toss game than hockey.) If you have grown butternuts of varying sizes, choose the smaller ones so they will fit a little more neatly on the plate.

This is a very simple recipe in which roasting the squash concentrates its flavor and natural sweetness. A complement to meat dishes, especially pork, it can take the place of a starch such as potatoes or rice, when served along with a green vegetable such as spinach. Place several on each person's plate or line them up on a platter.

The rounds can also be fried in butter in a skillet, but that is time-consuming if you're serving more than two people, and the oven route frees you up for other jobs.

1. Preheat the oven to 400°F.

2. Using a large heavy knife or a cleaver, slice the squash into rounds a little less than ½ inch thick. Lay them flat on a cutting board and chop off the tough peel on each one. (You'll find this is easier than trying to peel the squash whole.)

3. Put a large rimmed baking sheet in the hot oven for about 3 minutes. Then remove it and melt the butter on it.

4. Arrange the squash rounds on the baking sheet, rubbing each side in the hot butter. Roast for about 15 minutes.

5. Flip the rounds over with a spatula, and roast until they are soft inside and slightly browned and crisp on the outside, about 15 minutes. Sprinkle them with salt to taste, and serve hot or warm.

2 butternut squash necks
   (each about 1 pound)
3 tablespoons butter
Salt

Baking Butternut Squash

CUTTING. Winter squash can be hard to cut. Pounding the back of a cleaver with a rubber mallet does the trick.

SLICING AND TRIMMING. Use your cleaver, or a heavy knife, to trim the skin of the slices.

BAKING. Bake on a buttered sheet until softened and slightly browned.

ROASTED SUNCHOKES

SERVES 4 TO 6

2 pounds sunchokes, scrubbed but not peeled

3 tablespoons olive oil

1 teaspoon coarse sea salt

Freshly ground black pepper, to taste

1 whole head of garlic, cloves separated but not peeled

1 tablespoon finely chopped fresh rosemary or sage leaves (see Note)

I was skeptical about these strange, knobby little tubers (also known as Jerusalem artichokes) until I was served them roasted. Now they are a favorite. There is no need to peel them as long as you scrub them very clean with a stiff kitchen brush. Roasting at a fairly high heat makes them puff up, with a crisp exterior and a soft interior with a wonderful sweet, nutty flavor. Try these surrounding the Meat Loaf with Vegetables (page 413).

1. Preheat the oven to 400°F.

2. Combine the sunchokes, olive oil, salt, and pepper in a large baking dish and toss until the sunchokes are thoroughly coated. Roast for 30 minutes.

3. Remove the baking dish from the oven, turn the sunchokes over, and add the garlic cloves to the dish. Return it to the oven and roast until the outsides of the sunchokes are brown but not charred and they are soft inside when pricked with the tip of a knife, about 30 minutes.

4. Remove the baking dish from the oven and squeeze the garlic cloves out of their papery coverings. Toss the garlic, sunchokes, and rosemary together in a serving bowl, and serve hot or warm.

NOTE: If neither rosemary nor sage is available fresh, substitute 1 teaspoon dried thyme, adding it when you turn the sunchokes over halfway through the cooking time.

BABY TURNIPS WITH HONEY AND MINT

SERVES 4 TO 6

These white mini golf balls are so mild-tasting that people are often surprised to hear they are eating turnips. Look for one of the Japanese varieties such as Hakurei, and harvest them in spring or fall when they are no more than 2 inches in diameter. One inch is even better. This recipe is one of my favorite ways to serve them as a side dish, but they would also be delicious as a garnish surrounding a pork roast.

When harvesting turnips for this dish, cut off the green tops, leaving a half-inch tuft of green stem. This is more colorful, and celebrates how fresh the turnips are. If you have pulled ones of varying sizes, use small ones for this recipe and leave the large ones for another dish. You can cut the larger ones in halves or quarters, but small ones cooked whole will lose less of their juices.

3 tablespoons butter

About 30 baby white turnips, preferably about 1 inch in diameter

2½ tablespoons honey

¼ cup finely chopped fresh mint leaves

Salt and freshly ground black pepper

1. Melt the butter in a large skillet over medium heat until the foam subsides, about 2 minutes.

2. Add the turnips. (If including all of them would crowd the skillet, cook them in two batches to keep them from steaming.) Reduce the heat to low, cover the skillet, and cook, stirring the turnips every minute or two so they brown uniformly. They should be lightly browned and just barely tender when pricked with the tip of a knife, 10 to 20 minutes depending on their size. Using a slotted spoon, transfer the turnips to a warmed serving bowl.

3. Add the honey and mint to the skillet, and stir rapidly with a spatula, scraping up any brown bits. If the turnips have given up more than a tablespoon of liquid, boil it down over medium heat to reduce it to a thickened syrup.

4. Pour the sauce over the turnips, and stir briefly to coat them well. Season with salt and pepper to taste, and serve immediately.

Red Thai Curry with Fall Vegetables

SERVES 4 AS A MAIN DISH, OR 4 TO 6 IF SERVED OVER RICE OR AS A SIDE DISH

2 cans (each 14 ounces) unsweetened coconut milk (see Notes)

1 tablespoon red curry paste (see Notes)

1 tablespoon ground turmeric

1 tablespoon mild paprika

2 large sweet potatoes (about 1 pound total), peeled and cut into 1-inch chunks

4 medium-size onions, peeled and quartered

½ head cauliflower, cut into 1-inch florets (2½ cups)

Salt, to taste

3 scallions (green parts only), chopped

Thai hot sauce or Tabasco sauce, for serving (optional)

Making a Thai curry is a great way to feature the season's best vegetables. If you always keep coconut milk and Thai curry paste on hand, you can combine just about any fresh vegetables in a main dish that takes less than an hour. The terms "red curry" and "green curry" are not always an indication of the color of the final dish—they simply represent the color of the hot chiles the curry paste is made from. (And unless you have an asbestos palate, this is a small amount, whether red or green.) When making a red curry, I like to add mild paprika, turmeric, and at least one red or orange vegetable to heat it up visually, but you can also turn up the burn with more curry paste if your diners like it that way. I usually pass hot sauce at the table in an effort to please all.

This curry can be served on top of rice, can stand alone as a rich stew, or can be served as a side dish with grilled seafood or meat.

1. Shake 1 can of the coconut milk vigorously, open it, and pour 1 cup of the coconut milk into a large saucepan. Stir over medium heat until it has thickened slightly, 3 minutes.

2. Gradually add the red curry paste, turmeric, and paprika, stirring constantly with a spatula or whisk. Reduce the heat and simmer, stirring, for 3 minutes.

3. Shake the remaining can of coconut milk, open it, and add it along with the remainder in the first can. Stir in the sweet potatoes and the onions. Cook over medium-low heat, stirring frequently, for 15 minutes.

4. Add the cauliflower and cook until all the vegetables are tender and the sauce has thickened, 15 minutes. Season with salt.

5. Sprinkle the scallions over the top, and pass the hot sauce at the table.

NOTES:

✦ Coconut milk, usually sold in 13½- or 14-ounce cans, is very perishable once the can is opened, but an opened can can be stored in the refrigerator for a few days.

✦ You can use "light" coconut milk here, but the sauce won't be quite as thick and flavorful.

✦ Some Thai curry pastes come in glass jars, some in cans. Both will keep for several months after opening if refrigerated. When using the canned type, remove any unused paste and refrigerate it in a sealed glass container.

TRY THIS TOO . . .

Virtually any vegetable can be included in a curry. This fall-to-winter version might also be made with winter squash, broccoli, Swiss chard (both stem and leaf), and turnips. In summer we like to combine red bell peppers, plum tomatoes, eggplant, and yellow summer squash.

In summer we like to combine red bell peppers, plum tomatoes, eggplant, and yellow summer squash, but virtually any vegetable can be included in a curry.

ROOT VEGETABLE RIBBONS

SERVES 4 TO 6 AS A SIDE DISH

This looks almost like a pasta dish, with vegetables in long fettucine-like strands. (To grow leeks with a long white shank, see page 141.) It is a rather sweet mixture, thanks to the parsnips and to the fact that all the vegetables caramelize a bit as they cook down. Serve it as an accompaniment to a rich meat dish such as roast pork or beef brisket.

1. Slice the leeks lengthwise into narrow strips, and set them aside.

2. Cut the top inch off the carrots. Then, holding the tip, slice each one into ribbons with a vegetable peeler, moving from the narrow bottom to the top. Discard the core if it is pale in color.

3. Trim the top inch off the parsnips, and holding the tip, slice each one into ribbons with a vegetable peeler, turning as you go to get ribbons of even width.

4. Heat the olive oil and the butter in a large skillet over medium-low heat. Add the leeks, carrots, and parsnips, and season with salt and pepper. Cover the skillet and cook slowly, stirring the vegetables every 5 minutes or so to caramelize them evenly and prevent them from sticking, until they are soft, golden-brown in places, and reduced in volume. This should take about 25 minutes, but stop sooner if they get too brown.

5. Sprinkle with the parsley and serve hot or warm.

NOTE: To clean leeks, slice them in half lengthwise and then hold them under cold running water, spreading the layers open to rinse away any soil.

TRY THIS TOO . . .

For a daintier version, use the fine setting on a mandoline to create tangled nests of veggies rather than long strands. These will take less time to cook.

---

4 medium-size leeks, white parts only, cleaned (see Note)

6 medium-size carrots, peeled if necessary

2 medium-size parsnips, scrubbed, and peeled if rough-skinned or blemished

2 tablespoons olive oil

2 tablespoons butter

Salt and freshly ground black pepper, to taste

2 tablespoons finely chopped fresh flat-leaf parsley leaves

LAMB SHANKS WITH EARLY ROOT VEGETABLES | PAGE 418

Meat and Seafood Dishes

MEAT, RAISED BY US OR BY NEIGHBORING FARMERS in ways we consider humane, is a part of our family's diet. It's healthy for us and ecologically sound. Since we live near the ocean, we eat a good deal of seafood as well. Often meat and fish figure as ingredients in a dish rather than as stand-alone elements. Combined with produce from the garden, animal protein might be a major player, as in the Provençal Pot Roast on page 410, an equal one, as in the Shepherd's Pie on page 416, or a minor one, as with the Roasted Sweet Potatoes with Onions and Bacon on page 397 where the bacon merely lends a little richness and flavor.

Our use of meat is different from that in most households, in that we start with a whole, half, or quarter of an animal, freeze it, and make use of nearly all its edible parts—not just the chops, steaks, and roasts. There is nothing inherently superior about buying meat this way, but it has taught me to cook with it more creatively and economically. I've come to enjoy, and even prefer, the "lesser" cuts that may require more cooking but usually have the most flavor. We're big on stews, braises, meaty soups, and casseroles or rice dishes with varying amounts of meat or fish added—historically the diet of a well-fed peasant. And it's garden vegetables that give this hearty fare a good deal of its flavor, whether it's the storage roots that form the bedrock of stews the world over or the fresher, more delicate vegetables in the Springtime Fish Chowder with Fresh Herbs on page 430. Even if money were no object, I wouldn't cook any other way.

Our diet is that of the well-fed peasant.
Even if money were no object,
I wouldn't cook any other way.

PROVENçAL POT ROAST

SERVES 4 TO 6

Most long-simmered meat dishes are cold-weather dishes, but this one has summery flavors. Make it on a rainy day, or during the cooler morning or evening hours in the summertime. I've found that this pot roast reheats well and freezes well, which is good, because it is best made in quantity. Serve it with a bowl of steamed fresh-dug red-skinned potatoes, sprinkled with parsley. If you don't have good, flavorful potatoes, use noodles or rice.

1. Position a rack in the center of the oven and preheat the oven to 325°F.

2. Meanwhile, cook the bacon, stirring it constantly with a spatula, in your largest skillet over medium heat until it is just crisp, about 5 minutes. Remove it with a slotted spoon and set it aside in a cup or bowl, leaving the fat in the skillet.

3. Pat the beef dry with a paper towel. Add 2 tablespoons of the olive oil to the bacon fat in the skillet over medium-high heat, and when it is hot, add the chuck roast. Sear the beef, browning it thoroughly on all sides, about 7 minutes per side. Sprinkle it with salt and pepper to taste.

4. Transfer the roast to a flameproof casserole or Dutch oven that is large enough to hold it with a bit of room to spare. Retain the fat in the skillet.

5. Place the casserole over medium-low heat and warm it for a minute or two. Remove the casserole from the heat and away from anything flammable. Then pour the cognac over the meat and carefully ignite it with a wooden kitchen match. (If this job makes you uncomfortable, leave the cognac unlit.) When the flame has burned out, set the casserole aside.

6. Add the onions and carrots to the skillet and, if needed, add the remaining 1 tablespoon oil. Sauté, stirring frequently, until the vegetables are browned, taking care not to burn them, about 10 minutes.

7. Pour the wine over the roast. Then add the onions and carrots, thyme sprig, bay leaves, orange zest, anchovies, and garlic, stirring them all into the wine. Bring to a simmer over medium-low heat.

8. Tightly cover the casserole with a lid or with aluminum foil, transfer it to the oven, and cook until the meat is very tender, about 3 hours. Check from time to time and add a little water if needed to keep a scant amount of liquid in the pot.

9. Take the casserole out of the oven, and using a fork and tongs, transfer the roast to a cutting board or carving platter.

10. Tilt the casserole over a large strainer or colander set over a bowl, and using a large spatula, scrape all the contents into the strainer. Mash the vegetables against the strainer with the back of a large spoon to extract as much liquid as possible. Remove the strainer. Skim off most of the fat with a spoon, and then pour the strained liquid back into the casserole.

11. Add the bacon, tomato puree, and olives to the casserole, stirring to combine. If the gravy is very thin, reduce it over medium heat until slightly thickened. If it is too thick, add a little water. There should be 1½ to 2 cups of liquid. Taste, and add salt and pepper if needed.

4 ounces slab bacon or salt pork, cut into ¼-inch cubes

1 beef chuck roast, preferably bone-in (3 to 4 pounds)

3 tablespoons olive oil

Salt and freshly ground black pepper

2 tablespoons cognac or brandy

2 medium-size onions, peeled and quartered

2 medium-size carrots, scrubbed but not peeled, cut into 2-inch lengths

2 cups dry white wine

1 large fresh thyme sprig

2 bay leaves

Grated zest of 1 medium-size orange (about 1 tablespoon)

2 canned anchovy fillets, very finely minced, or 1 teaspoon anchovy paste

2 large cloves garlic, pressed or minced

1 cup tomato puree

½ cup small, strongly flavored, pitted and halved olives, either black or green

2 cups cherry tomatoes, preferably small ones

1 tablespoon finely chopped fresh basil leaves

12. Use a large sharp knife to slice the beef on the diagonal, making ½-inch-thick slices. Lay them in the gravy in the casserole. Cover and set aside.

13. Fill a medium-size saucepan halfway with water and bring it to a slow boil. Drop in the cherry tomatoes and cook for 15 seconds. Drain the tomatoes, and use a sharp paring knife to pierce the skins and slip them off, taking care to keep the tomatoes whole.

14. When you are ready to serve the pot roast, place the casserole over medium heat and bring the liquid to a simmer. Then reduce the heat to low and cook, basting the meat until the slices are heated through, about 5 minutes.

15. Arrange the meat slices in the center of a warmed platter and pour the gravy over them. Scatter the tomatoes over all, and then sprinkle with the basil. Serve hot or warm.

MEAT LOAF WITH VEGETABLES

SERVES 4 TO 6

Ample bread crumbs and vegetables keep this meat loaf moist and light. With a green salad alone, it could be a well-rounded meal, but add mashed potatoes if you're extra-hungry for comfort food.

I'm always glad when there is meat loaf left over, because it is equally fine the next day, reheated. And sliced about 1/2-inch thick, it's great in sandwiches, either warmed or at room temperature, with mayonnaise or aioli and lettuce from the garden.

1. Preheat the oven to 350°F.

2. While the oven is heating, melt the butter in a medium-size skillet over low heat. Add the onion, carrots, and celery, and sauté, stirring occasionally, until the vegetables are soft but not browned, about 15 minutes. Add a little water to the pan if the vegetables look dry before the carrots have softened.

3. Place the meat and the sautéed vegetables in a large bowl. Add the bread crumbs, beaten egg, thyme, parsley, nutmeg, salt, and pepper. Using your hands (best!) or a large wooden spoon, mix the ingredients together thoroughly.

4. Gather the mixture into a ball and press it firmly into a standard loaf pan or another deep baking dish. Bake for 1 hour.

2 tablespoons butter

1 medium-size onion, very finely chopped (1 cup)

2 medium-size carrots, scrubbed but not peeled, very finely chopped (1 cup)

3 ribs celery, very finely chopped (½ cup)

2 pounds lean ground beef, at room temperature

1¾ cups coarse dry whole-grain bread crumbs (see Note)

1 large egg, well beaten, at room temperature

1 teaspoon fresh thyme leaves, or ½ teaspoon dried

½ cup finely chopped fresh flat-leaf parsley leaves

½ teaspoon nutmeg, preferably freshly grated

½ teaspoon salt

Freshly ground black pepper, to taste

To feed more people, I double this recipe and cook the meat loaf in a Bundt pan. Unmolded, it is easy for guests to slice at a buffet.

5. Let the meat loaf rest for a few minutes. Then unmold it onto a warmed serving dish, slice it, and arrange the slices in an overlapping pattern. (If the meat loaf sticks in the pan, it can be sliced in the pan and removed with a spatula, piece by piece.)

NOTE: Homemade dry bread crumbs can be made by toasting slices of bread, removing the crusts, and pulsing the bread in a food processor until the crumbs have the texture you want.

TRY THIS TOO . . .

Traditional meatloaf is often made with a combination of beef, veal, and pork, which is not easy to have on hand. To impart some pork flavor, try laying half-strips of bacon on top of the meatloaf before baking it. After an hour the bacon will be crisp and the fat will have permeated the loaf. If you use bacon, reduce the amount of salt by half.

PORK AND VEGETABLE STEW WITH COCONUT MILK

SERVES 4

2 pounds pork rump steaks, country-style ribs (blade chops), or shoulder chops

Salt and freshly ground black pepper, to taste

1 tablespoon butter

2 tablespoon sunflower oil or peanut oil

1 can (about 14 ounces) unsweetened coconut milk, shaken

2 teaspoons minced garlic

1 large bay leaf

INGREDIENTS CONTINUED ▶

This rich, pungent stew with hearty storage vegetables is perfect for cold weather. It makes use of the flavorful and less expensive cuts of pork, tenderizing them by long braising in the oven. The long cooking helps to blend the flavors, and it tastes just as good, or even better, the next day. Apart from some bread to mop up the juices, this stew needs no accompaniment.

1. Preheat the oven to 350°F.

2. If the pork is in very large pieces, cut it into pork-chop-size portions. Blot the meat dry with a paper towel. Season it with salt and pepper.

3. Heat the butter and 1 tablespoon of the oil in your largest skillet over medium heat until the butter's foam subsides, 1 to 2 minutes.

4. Raise the heat to medium-high and add a batch of the meat. Sear on all sides, about 3 minutes per side. As the pieces are done, place them in a casserole (preferably flameproof) or Dutch oven. Repeat until all the meat has been seared. Leave the fat in the skillet and set it aside.

5. Add the coconut milk and ½ cup water to the meat in the casserole. Stir in the garlic, bay leaf, paprika, hot pepper flakes, cardamom, cumin, and cloves. If the casserole is one you can set on a stovetop burner, bring the mixture to a simmer over medium heat before you put it in the oven. Otherwise, just skip that step. Cover the casserole tightly with a lid or with aluminum foil, and bake in the oven for 1½ hours.

6. While the pork is cooking, sauté the onion in the fat in the reserved skillet, adding the remaining 1 tablespoon oil if necessary to keep it from scorching. After a minute or two, cover the skillet and sweat the onion for about 5 minutes, stirring once or twice with a spatula to incorporate all the tasty brown bits of the pork. Add the wine and scrape vigorously to loosen any remaining brown bits. Set aside.

7. Remove the casserole from the oven and add the onions, leeks, celery, carrots, and kohlrabi. Replace the cover so it is slightly ajar, return the casserole to the oven, and bake until the meat is very tender and the vegetables are cooked through, about 1 hour.

8. Remove the bay leaf, and add salt to taste. Serve hot or warm.

◀ INGREDIENTS CONTINUED
FROM PREVIOUS PAGE

4 teaspoons mild paprika

1 teaspoon hot pepper flakes

½ teaspoon ground cardamom

½ teaspoon ground cumin

6 whole cloves

1 medium-size onion, peeled and coarsely chopped

2 tablespoons white wine

2 medium-size leeks (white parts only), cleaned (see page 392) and cut crosswise into 1-inch pieces

1 large rib celery, coarsely chopped

2 medium-size carrots, scrubbed but not peeled, cut into 1-inch pieces

1 medium-size kohlrabi or white turnip, trimmed and cut into small chunks

Lamb shanks, beef chuck roasts, pork rump steaks—cuts like these are the flavorful ones, made tender and delicious by long, slow braising.

SHEPHERD'S PIE

SERVES 4 TO 6

- 6 medium-size baking potatoes (about 2 pounds total), scrubbed but not peeled, cut into 2-inch chunks
- 1 cup heavy (whipping) cream, half-and-half, or whole milk
- Salt and freshly ground black pepper
- 4 tablespoons (½ stick) butter
- 2 ribs celery, finely chopped
- ½ medium-size onion, peeled and finely chopped
- 3 medium-size carrots, scrubbed but not peeled, finely chopped
- Kernels from 2 ears fresh corn
- 1 large clove garlic, peeled and finely chopped
- 1 bay leaf
- 1½ pounds ground lamb
- 2 tablespoons whole wheat flour
- ½ cup dry red wine
- 1 tablespoon balsamic vinegar
- ½ teaspoon nutmeg, preferably freshly grated
- 1 teaspoon fresh thyme leaves, or ½ teaspoon dried
- 3 slices whole-grain bread, crusts removed, slices torn into pieces

Long popular in English pubs, shepherd's pie has become a staple in our household. (If made with beef instead of lamb, it is called "cottage pie.") With lots of vegetables included and a seasonal green salad alongside, it's a hearty meal. Instead of ground meat, I will sometimes use leftover meat from a lamb or beef roast, cut into ¼-inch to ½-inch cubes. This is also a good way to use up leftover mashed potatoes.

1. Preheat the oven to 350°F.

2. Place the potatoes in a large saucepan or stockpot, add salted water to cover, and bring to a boil over high heat. Then reduce the heat to low and simmer until the potatoes are tender when pierced with a knife, 10 to 15 minutes.

3. Drain the potatoes and return them to the saucepan. Add the cream and return the pan to medium heat. When the cream has reached a simmer, reduce the heat to low and simmer for 2 minutes. Then mash the potatoes thoroughly with a potato masher or an immersion blender. Season the potatoes with salt and pepper to taste, and set aside.

4. Melt 2 tablespoons of the butter in a large skillet over low heat. Add the celery, onion, carrots, corn kernels, garlic, and bay leaf, and raise the heat to medium-low. Sauté, stirring from time to time, until the vegetables are tender, about 8 minutes. Using a slotted spoon, transfer the vegetables to a large bowl. Remove and discard the bay leaf.

5. Add the lamb to the skillet and set it over medium heat. Cook, stirring with a spatula to break up any clumps, until the meat has a crumbled texture and is no longer pink, about 5 minutes.

6. Sprinkle the flour over the lamb and stir for 2 minutes. Then add the wine, balsamic vinegar, nutmeg, thyme, and salt and pepper to taste. Stir well. Add the vegetables and stir, scraping the brown bits off the bottom of the skillet. To make serving easier, the mixture should be slightly dry, so continue to cook, stirring, until the liquids have evaporated, about

5 minutes. Spread the mixture in a 9 by 13-inch baking dish and pat it with the back of a spoon to make it level.

7. Spread the mashed potatoes over the meat mixture, smoothing them with a rubber spatula or the back of a spoon to make an even layer. Place the baking dish in the oven and bake for 25 minutes.

8. While the shepherd's pie is baking, make the crumb topping: Melt the remaining 2 tablespoons of the butter in a small pan over low heat.

9. Put the bread in a food processor and whirl until it turns into crumbs. With the motor running, slowly pour in the melted butter. (You can also crumble the bread by hand into a bowl, pour in the butter, and toss.) Set the topping aside.

10. Remove the baking dish from the oven and sprinkle the crumb topping over the potatoes. Return it to the oven and bake, watching carefully that the topping browns but does not burn, for another 20 minutes.

11. While the shepherd's pie is still hot, cut it into squares or rectangles. Using a spatula, transfer the servings to warmed plates, taking care to keep the layers intact.

TRY THIS TOO . . .

✦ Add or subtract vegetables as the seasons dictate. For example, fresh peas could replace the corn in early summer.

✦ The potato topping can also be varied in endless ways—by incorporating grated Cheddar cheese into it, for example, or by mashing and mixing in another root vegetable such as celery root, kohlrabi, rutabaga, or winter squash.

Lamb Shanks with Early Root Vegetables

SERVES 4

1 tablespoon butter

1 tablespoon olive oil

4 lamb shanks (about 12 ounces each)

Salt and freshly ground black pepper

1 cup dry white wine

3 cups beef stock (see page 291) or lamb stock

1 medium-size fresh thyme sprig, or ½ teaspoon dried thyme leaves

1 large bay leaf

16 new potatoes (each about 1½ inches long)

12 small round onions (white, yellow, or red), peeled

10 young carrots, scrubbed but not peeled, cut into 2-inch lengths

12 baby turnips (no larger than golf ball size), trimmed but not peeled

1 tablespoon coarsely chopped fresh celery leaves, or 1 teaspoon finely chopped fresh lovage leaves

2 tablespoons coarsely chopped fresh flat-leaf parsley leaves

Lamb is often associated with spring and early summer, even though these days fresh new lamb is more often available later in the year. Although you could make this hearty stew at any time, it certainly is at its best when the root vegetables are young, tender, and freshly dug. If using larger ones, cut them in halves or chunks.

This is a stand-alone meal, but a loaf of crusty bread with which to mop up the broth would be most welcome.

1. Position a rack in the center of the oven and preheat the oven to 350°F.

2. Melt the butter in the olive oil in a large skillet over medium-high heat until the butter's foam subsides, about 2 minutes. Add the lamb shanks and brown them on all sides, about 15 minutes. Transfer the lamb shanks to a large flameproof casserole or Dutch oven (since all the vegetables will be added to the pot eventually, be sure to use one with lots of room—at least an 8-quart size). Sprinkle the shanks with a dash of salt and a generous amount of black pepper.

3. Pour out most of the fat in the skillet, leaving any meat juices and brown bits. Deglaze the skillet by pouring in the wine, bringing it to a boil, and cooking for 2 minutes while scraping the bottom of the skillet with a spatula. Pour this liquid into the casserole. Set the empty skillet aside to use later.

4. Add the stock, thyme, bay leaf, and some more ground pepper to the casserole, and stir to combine. Then bring to a simmer over medium heat.

5. Tightly cover the casserole with a lid or with aluminum foil, transfer it to the oven, and bake for 45 minutes.

6. Remove the casserole from the oven and turn the shanks over—you will see that the meat has started to retract from the bone. Return the casserole to the oven and bake, covered, for another 30 minutes.

7. Take the casserole out and arrange the potatoes on top of the lamb shanks. Add the onions, and then the carrots. Return it to the oven and bake, covered, for 15 minutes.

8. Remove the casserole again and add the turnips. Return it to the oven and bake, covered, until all the vegetables are just tender, about 10 minutes.

9. Remove the casserole from the oven, and using tongs, carefully lift the lamb shanks by the end of the bone, keeping the flesh intact, and transfer them to a bowl. Remove and discard the thyme sprig and bay leaf.

10. Use a slotted spoon to transfer the vegetables to the bowl containing the lamb.

11. Using a spoon or a fat separator, skim and discard most of the fat from the liquid in the casserole. Pour the liquid into the same large skillet you browned the meat in, and bring it to a boil. Boil until it has reduced to about 1½ cups, about 10 minutes to make a more concentrated broth. It does not need to thicken.

12. Return the lamb and vegetables to the casserole and place it over low heat. Simmer until all the ingredients are heated through, about 5 minutes. Taste, and add salt if needed. Stir in the celery leaves or lovage and parsley.

13. Place 1 lamb shank in each of four warmed shallow bowls, and surrounded each one with the vegetables. Distribute the broth over the top, and serve hot or warm.

LAMB CHOPS WITH FRESH MINT

SERVES 4

8 small loin lamb chops

Salt and freshly ground black pepper, to taste

4 tablespoons (½ stick) butter

2 tablespoons olive oil

¼ cup white wine

2 tablespoons maple syrup

4 tablespoons finely chopped fresh mint leaves

Mint sauce is traditional with lamb, but many of us have only had it as an artificially green packaged product. Here the mint is sprinkled on, garden-fresh.

1. Blot the chops dry with a paper towel, and season them with salt and pepper on both sides.

2. Combine 2 tablespoons of the butter with the olive oil in a large, heavy skillet over medium heat, and cook, stirring with a spatula, until the butter's foam subsides, about 3 minutes.

3. Add 4 of the lamb chops to the skillet, and sauté, turning them occasionally, until they are medium-rare and both sides are browned but not charred, about 10 minutes. Transfer the chops to a warmed platter and sauté the remaining 4 chops. Add them to the platter and keep warm.

4. Drain the fat from the skillet, retaining any brown bits. Add the wine and maple syrup and raise the heat to high. Cook, swirling the skillet and scraping constantly with the spatula to incorporate the pan drippings, until the liquid has reduced by a third, about 5 minutes.

5. Remove the skillet from the heat and gradually swirl in the remaining 2 tablespoons butter, 1 teaspoon at a time. Pour the sauce over the chops, sprinkle them with the mint, and serve immediately.

Most people know mint as a flavor, not a leaf. This sauce is simple, but it's the real thing.

ROAST CHICKEN WITH POTATOES AND SAGE

SERVES 4

Few dishes are as satisfying and as often prepared in our household as roast chicken. If I make it for the two of us, we get at least two more dinners out of the remains, even with a small bird. One might involve reheating any remaining breast, leg, and thigh meat in what is left of the gravy, along with a little extra white wine and cream. Another might be a chicken salad, made from the wing and back meat. And there still might be a little meat left for a soup, with stock made from the carcass and giblets (see Chicken Soup with Apples, page 270).

Inserting herbs under the skin is a great way to season a chicken as it roasts. In the summer I tend to use tarragon, at other times sage or rosemary, both of which we bring indoors to grow in pots. If you have a V-shaped rack on which to roast the chicken, it is easy to place the potatoes both under and around the bird to brown in the drippings. Sometimes I toss in a few carrots as well. (Before I had a rack I would set the chicken right on the potatoes. They supported it well, but neither the chicken nor the potatoes browned as uniformly as they do with a rack.)

Use a larger chicken if you are feeding more than four. Increase the amounts of the other ingredients accordingly, and use your biggest roasting pan.

- 1 chicken (3½ to 4 pounds), preferably organic
- 8 fresh sage, rosemary, or tarragon sprigs
- 8 medium-size baking potatoes, scrubbed but not peeled
- 2 tablespoons olive oil
- 12 large garlic cloves, peeled
- 2 tablespoons butter
- Salt and freshly ground black pepper, to taste
- 1 cup dry white wine
- 1 cup heavy (whipping) cream
- Juice of 1 lemon (about ¼ cup)

1. About 1 hour ahead of time, remove the chicken from the refrigerator to take the chill off it. Remove the giblets and refrigerate or freeze them for a future use.

2. When you are ready to cook the chicken, preheat the oven to 450°F.

3. Set the chicken on a work surface with the breast up and the legs pointing toward you. Remove any loose globs of fat from the interior. Then poke your fingers gently under the skin of the breast to loosen it. Loosen the skin of the legs and thighs as much as you can without tearing it, and poke a sprig of sage into the pockets where leg and thigh join. Distribute 4 sprigs under the breast skin, and then place the remaining ones in the cavity.

4. Slice the potatoes in half lengthwise and put them in a large bowl. Add the olive oil and garlic, and toss until they are thoroughly coated with the oil.

5. Set the chicken, breast side down, on a rack in a large roasting pan, preferably one that can also be used on top of the stove. Distribute the potatoes and garlic around the chicken. Place the pan in the oven and roast for 5 minutes.

6. Remove the pan from the oven, and using a fork, rub 1 tablespoon of the butter over the skin. Salt and pepper the chicken generously. Return the pan to the oven and roast for 20 minutes. The skin will have started to brown.

7. Remove the pan from the oven. Using tongs, get a firm hold on the bird, with one wing of the tongs in the cavity and the other on the outside. Supporting the other end with a serving spoon, tilt the bird so that most of the pink juices run out of the cavity into the pan. Then flip the chicken over so the breast side is up. Rub the remaining 1 tablespoon butter over the breast and legs, and sprinkle with salt and pepper. Use the tongs to flip the potatoes over. Return the pan to the oven and roast until the skin is crisp and golden brown and the juices run clear when a thigh is pricked with a fork or skewer, about 20 minutes.

Use a larger chicken if you are feeding more than four. Increase the amounts of the other ingredients accordingly, and use your biggest roasting pan.

8. Set the chicken on a warmed platter and cover it loosely with aluminum foil.

9. Drain off any excess fat from the pan, either by pouring it into a fat separator or by carefully tipping the pan and pouring slowly from a corner so that whatever juices you might have remain. It's okay if there's still a little fat in the pan juices.

10. Pour the wine into the pan and set it over high heat. (If your pan is not one you can heat on a stovetop, scrape all the brown bits up with a spatula and pour them, with the wine, into a skillet.) Stirring constantly, scrape the bottom vigorously with a spatula until all the delicious brown bits have been loosened. Cook until the liquid has thickened and reduced by half, about 3 minutes. Then slowly add the cream and continue to stir vigorously as the gravy thickens again, 3 to 4 minutes.

11. Reduce the heat to low, and drizzle in the lemon juice while stirring. Simmer, still stirring, for a minute or two. Then pour the gravy into a warmed gravy boat or small pitcher.

12. Serve immediately, with the potatoes and garlic either surrounding the chicken or in a separate bowl. Pass the gravy.

sesame CHICKen BReasTS WITH VeGeTaBLes

SERVES 4

Versions of this dish, traditionally called "Chicken Strange Taste" or "Strange Flavor Chicken," turn up occasionally in restaurants and in cookbooks. I don't know the origin of the name—an odd translation from the Chinese, perhaps. In any case, the flavor of sesame predominates, and the sauce does wonders for chicken breasts, which can be bland and dry. Broiling also helps keep them moist and tender. We serve the chicken over an Asian slaw made with crisp, succulent little heads of bok choy (also called pac choi).

4 boneless, skinless chicken breast halves

4 tablespoons toasted sesame oil (see Note)

4 heads baby bok choy (pac choi), each 6 to 8 inches long, thinly sliced crosswise (substitute an equal amount of tatsoi or Chinese cabbage if bok choy is not available)

8 ounces daikon radish, peeled and cut into matchsticks

2 medium-size carrots, scrubbed but not peeled, cut into matchsticks

8 scallions, white and green parts chopped separately

6 tablespoons sesame seeds, preferably unhulled

¼ cup tahini (sesame paste)

¼ cup soy sauce

2 tablespoons rice vinegar or white wine vinegar

2 teaspoons thick red chili sauce, such as Sriracha

¼ cup dry vermouth

1 tablespoon honey

1 large clove garlic, put through a garlic press or mashed to a paste with the tip of a knife

¼ teaspoon ground ginger

1. Place the chicken breasts between two sheets of wax paper and flatten them by gently pounding them with a mallet or with the bottom of a heavy frying pan. (The goal is to gently flatten them to an even thickness of about ¼ inch, not to pulverize them, so resist the temptation to use a hammer.) Set them on a plate or in a shallow bowl, pour 2 tablespoons of the toasted sesame oil over them, and rub to coat them thoroughly with the oil. Set aside.

2. To make the slaw, combine the bok choy, daikon, and carrots in a large bowl. Set aside 2 tablespoons of the chopped scallion greens, and add the rest of the greens to the other vegetables. Toss together thoroughly, cover the bowl with a towel, and set aside.

3. Place a medium to large dry skillet over very low heat, add the sesame seeds, and toast, stirring, until they are fragrant but not browned, about 10 minutes. Set 3 tablespoons of the toasted sesame seeds aside in a small bowl, and put the rest in a small saucepan.

4. Preheat the broiler to high, with the broiler rack set 6 inches below the heating element. Have ready a rimmed baking sheet with a cake rack set on it (easier to clean than a broiling pan).

5. While the broiler is heating, add the tahini, soy sauce, vinegar, chili sauce, vermouth, honey, garlic, ginger, and remaining 2 tablespoons of sesame oil

to the sesame seeds in the saucepan. Whisk to combine, and then bring to a simmer over medium heat. Simmer, stirring, until the sauce is slightly thickened, 2 to 3 minutes. Set aside in the pan.

6. Place the chicken breasts, skin side up, on the prepared baking sheet and broil for 7 minutes. Flip them over and broil until just cooked through, about 4 minutes.

7. When the chicken breasts are done, set them, skin side up, on a cutting board and slice them diagonally into ½-inch-thick strips.

8. Spread the slaw out on a platter, and arrange the chicken strips on top, leaving a border of slaw visible at the edges. Reheat the sauce if it has cooled, and pour it over the chicken. Sprinkle the remaining sesame seeds, then the chopped scallion whites and the reserved scallion greens, over the chicken and serve immediately.

NOTE: Toasted sesame oil is available in health food stores, Asian markets, and many supermarkets. The untoasted kind can be substituted but is not as flavorful.

TRY THIS TOO . . .

Serve the chicken over rice instead of the slaw, with a vegetable dish on the side.

BRIGHT RED CHICKEN PAPRIKASH

SERVES 4

Originally a Hungarian dish, this long ago became a popular standard because of its rich color and flavor. To keep it from turning out a dull brown, I up the ante with plenty of paprika, tomato puree, lots of red peppers, and chicken that is only lightly browned. If you don't grow, dry, and grind your own sweet paprika (page 179), seek out the real Hungarian kind, which makes a difference. Egg noodles or dumplings are traditional; use bright yellow saffron noodles, if available, for an extra festive dish.

- 4 tablespoons (½ stick) butter
- 8 chicken bone-in thighs (3 pounds), skin left on
- ½ teaspoon salt
- Freshly ground black pepper
- 3 medium onions, sliced in medium-thin strips
- 2 large red bell peppers, stemmed, seeded, and sliced in medium-thin strips
- 3 tablespoons sweet paprika, preferably Hungarian
- 1 cup tomato puree
- ½ cup chicken stock
- 1 cup sour cream
- ½ pound egg noodles

1. Melt the butter in a large skillet or Dutch oven over medium-high heat until the foam subsides. Season the chicken thighs with salt and pepper and add them to the skillet taking care not to crowd the pan. Cook until lightly browned on both sides. You'll probably need to cook the chicken in two batches for a total of 10 to 15 minutes. Set the chicken aside, but leave the fat in the pan.

2. Add the onions to the skillet and cook over medium heat, stirring frequently, until softened, 3 minutes. Add the bell peppers and cook 1 minute more.

3. Combine the paprika, tomato puree, and chicken stock in a bowl and stir to mix. Add to the chicken pieces and stir to coat them thoroughly.

4. Bring the ingredients to a hearty simmer, then cover the skillet and lower the heat. Turn the chicken pieces over after 15 minutes and continue simmering until the chicken is cooked through, 15 minutes more.

5. When the chicken is done, remove it to a warm bowl, leaving the tomato and paprika sauce in the skillet. Add the sour cream and stir thoroughly to mix. Simmer, uncovered, over low heat, stirring frequently, to reduce and thicken the sauce as needed, about 10 minutes. It should have the consistency of gravy. Taste and add salt and pepper if needed.

6. Cook the noodles according to directions on the package, drain, and spread out on a warm platter. Place the chicken on top of them, then pour the sauce over the chicken and serve hot.

CHICKEN STEW WITH HORSERADISH CREAM

SERVES 4

1 chicken (4 pounds)

2 large carrots, scrubbed but not peeled, sliced diagonally into 1-inch-thick pieces

2 medium-size ribs celery, cut into 1½-inch lengths

1 medium-size onion, peeled and quartered

3 medium-size leeks (white and light green parts), split lengthwise, well rinsed, and cut into 2-inch sections

4 to 6 small white turnips, about golf ball size, unpeeled and left whole

1 quart chicken stock (see page 289)

1 cup dry white wine

2 bay leaves

4 whole cloves

INGREDIENTS CONTINUED ▶

This rustic dish of chicken and vegetables, perfect for a family supper, is light but rich in flavor. A complete meal in itself, it's easy on the stomach at times when you're not feeling well, or when you are recovering from heavy holiday fare. I often make a lot of it, then eat it for several days. Since the solids and the broth are served separately, each diner can pour or ladle in as much broth as they like. A horseradish cream topping adds even more flavor and a bit of zip.

1. Cut the chicken into pieces, separating drumsticks from thighs, severing the wings, and splitting the breast down the middle, then cutting in half crosswise to make 4 pieces. Cut the back in half. (One easy way to make all these cuts is to hold the blade of a meat cleaver on the spot where the cut should be, then strike a blow on the back edge of the cleaver with a mallet or hammer. Poultry shears are also useful for splitting the breastbone.) Remove the skin from all the pieces except the wings.

2. Place the carrots, celery, onion, leeks, and turnips in a large soup pot. Add all the chicken pieces, including the giblets (minus the liver). Pour in the stock and the wine.

3. Place the pot over high heat and bring just to a boil, skimming off any thick foam that floats to the surface.

4. Reduce the heat to a simmer, and add the bay leaves, cloves, tarragon, thyme, salt, and pepper. Simmer until the chicken pieces are all cooked through and the vegetables are tender, 1 hour or a bit more.

5. While the stew is cooking, combine the sour cream, yogurt, and horseradish in a small bowl, and whisk together. Spoon the horseradish cream into a sauceboat or small serving bowl, and set it aside at room temperature.

6. When the stew is done, taste for salt and add if more needed. Using a slotted spoon and/or tongs, lift out the chicken pieces. Remove the meat from the bones (discard the bones).

7. Using the slotted spoon, lift out the vegetables and place them on a large warmed platter (if a few bits of vegetable remain in the broth, that's okay). Remove the bay leaves. Add the chicken meat to the vegetables.

8. Pour the broth into a warmed soup tureen or Dutch oven and serve it alongside the platter of meat and vegetables. Give each person a generous soup bowl, and let them help themselves to stew and broth. Pass the horseradish cream.

TRY THIS TOO . . .

For a simpler dish, substitute water for the stock, since simmering the chicken will create a flavorful broth. But creating what is called a "double chicken stock" makes this even more satisfying.

◀ *INGREDIENTS CONTINUED FROM PREVIOUS PAGE*

1 teaspoon dried tarragon leaves, or 2 teaspoons chopped fresh

½ teaspoon dried thyme leaves, or 1 teaspoon fresh

1 teaspoon salt (less if the stock is salty)

Freshly ground black pepper, to taste

½ cup sour cream

½ cup whole-milk yogurt

¼ cup prepared horseradish (not creamy style)

Striking a blow with a rubber mallet on the back edge of a cleaver is a handy way to cut up a chicken . . . or a winter squash.

PACIFIC HALIBUT WITH SWISS CHARD

SERVES 4

2 pounds Pacific halibut steak

2 cups dry white wine

1 large carrot, scrubbed but not peeled, cut into medium-fine pieces

1 medium-size onion, peeled and cut into medium-fine pieces

1 large rib celery, cut into medium-fine pieces

1 bay leaf

1 small handful fresh thyme sprigs, or 2 teaspoons dried thyme leaves

Salt

12 small to medium-size Swiss chard leaves, ribs removed, leaves sliced crosswise into narrow ribbons (about 6 cups)

1 cup heavy (whipping) cream

Pinch of saffron threads (optional)

Juice of ½ lemon

Freshly ground black pepper

Fish stocks, and the soups or sauces you create with them, are wonderfully flavorful and enriched with gelatin from the fish bones. But in today's markets it is not always possible to find fish heads or bones with which to make stock. Halibut steaks are not only delicious, they are also among the few fish commonly sold with the bones in, and it is worth creating a quick stock from them, as we do here.

Swiss chard is a good vegetable to use as a bed for sauced fish. Softer greens, such as spinach, hold more water after draining and tend to make the sauce runny.

I would serve this alone on individual plates. The saffron will brighten it up, but if you'd rather not use it, serve the halibut with a brightly colored, self-contained vegetable such as baked sweet potatoes in their skins or halves of baked winter squash.

1. About 2 hours before dinnertime, take the halibut out of the refrigerator and lay it on a cutting board. Using a sharp knife, cut out the bone(s) and remove (but do not discard) both the brownish top skin and the white underside skin. Cut in half any fish pieces that are more than about 4 inches long. Feel the flesh with your fingers to make sure all pieces of bone have been removed. Place the fish in a covered container and return it to the refrigerator.

2. Place the fish bones and skin in a large saucepan, and add the wine, carrot, onion, celery, bay leaf, thyme, and a dash of salt. Pour in 2 cups of water and bring to a simmer over high heat. Then reduce the heat and simmer, uncovered, for about 1 hour, making sure the liquid does not all evaporate.

3. Pour the contents into a strainer set over a bowl, and press on them with a spoon to extract as much liquid stock as possible. Discard the solids, and then measure the stock. If there is less than

1¼ cups, add water until it reaches that volume. Set the stock aside.

4. When you are ready to prepare the meal, bring water to a simmer in the bottom of a vegetable steamer, add the chard to the steamer basket, cover, and steam until tender, about 5 minutes. Remove the steamer from the heat and leave the chard to drain in the steamer basket, covered, to keep it warm.

5. Pour the reserved stock into a skillet, preferably one that is large enough to hold all the fish pieces in one layer. Heat it to a low simmer and then add the fish. Simmer for about 3 minutes. Then carefully turn the fish over with a spatula and cook on the other side until just cooked through, 2 to 3 minutes depending on its thickness. Remove the skillet from the heat.

6. Press any liquid out of the chard with the back of a large spoon, and then divide it among four warmed plates to make a bed for the fish. Distribute the fish on top of the chard, and keep warm.

7. Place the skillet over high heat and boil the liquid rapidly until it is quite thick and reduced to about ½ cup, about 5 minutes. Add the cream and the saffron, if using, stirring constantly with a spatula or whisk, and continue to boil until the liquid is reduced to about ⅔ cup, 5 to 10 minutes. Then drizzle in the lemon juice, stirring, and cook over low heat for about 1 minute more. Season with salt and pepper to taste.

8. Pour the sauce over the fish and serve immediately.

SPRINGTIME FISH CHOWDER WITH FRESH HERBS

SERVES 4

Hake is a white fish, similar to cod and haddock, and both could be substituted in this recipe. It is a good fish for a chowder, especially one made with spring vegetables. Since it is neither 3oily nor strongly flavored, it lets the delicacy of these early treats shine. Ideally, you'll make this soup when you are harvesting peas, baby new potatoes, scallions, and—best of all—some large sweet onions of the Vidalia type, which are winter-grown in the southern United States, or the Walla Walla type, which are fall-planted and over-wintered in the central and northern states. Together with the cream, all these elements contribute a degree of sweetness. (If you have no fresh herbs in the garden, use purchased fresh ones rather than dried.)

In the warm parts of the country, you could have all the vegetable fixings in the garden from April on. In Maine, they'd be ready by at least the Fourth of July.

1. In a large soup pot or Dutch oven, sauté the bacon over low heat, stirring, until it is just crisp, about 2 minutes. Remove the bacon to a plate with a slotted spoon and set it aside, leaving the fat in the pot.

2. Add the butter to the bacon fat, and let it melt. Then add the onion and sauté over low heat, stirring frequently, until it is translucent but not browned, about 10 minutes.

3. Add the potatoes, pepper, and water to cover. Bring to a simmer and cook over medium-low heat until the potatoes are fork-tender, 10 minutes.

4. Add the hake, scallions, peas, and the bacon, and cook over low heat for 5 minutes.

5. Add the parsley, dill, tarragon, and cream. Cook, stirring, until the soup reaches a simmer again and steam is rising, about 2 minutes. This should be a thick, chunky soup, but if it seems too thick, add a little water or cream. Season with salt and pepper to taste, and serve immediately.

TRY THIS TOO . . .

Small white onions would also be delicious in this chowder, as would a few thinnings from the garlic patch, harvested as green garlic. You could also add a few tender young carrots, chopped, along with the potatoes and onions.

- 2 ounces slab bacon or salt pork, very finely diced (¼ cup)
- 2 tablespoons butter
- 1 large sweet onion, chopped into medium-fine pieces
- 12 ounces new potatoes, cut into ½-inch cubes
- Freshly ground black pepper
- 1 pound hake, cut into 1-inch cubes
- ½ cup chopped scallions (white and green parts)
- 1 cup fresh green peas
- 2 tablespoons coarsely chopped fresh flat-leaf parsley leaves
- 1 tablespoon coarsely chopped fresh dill leaves
- 1 teaspoon coarsely chopped fresh tarragon leaves
- 1 cup heavy (whipping) cream
- Salt (unless the bacon is extra-salty)

This should be a thick, chunky soup, but if it seems too thick, add a little water or cream.

Desserts

A LITTLE SOMETHING SWEET AFTER A MEAL is not only satisfying, it seems to help the digestion, too. We keep these finales simple rather than grand. Apart from the occasional nibble of dark chocolate, our desserts usually involve fruit, preferably homegrown: a bowl of apples, a ripe melon sliced open on a cutting board, a bunch of grapes plucked from the arbor above our outdoor table.

Sometimes I make a more ambitious dessert—usually for visitors or for a special occasion. Often it's something small but rich, like a quivering Lemon Verbena Panna Cotta (page 442) or a foamy Strawberry Fool (page 446). My favorite desserts tend to be basic templates to which I can add whatever fruits are in season at the time. And then there's the direction I love to give to children at the table after a summer lunch: "The Pick-Your-Own Farm is that-a-way!" And off they gallop in a pack to the berry rows, to eat their fill.

RUSTIC APPLE TART

SERVES 6 TO 8

4 medium-size apples,
   peeled, quartered,
   cored, and sliced

1 unbaked 9-inch Butter
   Pastry Crust tart shell
   (recipe follows) in a
   shallow tart pan with
   a removable bottom

3 tablespoons unsalted
   butter

½ cup maple syrup

BUTTER PASTRY CRUST:

1¼ cups all-purpose flour

½ teaspoon salt

7 tablespoons cold
   unsalted butter,
   cut into pieces

This informal tart, long a household favorite, is quick to assemble and has a simple maple syrup glaze. Since apples keep so well, it is the fruit dessert I make when nothing else is in season. A scoop of vanilla ice cream alongside will help you to stretch the yield, but I usually prefer to pass a few firm cheeses such as a sharp Cheddar, an aged Gouda, and a Manchego.

1. Preheat the oven to 350°F.

2. Starting at the outside edge, arrange the apple slices in a ring in the Butter Pastry Crust tart shell, standing them up on edge to form a thick single layer. Make a second ring inside the first to make a rosette, saving a few short pieces for the center. You may have some pieces left over for nibbling while you work.

2. Prepare the basting sauce: Melt the butter in a small saucepan over low heat, and add the maple syrup. Simmer, stirring, until the mixture starts to thicken, about 4 minutes. It will bubble furiously, so make sure that it doesn't boil over.

3. Drizzle half of the basting sauce over the apples. Some of it will run down between them to form a base.

4. Bake the tart for 25 minutes. Then drizzle the rest of the basting sauce over the apples, and bake until the apples have softened and browned, 40 to 60 minutes, checking frequently toward the end to make sure the top has not burned. Serve warm.

BUTTER PASTRY CRUST

ONE 9-INCH TART OR PIE SHELL

BECAUSE ELIOT AND I love the flavor of butter, I use this recipe almost every time I make pastry, whether it's for a savory tart or a fruit pie. This makes enough for one 9-inch tart or pie shell. Double it for a double-crust pie or to freeze the extra dough for later use. On a busy day when a dessert is in order, having one or two disks of dough in the freezer gives me a head start.

There are three different ways to bake this crust. For most baked pies, and for the Apple Tart, I put the filling in an unbaked crust and then bake them together. For the Summer Tart with Roasted Tomatoes (page 368), I bake it partially, add the tomato-onion filling, and then finish baking them together. For the Chilled Raspberry Pie on page 436, I bake the unfilled crust completely, cool it, and then add the cold filling.

1. Place the flour and salt in a food processor and pulse five times. (You can also mix the dough by hand.) Add the butter and pulse about ten times. There should be some pea-size pieces of unmixed butter visible, but no chunks larger than that.

2. Remove the processor lid and sprinkle 3½ tablespoons cold water over the flour mixture. Close, and pulse five to ten times, until the dough starts to clump together.

3. Transfer the dough to a long sheet of wax paper, shape it into a ball, and then flatten it into a 6-inch disk. Wrap the disk in the paper. Chill in the refrigerator for at least 1 hour. (If you're making the dough several days in advance, it may be frozen in the wax paper. Let it defrost on the kitchen counter before rolling it out.)

4. Overlap two long sheets of wax paper on a work surface. Dust the wax paper lightly with flour. Unwrap the dough. If it's too stiff to roll out when you remove it from the fridge, let it rest until it softens a bit first. Roll the dough out to a diameter of at least 12 inches for a 9-inch pie (11 inches for a 9-inch tart with 1-inch sides). Having enough dough to make a generous, solid rim will reduce the chance of its shrinkage. Dust the rolling pin with a little flour if the dough sticks.

5. Place a 9-inch pie plate or tart pan next to the wax paper. With one hand underneath the wax paper and the other on top of the rolled-out dough, flip the dough over and let it fall gently onto the plate. Carefully peel off the wax paper. Lift the edges of the dough and use gravity to fit it into the plate without stretching it.

6. Fold the excess overhanging dough back up over the rim, piecing it as needed to make a rim of even thickness. Flute it with your fingers or press it flat with the tines of a fork. (If it's in a tart pan, cut off the excess overhanging dough and use it as needed to reinforce the sides of the tart.) Prick the bottom in about ten places with the tines of a fork (to release air and prevent buckling while cooking).

7. *To bake the shell filled:* Follow the directions for filling and baking the pie in the recipe you have chosen.

To partially bake the shell: Preheat the oven to 400°F. Cover the dough with a sheet of aluminum foil that is large enough to hang over the sides of the pie plate, and gently fit it to the shape of the pie (or do this with an 8-inch foil pie plate). Fill the foil all the way to the top with pie weights,

Instead of the weights designed for pies, I use ½-inch marble slingshot ammo.

to keep the sides from shrinking (see Note). Bake for 20 minutes. Then lift out the foil and weights, and proceed as your recipe directs.

To bake the shell completely: Partially bake the shell as described above. Then, after removing the foil and weights, put the shell back in the oven and bake until it is golden brown, another 10 minutes.

NOTE: Instead of the weights designed for pies, I use 1/2-inch marble slingshot ammo. These heavy white balls are available in 5-pound bags and work perfectly. You can also use uncooked rice or dried beans.

CHILLED RASPBERRY PIE

SERVES 6 TO 8

1 quart fresh raspberries

1 cup sugar, preferably turbinado or raw sugar

2 tablespoons cornstarch

Juice of 1 lemon (about 1/4 cup)

1 fully baked 9-inch pie shell (see page 434), cooled

1 cup heavy (whipping) cream

Summer is not complete until I have made this pie at least once while the raspberries are in season. What makes it so delicious is the combination of raw and cooked berries. The filling, topped with unsweetened whipped cream, is simple and foolproof. I often adapt this recipe to other fruits as well. Just be sure to make this dessert well ahead of time, to cool the filling and then chill the pie.

1. Put half of the berries in a medium-size saucepan and crush them with a potato masher. Add the sugar, cornstarch, and lemon juice, and stir to combine.

2. Cook the berry mixture, stirring, over medium heat until the sugar dissolves and the mixture thickens, about 10 minutes. Let it cool completely. (This can take at least an hour and can be hastened by putting the berry mixture in the refrigerator.) Then gently fold in the remaining berries.

3. Two hours before serving, spoon the filling into the pie shell and refrigerate it.

4. When you are ready to serve the pie, whip the cream until upright peaks form, and spread it over the pie.

TRY THIS TOO . . .

Make this pie with any summer berries, and with peaches, apricots, or nectarines. You might also combine two fruits, with one of them mashed and the other whole. I have also made it with berries I have frozen, all of them mashed; the filling will take a little longer to solidify and the pie lacks the flavor you get from the uncooked berries, but it tastes great in January!

HAZELNUT TORTE WITH SUMMER BERRIES

SERVES 6 TO 8

Tortes are cakes, usually constructed in layers, that rely more on nuts than on flour for their substance. This one has been a favorite special-occasion dessert for three generations of my family. I like to vary it with seasonal fruits, and for summer family get-togethers this means berries from the garden. The torte's popularity has a lot to do with its light texture, its rich nutty taste, and its adaptability, but truth be told, it is also a snap to make. Most of the work is done by the food processor or blender, and the frosting is simply flavored whipped cream. Other nuts might well be substituted, but hazelnuts are often favored for tortes, and are even a crop we have raised successfully at home.

This family favorite takes us through a year of celebrations.

2 tablespoons butter,
   at room temperature

2 tablespoons whole
   wheat flour

2½ teaspoons baking
   powder

4 large eggs

¾ cup plus 3 tablespoons
   sugar, preferably
   turbinado or raw sugar

1 cup hazelnuts

1½ cups heavy (whipping)
   cream

2 tablespoons Kirsch
   (see Note), or
   1 teaspoon pure vanilla
   extract

2 cups fresh strawberries,
   raspberries, or
   blueberries, either
   mixed or singly,
   depending on
   availability

1. Preheat the oven to 350°F.

2. Smear the bottoms and sides of two 8-inch, 1½-inch-deep layer cake pans with the butter. Line the bottoms with rounds of wax paper cut to size.

3. Mix the flour and baking powder together in a cup or small bowl, and set it aside.

4. Combine the eggs and the ¾ cup sugar in a food processor or blender, and process until smooth, about 1 minute. Add the hazelnuts and continue processing until the nuts are finely grated, about 1 minute. Add the flour mixture and process until just mixed, about 2 seconds.

5. Pour the batter into the prepared cake pans, dividing it equally. Bake until the layers are light tan in color and no longer jiggle when shaken, about 20 minutes.

6. Let the layers cool in the pans on a wire rack. They will deflate slightly.

7. To make the frosting, whip the cream, gradually adding the Kirsch and the remaining 3 tablespoons sugar, until soft peaks form.

8. Gently rap the edge of one of the cake pans on the counter to jar the cake loose, and invert the layer onto a flat serving dish. The wax paper will likely stay in the pan, but if not, just peel it off.

9. Spread a third of the whipped cream over the top of the layer, and then add half of the berries.

10. Holding the second cake pan upside-down, and gently rapping the edge of the pan on the counter if needed, catch the cake with your hand (easy to do with an 8-inch layer) and carefully place it on top of the first layer, topside down. Remove the wax paper if needed.

11. Spread the remaining whipped cream over the top of the cake, and then decorate with the remaining berries.

12. Keep refrigerated until just before serving.

NOTE: Kirsch, or Kirschwasser, is a cherry-flavored liqueur that is highly suitable for flavoring fruit desserts.

TRY THIS TOO . . .

✦ Peaches make an excellent substitute for berries, or may be combined with them.

✦ In winter, when there are no fresh soft fruits, I use fruit jam between the layers. Or I warm 1½ cups orange marmalade with ¼ cup Grand Marnier to make a thin syrup and drizzle that on, then spread the whipped cream. You could also use the Blueberry Lemon Sauce on page 449.

BLUEBERRY-PEACH COBBLER

SERVES 10 TO 12

10 fresh peaches
   (about 2½ pounds),
   peeled, pitted, and
   cut into 1-inch pieces
   (4 cups)

8 cups fresh blueberries

¼ cup cornstarch

1 cup honey

2½ cups all purpose-flour

1 cup whole wheat flour

2 tablespoons baking
   powder

4 tablespoons turbinado
   sugar or light brown
   sugar

1 teaspoon salt

1 cup (2 sticks) cold butter

3 cups heavy (whipping)
   cream

A cobbler is a wonderful dessert—easy to make and, above all, forgiving. A simple matter of a biscuit-like crust baked on top of fruit, it requires no special finesse. The topping can be casually arranged, and if the fruit has not thickened quite as much as you'd planned, no matter. Unlike a proper pie filling, it is best when it oozes a bit, and could just as well be considered a thick sauce.

Almost any fruit will make a cobbler, although I would avoid watery ones such as citrus and melons. For this recipe, I go for a combination of fleshy and juicy. I make it with any berry that is in season, combining several when their bearing times overlap. In late summer, when peaches and blueberries are both plentiful, they make a good pair. Frozen fruit (thawed) can also be used.

This is the summer dessert I turn to if I am very busy and have lots of guests to feed. Any left over is great warmed up the next day, especially for breakfast.

1. Preheat the oven to 375°F.

2. Combine the peaches and blueberries in a large baking dish (or in a large mixing bowl if you will be cooking this in two smaller baking dishes; divide and place in the dishes after Step 4).

3. Sprinkle the cornstarch over the fruit, and stir until thoroughly mixed.

4. Pour the honey over the fruit and stir to combine thoroughly. (If the honey does not pour freely, warm it slightly in a small saucepan over low heat, just enough to liquefy it; then pour.) Set the baking dish aside.

5. Sift both flours and the baking powder together into a large bowl. Add 2 tablespoons of the sugar, then the salt, and mix thoroughly.

6. Cut 1½ sticks of the butter into small pieces. Using a pastry blender or two knives, cut the butter pieces into the flour mixture. Then mix briefly with your fingers until the butter pieces are the size of peas.

7. Stir in 1½ cups of the cream, and then mix with your fingers until the dough forms a single ball.

8. Break off pieces of the dough, flatten them with your fingers to about ½-inch thickness, and cover the top of the fruit with them, leaving spaces here and there for steam to escape.

9. Melt the remaining ½ stick butter in a small saucepan over low heat, and pour it over the crust. Sprinkle with the remaining 2 tablespoons sugar.

10. Bake until the fruit has thickened somewhat and the crust is golden brown, about 50 minutes. The fruit

Try adding a scoop of vanilla ice cream instead of the cream topping.

will be slightly runny, but it will start to set after you remove it from the oven. Let the cobbler stand for at least 15 minutes before serving, but do not chill it. It is best slightly warm or at room temperature, in bowls.

11. Pass the rest of the cream in a pitcher to add a creamy, rich element to the buttery crust and sweet, juicy fruit.

TRY THIS TOO . . .

If you prefer, whip the cream topping, or add a scoop of vanilla ice cream to each bowl in place of the cream topping.

Lemon Verbena Panna Cotta

SERVES 4

- 1 to 2 teaspoons sunflower oil or other neutral-flavored oil
- 1 tablespoon ice water
- 1 teaspoon granulated gelatin
- 1 cup heavy (whipping) cream
- 12 large lemon verbena leaves, preferably fresh, plus 4 fresh leaves for optional garnish
- ¼ cup clover honey or other mild-flavored honey
- 1 cup buttermilk
- 1 cup fresh raspberries or strawberries (optional)
- Grated zest of 1 lemon (see Note)

Panna cotta, Italian for "cooked cream," is a simple molded pudding—essentially warm flavored, sweetened cream, barely solidified with gelatin. It's simple, but the proportions must be just right: Too much gelatin and you've got a rubbery puck of cream Jell-O. To get a delicate, smooth texture, you need to use just enough gelatin to hold the chilled mixture together when it is unmolded on the plate. This version uses lemon verbena, one of my favorite herbs, and buttermilk for a little tang.

1. Set out four small ramekins with sloping sides. Using your fingers, rub the interior of the ramekins with a thin film of the oil, and then refrigerate the ramekins.

2. Put the ice water in a small cup. Sprinkle the gelatin over the surface of the water, and stir briefly to keep the granules from clumping. Set aside.

3. Bring water to a simmer in the bottom of a double boiler. Combine the cream, lemon verbena leaves, and honey in the top of the double boiler, and cook over the simmering water, stirring occasionally, for 10 minutes. The cream may foam just a bit, with wisps of steam, but it should not boil. (If you do not have a double boiler, use a heatproof bowl set over a saucepan.)

4. Remove the pan from the heat. Using tongs, fish out and discard the lemon verbena leaves. Immediately pour the gelatin mixture into the cream, and stir until it is completely dissolved, about 2 minutes.

5. Gradually add the buttermilk, stirring until well mixed. Pour the mixture into the chilled ramekins and refrigerate for at least 3 hours or overnight.

6. When you are ready to serve the dessert, set the ramekins in a pan of hot water that reaches about halfway to their rims. Leave them there for 1 minute to loosen the panna cotta, and then remove them. Run a blunt knife around the sides of the ramekins to loosen the panna cottas a bit more. Then invert a small plate over a ramekin, and holding the plate and ramekin together firmly, flip them over, allowing the panna cotta to drop onto the plate. Repeat with the remaining ramekins. (If necessary you can hold the unmolded panna cottas in the refrigerator for a day or so.)

7. When it is time for dessert, scatter ¼ cup of the berries around each panna cotta, sprinkle some lemon zest on top, garnish with a fresh lemon verbena leaf, if available, and serve.

NOTE: My zester has a row of little sharp-edged holes that make tiny curls, and there is no need to mince the zest further. A fine-toothed Microplane also makes perfect zest. If you have neither, use a sharp knife to peel off a curl of zest and then mince it very fine. Use only the yellow part of the lemon skin, not the bitter white layer beneath.

TRY THIS TOO . . .

✦ The classic flavoring for panna cotta is vanilla, made by steeping a vanilla bean in the hot cream. Steeping a pinch of saffron in it is another great version. Try other herbs too, such as thyme, hyssop, or bay leaf.

✦ Experiment with unsweetened savory panna cottas, too. Flavor them with herbs and surround them with choice baby salad greens or steamed asparagus tips.

PLUM CUSTARD

SERVES 4 NORMAL PEOPLE (SEE STEP 7)

Fruit custards are at the top of our list of favorite desserts, and this one is so simple and quick that it can be made on a whim. It has a soft texture balanced by a crunchy topping. Although other stone fruits can be used, plums have a firmness that keeps them from diluting the custard.

1 tablespoon unsalted butter, for the pie dish

3 large eggs

1⅓ cups heavy (whipping) cream

3 tablespoons agave syrup (see Note)

1 teaspoon pure vanilla extract

3 large plums or 4 smaller ones, ripe but just slightly firm

2 tablespoons turbinado sugar or light brown sugar

1. Preheat the oven to 350°F. Butter a 9-inch ovenproof glass or ceramic pie dish.

2. Combine the eggs, cream, agave syrup, and vanilla in a bowl and beat with a whisk or eggbeater until thoroughly mixed.

Making Plum Custard

ARRANGE plum slices in a buttered baking dish in concentric circles.

POUR in the batter. A bit of the pinwheel pattern will show after the custard is baked.

3. Cutting from the stem end to the bottom, slice each plum into 8 vertical sections; then cut around the pit so that the slices fall away.

4. Arrange the plum slices in a pinwheel pattern on the prepared pie dish, with one pinwheel touching the outer edge of the dish and a smaller pinwheel in the center. (If your dish is square or oblong, arrange the slices in rows.)

5. Pour the batter over the fruit, transfer the dish to the oven, and bake for 30 minutes.

6. Remove the dish from the oven and sprinkle the sugar over the top. Return it to the oven and bake until the custard is puffed up and golden brown on top, 15 to 25 minutes. (It is done when the center no longer jiggles when the dish is gently shaken and a knife inserted into the custard comes out clean.) Let the custard sit for at least 5 to 10 minutes.

7. Serve this warm or at room temperature. Since the fruit's pattern will be partially visible, I like to serve it at the table, cutting it into wedges. If the fruit is very ripe and juicy the wedges may fall apart slightly, but no one will care. I'm told that the leftovers taste fine, cold, for breakfast, but the two of us have never once refrained from eating the whole thing, so I can't vouch for this.

NOTE: Agave syrup is available at many stores and is worth tracking down.

It dissolves well in the batter and has a much more neutral flavor than that of maple syrup or honey.

TRY THIS TOO . . .

For more than 4 people, it is best to make 2 custards this size, rather than increase the amounts and go to a larger dish, because the larger the custard, the harder it is to serve in wedges. Alternatively, serve it with a spoon, like a pudding, or in individual ramekins.

Adding 1 tablespoon of flour to the batter turns this into a French dessert called a *clafouti*. It will hold together better, but the texture will be slightly firmer, without the delicate creaminess of the flourless version.

Many other fruits can be substituted—especially apricots, nectarines, or peaches. For a more tropical version, try guavas or mangoes. In winter, use apple wedges sautéed in butter. Very juicy, ripe acid fruits, such as overly ripe plums or pluots, can make the batter quite runny—the custard will be almost curdled. Adding 1 egg yolk will prevent this, though the texture will be a bit less tender and silky. We prefer to enjoy it as is—like a wonderful adult baby food.

GRAPE RAITA

SERVES 4

As described on page 361, a raita can be made with a variety of ingredients, including most fruits. As simple, quick desserts, raitas make use of the season's best flavors and are light enough to top off a heavy meal.

1 cup whole-milk yogurt

⅓ cup sour cream

1 tablespoon honey

¼ teaspoon nutmeg, preferably freshly grated

2 cups large flavorful grapes, sliced in half lengthwise, any seeds removed

1. Combine the yogurt, sour cream, honey, and nutmeg in a medium-size bowl and stir gently until thoroughly mixed. Add the grapes and stir to combine.

2. Cover and refrigerate for 1 hour, or until ready to eat. Serve chilled.

TRY THIS TOO . . .

Earlier in the season, try making this with strawberries, peaches, or nectarines.

STRAWBERRY FOOL

STRAWBERRY FOOL

SERVES 4

A fruit fool is an old-fashioned dessert, often made with custard. This is a quicker, simpler version, the kind of dish you make on a hot summer day when you can't even think about baking a fruit pie. It's just berries and cream, but a little more constructed. Almost any soft fruit will work in this recipe, but this is my favorite because of its color.

4 cups fresh strawberries, hulled

2 tablespoons honey

1 tablespoon orange liqueur, such as Cointreau or Grand Marnier

1 cup heavy (whipping) cream

Leaves from 2 fresh mint sprigs, very finely sliced (about 2 tablespoons)

1. Set aside 1 cup of the nicest-looking strawberries. Combine the remaining 3 cups berries, 1 tablespoon of the honey, and the orange liqueur in a food processor or blender, and puree until very smooth. (You can also use a food mill.) Transfer the puree to a medium-large bowl.

2. In another bowl, whip the cream until soft peaks form. Add the remaining 1 tablespoon honey and whip until the peaks are stiffer but still glossy.

3. Gently fold half the whipped cream into the puree until just mixed. Do not beat. Carefully spoon the mixture into four large wineglasses (either stemmed or stemless) or small clear glass bowls.

4. Halve the reserved strawberries vertically and gently distribute them over the puree. Spoon the remaining whipped cream uniformly on top to make a final layer. Sprinkle the mint on top. Refrigerate for about 1 hour before serving.

I love desserts that are pretty and celebratory without taking a lot of work.

PINK APPLESAUCE

SERVES 4

8 small apples
(about 2 pounds)

1 tablespoon maple
syrup

1 small beet
(about 2 ounces),
peeled and grated
medium-fine to yield
1 tablespoon

½ cup heavy (whipping)
cream

Applesauce is a convenient, healthy dessert. If you have some put up in jars, you can serve it up in seconds. Even when made fresh, it takes little time. Not limited to the end of the meal, it is always welcome on the plate next to pork chops, ham, sausage, bacon, or liver.

There is nothing wrong with the typical brownish color that apples take on when they cook, but some with highly pigmented skin or flesh can tint the sauce bright pink—a seductive addition, though such apples are not always easy to find. In this recipe you'll find a shortcut I use when I want to make applesauce a bit more special.

This is also a good dish for cleaning out the cellar in the spring, when stored apples and beets have lost some of their moisture. You might even freeze or can some applesauce to tide you over until new apples come along in late summer.

1. Cut the apples into quarters (do not peel or core them), and put them in a medium-size saucepan. Add the maple syrup, 1 cup of water, and the grated beet.

2. Cover the pan and bring the mixture to a simmer over medium-low heat. Cook until the apples are soft, 20 to 30 minutes, depending on the variety. Lift the lid from time to time to stir and add water as needed, making sure the apples don't stick to the bottom and burn.

3. Put the mixture through a food mill to strain out the skins, seeds, stems, core walls, and any hard bits of beet. (You can also use a coarse strainer, but a food mill does the best job.)

4. Serve warm or at room temperature, either in individual bowls or in one shallow serving bowl. Drizzle the cream in a spiral design on top, or pass it separately.

BLUEBERRY LEMON SAUCE

MAKES ABOUT 1 CUP

Here's a quick, healthy sauce that can turn a few scoops of ice cream into a special dessert. Pour it on pound cake or angel food cake for an instant topping. Drop a spoonful next to an unmolded custard or panna cotta. When blueberries are not in season I use frozen ones, or better yet, I'll make up a large batch of the sauce in the summer and freeze or can it in half-pint jars.

2 cups blueberries, fresh or frozen

2 tablespoons fresh lemon juice (½ lemon)

3 tablespoons honey

1. Combine the blueberries, lemon juice, and honey in a small saucepan. Cover the pan and cook, stirring occasionally, over very low heat for 15 minutes.

2. Strain the sauce through a fine-mesh strainer into a medium-size bowl, extracting as much pulp as possible to thicken the juice (scrape the bottom of the strainer with a blunt knife from time to time). I usually end up with only a tablespoon or so of the skins left in the strainer. If your berries are on the firm side, a food mill may be needed to extract more of the pulp.

3. Stir briefly and then store in the refrigerator, where the sauce will retain its syrupy consistency. It can be warmed over low heat if desired, though I most often serve it cold.

CONVERSION TABLES

Please note that all conversions are approximate but close enough to be useful when converting from one system to another.

OVEN TEMPERATURES

FAHRENHEIT	GAS MARK	CELSIUS
250	1/2	120
275	1	140
300	2	150
325	3	160
350	4	180
375	5	190
400	6	200
425	7	220
450	8	230
475	9	240
500	10	260

NOTE: Reduce the temperature by 20°C (68°F) for fan-assisted ovens.

APPROXIMATE EQUIVALENTS

1 stick butter = 8 tbs = 4 oz = 1/2 cup = 115 g

1 cup all-purpose presifted flour = 4.7 oz

1 cup granulated sugar = 8 oz = 220 g

1 cup (firmly packed) brown sugar = 6 oz = 220 g to 230 g

1 cup confectioners' sugar = 4 1/2 oz = 115 g

1 cup honey or syrup = 12 oz

1 cup grated cheese = 4 oz

1 cup dried beans = 6 oz

1 large egg = about 2 oz or about 3 tbs

1 egg yolk = about 1 tbs

1 egg white = about 2 tbs

LIQUID CONVERSIONS

U.S.	IMPERIAL	METRIC
2 tbs	1 fl oz	30 ml
3 tbs	1 1/2 fl oz	45 ml
1/4 cup	2 fl oz	60 ml
1/3 cup	2 1/2 fl oz	75 ml
1/3 cup + 1 tbs	3 fl oz	90 ml
1/3 cup + 2 tbs	3 1/2 fl oz	100 ml
1/2 cup	4 fl oz	125 ml
2/3 cup	5 fl oz	150 ml
3/4 cup	6 fl oz	175 ml
3/4 cup + 2 tbs	7 fl oz	200 ml
1 cup	8 fl oz	250 ml
1 cup + 2 tbs	9 fl oz	275 ml
1 1/4 cups	10 fl oz	300 ml
1 1/3 cups	11 fl oz	325 ml
1 1/2 cups	12 fl oz	350 ml
1 2/3 cups	13 fl oz	375 ml
1 3/4 cups	14 fl oz	400 ml
1 3/4 cups + 2 tbs	15 fl oz	450 ml
2 cups (1 pint)	16 fl oz	500 ml
2 1/2 cups	20 fl oz (1 pint)	600 ml
3 3/4 cups	1 1/2 pints	900 ml
4 cups	1 3/4 pints	1 liter

WEIGHT CONVERSIONS

US/UK	METRIC	US/UK	METRIC
1/2 oz	15 g	7 oz	200 g
1 oz	30 g	8 oz	250 g
1 1/2 oz	45 g	9 oz	275 g
2 oz	60 g	10 oz	300 g
2 1/2 oz	75 g	11 oz	325 g
3 oz	90 g	12 oz	350 g
3 1/2 oz	100 g	13 oz	375 g
4 oz	125 g	14 oz	400 g
5 oz	150 g	15 oz	450 g
6 oz	175 g	1 lb	500 g

RESOURCES FOR THE GARDENER

Seeds

In addition to vegetable and herb seeds, many of the catalogs listed below sell seeds for green manures, cover crops, and grains, although it is best to check first with your local feed or agricultural supply store before having bulky items such as these shipped to you.

JOHNNY'S SELECTED SEEDS
955 Benton Ave.
Winslow, ME 04901
877-564-6697
johnnyseeds.com

The widest selection of garden seeds, including seed potatoes, sunchoke tubers, and onion and shallot sets, as well as plants such as asparagus, onions, sweet potatoes, and berries.

JOHN SCHEEPERS KITCHEN GARDEN SEEDS
23 Tulip Drive, P.O. Box 638
Bantam, CT 06750
860-567-6086
kitchengardenseeds.com

A cook-friendly catalog with interesting European varieties and tips for use in the kitchen.

TERRITORIAL SEED CO.
P.O. Box 158
Cottage Grove, OR 97424
800-626-0866
info@territorialseed.com

The broad selection includes many cold-resistant crops.

FEDCO SEEDS
P.O. Box 520
Waterville, ME 04903
207-873-7333 or 207-430-1106
fedcoseeds.com

A cooperative seed and garden supply company with a wonderfully written, amusingly illustrated catalog.

HIGH MOWING ORGANIC SEEDS
76 Quarry Road
Wolcott, VT 05680
802-472-6174
highmowingseeds.com

This one specializes in seeds for growing under organic conditions.

SEED SAVERS EXCHANGE
3094 North Winn Rd.
Decorah, IA 52101
563-382-5990
seedsavers.org

A major force in the seed preservation movement, Seed Savers publishes a fine catalog in addition to its seed swap yearbook.

BAKER CREEK HEIRLOOM SEED CO.
Baker Creek Rd.
Mansfield, MO 65704
417-924-8917
rareseeds.com

Baker Creek offers a unique collection of international heirlooms. Get the print catalog for fascinating reading.

SEEDS OF CHANGE
P.O. Box 4908
Rancho Dominguez, CA 90220
888-762-7333
seedsofchange.com

Organic seeds, with a focus on heirloom varieties.

WILD GARDEN SEED
P.O. Box 1509
Philomath, OR 97370
541-929-4068
wildgardenseed.com

The home source for seed breeder Frank Morton's brilliant output; includes many unusual greens.

SOUTHERN EXPOSURE SEED EXCHANGE
P.O. Box 460
Mineral, VA 23117
540-894-9480
southernexposure.com

A cooperative seed company specializing in open-pollinated and heirloom varieties, with an emphasis on the Middle Atlantic region.

SEEDS FROM ITALY
P.O. Box 3908
Lawrence, KS 66046
785-748-0959
growitalian.com

The U.S distributor of Franchi Seeds, a popular source of authentic, hard-to-find Italian varieties.

EVERGREEN Y. H. ENTERPRISES
P.O. Box 17538
Anaheim, CA 92817
evergreenseeds.com

A very wide selection of Asian vegetable seeds in an informative online catalog.

WOOD PRAIRIE FARM
49 Kinney Rd.
Bridgewater, ME 04735
800-829-9765
woodprairie.com

An excellent source of organic seed potatoes.

FILAREE FARM
182 Conconully Hwy.
Okanogan, WA 98840
509-422-6940
filareefarm.com

A reliable source of seed garlic.

HARRIS SEEDS
355 Paul Rd.
Rochester, NY 14624
800-544-7938
harrisseeds.com

A good old-fashioned seed company.

STOKES
P.O. Box 548
Buffalo, NY 14240
716-695-6980
stokeseeds.com

A well-established seed company with an informative catalog, catering to farmers and gardeners alike.

W. ATLEE BURPEE & CO.
300 Park Ave.
Warminster, PA 18974
800-888-1447
burpee.com

A long-established seller of seeds and plants, popular with home gardeners.

Plants

Although many seed companies ship annual vegetable seedlings, it's best to check your local area first. The same goes for plants such as asparagus, fruit trees, and small fruits—even onions and sweet potatoes if they are available in your area. But the following offer good mail-order selections.

NOURSE FARMS
41 River Rd.
Whately, MA 01093
413-665-2658
noursefarms.com

A first-class source of small fruits such as berries, including Mara des Bois strawberries.

MILLER NURSERIES
5060 County Rd. 16
Canandaigua, NY 14424
800-836-9630
millernurseries.com

We've found this a good source of young fruit trees.

BURNT RIDGE NURSERY AND ORCHARDS
432 Burnt Ridge Rd.
Onalaska, WA 98570
360-985-2873
burntridgenursery.com

Specializes in trees, shrubs, and vines that produce edible nuts or fruits.

DIXONDALE FARMS
P.O. Box 129, Department WP12
Carrizo Springs, TX 78834
877-367-1015
dixondalefarms.com

A good source of onion plants.

STEELE PLANT CO.
202 Collins St.
Gleason, TN 38229
731-646-5476
sweetpotatoplant.com

A good source of sweet potato plants.

RICHTERS
357 Highway 47
Goodwood, Ontario L0C 1A0
Canada
800-668-4372
richters.com

A very wide selection of herb plants and seeds, many of them unusual; ships to Canada and the United States.

APPLEWOOD SEED
5380 Vivian St.
Arvada, CO 80002
303-431-7333
applewoodseed.com

Seeds for nectar plants that attract bees and other pollinators.

Tools, Equipment, and Supplies

Most of the tools that home gardeners use, such as spades, shovels, rakes, and digging forks, can be easily found at your local hardware or home improvement store. Since developing or finding more efficient garden tools is one of our chief interests, we have mentioned a number of them in this book that may not be familiar to you. Listed below are some companies that sell them. Soil amendments such as lime, potting soil, greensand, and rock phosphate are best found locally, as they are very bulky and expensive to ship, but many of the sources below offer them for times when there is no other way to obtain them.

Garden hod.

JOHNNY'S SELECTED SEEDS

(See page 451.) Besides basic tools, Johnny's offers the following items highlighted in this book:

• Broadforks .

• Collinear hoes and stirrup hoes.

• Three-tooth cultivator.

• Bed preparation rake with row markers.

• Wire weeders.

• Soil block makers in a range of sizes.

• Soil thermometer.

• Hortonova 9FA trellis. This plastic mesh is designed to be used horizontally to support long-stemmed plants such as cut flowers. We also use it vertically to support climbing vegetables.

• Plastic Tomato Trellis Clips, useful for trellising vertical crops on strings.

• Precision seeders.

• Infrared-transmitting plastic; theirs is sold as Solar Mulch.

• Trap wire compost bins.

• The pipe benders used to make the Quick Hoops described in Chapter 3. This process is illustrated by a video on the Johnny's website.

• Row covers, clear plastic, and shade cloth in 10-foot widths, to be used for the Quick Hoop system, as well as plastic Snap Clamps to hold them in place.

• Johnny's "512 Mix" and the finer-textured "Germination Mix" can be used if there is no local source of organic seed-starting mix.

LOST CREEK GREENHOUSE SYSTEMS
245 C. R. 265
Mineola, TX 75773
903-569-8541
lostcreek.net

This innovative company sells bending forms for making your own greenhouses.

A. M. LEONARD, INC.
241 Fox Drive
Piqua, OH 45356
800-433-0633
amleo.com

An extensive catalog of tools and supplies, including high-quality soaker hoses.

PEACEFUL VALLEY FARM & GARDEN SUPPLY
P.O. Box 2209, 125 Clydesdale Court
Grass Valley, CA 95945
888-784-1722
groworganic.com

In addition to carrying many of our favorite implements, such as soil blockers and wheel hoes, Peaceful Valley is a good place to order soil amendments such as greensand if you cannot find them locally. They also sell BCS rototillers, our favorite choice.

GRIFFIN GREENHOUSE & NURSERY SUPPLIES
1629 Maine St.
Tewksbury, MA 01876
800-888-0054

Go to griffins.com/locations and click on the your region to find the nearest branch.

Source for "Wobbler" irrigation heads, and stands (page 236).

MAINE GARDEN PRODUCTS

The cold frame shown on page 89.

Cold frame automatic opener.

Maine Garden Hod (harvest basket with wire bottom noted on page 21 and shown at left).

BETTER GREENHOUSES
P.O. Box 995
Carbondale, CO 81623
bettergreenhouses.com

Sells all-polycarbonate transparent cold frames.

GREENHOUSE MEGASTORE
1644 Georgetown Rd.
Danville, IL 61832
888-281-9337
greenhousemegastore.com

Sells Netafim overhead sprinkler systems.

DRIPWORKS, INC.
190 Sanhedrin Circle
Wilits, CA 95490
800-522-3747
dripworks.com

Drip irrigation systems.

NORTHERN TOOL
northerntool.com
800-221-0516

Source of Gilmour fiber soaker hoses, which are easy to handle.

GARDENER'S SUPPLY CO.
128 Intervale Rd.
Burlington, VT 05401
888-833-1412
gardeners.com

Handy items such as French-style watering cans and bamboo poles of varying lengths and thicknesses.

DEERBUSTERS
9735A Bethel Rd.
Frederick, MD 21702
888-422-3337
deerbusters.com

Sells Tenax black plastic mesh fence pictured on page 245.

WOMANSWORK
P.O. Box 728
Pawling, NY 12564
800-639-2709
womanswork.com

Wide selection of gardening gloves that fit women's hands.

ULINE
12575 Uline Drive
Pleasant Prairie, WI 53158
800-958-5463
uline.com

Sells woven polypropylene sandbags
in an unobtrusive green color, for
holding down the plastic on Quick
Hoops and movable greenhouses.

LEHMAN'S
P.O. Box 270
Kidron, OH 44636
877-438-5346
lehmans.com

Source of non-electric household
equipment including corn mills, corn
cutters, and corn shellers.

HORIZON HERBS
P.O. Box 69
Williams, OR 97544
541-846-6704
horizonherbs.com

Source of seed-cleaning screens.

KEN-BAR, INC.
Garden Trends, Inc.
355 Paul Rd.
P.O. Box 24966
Rochester, NY 14624-0966
800-336-8882

Go to ken-bar.com to locate a dealer in
your area.

Source of wire for making wire wickets.

Books

Alltrista Consumer Products.
*The Ball Blue Book Guide to
Preserving.* Originally published
in 1909 by Ball Brothers.

Ashworth, Suzanne. *Seed to Seed: Seed
Saving Techniques for the Vegetable
Gardener.* White River Junction, VT:
Chelsea Green Publishing, 2002.

Coleman, Eliot. *The New Organic
Grower.* Revised edition. White
River Junction, VT: Chelsea Green
Publishing, 1995.

——. *Four-Season Harvest.* Revised
edition. White River Junction, VT:
Chelsea Green Publishing, 1999.

——. *The Winter Harvest Handbook.*
White River Junction, VT: Chelsea
Green Publishing, 2009.

Corey, Paul. *Buy an Acre: America's
Second Frontier.* New York: Dial Press,
1944.

Creasy, Rosalind. *Edible Landscaping.*
San Francisco: Sierra Club Books,
2010.

Damrosch, Barbara. *The Garden
Primer.* Revised edition. New York:
Workman Publishing, 2008.

Engeland, Ron L. *Growing Great
Garlic.* Okanogan, WA: Filaree Farm,
1991.

Goldman, Amy. *Melons for the
Passionate Grower.* New York:
Artisan, 2002.

Hall, Bolton. *The Garden Yard: A
Handbook of Intensive Farming.*
Philadelphia: David McKay, 1909.

Hertzberg, Ruth, Janet Greene, and
Beatrice Vaughan. *Putting Food By.*
Fifth edition. New York: Plume, 2010.

Hubert, Philip G., Jr. *Liberty and a
Living: The Record of an Attempt to
Secure Bread and Butter, Sunshine
and Content, by Gardening, Fishing
and Hunting.* New York and London:
G. P. Putnam's Sons, 1904.

Johnston, Robert Jr. *Growing Garden
Seeds.* Albion, ME: Johnny's Selected
Seeds, 1983.

Kourik, Robert. *Drip Irrigation for
Every Landscape and All Climates.*
Occidental, CA: Metamorphic Press,
2009.

——. *Designing and Maintaining Your
Edible Landscape Naturally.* White
River Junction, VT: Chelsea Green
Publishing, 2005.

Larkcom, Joy. *Oriental Vegetables.*
Revised edition. New York: Kodansha
America, 2008.

Lowenfels, Jeff and Wayne Lewis.
*Teaming with Microbes: The Organic
Gardener's Guide to the Soil Food Web.*
Revised edition. Portland, OR: Timber
Press, 2010.

Male, Carolyn. *100 Heirloom
Tomatoes for the American Garden.*
New York: Workman Publishing, 1999.

Nearing, Helen and Scott. *Living the
Good Life: How to Live Sanely and
Simply in a Troubled World.* New York:
Schocken Books, 1970.

——. *Building and Using Our Sun-
Heated Greenhouse: Grow Vegetables
All Year-Round.* Charlotte, VT:
Garden Way Publishing, 1977.

Phillips, Michael. *The Apple Grower:
A Guide for the Organic Orchardist.*
Second edition. White River Junction,
VT: Chelsea Green Publishing, 2005.

——. *The Holistic Orchard: Tree
Fruits and Berries the Biological Way.*
White River Junction, VT: Chelsea
Green Publishing, 2011.

Reich, Lee. *Growing Fruit Naturally.*
Newtown, CT: Taunton Press, 2012.

——. *Uncommon Fruits for Every
Garden.* Portland, OR: Timber Press,
2004.

Rodale, J. I. *How to Grow Fruits and Vegetables by the Organic Method.* Emmaus, PA: Rodale Press, 1976.

Rombough, Lon. *The Grape Grower: A Guide to Organic Viticulture.* White River Junction, VT: Chelsea Green Publishing, 2004.

Seymour, John and Sally. *Self-Sufficiency: The Science and Art of Producing & Preserving your Own Food.* London: Faber and Faber, 1973.

Weaver, William Woys. *Heirloom Vegetable Gardening.* New York: Henry Holt, 1997.

Periodicals

THE AVANT GARDENER
P.O. Box 525
Pipersville, PA 18947
avantgardener.info

Monthly newsletter stuffed with horticultural news. Available in print and online.

HORTIDEAS
750 Black Lick Rd.
Gravel Switch, KY 40328
users.mikrotec.com

In-depth bimonthly horticultural newsletter, now online only.

MOTHER EARTH NEWS
1503 SW 42nd St.
Topeka, KS 66609
800-234-3368
motherearthnews.com

This bimonthly magazine devoted to earth-friendly living in general covers food growing in more depth than most publications devoted solely to gardening. Free access to archives of past articles.

ORGANIC GARDENING
Published by Rodale, Inc.
33 E. Minor St.
Emmaus, PA 18098
800-666-2206
organicgardening.com

Bimonthly. Not the jam-packed, thick little magazine of bygone days, but worth keeping up with for its willingness to cover food growing, and its devotion to organic methods.

Construction Details

For more information on building Quick Hoops, movable greenhouses, chickshaws, and Duckingham Palace, visit our website fourseasonfarm.com.

Organizations

U. S. DEPARTMENT OF AGRICULTURE COOPERATIVE STATE RESEARCH, EDUCATION, AND EXTENSION SERVICE

Now formally known as the National Institute of Food and Agriculture, has offices in every state's Land Grant University as well as regional offices. It provides regionally based information in the form of articles, fact sheets, tables of planting dates, locally appropriate crop varieties, and so forth. Browse the site (see below) for topics that interest you, and click on your state at the site's map or on a list to find experts at the Extension Service office closest to you.

Contact by mail:

UNITED STATES DEPT. OF AGRICULTURE
National Institute of Food and Agriculture

1400 Independence Avenue SW., Stop 2201
Washington, DC 20250
202-720-4423
csrees.usda.gov/Extension/

STATE AND REGIONAL ORGANIC ORGANIZATIONS

These represent both farmers and home gardeners, and every state or region in the U. S. has at least one. Some examples are MOFGA (Maine Organic Farmers and Gardeners Association) and MOSES (Midwest Organic and Sustainable Education Service). Such groups offer publications, online forums, educational programs, and events where you can both learn gardening skills and interact with other gardeners. A list can be found on the ATTRA website (see below) attra.ncat.org/other.html#State.

ATTRA (NATIONAL SUSTAINABLE AGRICULTURE INFORMATION SERVICE)
P.O. Box 3838
Butte, MT 59702
Free hotline: 800-346-9140
attar.ncat.org

Offers a wealth of useful gardening and farming information on its website.

PLANTING IN FALL FOR WINTER HARVEST

CROP	DAYS FROM PLANTING TO 10-HOUR DAY
Arugula	45
Beet leaves	55
Carrots	85
Chard	90
Claytonia	40
Endive	50
Kale	90
Lettuce	40
Mâche	35
Mizuna	35
Parsley	100
Scallion	90
Spinach	45
Tatsoi	45

WHEN PLANTING IN fall to grow winter vegetables, it's very important to consider day-length, even when the crops are adequately protected from the cold. This table gives you the period during which winter day-length is 10 hours or less, calculated for different parallels of latitude, in order to determine when to sow.

The length of winter days depends on how far north (or south) of the equator you are. You can calculate winter day-length according to the latitude of where you live. Latitude is your position on the earth in relationship to the equator. Most maps of the U.S. in a good atlas will indicate the lines of latitude circling the earth parallel to the equator.

When winter day-length drops below 10 hours, plant growth slows considerably.

For best results, winter crops need to be planted early enough to become well established before the beginning of the below-10-hour period. The table at left gives the number of days before the onset of the below-10-hour period, at your location, to plant the most popular winter crops, and the map below allows you to find your latitude. For example, someone on the 40th parallel would want to plant spinach by September 29, which is 45 days before November 14, when the day drops to 10 hours.

We have calculated these figures from our experience here on the 44th parallel. They are a good place to start, but you will want to fine-tune them from your own experience at your location.

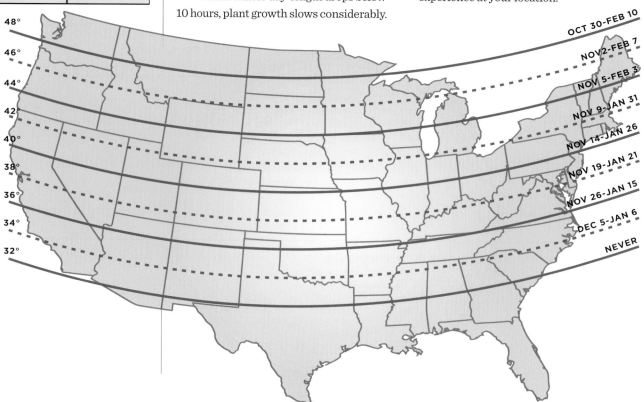

SOWING FOR SPRING, SUMMER, AND FALL HARVEST

THE MOST SPECIFIC planting information for your area can best be obtained from your local Extension Service or your state's Land Grant University (see page 455). Most states publish tables that show the date of the average last frost in spring, the first frost in fall, and the right time to plant specific crops. Often these are broken down into specific areas of your state.

The table below shows which crops are best sown directly into the garden; which should be started indoors and put out as transplants, and at what age; and which crops will work with either method. The spacings of the crops are the ones we use for maximum production from a small area, with suggestions for repeat sowings to prolong the harvest. They are based on our system of 30-inch-wide beds described on page 41. They represent the spacing achieved after any necessary thinning has been done.

CROP	SOW DIRECTLY IN THE GARDEN	SOW INDOORS, THEN TRANSPLANT INTO THE GARDEN	ROWS PER 30-INCH-WIDE BED	INCHES APART IN THE ROW
Artichokes		Sow 6–8 weeks before first hard frost, then transplant.	1	24
Arugula	Sow from early spring on, then every 2–3 weeks until 1 month before average first frost date.		6	1
Asian Greens	Can be sown in succession from early spring through midsummer.	Sow in early spring; transplant after danger of hard frost has passed.	3	6
Asparagus		Sow 12–14 weeks ahead; set out after frost danger. If purchased plants, set out in early to mid-spring.	1	15
Basil	Make outdoor sowings after frost, every 3 weeks through midsummer.	Sow 3 weeks before end of frost danger, then set out.	3	10
Beans	Sow after danger of frost, when soil is at least 60 degrees.		1	6
Beets	Sow from mid-spring through late July every 2 weeks for a steady supply. Sow storage beets 10 weeks before expected hard freeze.	Sow 4 weeks before setting out after danger of frost has passed.	3	3
Broccoli		Sow 3 weeks before danger of hard frost is past. Set out 3-week-old plants until midsummer (late summer in warm climates).	2	16
Brussels Sprouts		Sow 4 weeks before last spring frost or about 4 months before first expected fall frost.	1	16
Cabbage		Sow 3 weeks before last frost for summer eating. For storage varieties, set out 3-week-old plants up to 4 months before first fall frost.	2	16
Carrots	Make sowings from early spring to mid-August.		6	1
Cauliflower		Sow earliest planting as for Broccoli. Set out 3-week-old plants until 2 months before first fall frost.	2	16
Celery and Celery Root		Sow 8 weeks before setting out, after danger of frost has passed.	3	12

CROP	SOW DIRECTLY IN THE GARDEN	SOW INDOORS, THEN TRANSPLANT INTO THE GARDEN	ROWS PER 30-INCH-WIDE BED	INCHES APART IN THE ROW
Corn	Sow after last frost date in spring, with soil temperature at least 65°, then succession plantings into early summer.		1	6
Cucumbers	Sow after danger of frost, when soil temperature is at least 70°.	Sow 3 weeks before last frost, then set out 1 week after last frost.	1	24
Dill, Chervil, and Coriander	Sow as soon as the soil can be worked, then every few weeks through midsummer.		3	6
Eggplant		Sow 9 weeks before last spring frost and set out 1 week after.	1	24
Endive	Sow as soon as garden soil is prepared, then every 3 weeeks.	Sow 3–4 weeks before setting out after hard frost, then every 3 weeks for a steady supply.	3	6
Escarole	Same as for Endive.	Same as for Endive.	2	15
Fennel		Sow 3–4 weeks before transplanting. Set out from mid-spring to late summer.	3	9
Garlic and Shallots	Plant the cloves in mid-fall, at the same time you would plant flower bulbs in your area.		3	6
Kale and Collards		Sow 3 weeks before danger of frost is past. Set out 3-week-old plants until 3 months before first fall frost.	3	12
Kohlrabi	Sow in midsummer for a fall crop. Spacing depends on size of the variety.		2–3	8–18
Leeks		Sow at least 2 months before setting out in mid to late spring, when at least 10 inches tall.	3	6
Lettuce, Head		Sow indoors 3–4 weeks before setting out, after danger of hard frost. Sow every 2–3 weeks for steady supply.	3	12
Lettuce, Baby Leaf	Direct-sow as soon as garden soil is prepared, then every 2–4 weeks for a steady supply.		6	1
Melons		Sow 3 weeks before last frost, then set out 1 week after last frost.	1	30
Onions	Sow onion sets as early as garden soil can be worked, in clusters of 4.		3	12
Oregano and Sage	Sow in spring as soon as garden soil can be worked.	Sow transplants 8–10 weeks before setting out after last frost, or buy started plants.	2	12
Parsnips	Sow in early spring.		3	4

CROP	SOW DIRECTLY IN THE GARDEN	SOW INDOORS, THEN TRANSPLANT INTO THE GARDEN	ROWS PER 30-INCH-WIDE BED	INCHES APART IN THE ROW
Parsley	Sow after danger of frost.		4	8
Peas	Sow in spring as soon as the garden soil is ready. For a fall crop sow 2 months before the first expected frost.		2 (see page 185)	2
Peppers		Sow 9 weeks before last frost, then set out 1 week after last frost.	1	18
Potatoes	Sow 6 weeks before the end of hard frosts.		1	8
Pumpkins	Sow after last frost.		1	48
Radicchio		Sow from early spring through summer, setting out 4-week-old transplants.	3	12
Radishes	Sow small type any time, starting in early spring; large spring varieties in mid to late spring; large fall varieties in early to late summer. Spacing depends on variety.		3	2-4
Scallions	Sow in early spring. Sow in July and August for fall, winter, or spring harvest.		3	1
Squash, Summer	Sow after danger of frost, with soil temperature above 60°.	Sow 2-3 weeks before transplanting after danger of frost.	1	36
Squash, Winter	Sow 1 week after last frost date, with soil temperature above 60°.		1	48
Spinach	Begin sowing in early spring as soon as the ground can be worked.		5	3
Strawberry, Alpine		Sow 10–12 weeks before last frost.	3	8
Swiss Chard	Sow 4 weeks before setting out after danger of frost, then any time from mid-spring through summer.		3	12
Thyme	Same as Oregano and Sage	Same as Oregano and Sage	3	10
Tomatillo		Sow 4–5 weeks before setting out 1–2 weeks after frost.	1	18
Tomato		Sow 6-8 weeks before setting out after danger of frost.	1	18
Turnips and Rutabagas	Sow in early spring, then late summer for a fall crop. Spacing depends on size of root desired.		3	6

USDA PLANT HARDINESS ZONE MAP

THE 2012 USDA Plant Hardiness Zone Map illustrates for gardeners the average minimum winter temperature for locations throughout the country, divided into 10°F zones, or 5°F half-zones.

The online version at **planthardiness.ars.usda.gov/PHZMWeb** allows you to click on your state for a more detailed view.

HAWAII

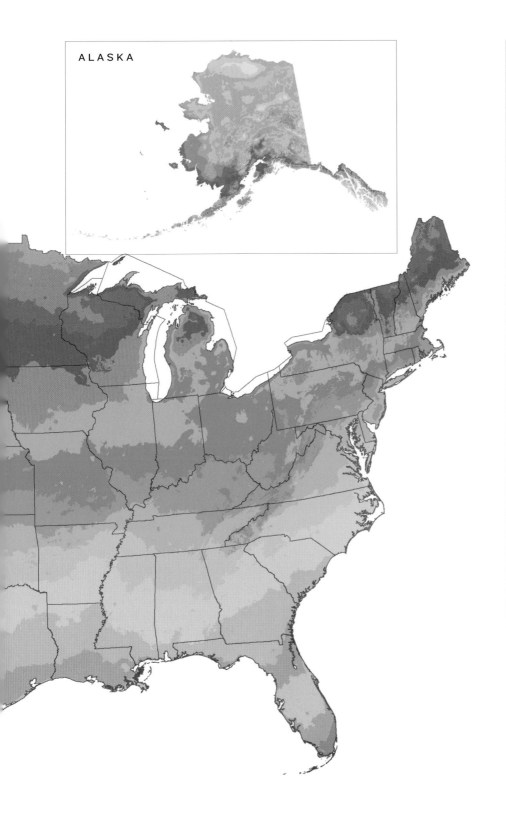

ALASKA

Average Annual Extreme Minimum Temperature 1976-2005

Temp (F)	Zone	Temp (C)
-60 to -55	1a	-51.1 to -48.3
-55 to -50	1b	-48.3 to -45.6
-50 to -45	2a	-45.6 to -42.8
-45 to -40	2b	-42.8 to -40
-40 to -35	3a	-40 to -37.2
-35 to -30	3b	-37.2 to -34.4
-30 to -25	4a	-34.4 to -31.7
-25 to -20	4b	-31.7 to -28.9
-20 to -15	5a	-28.9 to -26.1
-15 to -10	5b	-26.1 to -23.3
-10 to -5	6a	-23.3 to -20.6
-5 to 0	6b	-20.6 to -17.8
0 to 5	7a	-17.8 to -15
5 to 10	7b	-15 to -12.2
10 to 15	8a	-12.2 to -9.4
15 to 20	8b	-9.4 to -6.7
20 to 25	9a	-6.7 to -3.9
25 to 30	9b	-3.9 to -1.1
30 to 35	10a	-1.1 to 1.7
35 to 40	10b	1.7 to 4.4
40 to 45	11a	4.4 to 7.2
45 to 50	11b	7.2 to 10
50 to 55	12a	10 to 12.8
55 to 60	12b	12.8 to 15.6
60 to 65	13a	15.6 to 18.3
65 to 70	13b	18.3 to 21.1

Agricultural Research Service

Oregon State UNIVERSITY

Mapping by the PRISM Climate Group, Oregon State University.

INDEX

Forming beds, page 42

Blueberry basics
page 211

Beef Borscht, page 272

Carrot(s), 44, 51, *68*
  basics, 152–54
  Beef Borscht, 272–73
  crop rotation and, 47, 48–49
  finger-size, 120
  Fried Rice with Pork and
    Vegetables, 350–51
  in Hard Times Garden, 76, 77, 80
  with Honey and Rosemary, 386
  Lamb Shanks with Early Root
    Vegetables, *408,* 418–19
  in mirepoix or soffrito, 153, 154
  Nelson, *152*
  and Parsnip Puree, 387
  Pork and Vegetable Stew with
    Coconut Milk, 414–15
  in Practical Garden, 68, 69, 70
  Provençal Pot Roast, 410–12
  and Raisin Sandwiches, 267
  return per square footage of, 246,
    247
  Rice Salad with Summer
    Vegetables, 314
  Root Vegetable Ribbons, *384,* 407
  in Savory Garden, 118, 120–21
  seed saving and, 113, 115
  in Self-Reliant Garden, 104, 113,
    115
  Sesame Chicken Breasts with
    Vegetables, 423–24
  in colors other than orange, 120,
    152–53
  Shepherd's Pie, 416–17
  Soba Noodles with Vegetables
    and Tahini Sauce, 347–48, *348*
  Spaghetti with Summer
    Vegetables, 344–45
  Spicy Shrimp Soup, 280
  sprouting indoors, 80
  Vegetable Stock, 292–93
  watering not-yet-germinated
    seeds of, 153, 239
  in Winter Garden, 88, 95, 96,
    97–99, 101, 120–21
Carrot family (Apiaceae,
    Umbelliferae), 44, 70
  basics, 152–61

  cooking with flowers of, 166
  herbs in, 159–61
Carson, Rachel, 58
Carts, two-wheeled, 41
Cattle, 28–29
Cauliflower, 44, 72, *118*
  basics, 133–34
  blanching of, 133
  Cheddar, *44, 133*
  in colors other than white, 121,
    133
  controlling size of, 121, 235
  Creamed, on Toast, 393
  with Pine Nuts and Brown Butter,
    389
  Red Thai Curry with Fall
    Vegetables, 404–6, *405*
  return per square footage of, 247
  Roasted, Gremolata, 388
  Romanesco, 121, *121,* 133
  in Savory Garden, 118
  Soufflé, 333
  Spaghetti with Summer
    Vegetables, 345
  starting indoors and setting out
    as transplants, 133, 226
  see also Cabbage family
Celery, 44, 70, *156*
  basics, 156–57
  crop rotation and, 48
  Green Gazpacho, *286,* 287
  growing indoors, 80
  Heart Salad, 305–6
  in mirepoix or soffrito, 153
  in Savory Garden, 118
  Vegetable Stock, 292–93
Celery root (celeriac), 44, 70, *157,*
    397
  basics, 157–58
  crop rotation and, 48
  Cutlets, 390–91
  in Hard Times Garden, 76, 77, 80
  and Potato Mash with Brown
    Butter, 396–97
  in Savory Garden, 118
  seed saving and, 113
  in Self-Reliant Garden, 104, 113

  sprouting indoors, 80
Chard. *See* Swiss chard
Cheddar cheese:
  Cold-Weather Salad with Apples
    and Cheese, 300–301
  Open-Faced Sandwiches with
    Tomato and Pesto Topping,
    256, 265–66
  Spinach Quiche with Buckwheat
    Crust, 336–37
Cheese:
  Baked Spaghetti Squash with,
    398–400
  blue, in Lettuce with Pan-Roasted
    Pears, 297
  Brie and Apple Topping, Open-
    Faced Sandwiches with,
    266–67
  Cold-Weather Salad with Apples
    and, 300–301
  goat, in Savory Custards with
    Garlic and Tarragon, 329–30
  grated, approximate equivalents
    for, 450
  Gruyère, in Asparagus
    Goldenrod, *334,* 335–36
  Orzo Pasta with Shrimp, Peas
    and, 342–44, *343*
  Parmesan and Onion Topping,
    Open-Faced Sandwiches with,
    266
  Peruvian Potatoes, 312, *313*
  Stuffed Squash Blossom Fritters,
    262–64, *263*
  see also Cheddar cheese; Feta
    cheese
Chemical contamination, 26, 29
Cherries, 58
  fruit tree basics and, 214–19
Chervil, 44, 159, *160,* 166
  basics, 161
  Dressing, Creamy, 318
Chicken(s):
  Breasts, Sesame, with Vegetables,
    423–24
  cutting with cleaver and mallet,
    401

Cold Frames, page 87

Strawberry Fool page 446

Garden forks, page 223

Lavender, page 161

Melon basics, page 173

Peruvian Potatoes, page 312

Q

R

Radish basics, page 134

Starting seedlings page 226

Rustic Apple Tart, page 434

Yoke, page 239

PHOTO CREDITS